JUL 1 8 2016

Praise for *Mockingbird*

"If there is a great American novel, certainly *To Kill a Mockingbird* is it. But, for all of us who love it, its author has always been an enigma. Did Harper Lee really write this classic? And if she did, why didn't she ever write another book? And who is Harper Lee, anyway? Finally, a writer has done the necessary research to reveal the surprising answers. To every *To Kill a Mockingbird* reader, I send this message: The story isn't over. There's so much more to come, and you'll find it all in Charles Shields' delightful and insightful *Mockingbird*."

—HOMER HICKAM, author of *Rocket Boys*

"A worthwhile portrait of the artist."

—JANET MASLIN, *The New York Times*

"As readable, convincing and engrossing as Lee's literary wonder."

—*Orlando Sentinel*

"Lively, absorbing. *Mockingbird* reads briskly.... If you treasure Scout, one of literature's more endearing characters, you'll like the woman who emerges in *Mockingbird*."

—*The Miami Herald*

"A literary portrait that could stand as definitive for years to come.... The portraits Shields presents will captivate those who enjoy *To Kill a Mockingbird* in print or on film."

—*The Tennessean*

"An impressively unauthorized biography of the famously reclusive author."

—*New York* magazine

"Shields has been enterprising [in his research]. He offers the book as a kind of homemade present."

—*The New Yorker*

"Harper Lee caught the beauty of America with *To Kill a Mockingbird*, but has remained something of a mystery ever since. Charles J. Shields's portrait of her, *Mockingbird*, shows us a quietly reclusive, down-to-earth woman with an enormous gift and documents her struggle to live with that gift for the rest of her life. Shields's evocation of both the woman and her beautiful, sleepy, and smoldering South are pitch perfect."

—ANNE RIVERS SIDDONS,
author of *Sweetwater Creek* and other books

"This biography impresses for both its breadth and depth. . . . Comprehensive, readable and fascinating."

—*The Buffalo News*

"The chief value of *Mockingbird*—and it is an extraordinarily important one—is Mr. Shields' meticulous and fascinating account of how Ms. Lee came to write her novel."

—*The New York Sun*

"This biography will not disappoint those who loved the novel and the feisty, independent, fiercely loyal Scout, in whom Harper Lee put so much of herself."

—GARRISON KEILLOR, *The New York Times Book Review*

"With a journalist's healthy appetite for research, Shields has unearthed every article and archive mentioning Harper Lee. He susses out which characters from *To Kill a Mockingbird* correspond to Lee's childhood, and he's included useful civil rights history. His portrayal of Lee's brusque personality and socially eccentric ways as a [university] student and humorist help explain her unorthodox individuality later in life."

—*San Francisco Chronicle*

"A work that all future biographies of Harper Lee will need to consult for its many commendable aspects."

—*The Washington Times*

"Captivating."

—*The Denver Post*

"Highly readable . . . This is an easy sell."

—*Daily News* (New York)

"Admirable . . . *Mockingbird* makes the reader look at Harper Lee with new and respectful eyes."

—*USA Today*

"Harper Lee's intense personal privacy sets daunting limitations for a biographer, but Charles Shields has ingeniously recovered the feel of her childhood world of Monroeville, Alabama, and the small-town Southern customs and vivid personalities that shaped her prickly independence. Detailed memories of Lee's classmates and friends are interwoven with dramatic recreations of key events and stories of her friendships and literary collaborations, all fleshing out the general narrative of her development as a novelist. Close attention to her friendship with Truman Capote and the conditions of the writing and then the filming of *To Kill a Mockingbird* offer special fascination."

—LOUISE WESTLING, professor emerita, University of Oregon, author of *Sacred Groves and Ravaged Gardens: The Fiction of Eudora Welty, Carson McCullers, and Flannery O'Connor*

"A superb biography."

—WILLIAM GIRALDI, *The New Republic*

"Entertaining and enlightening."

—*The Dallas Morning News*

"A must-read."

—*NEA Today*

"Shields earns As for effort and for his evocation of the Depression-era South."

—*Bookpage*

"An informative and genial biography that literary fiction lovers will flock to."

—*Booklist*

"An affectionate biography."

—*Publishers Weekly*

"A well-written profile."

—*Library Journal*

"A moving story . . . Shields has a lilting style and a way of inventively filling the gaps without resorting to fabrication. It's nice to imagine Lee, who knows a good human story when she sees one, stepping outside of herself and admiring his achievement."

—*C-ville Weekly*

Mockingbird

Mockingbird

A Portrait of Harper Lee,
from Scout to
Go Set a Watchman

Charles J. Shields

Henry Holt and Company

New York

Henry Holt and Company, LLC
Publishers since 1866
175 Fifth Avenue
New York, New York 10010
www.henryholt.com

Henry Holt ® and 🅷® are registered trademarks of
Henry Holt and Company, LLC.

Distributed in Canada by Raincoast Book Distribution Limited

Library of Congress Cataloging-in-Publication Data is available.

ISBN: 978-1-250-11583-6

Our books may be purchased in bulk for promotional, educational, or business use.
Please contact your local bookseller or the Macmillan Corporate and
Premium Sales Department at (800) 221-7945, extension 5442, or by e-mail at
MacmillanSpecialMarkets@macmillan.com.

Revised Edition 2016

Originally published in hardcover in 2006 by Henry Holt and Company and in
paperback in 2007 by St. Martin's Griffin.

Map by Laura Hartman Maestro

Designed by Meryl Sussman Levavi

Printed in the United States of America

1 3 5 7 9 10 8 6 4 2

To my wife, Guadalupe

If nothing but the bright side of characters should be shown, we should sit down in despondency, and think it utterly impossible to imitate them in *anything*.

—SAMUEL JOHNSON, on the writing of biography

Contents

Chronology

1880 July: Amasa Coleman Lee born in Georgiana, Butler County, Alabama: model for Atticus Finch in *To Kill a Mockingbird*.

1890: Frances Cunningham Finch born in Finchburg, Alabama.

1901: Monroeville, Alabama: population 215 white and 215 black; no paved streets or sidewalks; no streetlights; dwellings unpainted.

1905: Lillie Mae Faulk born in Brewton, Alabama.

1910: Frances and Amasa marry.

1911: Alice Finch Lee born.

1913: A. C. Lee: Monroeville law firm hires him to come to Monroeville.

1915: A. C. Lee admitted to the bar.

1916: Francis Louise Lee born.

1916: Law firm changes its name to Barnett, Bugg & Lee.

1919: Brown and Frank Ezell defended by A. C. Lee on charge of murdering a white man; both are hanged and mutilated: partial basis of *To Kill a Mockingbird*.

1920: Edwin Coleman Lee born: Jem in *To Kill a Mockingbird.*

1920 Alfred R. Boulware, Jr., age 9 (model for Boo Radley), listed on the 1920 federal census; father, Alfred R. Boulware, age 47, merchant of a general store; mother, Annie, age 45; sisters Mary A., age 18, and Sally C., age 15.

1920–1930: A. C. Lee on the Monroeville city council.

1923: Monroeville gets electricity.

1923: Arch Persons and Lillie Mae Faulk marry at the Faulks' home.

1924: Truman (Persons) Capote born in New Orleans: Dill in *To Kill a Mockingbird.*

1926: Nelle Harper Lee born: Scout in *To Kill a Mockingbird.*

1927–1938: A. C. Lee serves in State House of Representatives.

1928: Truman's parents divorce; the four-year-old moves to Monroeville, where he lives until 1933.

1929: Alice graduates from high school.

1929–1947: A. C. Lee is editor and partner of the *Monroe Journal.* Alice Lee becomes associate partner and editor, along with two other partners.

1931: The first brick residence is built in Monroeville.

1931: New Monroeville Methodist Episcopal Church opens, where the Lee family worships.

1932: Monroeville's only library opens in the upstairs of Jenny Faulk's millinery store.

1933: Truman moves to New York to be with his mother and stepfather.

1933: Walter Lett arrested near Monroeville on charge of raping Naomi Lowery, a white woman: basis of *To Kill a Mockingbird* trial.

1934: Walter Lett pleads not guilty to rape; tried and found guilty. Jury recommends death by electrocution; judge sentences him to death.

1934 summer: *Monroe Journal,* "Mad Dog Warning Issued"; basis of rabid-dog scene in *To Kill a Mockingbird.*

1935: Truman's name changed to Truman Garcia Capote.

1936: New public high school for whites only completed in Monroeville.

1937: Alice goes to Birmingham, Alabama, to work for IRS; at night attends the Birmingham School of Law.

1940: Population of Monroeville fewer than 2,500.

1940 January: The Faulks' house burns down: basis of Miss Maudie's fire in *To Kill a Mockingbird*.

1942: Alfred "Son" Boulware dies at home at age 42; "Boo" Radley in *To Kill a Mockingbird*.

1943 August: Alice Lee admitted to the Alabama bar; joins father's law firm in Monroeville in January 1944.

1944: Nelle graduates from high school; starts at Huntingdon College in Montgomery that summer.

1945: Capote returns to Monroeville to begin *Other Voices, Other Rooms*: Nelle Lee is model for Idabel Thompkins.

1945: Nelle Lee enrolls at University of Alabama for law school.

1946: Monroeville Methodist Episcopal Church supports full-time missionary and family in Southern Rhodesia: basis for the "missionary ladies" in *Go Set a Watchman* and *To Kill a Mockingbird*.

1946: Lee writes the column "Caustic Comment" for University of Alabama campus newspaper.

1947: Sara Ann McCall marries Edwin Coleman Lee.

1946–1947: Nelle Lee edits *Rammer Jammer*, campus humor magazine.

1948: Random House publishes Capote's first novel, *Other Voices, Other Rooms*.

1948: Lee drops out of the University of Alabama, returns home.

1949: Nelle leaves Monroeville for New York City.

1950s: Union High School built in Monroeville for black students; Monroe County schools not integrated until late 1960s.

1951: Frances Cunningham Finch dies in Selma, Alabama.

1951: Edwin Coleman Lee dies at Maxwell Air Force Base in Montgomery.

1952: Alice Lee and A.C. move into a brick home, six blocks west of their former home, where they will spend the rest of their lives.

1954: *Brown v. Board of Education* is decided by the U.S. Supreme Court; finds school segregation unconstitutional.

1955: Rosa Parks refuses to give up her bus seat to a white man in Montgomery, leading to a bus boycott by African-Americans.

1956: Rev. Whatley dismissed from Monroeville Methodist Episcopal Church for sermons about social justice; joins St. Mark's in Montgomery; serves on civil rights board with Dr. Martin Luther King.

1956: Montgomery bus boycott ends.

1956 November: Nelle Lee brings short stories to the offices of Maurice Crain and Annie Laurie Williams, literary agents.

1956 Christmas: Joy and Michael Brown give Lee a full year of financial support to complete her novel.

1957 January–February: Lee brings sections of *Go Set a Watchman* to her agent, Maurice Crain.

1957 May: *Go Set a Watchman* is submitted to Tay Hohoff at J. B. Lippincott in New York City.

1957: Lee brings 111 pages of "The Long Goodbye" to Crain (no date of return).

1957 September: Federal troops sent to Little Rock, Arkansas, to protect nine African-American students at Central High School from the white mobs trying to block the school's integration, and to enforce court-ordered desegregation of schools.

1957 October: *Go Set a Watchman* sold to J. B. Lippincott; no title in contract.

1959 Spring: Lee completes third draft of manuscript; final draft accepted in November.

1959 November: Clutter family members found murdered in Holcomb, Kansas, home.

November 19: Capote and Lee arrive in Garden City, Kansas, to research *In Cold Blood*.

1959 December: Christmas parade in Monroeville canceled after threats from Ku Klux Klan.

1960 March: Perry Smith and Richard Hickock's trial begins.

1960 March: *To Kill a Mockingbird* chosen by the Literary Guild and *Reader's Digest*.

1960 July: Civil rights sit-ins at Woolworth's in Greensboro, North Carolina.

1960 August: *To Kill a Mockingbird* is 7th on the *New York Times* bestseller list.

1961 May: Harper Lee awarded Pulitzer Prize for fiction.

1962 January: Gregory Peck visits Monroeville; meets A. C. Lee, the man he will play in the film version.

1962: Monroeville Chamber of Commerce films A. C. Lee holding a copy of *To Kill a Mockingbird*. "We are looking for Atticus Finch." "Yes, I am Atticus."

1962 April: Amasa Coleman Lee dies.

1962 October: James Meredith becomes first African-American student admitted to University of Mississippi. Violence necessitates deployment of federal troops.

1962 December: Premiere of film *To Kill a Mockingbird* in Hollywood. The film is nominated for eight Academy Awards.

1963 May: Crowds jam Birmingham, Alabama, theater to see *To Kill a Mockingbird*; during nearby civil rights protests in the city, Police Commissioner Eugene "Bull" Connor employs dogs, clubs, and cattle prods to disperse four thousand demonstrators.

1963 June: James Chaney, Andrew Goodman, and Michael Schwerner, voter registration workers, ambushed and killed in Neshoba County, Mississippi.

1963 August: Quarter of a million people join March on Washington; King delivers "I Have a Dream" speech.

1964 July: President Lyndon Baines Johnson signs 1964 Civil Rights Act.

1964 December: Combined sales of *To Kill a Mockingbird* reach eight million.

1965 April: Perry Smith and Richard Hickock hanged for Clutter murders.

1966: *To Kill a Mockingbird* banned by Richmond, Virginia, school board.

1966: *In Cold Blood* published. Capote appears on cover of *Time* magazine.

1969: Christopher Sergel adapts *To Kill a Mockingbird* into a play.

1970: Maurice Crain, Lee's agent, dies.

1971: Annie Laurie Williams, Crain's wife, closes the office.

1974: Tay Hohoff, Lee's editor on *To Kill a Mockingbird,* dies.

1984: Truman Capote dies.

1990: Monroeville begins annual performances of *To Kill a Mockingbird*.

1999: *Library Journal* votes *To Kill a Mockingbird* the best novel of the century.

2007: Lee inducted into the American Academy of Arts and Letters in May, an honor society of two hundred and fifty architects, composers, artists, and writers; she suffers a stroke in June; Lee receives Presidential Medal of Freedom in November.

2010: Fiftieth anniversary of the publication of *To Kill a Mockingbird*.

2011: Unpublished manuscript of *Go Set a Watchman* found in Monroeville.

2013: Lee files a lawsuit against her literary agent.

2014: Alice Finch Lee dies, age 103.

2015: *Go Set a Watchman* published.

February 19, 2016: Nelle Harper Lee passes away at age 89 in Monroeville, Alabama.

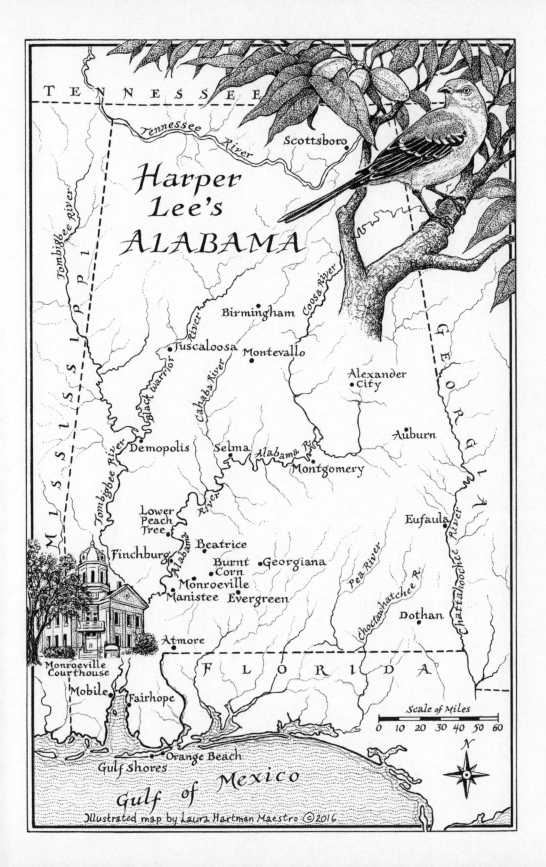

Harper
Lee's
ALABAMA

TENNESSEE

Tennessee River

Scottsboro

Tombigbee River

MISSISSIPPI

Birmingham

Coosa River

Tuscaloosa

Black Warrior River

Cahaba River

Montevallo

Alexander
City

Auburn

GEORGIA

Demopolis

Selma

Alabama R.

Tombigbee River

Montgomery

Alabama River

Lower
Peach
Tree

Eufaula

Chattahoochee River

Finchburg

Beatrice

Burnt
Corn

Georgiana

Pea River

Monroeville

Choctawhatchee R.

Manistee Evergreen

Atmore

Dothan

Monroeville
Courthouse

FLORIDA

Mobile

Fairhope

Scale of Miles

0 10 20 30 40 50 60

N

Orange Beach

Gulf shores

Gulf of Mexico

Illustrated map by Laura Hartman Maestro ©2016

Mockingbird

Introduction

Harper Lee's *To Kill a Mockingbird*, published in 1960, became one of the most beloved novels of the twentieth century. Lee's fellow Southerner and contemporary Flannery O'Connor was mystified by its success. "It's interesting that all the folks that are buying it don't know they are buying a children's book." O'Connor, one of the finest short-story writers in American literature, failed to appreciate Lee's caustic sense of humor and subversive social criticism. In the same category is another classic often mistaken for a children's book, *The Adventures of Huckleberry Finn*.

There will always be a place on library shelves for good stories, and *To Kill a Mockingbird* certainly is one. It draws the reader into a deep fictional landscape. Readers return to *To Kill a Mockingbird* because they want to walk the dusty streets of 1930s Maycomb, run madly through Boo Radley's backyard at night, or watch the trial of Tom Robinson play out to its disastrous end. Lee's storytelling voice is strong.

Also, the novel's emphasis on justice and compassion is timeless. You don't need to be a Southerner, or for that matter an American, to understand its importance. A harmless man, Boo Radley, is feared because he's peculiar. A good man, Tom Robinson, is denied the protection of the law because he isn't white. The primitive fear of otherness is the root of most of the world's evils.

And finally, *To Kill a Mockingbird* has the hallmark of all great works of literature: it reads you, the reader, as you read it. Great books and stories probe your convictions; silently, they ask what *you* stand for. As Atticus Finch leaves the courtroom—defeated but still true to himself—we wonder what it would be like to have people get to their feet out of respect for us, and what we would have to do to deserve it.

Consequently, no one could have anticipated how painful Atticus's moral fall would be when *Go Set a Watchman*, Lee's first published novel after fifty-five years, appeared in 2015. The hero of Depression-era southern Alabama, its moral compass, has turned into just a pleasant old man by the late 1950s when the novel is set, agreeing in spirit with Alabama Governor George Wallace, "Segregation now, segregation tomorrow, segregation forever!" And because *Go Set a Watchman* arrived in bookstores, by coincidence, just two weeks after a white supremacist murdered nine people in a historic African-American church in Charleston, South Carolina, the overlap added to the disappointment—feelings of betrayal, even—that ran deep among many of Lee's admirers. "You double-dealing, ring-tailed old son of a bitch!" Jean Louise shouts at her father.

The purpose of this revision of *Mockingbird: A Portrait of Harper Lee* is to complete the picture of the author and her work, and to consider how she could have written two such completely different novels. In the ten years after the original version of this biography was published in 2006, Lee was more in the public eye than ever during the previous half century. Two films arrived in theaters: *Capote* and *Infamous*, with distinguished actresses playing her. Then Lee unknowingly signed over the copyright to *To Kill a Mockingbird* and had to fight to get it back. She also sued the Monroe County Heritage Museum in her hometown of Monroeville, alleging that the museum had profited from unauthorized use of her characters. More threats of litigation challenged the publication of a memoir in 2014 by a journalist who wrote about becoming her next-door neighbor and friend. Later that year, in November, Lee's sister, Alice—her confidante, protector, and financial adviser—passed away at age one hundred and three. Three months later came the announcement that *Go Set a Watchman*, a supposedly lost novel, had been found.

So much has happened; there's so much more to tell. Although one thing is constant: this revision, like the earlier version, was written without Lee's permission, encouragement, or assistance.

—CHARLES J. SHIELDS
Charlottesville, Virginia
2016

one

The Making of Me

On any person who desires such queer prizes, New York will
bestow the gift of loneliness and the gift of privacy.

—E. B. WHITE, *Here Is New York* (1949)

On a snowy night in the winter of 1958, in a one-bedroom cold-water
flat at 1539 York Avenue between Eighty-first and Eighty-second streets,
Nelle Harper Lee sat crying at her desk. Rolled into her typewriter was
a page from a novel she'd been working on for almost ten years, about
growing up in a little southern town. Thinking she was close to finishing, she had accepted a loan from friends—"an act of love" that would
be "the making of me" she had called it—and spent the small advance
from a publisher to stay home and write full-time.[1] That had been
months ago. Beside the typewriter lay the unfinished manuscript with
sentences and paragraphs crossed out, and her editor's comments and
suggestions written in red pencil in the margins.

When she had arrived in New York City from Alabama in 1949,
she had been twenty-three. Her send-off from her hometown of Monroeville had not been festive. Her mother was easily thrown off-kilter by
emotional and health problems. Her father was disappointed that his
youngest child had burned her bridges by dropping out of law school at

the University of Alabama a semester short of graduation. He had entertained an old man's hopes that she would join his law firm, where he had been a partner for more than twenty-five years. Instead, she was leaving to go to New York to write, an ambition that must have sounded obstinately romantic.

He was not a worldly man, but stereotypes of Southerners ran rampant in the North, and she would likely be perceived as just another hick coming to the big city. On the Fred Allen radio show, heard nationwide, a Connecticut-born actor was convulsing audiences with his portrayal of a blustering, pontificating southern politician named Senator Beauregard Claghorn. "When in New York ah only dance at the Cotton Club," intoned Claghorn solemnly. "The only dance ah do is the Virginia reee-ahl. The only train ah ride is the Chattanooga Choo-Choo." Just as popular was *The Jack Benny Program,* whose bandleader, Phil Harris, was from Tennessee and pretended to be drunk. His signature song—a jazzy number called "That's What I Like About the South"—sold millions after it was featured in a hit movie of 1945, *I Love a Bandleader.*

Won't you come with me to Alabamy?
Let's go see my dear old mammy,
She's frying eggs and broilin' hammy,
That's what I like about the South!

Moreover, it was unlikely that lightning would strike twice in the same place: Monroeville had already produced one literary star Nelle Harper Lee's age.

As a child, she had been as close as a sister to the boy next door, Truman Capote. They had played, wrestled, fought, and even written childish stories together. He was something of a sensation now in the literary world, writing for the *New Yorker,* and his first novel, *Other Voices, Other Rooms* (1948) had received an ecstatic review in the *New York Times*: "Only twenty-three now, precocious, self-confident and genuinely gifted, Mr. Capote has been getting himself a reputation by his short stories. . . . In a few years he has mastered a bewildering variety of jobs and acquired an amazingly finished literary technique . . . emotional, poetic, symbolical, filled with sibilant whispering and enigmatic verbal mysteries."[2] No doubt Nelle's desire to emulate her friend was drawing her to New York, but a town of two thousand souls was not likely to produce two published writers in the same generation.

It seemed, however, that nothing could change her mind. After dropping out of law school, she had lived at home and worked as a waitress, saving her money for the day when she could strike out for New York. Finally that day had arrived, and now the family's black Chevy was being loaded for the trip to the train station in Evergreen, an hour away. After she bade everyone adieu, father and daughter drove down South Alabama Avenue, where she had played tag as a child, caught fireflies in jars, shot marbles, and stolen fruit from neighbors' trees. On their way out of town, they passed rickety picket fences, hundred-year-old trees, and homes where people had been born, lived, and died without ever feeling the need to venture far.

To a pair of young eyes like Nelle's, though, Monroeville was just a dusty old hamlet. Even after electric power had arrived in 1923, the town seemed reluctant to leave the nineteenth century. When she was a child, the sawmill whistle at noon announced when it was time for the midday meal; when it blew again, at five o'clock, wives checked their progress on making supper. The metallic clink of blacksmiths' hammers rang from several shady alleys because horse-drawn wagons were still in use. Folks shared "pass-around perennials" to save on expense: calla lilies, coreopsis, dianthus, gladiolas, phlox, and fragrant chocolate vines. In hot weather, a friendly wave from a porch beckoned passersby to come on up for a glass of sweet tea. For conversation, there was news from church, and gossip was always welcome. With as many as ten households on the same telephone party line, everyone eavesdropped on everybody else's business anyway. In times of sickness or trouble, neighbors brought over covered dishes—casseroles, biscuits, collard greens, and ham—whatever they could spare. In the late summer, the air sometimes sparkled at dusk with sawdust from the mills. In winter, the red clay streets turned sloppy, and cars splashed along in axle-deep tire ruts. The week before Christmas, farmers tended not to mind trespassing on their land, so long as anyone hunting for just the right pine tree to decorate respected the fences and closed the gate behind them when they left. About the time everyone turned in for the night, Monroeville's sole watchman began his quiet rounds in the square.

Nelle Lee, who had begun using the byline "Harper Lee" on articles she contributed to the University of Alabama campus newspaper, would have all this to remember whenever she looked back. Mr. Lee turned south out of the square and left Monroeville behind, the white dome of the courthouse receding in the rearview mirror. At Repton, he caught Route 84 to Evergreen, where the Louisville and Nashville Railroad, pulling a line of Pullman cars, would take on passengers. From there, his headstrong daughter could begin the 1,110-mile journey to New York City.

Nelle's first hurdle after arriving in Manhattan with a suitcase and typewriter was finding a decent place to live. The wartime housing shortage wasn't nearly over, and thousands of ex-GIs and their families were living in temporary Quonset huts in Manhattan Beach, Brooklyn, Fox Hills, and Staten Island. Some took whatever they could get. A Marine Corps veteran living with his wife in Queens had to settle for a place that was "seventy dollars a month, hardly furnished, stall shower, ice box. The door down to the basement got water rats. They were banging on the door."[3]

And then there was the sheer size of the city for a small-town girl to reckon with. Eight million people lived in the five boroughs. The skyscrapers of New York resembled colossal outcroppings of rock scraping the clouds. There were twenty bridges, eighteen tunnels, seventeen scheduled ferries, fifteen subways, and eleven thousand taxis. Was it rumor or fact that alligators lived in the sewers, dumped there when they grew too large to be pets?[4]

Finally, Nelle found a cold-water flat in the Yorkville neighborhood on the East Side of Manhattan; by coincidence, it wasn't far from where Capote had rented his first apartment a few years earlier: "one room crowded with attic furniture, a sofa, fat chairs upholstered in that itchy particular red velvet that one associates with hot days on a train.... The single window looked out on a fire escape. Even so, my spirits heightened whenever I felt in my pocket the key to this apartment; with all its gloom, it still was a place of my own, the first, and my books were there, and jars of pencils to sharpen, everything I needed, so I felt, to become the writer I wanted to be."[5] Nelle's place unfortunately came without a stick of furniture.

Yorkville was one and a half square miles of rathskellers, grocery stores, newsstands with papers in East European languages, Brauhauses, delicatessens, coffeehouses, flower shops, drugstores, and German-language movie theaters. Geraniums and catnip grew in window boxes; ivy and myrtle on brick walls; boxwood, yew, and laurel in tubs around sidewalk cafés. A few of the better restaurants, such as the Café Geiger, attracted tourists with loud polka music on weekends for plates of pigs' knuckles and sauerkraut, plockwurst, or Bavarian sauerbraten. In the cellar taverns, a regular topic of conversation was the fallen Nazi Party or, on a happier note, the legend of local boy Lou Gehrig. A block from Nelle was a branch of the New York Public Library.

It was a working-class neighborhood. Children dashed in and among cars after balls and shouted to friends to come out and play. During a recent garbage strike, some residents had protested by dumping their trash in the gutters. On windy days, cyclones of newspapers, bread wrappers, and cigarette cellophane whirled through the air. Squashed fruit rotted and stank and the flies were as big as raisins.[6]

Nelle found a job fairly quickly—Capote thought he could find her one, but that didn't pan out. Instead, she worked in a bookstore, somewhat in the orbit of the literary world, at least. But if any famous writers came in while she was unpacking shipments of books, shelving them, and ringing up sales, she didn't have time to notice. And quickly, she learned one of the first lessons of living in New York: a job that barely pays the rent isn't worth it. At night, if there were no police walking the beat, she slapped parking meters, hoping to dislodge a nickel or a dime.[7]

After a year or so of getting by, her finances improved when she was hired as a ticket agent at Eastern Airlines. She joined a union, the Brotherhood of Railway Clerks, and instantly doubled her take-home pay. Still, for someone with three years of college, showing customers a diagram of available seats wasn't exactly riveting employment. And she was afraid to fly, strangely enough. But she moved over to British Overseas Air Corporation (BOAC), and because she adored

Dickens and Jane Austen, it was exciting speaking familiarly about destinations such as London, Manchester, and Birmingham—the stuff of nineteenth-century novels.

In the evenings, she sat down to write. At first, the din of the city was hard to shut out. Bored taxi drivers blew their horns constantly; the sirens of fire engines made the windowpanes rattle, and radios blaring from open windows in hot weather created a bedlam of music, laughter, and talk up and down the open street. With time, however, she was able to settle into reveries at her desk—just a closet door propped up on blocks. For subject matter, she abided by the advice given to most novices: "Write about what you know." She wanted to write about the comforting ripples of incident and character back in Monroeville. She wanted to catch the rhythms of life in a small southern town: the eccentricities, the humor, and how folks spoke of the past as if it had only happened yesterday. She was lonely.

There was a party-loving bunch of ex-Alabamians in New York, and she had found them. One of the chief revelers was Eugene Walter, a modern-day Puck from Mobile who kept a stuffed monkey under a glass bell jar. His book *The Untidy Pilgrim*—a comic novel about "Mobile madness," a malady specific to the Gulf Coast—won the 1954 Lippincott Prize. He said he couldn't exist in New York except that all the Southerners "would get together about every ten days or two weeks and cry over Smithfield ham. There was a community, like a religious group except it wasn't a church. Southerners always, by secret gravity, find themselves together. . . . You always knew, if there was any kind of trouble, that was like [having] cousins in town."[8] Nelle, accompanied by Truman, put in an appearance from time to time, toting a bottle of scotch, but to most everyone else in the room the quiet girl in scruffy jeans and a tomboy haircut lacked essential cool. The wife of Zoot Sims, the jazz saxophonist, took her measure and was not impressed. "Here was this dumpy girl from Monroeville. We didn't think she was up to much. She said she was writing a book, and that was that."[9]

The years passed. It was 1957; she had spent almost ten years trying to get published. She hadn't submitted a single thing, fearing rejection, except to an agent she had met through a mutual friend. He liked her work, but suggested a change of direction. "Have you ever tried a novel? This story about the woman with cancer ought to be in a novel. Why don't you write one about the people you know so well?"[10] That was what she was *trying* to do, but she felt hopelessly lost. She was floundering, revising, discarding, and starting over.

It was dark and cold outside that night in 1958, and the words on the page in the typewriter might as well have been in Swedish. The whole book—an amalgam of stories, anecdotes, anything she could use—no longer made any sense.

Suddenly, she yanked the page out of the typewriter, gathered up the chapters, the notes, the drafts, walked over to a window on the alley, and threw the entire mess of paper outside into the snow. The wind blew away some of the pages, taking with them words spoken by characters named Atticus, Jean Louise, Uncle Jack, Aunt Alexandra . . . never to be heard from now. She went to the phone to call the editor she was working with, an older woman, and tearfully explained what she'd done.

Then not many minutes later, a young woman on York Avenue could be seen hurrying down the steps of her building, chasing after pieces of typewriter paper. Her editor had chewed her out good, and "since I knew I could never be happy being anything but a writer . . . I kept at it because I knew it had to be my first novel, for better or for worse."[11]

two

"Ellen" Spelled Backward

Hell is eternal apartness.

—HARPER LEE, *Go Set a Watchman* (2015)

"Get *offa* him!" Nelle roared. "Get off now!" She peeled the older boys from on top of their prey, uncovering Truman beneath flailing elbows and knees; he was lying on his back, red-faced and tearful, in the sandpit of the Monroeville Elementary School playground. The bigger boys had been playing a game called Hot Grease in the Kitchen, demonstrating their territorial prerogative by standing with arms crossed in front of the sandpit as they announced, "Hot grease in the kitchen, go round, go round!"[1]

Every other child had been wise enough to obey the injunction, but not Truman, who saw a dazzling opportunity to get attention. He had run straight toward the bigger boys, breaking their line for an instant, but then they dragged him down and piled on. Pain, darkness, and muttered curses between clenched teeth enveloped him for a few seconds, until Nelle leaped in, hauled him to his feet, and escorted him away from his antagonists, glancing backward as if daring any of them to pursue.[2]

But the boys knew better than to try that. Though she was only seven years old, Nelle Harper Lee was a fearsome stomach-puncher, foot-stomper, and hair-puller, who could talk mean like a boy.[3] Once, three boys had taken a shot at her, charging at her one at a time like knights galloping toward a dragon. Each one ended up facedown, spitting gravel, and crying "Uncle!" Watching the mêlée was George Thomas Jones, a sixth-grader in 1933. "In my mind's eye I can still see the fire in those big brown eyes as they stared dead ahead, her teeth clenched in jaws set as only could be akin to a full-blood bulldog. Her tiny hands balled into tight fists as she strode defiantly from the play-ground back toward her fourth-grade classroom."[4] Truman later based the character "Ann 'Jumbo' Finchburg . . . a sawed-off but solid tom-boy with an all-hell-let-loose wrestling technique" on his friend Nelle in his short story "The Thanksgiving Visitor."[5]

No one could dispute that Nelle was quick on the draw out on the playground, but she outstripped nearly all others in the classroom, too. Her vocabulary was prodigious, her skepticism a constant bother to teachers accustomed to obedient children. Classmates would turn around to watch in awe whenever Nelle began asking her usual slew of impertinent questions.[6] Mrs. Leighton McNeil was astonished to hear little Nelle greet her at the start of a new school year as "Leighton." When the child was upbraided, she expressed confusion. At home, she called her father by *his* first name. "The second grade was grim," Scout says in *To Kill a Mockingbird*, "but Jem assured me that the older I got the better school would be."

Further proof of Nelle's peculiarity was her taking on the job of guardian angel to Truman Streckfus Persons—as Capote was known then—because Truman, as every child at Monroeville Elementary knew, was a sissy, a crybaby, a mama's boy, and so on. Moreover, if he had worn a sandwich board to school with the words "Hate Me" painted on it two-feet tall, the advertisement would have been redundant. His clothes extended that invitation from a block away. It was the 1930s, the Great Depression, when children went to school in hand-me-downs that had been patched, taken down, taken up, or taken in several times. A girl in a dress made from a fifty-pound cotton flour sack had nothing to be ashamed of. (Manufacturers printed patterns on the inside just for that purpose.) Many children came to school with no shoes, their dirty heels thumping on the smooth pine floors. Truman, however, whose cousin Jenny Faulk owned a women's hat store in Monroeville, wore Hawaiian shirts, white duck shorts, blue socks, sandals, and Eton caps purchased from the best department stores in Mobile and Montgomery. He looked, as one teacher expressed it, "like a bird of paradise among a flock of crows."[7] The implied insult to the other children could not be ignored. Boys gave him his comeuppance by rubbing cockleburs into his fine blond hair and bruising his milky-white skin.

Nelle was five years old the summer she became acquainted with Truman, who was almost six and living with his late-middle-aged cousins next door, the three Faulk sisters and their brother. Barefoot, Nelle balanced like a tightrope walker along the top of the low rock wall separating the Lee and Faulk properties. (It's still there, falling into ruin.) Beside the wall grew a twin-trunk chinaberry tree supporting a tree house. From this outpost, Nelle could spy on Truman ambling among the lilacs and azaleas. "Beautiful things floated around in his dreamy head," she would later write of him, when Truman became Dill, the lonely boy next door in *To Kill a Mockingbird*. "[H]e preferred his own twilight world, a world where babies slept, waiting to be gathered like morning lilies."[8]

Some of Truman's loneliness gradually abated because of Nelle: "I had a very good friend by then though, so I really wasn't totally alone all the time."[9] Whatever his imaginative gifts, however, at first glance he hardly seemed the ideal candidate for friendship with a girl like Nelle. She was a female Tom Sawyer with large, dark brown eyes and close-cropped hair. Besides, she already had a playmate: her ten-year-old brother, Edwin. As a big brother, Edwin was a little sister's dream. Friends saw him horsing around in the backyard with Nelle, and he was good to her.[10] But when he left for an afternoon game of baseball on the courthouse lawn, she was out of luck. Next oldest in line was Nelle's sister Louise, a freshman in high school. An attractive girl and a smart dresser, Louise participated in 4-H and youth activities at the Monroeville Methodist Episcopal Church. But she was too old to play with Nelle, as was Alice, the Lees' eldest daughter, who was in her early twenties and working full-time at the *Monroe Journal.*

In fact, on the whole block of South Alabama Avenue there were no real peers for Nelle. A little girl lived across the street from the Lees briefly, but she moved away. To the south of the Faulks lived Mrs. Powell Jones and her blind, ex-Confederate husband. Their house was best avoided. The Joneses were very old, and Mrs. Jones, an invalid in a wheelchair, shouted constantly at her beleaguered husband. Children passing by her property were not exempt from her imprecations, either. (Many Monroeville residents would later recognize in Mrs. Jones the model for Mrs. Dubose in *To Kill a Mockingbird,* who tormented Scout and Jem with her vicious taunts.) To the north of the Lees lived Mr. Hendrix, a druggist, and his wife. Their children were grown.

Under these circumstances, Nelle turned to Truman, who was overjoyed. By the second summer of their friendship, 1931, they were partners in adventure. The Faulk residence, where Nelle spent a good deal of her time, was better appointed than most of the houses in town. It was a capacious, high-ceilinged dwelling. The entryway was decorated with potted ferns on special occasions. There was a formal parlor, a dining room with china cabinets displaying "Dresden, Meissen, and sparkling pieces of cut glass," a spacious kitchen where the cook, Little Bit, rustled up enormous meals; a bathroom, several bedrooms, and in every room a fireplace. In the backyard were two or three outbuildings for chickens and turkeys, as well as a smokehouse with hams, bacon, and bagged sausage suspended from the joists during autumn for curing. Also in the backyard was an in-ground birdbath, which the children called a "swimming pool," beside a rock wall. These are the only two remnants of the Faulk home remaining, both of which appear in the novel as part of the property belonging to Dill's aunt, Rachel Haverford.

Virginia "Jenny" Faulk, who was in her midfifties, had built the house as a communal dwelling for her sister Callie, two years younger than she; their brother, Bud, who managed a little farm and had acquired the nickname "Squire" Faulk among the wags in town; and their elder sister, Sook, who, despite being white-haired when Nelle knew her, had the mind and disposition of a preadolescent girl.

Despite the outward signs of gentility, the Faulks lived in a stew of door-slamming, tearful arguments, accusations, shouting, delicious schemes to subvert authority, and mock remorse when one was caught red-handed. Though elderly, the four siblings fought like teenagers. Jenny carried the weight of the household on her shoulders and refused to budge on matters unless she deigned to let Callie have her way; Sook, rarely comfortable with anyone except children, gave away her position as the eldest in return for scraps of kindness and respect. Brother Bud, using his male prerogative, absented himself from the frays downstairs by relaxing in his room. The atmosphere was quite a bit different from the Lees' home, which proceeded day-to-day with an air of managed restraint.

Nelle's favorite among the squabbling siblings was Sook. A prolific baker of fruitcakes—she was later immortalized in Truman's "A Christmas Memory"—Sook kept a plug of Brown's Mule tobacco tucked in her cheek. She dabbed away the juice from her lips with a cotton handkerchief. She was addicted to morphine, prescribed following a mastectomy; and when her medicine bottle went dry, the children saw her grow skittish and distracted until someone fetched her a refill from the pharmacy.

She fed Nelle and Truman sugar cookies dipped in morning coffee and they ate like open-mouthed birds. They sat in her skinny lap making up long, fantastic tales. When the *Mobile Register* landed on the porch, Sook opened to the "funnies" and together the three of them read their favorite strip, "The Meditations of Hambone," which lampooned, among other subjects, the Ku Klux Klan, the Republican Party, and all political elections. The *Montgomery Advertiser*, also widely read in Monroeville, often carried front-page stories by a reporter and columnist named Atticus Mullins, which may have been Nelle's first exposure to the distinctive first name she later gave the hero of *To Kill a Mockingbird*.

The children's private retreat from grown-ups was the tree house in the chinaberry tree.[11] The friends' talents at playing complemented each other. Nelle was best at shooting marbles, while Truman excelled at swiping jacks off the sidewalk so fast that his hand was a blur. As a matter of fact, he was not uncoordinated—the label "sissy" was undeserved; he just wasn't interested in the kinds of things most boys were. But when he played, he was quick, agile, and determined, and could leap up on the rock wall and turn cartwheels. Though he was too small for his punch to pack a real wallop, kids at school called him "Bulldog" because he had an underbite, and he lived up to the moniker by head-butting adversaries and knocking them down. One afternoon in the lobby of the Lyric movie theater in Mobile, Bulldog sailed in a bit low and collided with the other boy's genitals.[12]

So whether he actually needed her help or not, it was a point of pride for the roughest girl in school to be the bodyguard of her pip-squeak friend. In a funny way, they went together: She was tall for her age; he was small and delicate. She was too rough for the girls; he was too soft for the boys. That was how they appeared on the surface, any-way. But they also had a secret understanding about themselves. They were bound, said Harper Lee, "by a common anguish."[13] For both children disappointed their mothers' hopes—they were just too different.

Nelle's mother's side of the family began in Virginia, resurfacing in Monroe County, Alabama, in the early 1800s, probably as part of the migration of farmers who could no longer afford good land along the mid-Atlantic seaboard. Nelle's grandfather, James Cunningham Finch, the postmaster, grew up on his parents' farm near Belle's Land-ing. His wife, Ellen Rivers Williams, came from a family that owned a plantation nearby, about halfway between Montgomery to the north, and Mobile to the south. The land was excellent, bordered as it was by the Alabama River, flowing south to Mobile Bay. The river would flood the Williamses' bottomlands at least once a year, and sometimes several times, depending on the rainfall. It was deep enough, too, that steamboats arrived to offload goods and take on the Williamses' cot-ton. Enslaved farmhands stood at the top of the hill and slid the four-hundred-pound cotton bales down a steep chute to stevedores on the deck, who stopped them before they fell overboard.

James Finch's family was not as gentrified as Ellen Williams's, but they tried to rear their two daughters in genteel circumstances. When Nelle's mother, Frances, and Frances's sister, Alice, reached fifteen, they were enrolled in the new Alabama Girls' Industrial School in Montevallo, a progressive boarding school for whites created by Julia Tutwiler, a feminist leader in Alabama educational and penal reform.

The school was unusual, because it was both a vocational and a finishing school. All the girls took English, Latin, and other basic high school courses. Then they could add elective classes, including stenography, photography, typewriting, bookkeeping, indoor carpentry, electrical construction, clay sculpture, architectural and mechanical drawing, sewing, cooking, and "other practical industries," according to the school catalog. The catalog also expressly warned that "pupils are not here to enter society, but to be educated; therefore they are not allowed to correspond with gentlemen, and visits from them are positively prohibited under penalty of expulsion."[14] Trips off campus into Montevallo were forbidden without a chaperone. All the girls wore the school uniform: a navy blue dress and a beret with a white tassel. Frances Finch distinguished herself by excelling in music and appeared as a pianist and vocalist in concerts and recitals.

With such an education, Frances Finch was an artistic, some might say slightly pampered, young woman. Throughout her life, family members often used the word *gentle* to describe her.[15] An ambitious husband for her—one her parents approved of, although he was a bit older than Frances—would appear on the scene before long.

Amasa Coleman Lee, born July 19, 1880, in Georgiana, a village in Butler County, Alabama, was the middle of nine children: six boys and three girls, two of whom died in childhood. His family called him Coley. It's highly doubtful that these Lees are related to the famous Virginia tidewater Lees that include Robert E. Lee, as encyclopedia entries about Harper Lee continue to claim. The history of Harper Lee's family in North America began with John Lee, Esq., born in 1695 in Nanesmonds, Virginia. Her grandfather Cader Alexander Lee was a private in the 15th Alabama Regiment of the army of the Confederate States of America, who fought in twenty-two battles including Gettysburg. When the 15th surrendered at Appomattox, Private Lee was one of only a few hundred remaining from the original fifteen hundred recruits. General Lee may have tipped his hat to one of his most valiant soldiers, as well he should have, but that's as far as current genealogical research will take us about the relationship.[16] Nelle's grandmother, the former Theodocia Eufrassa Windham, was sister to one of Cader Alexander Lee's kinsmen who had been killed early in the war at the battle of Malvern Hill in Virginia.

Young Coley Lee's upbringing was Methodist with a stringent dose of evangelicalism, which emphasized the authority of the Bible, personal conversion, and salvation by faith. The Lees frowned on drinking, card playing, gambling, and other diversions considered a waste of time. On Sundays, his father hitched up the horses for the three-and-a-half-mile trip from their farm to services at the local Methodist church. The message delivered there—to act according to the teaching of the Gospel—became Coley's central philosophy as an adult. Respectable Christians needed to be concerned about their Divine Father's work. But farm chores took precedence over philosophizing or book reading. Some winter evenings during the school year, Coley ran out of daylight before finishing his lessons. At sixteen, he passed the examination to teach, which he did for three years at a school near Marianna, Florida.

By the time he was twenty, Coley was introducing himself as A. C. Lee. Eager for advancement, he relocated to Monroe County in Alabama, where sawmills were chewing into the piney woods, filling the air with their earsplitting shriek and the vinegary smell of fresh-cut lumber. He was a man on the go in those early years, which was fairly typical of the generation that came after the War Between the States. As the southern historian Edwards Ayers wrote, "Investors began to put money into sawmills, textile factories, and coalmines. Young people of both races set out for places where they could make a better living. Railroads connected the landscape, cutting into clay banks, running across long sandy and swampy stretches, winding their way through wet mountain forests. Enthusiastic young editors talked of a 'New South.'"[17] Deprived of victory on the battlefield, ambitious white Southerners looked to a New South to regain their pride.

A. C. Lee took a series of better-paying jobs as a bookkeeper, which brought him to the Bear Creek Mill at Finchburg, Alabama. While attending church one day, Lee, who was thirty, met the postmaster's daughter, nineteen-year-old Frances Cunningham Finch. They married in the bride's home on June 22, 1910.

As a provider, A.C. did not disappoint the new Mrs. Lee. In 1912, two years after their marriage, he accepted a position as financial manager for the law firm of Barnett & Bugg in Monroeville, which was then a small, segregated town of 750 residents.

Monroeville hadn't changed much from the days of the War Between the States, when a Confederate soldier passing through wrote to his folks that he had arrived in the "most boring place in the world."[18] But in the early 1900s, the town finally seemed about to live up to its potential. The year the Lees arrived, the first locomotive of the Manistee and Repton Railroad reached the downtown on freshly laid tracks. The railroad was the brainchild of Lee's employers, Barnett and Bugg, along with a third investor. The county newspaper, the *Monroe Journal,* proclaimed that the Manistee and Repton intended "to establish freight and passenger rates with the Louisville and Nashville Railroad, which will be a great convenience to all concerned."[19] The M&R did indeed begin hauling freight and passengers east from Monroeville to Manistee Junction, where it joined like a tributary the mighty Louisville and Nashville Railroad. And from there, it was possible to go to just about any major hub in the United States.

A. C. Lee's career flourished in Monroeville. First, he acquitted himself well as a financial manager. Then by reading for the law under the tutelage of his employers, he passed the bar examination in 1915. Steadily, he was ascending the rungs of respectability: from teacher in a country school, to bookkeeper, to financial manager, to attorney. The firm changed its name to Barnett, Bugg & Lee.

He was in every respect a New South man who had fought his way up from poverty—a replacement for the old ruling aristocracy that reluctantly yielded, as the historian W. J. Cash said, to the men of "Rotary, the sign-manual of the Yankee spirit, the distillate, as it were, of the Yankee mind," though every "Southern gentleman expressed contempt for money-grubbing Yankees as a way to ease his own mind about Yankee success."[20] By the time he was forty, Lee would have his finger in every pie in town: the bank, the newspaper, the Chamber of

Commerce, Kiwanis, and the local Methodist church. The New South meant economic growth and local pride.

The Lees had four children: Alice Finch Lee, born in 1911; Frances Louise Lee, born in 1916; and Edwin Coleman Lee, born in 1920. But the birth of their youngest, Nelle Harper Lee, on April 28, 1926, put an unexpected wrinkle in the upper-middle-class home life the Lees enjoyed. By naming her "Nelle"—her grandmother Ellen's name spelled backward—it was as if they had introduced a changeling into the quiet and sober Finch-Lee line. (Nelle's middle name, Harper, was a tribute to Dr. William W. Harper who had ministered to mother and child after baby Louise failed to thrive and Mrs. Lee suffered a nervous breakdown.[21]) Deliberately or not, she rebelled at everything her mother valued. Nelle would not go willingly into the "pink cotton penitentiary" of girlhood, any more than would her fictional self, Scout Finch.[22] Miss Tutwiler's Alabama Girls' Industrial School would not have been the place for her. She couldn't even accept, without squabbling with her teachers, the three Rs offered at the public school down the block. Consequently, Frances Lee and her headstrong daughter lived in two different worlds.

Truman disliked Nelle's mother, partly out of loyalty to his friend but also because Mrs. Lee was an "eccentric character" and an "endless gossip," he thought. He poked fun at her in a story he submitted to the *Mobile Register* for a children's writing contest. She was Old Mrs. Busybody, "a fat old widow whose only amusement was crocheting and sewing. She was also fond of knitting. She didn't like the movies and took an immediate dislike to anyone who did enjoy them. She also took great delight in reporting children to their mothers over the slightest thing that annoyed her. In other words no one liked her and she was considered a public nuisance and a regular old Busybody." Over the next twenty-seven pages of Truman's childish handwriting, Mrs. Busybody is driven to distraction by a visit from her loud and embarrassing in-laws, until they leave on the train for their home in "Slumtown."[23]

The story was so true to life, Capote claimed, that when it appeared in the newspaper, he instantly became a notorious character on South Alabama Avenue. "I'd walk down the street and people on their front porches would pause, fanning for a moment. I found they were very upset about it. I was a little hesitant about showing anything after that. I remember I said, 'Oh, I don't know why I did that, I've given up writing.' But I was writing more fiercely than ever."[24]

The differences between Nelle and her mother were sharpened because Mrs. Lee, sometime after Nelle's birth, began to show signs of mental illness. Truman's cousin, Marie Faulk Rudisill, visited the Lees now and then and saw evidence of it.

> She was very kind and very sweet to us. Always had a watermelon for us out on the back porch, but she didn't talk to us at all. I never saw her even speak to one of her children. She got up in the morning and started playing that darned piano all day long, or going outside on her front porch and tending to her nasturtiums in flower boxes on the end of the porch. Those were the only things I ever saw Mrs. Lee do, but as far as providing companionship for the children that wasn't so because Mrs. Lee never left the house.[25]

"She would speak to you. She would speak to you," remembered a visitor to the house. "She was a big, heavyset lady—but I don't think she was well."[26]

From the time she was small, Nelle mainly knew her mother as an overweight woman with a host of demons; her symptoms suggest what is now known as bipolar disorder. The "gentle soul" of the household could become inexplicably upset or unaccountably happy at the drop of a hat. On certain days, Mrs. Lee acted withdrawn: she might remain blank-faced in response to a greeting, as if she didn't know the person, or she might only nod in reply. On other occasions, she would veer to the opposite pole, her mind racing, words tumbling out; at these times she seemed to fear the worst. One hot day, Mrs. Lee spotted someone walking quickly past the house. Thinking he was going to get sunstroke, she charged out on the porch and—pointing to another passerby, who was strolling—she shouted with a note of desperation, "Walk like her!"[27]

How serious the situation was, no one could deny after an incident when Nelle was two. According to Truman, whose account was substantiated by others, one day Mrs. Lee tried to drown toddler Nelle in the bath. Mrs. Lee was an older parent, in her forties, and perhaps she was suffering postpartum depression after the birth of her fourth (and very difficult) child. In any case, Alice and Louise heard the commotion and rushed into the bathroom to save their sister. Truman claimed it happened again. In *To Kill a Mockingbird*, Scout says, "Our mother died when I was two, so I never felt her absence." Perhaps the emotional bond snapped between mother and daughter with lasting impact on Nelle's development, deprived as she was of approval from one of the most important figures in a child's life. Her mother's illness almost certainly denied her the constancy children need to feel secure.

The Lees coped with Frances's "nervous disorder," as they preferred to call it, as well as they could. Monroeville, especially during the hard-bitten years of the Great Depression, was a place with few resources for someone with mental health problems. After the stock market crashed in 1929, the town, like a boat unmoored, drifted back into the economic twilight that had preceded its two golden decades between 1910 and 1930. The standard of living in the South at the end of the 1920s was already the lowest in the nation. The South ranked at the bottom in almost everything: ownership of automobiles, radios, residence telephones; income per capita; bank deposits; homes with electricity, running water, and indoor plumbing. Its residents subscribed to the fewest magazines and newspapers and read the fewest books; they also provided the least support for education, public libraries, and art museums.[28]

To compensate for the lack of health care, Mr. Lee made it a practice to send his wife on long summer vacations to Orange Beach on the Gulf of Mexico, under the watchful eye of his secretary Maggie Dees. There Mrs. Lee was free to read and rest. (Capote said, "Mrs. Lee, who was a brilliant woman, could do a *New York Times* crossword puzzle as fast as she could move a pencil.") Meanwhile, he packed Nelle off to his sister-in-law's house in Atmore, hoping for a little peace and quiet for a few weeks. Daughter Alice, whose family nickname was "Bear," shifted some of her father's burdens onto herself by acting as his substitute helpmate in practical affairs. The two other Lee children had their own ways of getting by. Louise maintained an active social life and moved away as soon as she was old enough. Edwin, simply called Brother, stuck close to a few good friends, played sports, and kept his head down.

A.C. responded to his wife's maladies with a stiff upper lip. A quiet, thoughtful man, he went about his business without complaint, probably reasoning that everybody had some kind of cross to bear and that in the scale of things he had much to be grateful for.

Also, Mrs. Lee had hired help, as was customary among better-off white families.[29] Hattie Belle Clausell was the cook, housekeeper, and nanny; every day except Sunday, she walked over to South Alabama Avenue from the "colored" part of town, known as "the quarters," which was literally on the other side of the tracks.[30] Mrs. Clausell kept the house organized with a sort of Spartan plainness: there were no rugs to vacuum or shake out, the chairs were cane-backed, the iron bedsteads had been painted white, and the pine floors gleamed from regular rubbings with oil.[31] When Nelle barged through the screen door after a day of playing, sunburned and grass-stained, it was Mrs. Clausell who ordered "Miss Frippy Britches" out of her overalls, to be washed, combed, and given supper in the kitchen.[32]

Meanwhile, Mrs. Lee's health continued to deteriorate. Although she wasn't supposed to go out when she was feeling bad, she went out anyway, until steps were taken to keep her on the premises. Sympathetic neighbors spoke of her condition as "hardening of the arteries" or "having a second childhood"—expressions used at the time to describe mental illness including dementia in older people.

Truman's aunt, his mother's sister, Marie Rudisill, was a teenager in those days and used to visit with Mrs. Lee sometimes. "I think she loved people, but she had a very hard time expressing it."[33]

Nelle came into the world with a mother who was ill; Truman's unhappiness, on the other hand, began even before he was born. His mother simply didn't want him; in fact, she abandoned him.

Lillie Mae Faulk, five foot two, with brown eyes, had the reputation of being a "rare beauty" in Monroeville.[34] When she sold tickets at the

Strand Theater, the only movie house in town, teenaged boys gawked at her as if she were something wonderful on display inside the glass ticket booth.

Then in the spring of 1923, Archulus Julius Persons (pronounced "PEER-sons"), arrived in a chauffeur-driven Packard Phaeton.[35] He was in town visiting fraternity brothers from college. As a suitor, Arch had some considerable baggage: he was a huckster, a disbarred lawyer, and a world-class liar. But Lillie Mae was smitten, even if her suitor did wear spectacles as thick as magnifying glasses. More and more often, Persons came calling for his sweetheart at the Faulks' home, where Lillie, for reasons that are unclear, was living with Jenny, Callie, Sook, and Bud instead of with her parents. On August 14, 1923, a silver-haired probate judge named Murdoch McCorvey Fountain granted Arch and Lillie a marriage license. Arch was not quite twenty-six, and Lillie Mae was just sixteen. A week later, on a sweltering day, a Baptist minister conducted the wedding in the Faulk home, as guests consumed gallons of iced tea and lemonade. At the piano, Nelle's mother played classical music.

It only took a few weeks for the glamour of romance to wear off. In New Orleans, where the couple were kicking up their heels in the French Quarter, Arch confessed to his child-wife that he was in "straitened means"—in other words, he was broke and "between opportunities." Tearful and humiliated, Lillie Mae returned alone to Monroeville. Arch hung back in New Orleans, probably suspecting, with good reason, that Jenny Faulk would brain him with a skillet if he dared show his face. Once before, years earlier, she had driven off with a horsewhip a man she didn't think was fit to court her sister, Callie. The newlyweds reconciled and fell out again several times over the next year.

Their only child, Truman Streckfus Persons, was born on September 30, 1924. Arch named him "Truman" after one of his college friends; "Streckfus" was intended to flatter Arch's most recent employer, the Streckfus Steamship Line, a fleet of old-fashioned paddle wheelers called "tramps" that offered hot jazz by Louis Armstrong and other musicians during one-night trips on the Mississippi and Ohio rivers.

But the marriage was doomed. Threats of divorce smoldered as Lillie Mae and Arch both pursued extramarital affairs while Truman grew into a toddler. The Faulks' housekeeper, Corrie, was unsurprised, saying Lillie Mae "will never be content. She's born greedy for mens an' money."[36] Lillie Mae, determined to immerse herself in cosmopolitan excitement and sophistication, would check into hotels in places like New Orleans and Mobile. If Truman was with her, she would lock him in alone for the evening, instructing the front desk to ignore his hysterical screams.[37]

In the summer of 1930, Lillie Mae brought Truman to Monroeville to live indefinitely with his Faulk relatives; she divorced Persons the following year. Freed from the financial burdens of parenthood, Arch slipped away in a rented limousine in pursuit of get-rich-quick schemes, while Lillie Mae flew like a butterfly to New York, having won an Elizabeth Arden beauty contest. Truman started throwing red-faced tantrums, legs flailing in the air. "Lillie Mae was that most treacherous of mothers," wrote a reviewer of Gerald Clarke's *Capote* (1988), "a discontented small-town beauty who would appear in his life for a day or two, wafting the perfume of motherhood over him, then disappear." The metaphor is more than apt: once, after Lillie Mae had departed again, Truman drank a bottle of her perfume to try to keep some of her essence inside him.[38]

But there was an aspect of him he could never change, and Lillie Mae was repulsed by it: his behavior was effeminate. She resented her son for not conforming to her idea of what a boy ought to be. Lillie Mae continually attacked him; she rode him constantly.

"Truman, I swear, we give you every advantage, and you can't behave. If it were just failing out of school, I could take it. But, my God, why can't you be more like a normal boy your age? I mean—well, the whole thing about you is so obvious. I mean—you know what I mean. Don't take me for a fool."[39] So he was trapped. Craving his mother's love, he missed it keenly; on the other hand, there was an aspect about him that he couldn't change, and it repelled her. Like Nelle, he was who he was.

Gender expectations and sexual orientation troubled Nelle as a child as well, if we accept that Capote was portraying her accurately in his first published novel, *Other Voices, Other Rooms* (1948). She is Idabel

Thompkins in Capote's telling—a forceful personality, quick with a dirty joke, haughty, and angry about the constraints of her gender. When Joel, the main character, expresses embarrassment about undressing in front of Idabel, she retorts,

> "Son," she said, and spit between her fingers, "what you got in your britches is no news to me, and no concern of mine: hell, I've fooled around with nobody but boys since first grade. I never think like I'm a girl; you've got to remember that, or we can't never be friends." For all its bravado, she made this declaration with a special and compelling innocence; and when she knocked one fist against the other, as, frowning, she did now, and said: "I want so much to be a boy: I would be a sailor, I would . . ." the quality of her futility was touching.[40]

A reviewer for *Time* wrote, "For all his novel's gifted invention and imagery, the distasteful trappings of its homosexual theme overhang it like Spanish moss."[41]

Truman and Nelle were just, in Truman's phrase, "apart people," different from most other children their age.[42] ("Hell is eternal apartness," Jean Louise comments in *Go Set a Watchman*.) A classmate of theirs at Monroeville Elementary School recalled seeing them play a word game before the start of the Saturday matinee at the Strand Theater. "They were a little above the rest of the kids in town."[43]

In their defense, Monroeville during the Depression in the 1930s was not much to be above. There was no library, nor were there many ongoing activities outside of church. There were no books to take home from school because the school had none to loan. Movies at the Strand Theater tended to be escapist westerns, adventures, or romances, because people wanted to forget their problems for a few hours. "This was my childhood," Nelle said. "If I went to a film once a month it was pretty good for me, and for all children like me. We had to use our own devices in our play, for our entertainment. We didn't have much money. Nobody had any money. We didn't have toys, nothing was done for us, so the result was that we lived in our imaginations most of the time."[44] She might be overstating the case a bit here. During the Great Depression, when homeless men would rake leaves for a sandwich, the Faulks and the Lees barely felt the pinch. Truman's spanking-new clothes testify to that; and the Lees sent all four children, including the two girls, to private colleges. To invoke a word that's not often used any longer, the reason that Nelle Harper Lee acted up in class and did pretty much as she pleased may have been because she was the youngest and "spoiled."[45] "We were privileged," she admitted. "There were children, mostly from rural areas, who had never looked into a book until they went to school. They had to be taught to read in the first grade, and we were impatient with them for having to catch up."[46]

One day a glimpse of possibilities induced a moment of rapture in Monroeville children. In the fall of 1931, Nelle and her classmates thrilled to an announcement by the principal that everyone should go outside and look in the direction of Alabama Avenue. Poking its monstrous dark nose above the trees, a craft as big as a flying battleship churned into view. It was the eight-engine, 785-foot Navy dirigible U.S.S. *Akron*. One of the boys on the playground felt a sense of awe sweep over everyone: "And there it was, right before your eyes. A gigantic, sleek, grey giant silhouetted against an overcast morning sky. It was an eerie sight as it glided noiselessly, and so low to the ground that it seemed as if you could reach up and touch it. . . . [A] kind of mild hysteria set in and students bolted the campus, crossed the road, and chased the giant airship down the old M & R railroad tracks until it was out of sight." The airship churned away, pointing like a compass needle to the future.

One way "apart people" with time on their hands could feed their imaginations was by reading. Truman's cousin Jennings Faulk Carter recalled how Nelle and Truman created a bond over books that put them in splendid isolation.

> The year I began school, Truman and Nelle were knee-deep reading Sherlock Holmes detective books. Even though I hadn't learned to read with their speed and comprehension, we three would climb up in Nelle's big tree house and curl up with books. Truman or Nelle would stop from time to time to read some interesting event aloud. We'd dis-

cuss what might happen next in the story and try to guess which character would be the culprit. Sometimes Truman called me "Inspector." Nelle was "Dr. Watson." [47]

The Rover Boys, a series written by Edward Stratemeyer, was a favorite too, despite the stories' ridiculously stilted dialogue—" 'Hello, you fellows!' shouted a voice from behind the Rover boys. 'Plotting mischief?' " At least they featured a girlfriend-sidekick named Nellie. A better choice, in Nelle's opinion, was the Seckatary Hawkins series by Robert F. Schulkers, about a boys' club on the Kentucky River. The club's motto was "Fair and Square." (From *To Kill a Mockingbird*: "Atticus opened his mouth to say something, but shut it again. He took his thumb from the middle of the book and turned back to the first page. I moved over and leaned my head against his knee. 'H'rm,' he said. *'The Gray Ghost*, by Seckatary Hawkins. Chapter One . . .' ") Nelle wrote to the publisher requesting a club membership form. In her childish handwriting she signed the pledge: "I shall always be fair and square, possessed with strength of character, honest with God and my friends, and in later life, a good citizen." [48]

Just as satisfying as reading stories to herself was hearing stories read aloud. "When we were a bit too young to read, Brother, who was a voracious reader," Nelle said, "would read many, many stories to us. Then we'd dramatize the stories in our own ways, and Truman would always provide the necessary comic relief to break up the melodrama."

Sometimes Nelle's friendship with Truman was tested, though—he could be a handful. Being insecure and easily upset, he strained everyone's patience. But Nelle wouldn't let him get under her skin, even when he marred a nice afternoon spent cutting out magazine pictures of kites by raging at her.

" 'Stop that, Nelle. Keep your hands off my pictures. I hate you, Nelle. I really do.'

'You shut up, you silly little shrimp, or I'll knock your silly block off.' " [49]

He couldn't push her far.

When this sort of pleading failed, he tried playing the victim, to shame her into letting him have his way. "She was bigger than Truman. Lots bigger," said Jennings's mother, Mary Ida Carter. Nelle would hurl him to the ground, as if to demonstrate that weakness made one legitimate prey—"She was tough on me," he said.

Unable to overcome her in physical contests, he tried other methods to manipulate her. Once, smarting from one of their fights, he concocted a fabulous scheme to make her jealous: he decided to run away with another girl who was older. They hitched to Evergreen, probably with the idea of getting on the train and lighting out for parts unknown. But they were spotted and brought home by suppertime.[50]

Yet despite their spats, separations, and grudging reconciliations, the two friends remained inseparable. They swam in the pond at Hatter's Mill Creek, where speckled trout tickled their legs. Sometimes they hiked the dirt road that led to cousin Jennings's farm. They dug in when Truman's aunt Mary Ida spread the kitchen table with homemade biscuits, jam, butter, and fresh milk to welcome them. And if there was nothing else to do, they could always walk to the town square. As Scout says in *To Kill a Mockingbird*, "There was no hurry, for there was nowhere to go, nothing to buy and no money to buy it with, nothing to see outside the boundaries of Maycomb County."[51] But window-shopping was free. There were stores around the square—in the center of which was a grassy park with three enormous oaks—providing simple goods and services: hardware, jewelry repair, dry goods, and so on. At the pharmacy, cold drinks cost five cents. Expensive, but sometimes, a tin can on a string descended like bait from a second-floor window of the jail by the courthouse, meaning a prisoner up there needed someone to run an errand. In the bottom of the can would be money for cigarettes, and a tip left over.

The Barnett and Jackson Hardware Store was a dependable stop because the owner, Gus Barnett, had a wooden leg and never minded hiking up the cuff of his trouser to show it off. For pretty things, there was Meyer Katz's Department Store. Katz was a Russian Jew who had worked his way up from peddler in southern Alabama to patriotic merchant. "The only free cheese is in a rat trap!" he was fond of saying. He also had the distinction of selling the local Ku Klux Klan their sheets in the 1920s. When a member of the Invisible Empire, as they called themselves, said that maybe he shouldn't be purchasing his robes from a Jewish store owner, Katz replied, "That's all right because you know who I am and I know who you are. And you know that if you buy them somewhere else you will have to pay more for them."[52] (In *To Kill a Mockingbird,* Atticus recalls how the Klan paraded by "Mr. Sam Levy's house one night but Sam just stood on his porch and told 'em things had come to a pretty pass, he'd sold 'em the very sheets on their backs. Sam made 'em so ashamed of themselves they went away.")

Also on the square was the Home Café, which in *To Kill a Mockingbird* became the O.K. Café, "a dim organization on the north side of the square." Mrs. Dubose, trying to intimidate Scout, stops her with "What are you doing in those overalls? You should be in a dress and camisole, young lady! You'll grow up waiting on tables if somebody doesn't change your ways—a Finch waiting on tables at the O.K. Café— hah!"[53]

The Simmons Hotel advertised a fifty-five-cent brunch special on Sundays in the sunroom. Fifteen minutes before all was ready—chicken, mashed potatoes, okra, corn, gravy, cornbread, and pie—a black child wearing a white suit rang a handbell loudly like a town crier at the curb. The event was a treat for those who could afford it, although Sundays were special for everyone. Scout says, "Of all days Sunday was the day for formal afternoon visiting: ladies wore corsets, men wore coats, children wore shoes."[54]

And presiding over the square was the Monroe County Courthouse, open to the public during the week. A genial, moonfaced man named Judge Nicholas Stallworth had conceived it. He was convinced that Monroeville, the "hub of Southwest Alabama" needed a courthouse worthy of the distinction. In 1903, work got under way, until the blueprints disappeared and a new set had to be drawn. As construction proceeded, it was pointed out that the basement should have been scooped out first, causing another delay. As the costs continued to mount, predictions flew that the four-story citadel of brick, capped by a six-sided clock tower dome was going to be a financial fiasco at taxpayers' expense. They voted Judge Stallworth out of office and rued the day they had ever agreed to "Stallworth's Folly."[55]

But when at last the courthouse was complete, there was nothing foolish about its interior. On the contrary, it was, as the *Monroe Journal* boasted, "one of the handsomest and most conveniently appointed in the state and one that would do credit to a county far exceeding Monroe in wealth and population." Painted all white inside, with rows of wooden benches like pews, curving side aisles, and tall windows, the courtroom gave the impression of a small church with New England ties. (To this day, visitors tend to take off their hats when they enter, and to speak in a whisper.) The pine floor, tight as a ship's deck, was coated several times with black gum resin, to resist scuff marks from the boots of country folk. At the front was the judge's bench, on a dais enclosed by white balusters, where lawyers presented their forensic performances. To the right was the jury box.

From the second-floor gallery, Truman and Nelle sometimes watched Mr. Lee below as he presented cases. In fact, Nelle only seemed to have two favorite pastimes, Truman complained: either hanging around the courthouse and playing pretend golf.

Until, that is, the flint of their imaginations was sparked by an act of thoughtfulness: Nelle's father gave them a typewriter to share—a black, steel-chassied Underwood No. 5 with keys that made a satisfying "Clack! Clack!" Just operating it was fascinating. "Ding!" The tree house would have been the ideal office, but the typewriter was too heavy to get up there. Instead, they sat under the big yellow rose bushes in the Faulks' backyard. Truman would bring his tattered copy of Webster's dictionary, and together they would sit for hours, tapping out stories.[56] A girl from school tried to join in, but discovered that three's a crowd. "Nelle grabbed some paper and put it in the typewriter. Truman started telling a story, and while he talked Nelle typed it. Well, they would not let me help with the story, so I just grabbed my paper dolls and went home!"[57]

Before long, the residents of South Alabama Avenue unknowingly became dramatis personae in the first stories of coauthors Truman Streckfus Persons and Nelle Harper Lee.[58] Looking back, Nelle was of the opinion that small-town life "naturally produces more writers than, say, an environment like Eighty-second Street in New York. In small town life and in rural life you know your neighbors. Not only do you know everything about your neighbors, but you know everything about them from the time they came to the country."[59] One of their earliest efforts (since lost) bore the provocative title "The Fire and the Flame."[60]

And there was certainly no lack of interesting people in the vicinity to write about. As a source of mystery and speculation, for instance, nothing beat the tumbledown Boulware place just two doors south of the Lees'.

It was a dark, ramshackle house with all the paint gone from the boards. What went on inside was a matter of conjecture, because the shutters stayed closed as if the house were asleep. The owner was Alfred R. Boulware, sixty, a merchant and an influential man in town but a cheapskate. Boulware wouldn't spend a dime on his house, or its raggedy yard of tangled pecan trees. Regardless, his sagging realm belonged to him and nobody was permitted to put a foot on it without his permission. A well-hit ball from the schoolyard over the fence into Boulware's weeds might as well have landed in a minefield. Everyone knew better than to retrieve it. Even the pecans that fell from the trees were his, and he stood in the backyard, arms crossed, as if daring any kid to steal one.

He had three children—Mary and Sally, both in their late twenties, and Alfred, Jr., who was nicknamed "Son."[61] Every weekday morning Mary and Sally emerged looking fresh as daisies. They waved to Nelle and Truman like beauty queens on parade floats, and then continued on their way downtown to their respective jobs, Mary as a dental assistant and Sally as a secretary. This unaccountable behavior left Nelle and Truman astonished, because Son Boulware, whom nobody had seen in years, had become a southern Frankenstein's monster—a prisoner in his own home, tied to a bedstead.

His fate sounded like a campfire tale, but the tale was essentially true. Sonny Boulware and two schoolmates, one of them the sheriff's son, had been hauled before Judge Murdock Fountain in 1928 for breaking school windows with a slingshot and burglarizing a drugstore.[62] The judge decided that such enterprising young men could benefit from a year at the state industrial school. The two other boys' parents concurred, but not Mr. Boulware. He asked the judge to turn the boy over to him, promising that his Sonny would never trouble anyone again. (It's said by those who remember what happened that Mr. Boulware "was too proud to have his son sent to a correctional facility.")[63]

After that, Son was rarely seen by anyone.[64] At first, friends from high school would crawl on elbows and knees to his bedroom window to talk to him. Word got around that he would gladly do the football players' math for them. In return for his help, team members took him for rides in the darkness after midnight.

But eventually, his classmates grew up and moved on, and he was forgotten. Occasionally, as the years went by, he would appear on the porch at night, his presence only known by making the rockingchair creak and squeak. Children coming home from school held their noses while walking by, or crossed to the other side of the street to avoid inhaling evil vapors. Some neighbors reported hearing a parched voice from the Boulware place cry, "Caw, caw!" and incidents of peeping Toms were blamed on him. Nelle had seen him outside once, resting in the shade, and didn't find him so strange. But essentially, Sonny Boulware was erased from Monroeville forever. "Mr. Boulware ruined his son's life, I guess because it was shaming him," said a friend of the Lee family. "That man was *mean*."[65] Or as the Finches' housekeeper Calpurnia says bitterly in *To Kill a Mockingbird,* when "Boo" Radley's father dies, "There goes the meanest man God ever blew breath into."

Son Boulware never left the property again, until he was carried out on a stretcher in 1952, dead from tuberculosis. The marker placed at his grave in the First Baptist Church cemetery reads, TO LIVE IN HEARTS WE LEAVE BEHIND IS NOT TO DIE.

The splendid friendship between Nelle and Truman was interrupted suddenly in the mid-1930s, when Lillie Mae belatedly exercised her partial-custody rights and took Truman to New York City. Her second husband, a Cuban-American businessman named Joseph Capote, adopted him, and ten-year-old Truman took Capote as his surname. Lillie Mae, who was now calling herself Nina, enrolled him in prep school. From then on, until he was about eighteen, Truman returned to Monroeville only during the summers. He had always been an outsider, and now his connection grew more and more tenuous. In fact, he enjoyed letting people know he was different now, a New Yorker—a fact he liked to lord over everyone.

During one of his return visits, he ambled into a drugstore on the square one afternoon and sat down at the lunch counter, looking bored.[66] He was dressed in his prep school jacket and tie, and he flicked his long blond hair out of his eyes. "I'll have an ice cream," he said. The teenaged soda jerk behind the counter asked him what kind. Capote replied, "Oh, I don't know. . . . I guess I'll have a Broadway flip." The teenager shoved Truman backward off the stool, spilling him on the linoleum floor. "There you go!" he said. Capote stood up, straightened his jacket, and left.[67] His revenge came later. During an all-day rainstorm, he hired the only taxi in town and kept it for himself all day.

The Lees might have sent Nelle away to a private school, too. They were better off than most, and some parents in town who had the means sent their children to boarding schools in Birmingham and Montgomery. The Lees, however, knew their youngest was a nonconformist and bored with school already.[68] There was a chance that at a private school, she might be pigeonholed as a hopeless troublemaker. The Lees were too tenderhearted to resign her to a lonely fate like that. Instead, it seems that her father took her in hand.

By now Mr. Lee was in his midfifties, and he didn't seem the type to minister to a rowdy child young enough to be his granddaughter. His favorite caddy on the golf course, Joseph Blass, had trouble imagining it. "He seemed much more of an intellectual than a physical man. The image of shooting the mad dog or of facing down the crowd of roughnecks has never quite rung true to me. The strong intellectual stand, though, seems very natural."[69]

Truman's aunt Marie Rudisill agreed. "Mr. Lee was detached, not particularly friendly, especially with children. He was not the sort who came up to his children, ruffled their hair, and made jokes for their amusement."[70] As Scout says of Atticus, he "treated us with courteous detachment."

The era before World War II had a good deal to do with Mr. Lee's reserve. Professionals such as doctors and lawyers were expected to display a degree of gravitas around others. Southern gentlemen felt an obligation to set an example to the common whites: advise them, get them out of trouble, and hold them to a moral standard that was part Christian, part southern tradition, and a good fit with Rotarian ethics for the public man.[71] The impression Mr. Lee gave of being a bit stuffy was a function of the times, said a resident. "People seeing him in the normal course of affairs might interpret his formal habits of speech and behavior as signs of coldness and distance. For example, he and my father were good friends and golfing buddies, but I don't believe either ever called the other by his first name."[72] Younger members of the Kiwanis Club were too cowed by Lee's standing in the community to use his nickname, "Coley," even though he welcomed it in the spirit of fellowship; they preferred instead paying a quarter into the club treasury each time they respectfully called him A.C.[73]

Mr. Lee was of slightly taller than average height, with flat, pugnacious features like a boxer's. But his large-eyed, impassive expression, accentuated by a pair of big round glasses, seemed permanently impressed on his face from his days as a bookkeeper. Every weekday morning, like clockwork, he could be seen coming down the steps of the Lees' bungalow dressed in a rumpled three-piece suit. Passing beneath the fig trees, crape myrtle, and pecans in the front yard, he turned left to walk the two blocks north to his law office above the bank in the town square. Had someone pointed him out as a minister, a scholar, or a professor, instead of one of the most prominent businessmen in town, it would have seemed appropriate. His mannerisms were those of someone always preoccupied with his thoughts.

Stopping to converse with him required patience. His manner of speaking was almost comically precise and deliberate. He did not make conversation as much as offer pronouncements that began with "ah-hem!" progressed to "uh," and sometimes, for emphasis, ended with "ah-RUM!"[74] It was as though every matter he was invited to discuss had a potentially grave aspect, and he wanted to limit his personal liability by choosing his words with absolute care. He much preferred listening to talking, often while sucking thoughtfully on a piece of hard candy. He also had a distracting habit of absentmindedly fumbling with things, including his watch, a fountain pen, or his special favorite:

a tiny pocketknife that he flipped with his thumb and caught like a coin. Once a hardware store clerk waited while Mr. Lee selected and flipped different penknives until he found one with exactly the right weight and balance. It soothed him to do it.

He did not grope for words, however, when writing editorials for the *Monroe Journal.* In addition to being an attorney, in 1929 he had purchased a partnership in the newspaper. Founded in 1866, the *Monroe Journal* was not one of the more influential organs in a state that boasted the *Mobile Register,* the *Montgomery Advertiser,* the *Birmingham News,* and the *Birmingham World,* the most widely read black newspaper.[75] But the *Journal* was a dependable guide to goings-on in the county: a weekly farrago of mishaps, odd bits of local and national news, letters from readers, arrests, marriages, visits by out-of-town kin, births, and deaths. Residents of Monroe County looked to it as their source of local information and opinion. As the *Journal*'s editorialist, Lee used the paper as a bully pulpit from which to address his favorite topics: taxes, overreaching government, drinking, hooliganism, and political corruption. As a businessman and a civic leader, Lee was intent on keeping the peace, because peace facilitated progress; but such a stance also put him in a bind.

Whites were afraid of blacks getting out of control, forgetting their place; unless examples were made, some might take it into their heads to victimize whites who were alone in the back county or traveling on deserted roads.[76] Heinous crimes—and ones in which blacks were accused received particularly gruesome attention in newspapers— triggered cries for swift justice, and Southerners tended to be skeptical of official authority.[77] From the *Monroe Journal* in 1892: "Mr. Richard L. Johnson, an aged gentleman from the north who moved into the community only a short time previously, was called to the door and brained with an ax, his daughter outraged and the bodies of both consumed in their burning home. Four Negro suspects were arrested, and being confronted with circumstantial proof of guilt, were said to have confessed participation in the crime. They were lodged in the jail. In the dead hours of the night, a mob stormed the prison, took the miscreants therefrom and meted out punishment."[78] A willingness to believe the worst, added to a perverse sense of what constituted law and order, resulted in otherwise upstanding citizens attending lynchings with a clear conscience, like a posse out West riding out and hanging an outlaw. "Every mob in every little Southern town is always made up of people you know," Atticus tells Scout.

Violence also addressed maladies southern white men shared as a result of the War Between the States—wounded pride, loss of honor, loss of caste, loss of face.[79] The southern white man has "freed himself from every stigma," says Uncle Jack Finch in *Go Set a Watchman*, "but he sits nursing his hangover of hatred."[80]

Yet there were many who, like A. C. Lee, opposed nursing a "hangover of hatred" because disorder was not in the community's interest. Monroeville had only one police officer in the 1930s, and liquored-up mobs might destroy property; workers who resorted to rowdyism at every provocation made poor employees. According to one historian, membership in the Alabama Ku Klux Klan actually declined steeply from 115,000 in 1925 to 1,349 in 1930, because those who were otherwise in sympathy with its platform—Americanism, Protestantism, and the supremacy of the "Caucasian race"—"condemned its use of the mask, intimidation, and violence. Its own excesses virtually destroyed it, especially in the South; in fact, opposition to the hooded order was more serious and outspoken in the South than anywhere else."[81]

A. C. Lee belonged to the camp intent on keeping the peace for the sake of progress and social uplift. Nor was he merely talking through his hat about the importance of law-abiding behavior. One night in August 1934, just weeks before a state election, a hundred Klansmen gathered in the parking lot of Monroeville Elementary School to make a show of force. Marching up South Alabama Avenue in serried rows toward the courthouse, the hooded figures passed the Lee property. A.C. came down off the porch, his suspenders hanging in loops to his knees and confronted the local Grand Dragon. After an exchange of words in the street that lasted a few minutes, a compromise was reached. The marchers dropped the militant pose and walked the rest of the way like pedestrians.[82]

But it must be emphasized here that although Mr. Lee, on whom Harper Lee later based Atticus Finch, was a better educated man, a more enlightened man than most, he was no saint, no prophet crying in the wilderness with regard to racial matters. In most ways, he was typical of his generation, especially about issues surrounding blacks, the law, and segregation. He was a Southerner—the son of a Confederate soldier—and his heritage, even his religion as it was then practiced, shaped his views.[83]

On Sundays, A. C. Lee the public man took a few moments to be alone with his thoughts during services at the Monroeville Methodist Episcopal Church. Congregants noted that he preferred to sit in front by himself. Later during the service, in his capacity as church deacon, he would rise to lead his fellow worshippers in long improvised prayers, tapping the pew with his penknife to create a cadence for his deep, somnolent voice.

Lee's beliefs reflected the core of southern Methodism in the first half of the twentieth century, built as they were on the conviction, as he wrote in the newspaper, "that the destiny of this world in the years before us is very largely in the hands of the rather small percentage of mankind that have come to accept the Christian religion, and have recognized that in reality this is our Father's world, and that the way of life He has provided is the only way that holds any promise of endurance. And that way of life includes the acceptance of his rules and regulations for all creation, including mankind."[84]

In a roundabout way, segregationists and apologists for slavery found justification in words like these. Their argument ran something like this: "Every man was in his place because He had ordained it so. Hence slavery, and indeed, everything that was, was His responsibility, not the South's. . . . And change could come about only as He Himself produced it through His own direct acts, or—there was always room here for this—as He commanded it through the instruments of His will, the ministers."[85] This philosophy provided balm to many an uneasy mind, which preferred to believe that Southerners had "bled for God and Womanhood and Holy right; not one has ever died for anything so crass and unbeautiful as the preservation of slavery."[86]

But few people studying A. C. Lee while he was speaking about God and obedience in such uncompromising terms, in print and during Sunday services, could have guessed correctly what kind of parent he was under his own roof. The truth was, despite his reserve in public, he was a fond and indulgent father. At home, he encouraged Nelle to clamber up on his lap to "help" him read the newspaper or complete the crossword puzzle. And she did call him A.C., as Scout calls her father Atticus. They invented a word game, which they played together while Nelle toyed with A.C.'s pocket watch. One would think of a word and provide two clues: a letter and the total number of letters. Then the other would have to guess the word. Nelle's vocabulary shot up as a result. Scout recounts how her teacher, Miss Caroline, fresh out of college and eager to teach reading, "discovered that I was literate" and instructs her to "tell your father not to teach you anymore. It's best to begin reading with a fresh mind. You tell him I'll take over from here and try to undo the damage." Because Scout is one of the few girls in class, it's possible Miss Caroline's reaction of "faint distaste" arises also because she thinks a girl shouldn't be so bold.[87]

Mr. Lee used a light hand when it came to disciplining his children, overlooking misdemeanors for the sake of teaching a lesson. He spared the rod, preferring to reassure Nelle—even if it meant being too lenient at times—that she was growing up in a home where she was loved. Perhaps he leaned far over in this direction to compensate for what his wife seemed incapable of giving.

"Nelle just trotted at her father's heels, up and down the street," said Marie Faulk Rudisill.[88]

three

Without "Finishing Touches"

Poor child, is it that she believes she is a freak, too?

—WISTERIA, the carnival midget in
Truman Capote's *Other Voices, Other Rooms* (1948)

An era in Harper Lee's life seemed to end one winter night in January 1940. A bitter north wind rattled the strings of Christmas lightbulbs still hanging in trees on the courthouse square. It was so cold that her father was forced to throw extra coal in the furnace to keep their little bungalow warm. "For reasons unfathomable to the most experienced prophets in Maycomb County," says Scout in *To Kill a Mockingbird*, "autumn turned to winter that year. We had two weeks of the coldest weather since 1885, Atticus said."

Next door, Truman Capote's cousins, the Faulk sisters and their brother, were just getting ready for bed when the sound of frantic pounding on the front door sent Jenny Faulk downstairs again, expecting to find a lunatic on the porch. To her shock, the kitchen was ablaze and a neighbor was trying to force his way in to help.

Nelle heard the volunteer firefighter siren go off. The Faulk family, wearing only bathrobes and slippers, stumbled into the front yard, abandoning their home to the fire hose and the ax. Flames, leaping inside, pressed against the windows, shattered the glass, and burst upward into the darkness. The firefighters had trouble getting the hydrant at the curb to work properly because it was frozen.

Soon the whole house was a pyre, and the wind-driven flames roared through the trees toward the Lees' property, less than fifteen yards away. The "fire truck began pumping water on our house; a man on the roof pointed to places that needed it most," says Scout in *To Kill a Mockingbird*. The paint on the Lees' white bungalow began to blister and slough off from the heat. Nelle's mother feared the worst; her husband and neighbors guided her to a house across the street to calm her. A scene transpired that was almost identical to the one described in the novel. "At the front door, we saw fire spewing from Miss Maudie's dining room windows. As if to confirm what we saw, the town fire siren wailed up the scale to a treble pitch and remained there, screaming. . . . We stood watching the street fill with men and cars while fire silently devoured Miss Maudie's house."

The struggle lasted until 3:00 A.M. By dawn, the Faulk residence, where Jenny Faulk had been known to welcome any "smear of kin," was a carcass of blackened walls and bony icicles.[1] Even their smokehouse, stuffed with cured hams, bacon, and bagged sausage hanging from rafters, had collapsed. The exhausted volunteers trudged home. One of them removed his waterlogged wool overcoat and hung it on a hook outside his front door. Within a couple of hours, it was frozen like ice. He stood it on the porch steps, ghostly and uninhabited, to the delight of passing children.[2]

The destruction of Capote's childhood home coincided with the beginning of Harper Lee's adolescence, leaving behind a kind of golden age she would yearn for in her fiction.

In September 1940, she entered Monroe County High School with the United States' entry into World War II only a year away. All around her, the engines of the nation's economy were finally revving up after years spent idling during the Great Depression. After the attack on Pearl Harbor in December 1941, Monroeville awoke from its sleepy, magnolia-shaded lassitude, roused by a sense of national purpose. The Lees found a number of ways to pitch in, doing more than many families.

A.C. assisted his former law partner, J. B. Barnett, now president of the Monroe County Bank, in chairing local war bond drives; Alice volunteered for the Red Cross; Louise had settled down for the duration of the war in Eufaula, Alabama, with her infant son to await her husband's return from duty; and Edwin suspended his studies at Auburn University in 1943 to join the Army Air Corps. In addition, the governor appointed A.C. to the three-member state Alcohol Beverage Control Board. Knowing Lee's views about alcohol consumption, newspaper editors all over the state had a field day commenting about giving a teetotaler oversight for liquor. Mr. Lee, a strict Methodist, was, as everyone knew, "as dry as an old bleached bone."[3]

Nelle, only sixteen during the first full year of the war, navigated adolescence according to her own lights. Generally, she ignored conventions that applied to most girls. "You took her as she was. She wasn't trying to impress anyone."[4] During a game of touch football on the courthouse lawn, she straight-armed a boy out of the way, who protested as he fell, "Nelle, we're playing touch!"

"Y'all can play that sissy game if you want to," she shouted over her shoulder, "but I'm playing tackle!"[5] In a photograph taken during her sophomore year, she poses with her English class on the high school steps. Unlike nearly all the other girls, she isn't wearing lipstick, her hair doesn't look as if it's seen a curling iron recently, and her chin, held high, gives her unsmiling face a truculent expression.

Just how different she felt from girls her own age is suggested in Capote's *Other Voices, Other Rooms*, when her counterpart, Idabel, creates a weird moment of rapport with a circus performer named Miss Wisteria. Joel watches fascinated as Idabel, "borrowing [Miss Wisteria's] lipstick, painted an awkward clownish line across her mouth, and Miss Wisteria, clapping her little hands, shrieked with a kind of sassy pleasure. Idabel met this merriment with a dumb adoring smile. Joel could not understand what had taken her. Unless it was that the midget had cast a spell. But as she continued to fawn over tiny yellow-haired Miss Wisteria it came to him that Idabel was in love.

'Poor child,' Miss Wisteria asks Joel, watching Idabel scamper off, 'is it that she believes she is a freak, too?'"

* * *

Freakishness implies that there was no one a teenaged Harper Lee could identify with, no one she could emulate. Actually, there were two women who influenced her, both of whom possessed characteristics she admired.

There was Miss Watson, for example, her high school English teacher. Because the faculty of Monroe County High numbered only about a dozen teachers, students took Miss Watson's classes for three years—sophomore through senior English, which included a semester of British literature. Many students counted themselves lucky to have had a triple dose of "Gladys" (as some called her secretly). Her graduates who attended area colleges and universities were surprised to hear their English professors say, "Well, you must have taken Miss Watson."[6]

Tall and thin, she lived with her parents across the street from Nelle, in a two-story yellow house with a deep, wide veranda. Her father "Doc" Watson was a dentist, a three-hundred-pound giant of a man. In addition to being one of the best teachers in town, Miss Watson was an energetic gardener. Neighbors were accustomed to seeing her in her parents' yard pruning the lilacs, tending the potted succulents on the porch, and yanking out pernicious weeds in the grass, her fair face hidden beneath a big straw hat to keep off the sun. From her, Harper Lee created Scout's best adult friend, Miss Maudie Atkinson.

Of the characters in the novel, Miss Maudie is the most candid and also, for a woman, the least conventional. For forty years, Scout's Uncle Jack Finch has been shouting, "Marry me!" to her during his annual visits at Christmas. "Miss Maudie would yell back, 'Call a little louder, Jack Finch, and they'll hear you at the post office, I haven't heard you yet!'"[7] Her thoughts about racism, fairness, and human foibles—key themes of *To Kill a Mockingbird*—mirror Atticus's, putting her in the minority of Maycomb's residents. After Atticus says, "It's a sin to kill a mockingbird," Harper Lee leaves it to Miss Maudie to explain: "Your father's right," she said. "Mockingbirds don't do one thing but make music for us to enjoy. They don't eat up people's gardens, don't nest in corncribs, they don't do one thing but sing their hearts out for us. That's why it's a sin to kill a mockingbird."

Her alter ego, Miss Watson, introduced an unusual amount of intellectual rigor to Monroe County High School. Her classes began in September with students receiving a blue grammar rules booklet she personally had selected—a sort of early Strunk and White *Elements of Style*. It was going to be their Bible, she told them—they should never lose it.[8] Grammar was not a pointless academic exercise, but a tool—the key to being clear in written expression. She called on students to read their compositions aloud. As she listened, she leaned forward, sucking on an earpiece of her pink tortoiseshell glasses and interjecting now and then, "That was good, very good."[9] Little did her students know that she would have given anything to be a writer herself.[10]

Sometimes when the class had grown weary, she read them a story, a poem, or scenes from Shakespeare. *The Canterbury Tales* was a favorite because she read passages in Middle English, which she was proficient at.[11] One has to imagine the effect on students who were the sons and daughters of farmers, laborers, and merchants hearing their teacher drop into a version of their native tongue that was seven hundred years old. Harper Lee became devoted to British literature as a result, spending time in the school library looking up topics Miss Watson had mentioned in class. A well-thumbed copy of *Pride and Prejudice* opened for her the intimate world of Jane Austen.[12] "I cling to the old gentlemen, like Charles Lamb and Robert Louis Stevenson," she said later, "and to Jane Austen, writing, cameo-like, in that little corner of the world of hers and making it universal."[13]

A lifelong bond developed between Nelle and her sister Alice, too, though Alice was seventeen years her senior. Alice's disposition and outlook were very similar to her father's. To draw an analogy between life and fiction, Miss Maude is to Atticus what Alice was to A. C. Lee, although Nelle later reduced the comparison to "Alice is Atticus in a skirt."[14] For their shared qualities, Harper Lee admired her sister as much as she did their father.

Physically, however, Nelle and Alice were as alike, Capote said, "as a giraffe and a hippopotamus."[15] Alice was a polite, birdlike woman—traits that belied her forcefulness; Nelle, by the time she was an adult, had the carelessness and appearance of a man. Alice, always at the head of her class, graduated at sixteen from high school and enrolled at the Methodist-founded Women's College of Alabama in 1929, becoming the first member of her family to attend college. It was one of the happiest times of her life, she said.[16]

But then her sophomore year she returned to Monroeville, called home by her father. He needed her help: Mrs. Lee was not well, and Louise, Edwin, and Nelle were then thirteen, nine, and three, respectively. In addition, he in 1929 had purchased a majority share of the *Monroe Journal* and was now the publisher. At eighteen, in addition to her household responsibilities, Alice joined the small staff as associate editor.

She was needed there because purchasing the *Monroe Journal* was part of Mr. Lee's larger plan to run for the state legislature. In an advertisement appearing in the newspaper, he assured the electorate that his candidacy was "not prompted by any political or selfish motive, but with the sincere purpose to contribute to the general welfare." A Southern Democrat, an advocate of states' rights, and a fiscal conservative, in the August primary he thumped his opponent 281 to 116 (the Republicans had not bothered slating a candidate for seventy-five years), and in the November election he won the seat handily.[17] Alice continued to remain in Monroeville, "keeping the home fires burning."[18] Her spirit and intelligence suited her for a larger arena, but her devotion to her father came first.

Meanwhile, A.C. toiled away in the Alabama legislature, pursuing a political career that was not exceptional, but steady. During the years he represented Monroeville, he was proudest of making good on a campaign promise to push through a budget bill that put county fiscal systems on a pay-as-you-go basis, thus reducing deficit spending.[19] He also sponsored a bill that substantially raised the pension amount awarded to several thousand Confederate soldiers and their widows still living in Alabama in the 1930s. These were not bills put in the hopper by a firebrand: they reflected his conviction that states' rights trumped federal power.

But as the 1938 election approached, he decided he would not run again. After more than twenty years on the public scene, he was one of the most prominent figures in southern Alabama. In his hometown, he was a guiding spirit as a highly regarded attorney, newspaper publisher, bank director, civic leader, and church deacon. Also, there was the other side of the ledger to consider: he was coming up on sixty years of age. His legacy was on his mind when his law partner L. J. Bugg died. With Bugg departed, there was a once-in-a-generation opening in the firm.

By then, Alice was twenty-six; she had moved away from Monroeville and was living on her own for the first time, working as a clerk in Birmingham, Alabama, in the newly created Social Security department of the Internal Revenue Service. But her father raised another possibility: she could take night classes at the Birmingham School of Law and come in as a partner. She hesitated to accept, wondering if she would be perceived as Mr. Lee's "little girl." But he prevailed, and in July 1943, after four years of part-time study, Alice Lee became one of the few female lawyers practicing in Alabama. She acquitted herself well during her first case at the Monroe County Courthouse, too, and after that, she said, "I was treated as a member of the Bar and not as an aberration."[20] She never married or lived away from Monroeville for the rest of her very long life, which spanned almost the entire twentieth century and extended into the twenty-first.

Alice's family nickname, "Bear," hints at her patience and stamina. To Nelle, she was something of a hero, although how Alice felt about furthering their father's plans after her younger sister later left for New York City and freedom created some friction between them. Alice had been asked to step into her father's shoes; and in her role as surrogate parent, she was determined as time went on to take charge of her rambunctious sister.

Initially, Nelle too had followed her family's wishes, as young people tend to do. In 1944, she enrolled at the former Women's College of Alabama, where Alice had spent her freshman year. (It had been renamed Huntingdon College, for the Countess of Huntingdon, a sponsor of the Wesleyan movement in England that inspired Methodism.) Wasting no time, she signed up for summer classes beginning the June of her high school graduation, with an eye toward studying law eventually at the University of Alabama. Her father viewed this latest development with undisguised pleasure, which was evident from a little joke he was fond of telling when someone asked about the family. The way things were going, he said, feigning bemusement, he might have to change the name of the firm from Barnett, Bugg & Lee to "A. C. Lee and Daughters, Lawyers."[21]

But Huntingdon College, as it turned out, was a poor fit for his youngest; it was better attuned to young women who hoped to graduate with a "Mrs."—more like Frances Lee had been at that age.

Huntingdon was a picture of propriety in the mid-1940s. As freshman girls arrived through the front gate, they saw directly ahead John Jefferson Flowers Memorial Hall, styled in the collegiate Gothic architecture of Cambridge and Oxford, complete with a few gargoyles on the center steeple. The foyer led to the chapel (mandatory attendance every morning in the 1940s) with open-air cloisters to the Green, which was a park-cum-playing field and the site of an annual May festival with a maypole and May Queen. To the left and right of Flowers Hall, extending along a low semicircular ridge, were the library and the student center with a tea room, two dormitories, and the infirmary.

The girls' education included practice in the social graces. At dinner, students sat at tables of eight with a female instructor at the head. The correct piece of silverware was supposed to be used for the proper course, and everyone was expected to take a serving from the dishes out of politeness, even if they didn't care for any. Now and then the instructor would peek under the table to make sure none of the girls had her legs crossed—feet *flat* on the floor. Once a month, usually on a Sunday, the girls were expected to come down to dinner in evening dress. An appropriate outfit for a Saturday in Montgomery consisted of a skirt, a cardigan, pearls, a black Chesterfield coat, white gloves, and a white scarf worn in blustery weather; "We must have looked like a bunch of penguins," one alumna later said.[22] In their rooms, the girls could wear whatever they chose, but the instant they stepped outside— even to go to class—they were expected to adhere to a dress code deemed appropriate for young ladies.

Nelle shared a room with two other girls in Massey Hall, where the housemother was Mrs. Hammond or "Mother Hammond," a beloved figure on campus who enjoyed playing the role of nosy maiden aunt. When a young man arrived to pick up his date, Mrs. Hammond made a show of examining him up and down through her pince-nez as if she had never seen such a specimen in all her years. It was rumored she could smell beer at twenty feet.

There were many fine instructors at Huntingdon, but Nelle's favorite was Irene Munro, a graduate of Wesleyan and Columbia universities whose course on international affairs had extra relevance because of the war. In a number of ways, Professor Munro was like Gladys Watson. She peppered her lectures with sketches of notable people in arts and letters. She impressed upon her students the need to always think critically and emphasized that an education was not a commodity that could be purchased. "If you lost your lecture notes, would you forget everything you're learning here?" she asked regularly. "I certainly hope not."[23]

Lee made friends with a junior in Munro's class and they studied together, but it struck the other girl that Nelle was different from most of the students. "I don't think that there were others at Huntingdon—whom I knew and had ready access to—who had these same interests."[24]

It was true Miss Lee was probably better informed than most of her classmates about history and politics; after all, her father was a newspaper publisher and a former state representative. She also read a great deal. On the other hand, she was not as sophisticated, perhaps by choice, about politeness. The girls on her floor objected to her use of salty language, for instance. "We were taught that if you had to resort to ugly words, you had a very weak vocabulary and needed further English study. Actually we were not sure what a lot of bad words meant. We were ladies in every sense . . . at least, most of us were. So, a girl who used foul language was a misfit in every sense of the word. Nobody wanted to be around her."[25] Another criticism was her smoking—or, rather the way she smoked. Students were permitted to smoke in their rooms, but a girl passing by the door of Nelle's room did a double take when she saw Miss Lee at her desk puffing away meditatively on a pipe.

She skipped the monthly formal dinners rather than be forced to wear an evening gown. When Saturday night came and the girls left for a night of dancing, she found other ways to spend the evening, or she just went home for the weekend. "She wasn't like most of us. She wasn't worried about how her hair looked or whether she had a date on Friday night like the rest of us were. I don't remember her sitting around and giggling and being silly and talking about what our weddings were going to be like—that's what teenage girls talked about. She was not a part of the 'girl group.' She never had what we would call in the South 'finishing touches.' "[26]

At the end of first semester, her roommates kicked her out.

Against the larger canvas of the campus, however, she made a different impression. Seen from a distance, the traits that set her apart from the normal Huntingdon "penguins" were found intriguing. Walking across campus with her long stride, dressed in a simple navy cotton skirt, white blouse, and her brother's gift of a brown leather bombardier's jacket—he had enlisted in the Army Air Corps—she cut a figure that blurred gender distinctions. "She had a presence. I remember her better than I do anyone else at Huntingdon, except my roommate and maybe one or two other people. Everything about her hinted at masculinity. I think the word *handsome* would have suited her. . . . Having come from a family of privilege and money, she was unpretentious."[27]

She was not incapable of making friends, either, if given the chance. A chat with her after class revealed a bubbling, subversive wit. From her vantage point at the edge of Huntingdon's lively social mainstream, she confided that there was nothing she disliked about the place; she just found the experience a little humorous at times. Her conversation was rich in observations of campus life, spun into stories. Exhaling smoke slowly from her cigarette, she would watch the face of her entertained listener with an amused expression. It took a while to get to know Nelle Lee, but those who did realized that she was comfortable in her own skin. Her cussing was unconscious; the clothes she wore appealed to her because they were practical; she laughed when one of her teasing remarks drew a comeback delivered with equal zest. But she would not seek others' approval. The notion that she should do so never seemed to enter her head. Her right to live as she pleased was not up for negotiation, even if it ran against the grain of the milieu at Huntingdon. It was nobody's business. "That was an era when you did the proper thing," said a classmate. "And your mother was horrified if you didn't. That was never part of Nelle's persona—she didn't care! It must have taken a colossal amount of courage to be different."[28]

* * *

Although sidelined socially at Huntingdon, Lee contributed to the *Huntress*, the campus newspaper, and in April, she was inducted with seven other girls into the campus chapter of the national literary society, Chi Delta Phi. Also that spring, the second-semester edition of the Huntingdon literary magazine, the *Prelude,* featured her first two published pieces of fiction. They stand out not only because her storytelling voice comes through, but also because of the daring choice of subject matter.

"Nightmare" is about a child overhearing a strange commotion on the other side of a fence. It's a lynching—though, mercifully, Lee doesn't describe it; the child runs home and hides. A man passing by her window says, "Now maybe they'll learn to behave themselves."[29]

The second story, "A Wink at Justice," features a wise judge who knows the difference between the letter of the law and justice. It begins, "The tiny courtroom reeked of tobacco smoke, cheap hair oil, and perspiration," anticipating the description of Scout and Jem arriving at Calpurnia's church in *To Kill a Mockingbird*: "The warm bittersweet smell of clean Negro welcomed us as we entered the churchyard—Hearts of Love hair-dressing mingled with asafetida, snuff, Hoyt's Cologne, Brown's Mule, peppermint, and lilac talcum." The case in "A Wink at Justice" centers on eight black men arrested for gambling. Judge Hanks, who hears the case, is a dead ringer for A. C. Lee, right down to his mannerisms: "He carried a pocketknife which he twirled constantly, sometimes thumping it up and catching it. Fine lines ran down from his nostrils to the corners of his mouth. I noticed that they deepened when he smiled. A pair of rimless glasses perched precariously on his short nose."

Judge Hanks comes down from the bench and orders the accused to turn their palms up. "He went down the line inspecting each outstretched hand. To three of the men he said, 'You c'n go. Git out of here!' To the other five he barked, 'Sixty days. Dismissed.'" Then an unnamed "I" approaches the judge (Lee's struggles with shifting points of view dogged her writing even then). The narrator asks the judge how he reached his decision.

"Well, I looked at their hands. The ones who had corns on 'em I let go, because they work in the fields and probably have a pack of children to support. It was the ones with soft, smooth hands I was after. They're the ones who gamble professionally, and we don't need that sort of thing around here."[30]

Taken together, the two stories introduce ideas that would preoccupy Harper Lee for the rest of her writing career: childhood, a fatherly figure, racism, and the difference between law and justice.

After moving into a single room, Lee spent a lot of time alone. Sometimes seen at the library studying, she seemed "reclusive" to others. But she had no intention by then of staying until the end of her sophomore year to finish her requirements; she applied as a transfer student for the law program at University of Alabama. The departure after freshman year suggests that she had had enough of Huntingdon.

One of her instructors, a professor of history and economics mentioned to his teaching assistant that he was sorry to see Miss Lee go. "Several students were doing outstanding work and she was one of them. He was disappointed because he thought she had a lot of promise. He was interested in the girls he thought would go far."[31]

In June, the girls exchanged yearbooks for friends to sign. Lee scribbled a quick piece of farewell verse in one that ended, "you were so swell / and now I'll leave you / with love & all that hell!" The girl to whom it was written thought, "Hmm, typical Nelle."[32]

four

Rammer Jammer

I shall probably write a book some day. They all do.
—Nelle Lee, quoted in the University of Alabama's
campus newspaper, October 8, 1946

Harper Lee arrived on the Tuscaloosa campus in the autumn of 1945 with an optimistic heart, and added her name to the Panhellenic Association's list of young women participating in Rush Week. Perhaps it was a good-faith gesture, going Greek, to satisfy her mother.

At Chi Omega, the members serenaded newcomers with fraternity and drinking songs. Nelle liked the humor; they invited her back. And a few days later, the Chi Os' Nu Beta chapter accepted her. It was a house that "specialized in blondes," proclaimed the university yearbook, "long, short, thin and broad," including a recent Miss Alabama. Social events figured importantly in the lives of the girls, so after one of them got to know Nelle Lee better, she "wondered what she saw in a sorority to join it."[1]

It was, after all, an exciting time to be a single woman on campus. World War II had officially ended in September, and the student body of 7,500 was suddenly awash in green and khaki with veterans. The girls greeted them with open arms, and more than just figuratively.

The student newspaper, the *Crimson White,* added luster to their fantasies by featuring an undergraduate "Bama Belle" on the front page almost every week—lovely as a Hollywood starlet, sometimes with the enviable distinction of being a young man's fiancée. A few Bama Belles were married already and pictured in romantic settings with their husbands, suggesting that a princess had at last found her prince. During the war, men had been in such short supply that some college women had taken to calling each other Tom or Bill just to hear a man's name said.

But that was all over now, and the girls of Chi Omega prepared for action.

The sorority was a two-story brick house painted white and designed in the Jeffersonian Federal style. To the right of the main stairway was the sunroom; to the left, the dining room. A black butler served at table. Upstairs, the young women got ready for the day, and once they had left for class in the mornings, black maids scurried upstairs to dust, sweep, and change the sheets. None of the girls would have dared to come downstairs other than nicely dressed, and not just because there might be a young man or several down there. A masculine voice calling up the stairs, "Three for bridge!" was an invitation for anyone to play a few hands and socialize.

There was a country club atmosphere about the University of Alabama. Zelda Fitzgerald interrupting a football game in the 1920s to dance the Charleston on top of an automobile on the fifty-yard line captured the feeling: 'Bama was the demesne of smart, well-off white students, of whom Nelle Lee was one.

Yet she seemed so unlike other young women. She chain-smoked; she preferred men's flannel pajamas; she never came to breakfast because she hated eggs; she didn't like swing music and sang numbers by Gilbert and Sullivan in the shower. "She was a little mannish-looking," recalled one of her sorority sisters. "When girls had long hair and did things with it, her hair was short."[2] Another chose the word *matronly* to describe her: "A little bit thick in the middle. Nothing very stylish." However, "she had beautiful large, dark brown eyes that were quite piercing."

In the evenings, the girls chatted about their days and their beaux, but Nelle didn't. "She was just sort of a loner. She just sat there and looked. I don't remember any contact between her and anybody." At mealtimes, "she never entered into any conversations with the girls at the table, but was more of an observer. I always had the feeling that she found us very shallow, silly, and young, in which case she was absolutely right."[3] Most of the girls incorrectly assumed Nelle was a graduate student. She could be friendly, "but she was not going to bounce up to somebody and go, 'Hiya, I'm *Nail!*'"

On weekend nights, when the other Chi O girls were bustling around, getting ready for dates or dances, Nelle never had any plans. No one recalled seeing her with a beau. Saturday mornings, she tromped through the living room, golf bag slung over her shoulder, heading out for a few rounds. The way she dressed for eighteen holes raised a few eyebrows—just jeans and a sweatshirt. "That wasn't the way we dressed."[4] Nelle's style was pronounced "very different." And some found that offensive.

One morning, as she was passing the Phi Mu house, some girls went to the windows and sang "Three Blind Mice," the theme song of the dim-witted Three Stooges. Their voices were loud enough so that the target of their derision could hear every syllable. She looked like a drudge as she passed the fifteen houses on Sorority Row, one of the choirsters said, "long flat shoes, straight hair, a slight slump, probably because she carried a black, portable typewriter in one hand and a stack of books and papers in the other. I'm ashamed to admit that we made fun of her. Today she would be called a nerd."[5]

After a year living at the sorority house, Nelle moved out into New Hall, a female dormitory. She continued to take her meals at the house now and then, and attended chapter meetings too, but her sorority sisters lost interest in her: "I never saw her with anyone and wondered if she were lonely."[6]

Fortunately, it didn't take her long to find her way to the Alabama Student Union in search of opportunities to write. Up on the third floor was "the most casual colony" she was likely to find, she said, and they greeted her as one of their own. They were "the various editors, feature writers, proofreaders and kibitzers who sling together" the University of Alabama campus publications.[7]

Their meeting space was a large room divided in half by file cabinets: on one side was the staff of the *Crimson White*, the campus newspaper; on the other, the writers and editors for the *Rammer Jammer*, the campus humor magazine, named for the thunderous cheer shouted by Crimson Tide football fans: "Rammer jammer, rammer jammer, rammer jammer!"

Nelle introduced herself to the *Crimson White* editor in chief, who was, she said, "a lanky, Klan-hating six-footer from somewhere in Mississippi."[8] She offered her services as a stringer—someone to cover the odd meeting or event. But most of the news beats had already gone to journalism majors; also working against her was that she had no experience. Undeterred, she went around the file cabinets to the *Rammer Jammer* side; original submissions were needed there, and students interested in creative writing were fewer in number than campus journalists. Nelle got her hand in right away by submitting "Some Writers of Our Times" for the homecoming parody issue—a takeoff on *Esquire* magazine.

"Some Writers of Our Times" poked fun at the notion that in order to write, you must be tormented.

A factor in the development of creative talent is that a soul is required. Now there are several classifications of souls, namely: The Frustrated Soul, The Somnambulistic Soul, and The Warped Soul. (The W.S. results in the most profit these days.) But no matter what kind of soul the budding writer has, it must be flaunted before the eyes of his readers. . . . The element of frustration is another *must*. If a person is not frustrated, what would he have to write about? He must love himself to an unbearable degree, curse God at regular intervals, be scorned by the one person he loves better than himself. Then he will have the material with which to produce the most provocative novel of the century.[9]

Lee also scoffed at the trend of setting novels in "small towns, preferably Southern villages" (as both her novels would be!).

And he certainly must not omit his reflections upon the way justice is so casually administered by the crooked Judge in the broken down courthouse. Yes, it is to the writer's advantage if he comes from such surroundings. He has a chance to expose to the public the immoral goings-on in an out-of-the-way village, have himself hailed as the H. W. Beecher of the day, and instigate a movement which would do away with small towns forever.

She can't resist including a little in-joke, too. Among her acquaintances is an intense southern writer, a "blonde young gentleman" with a "soft voice" who lisps. "Honey, I'm thuck. My novel ith about a then-thitive boy from the time he'th twelve until he ith a gwown man"—a hint about Truman's first book, *Other Voices, Other Rooms* (1948), which Lee had seen in drafts.[10]

Already she's showing signs of mastering a key element of good writing: using a voice that the reader can hear. Such a voice also goes under the heading "style," but essentially it's the art of making the reader feel engaged with another person. A *Crimson White* staffer recalled overhearing Lee on the other side of the file cabinets—the *Rammer Jammer* side—and years later, when she read *To Kill a Mockingbird,* she said, "I could just hear her talking in the book."[11] In the December issue, the magazine's masthead listed her as a staff member.

The following summer, she stayed on campus, catching up on a few credits but also because she knew that the *Crimson White* would be strapped for writers. Pages were hard to fill while the university was dozing from June to August. For the editorial page, she began submitting "Caustic Comment," an irregular column that delivered doses of self-parody, exaggerated descriptions, and long-winded gags. John T. Hamner, a student journalist at Alabama, was struck by the tone of "bright, brittle, sophomoric but sharp humor. . . . Her specialty was debunking, taking quick sharp jabs at the idols and mores of the time and place."[12] The column was at its strongest when Lee took aim at inane advertisements on the radio, or the amount of red tape students had to endure; it was at its weakest when she got on her high horse about something. Also, a personal trait she didn't bother to rein in was her fondness for cursing, which prompted a few complaints from readers, including this one: "Irony is delightful; sarcasm is fine; 'Caustic Comment' is the best reading there is—but so much more fun if not slapped on like red paint on an old barn."[13]

But she was not to be denied when it came to tackling controversy.

And in the South, particularly on a campus like the University of Alabama—in the words of a former student, "a profoundly conservative community"—there were few topics considered more impolite than racism. "There were a few faculty members who expressed reservations about some of the prevailing political and social orthodoxies, but they received little student support and were generally regarded as harmless eccentrics. The one subject never discussed, in my experience, was race relations. The prevailing view was that there was no reason to upset the status quo, and most were willing to continue existing conditions indefinitely."[14]

To Lee, who was making a career of nonconformity, that was an invitation to let fly, as she did in a review of *Night Fire* (1946), a novel by a university instructor named Edward Kimbrough:[15] "Almost since the time the first slaves were shipped into the South by the Yankees, various authors have taken it upon themselves to probe, explain and hash over the problems that came with them. The South has been repeatedly embarrassed by the Smiths [in reference to Lillian Smith, author of *Strange Fruit*], Faulkners, Stowes, et al., who either wrote delicately of the mint julep era or championed the dark eddies of 'niggertown.'"

Lee praised *Night Fire* for its realism, relishing Kimbrough's portrayal of "Turkey Littlepage, who is reminiscent of all the county sheriffs in South Alabama and Mississippi. Mean, utterly stupid, and with violent prejudices, Turkey tramps through the pages of *Night Fire* as a living memorial to all the miserable incompetents the South elects as enforcers of the law."

Such language was not often seen in print on campus. But, among the "casual colony" of young journalists working on the newspaper, Nelle's contempt for "miserable incompetents" being elected to public office wasn't unique. That summer, Governor Theodore G. Bilbo of Mississippi was campaigning for the U.S. Senate. With the November elections just a few months off, he declared, "I call upon every red-blooded white man to use any means to keep the nigger away from the polls. The best way to keep a nigger from voting is to have a little talk with him the night before."[16] The "Klan-hating" editor in chief of *Crimson White* countered in his final editorial, "When a shrewd politician will boast of his Klan membership, the average citizen may rest assured that the power of that organization is pretty great. . . . Now is the time to stamp out this malignant growth. If we have any legacy to leave our successor, we would make it a thoroughgoing hatred of Alabama's—and the nation's—Ku Klux Klan."[17]

Come September of her junior year, Lee might have stayed on as a contributor to the *Crimson White* newspaper. Recently a lengthy article she wrote for a national magazine has come to light—discussed in Chapter 8, "'See NL's Notes'"—that demonstrates she was a natural journalist. But the *Rammer Jammer* was a better place to showcase her talents as a creative writer. Also, she had scored quite a coup after one year on the magazine: she was offered the spot of editor in chief. It would be a heavy responsibility. Finished with her prelaw classes, she had been accepted into the law school.

She decided she could do both, which probably struck her young mind as compromise; but it was also the first sign that writing mattered as much to her as fulfilling her father's hopes for "Lee & Daughters, Attorneys." A profile of her in an October 1946 issue of the *Crimson White* described how she was coping with her dual responsibilities:

[She is an] impressive figure as she strides down the corridor of New Hall at all hours attired in men's green striped pajamas. Quite frequently she passes out candy to unsuspecting freshmen; when she emerges from their rooms they have subscribed to the *Rammer Jammer*. . . . [H]er idea of heaven is a place where diligent law students and writers ascend after death and can stay up forever without Benzedrine. . . . Wild about football, she played center on the fourth grade team in Monroeville, her hometown. Her favorite person is her sister "Bear." . . . Lawyer Lee will spend her future in Monroeville. As for literary aspirations she says, "I shall probably write a book some day. They all do."[18]

She cared nothing about being perceived as a demure "Bama Belle." There were only five women in the law school program, and Lee issued a call for more. "If you are an earnest student, not afraid of hard work (by that we mean hard, brother) and are of a high moral character (you have to get five affidavits to prove it) the Law school wants you!"[19] And because she courted controversy, her parody of "Yes, Virginia, There Is a Santa Claus" for the winter issue of *Rammer Jammer* included a reference to homosexuality. "Believe in Santa Claus! You may as well believe in fairies! Of course, there are fairies, but not the kind you read about in Anderson's fairy tales. While we are on the subject, I may as well disillusion you further. The authorities tell us that fairies cannot be seen. Don't you believe it! I saw two of them huddled together reading *The Well of Loneliness*."[20] For decades, *The Well of Loneliness* (1928) was the best-known lesbian novel in English.

In any case, she sallied forth with equal fervor both as the editor of the *Rammer Jammer* and as a law student. It was demanding, preparing for a day's classes in torts, real estate, and contract law; yet along with that, Lee managed the *Rammer Jammer*'s staff of sixteen, too. Her quirkiness was a particularly good fit with the magazine's reputation, and she enjoyed acting eccentric. The yearbook photographer caught her hamming it up as a harried writer glaring at a typewriter, a cigarette burning perilously low in one hand. The southern novelist Elise Sanguinetti was a self-described "lowly person" on the staff—Nelle, she said, "was a lot of fun; she just made it go."[21]

Racism came in for ridicule again in her one-act play, published in the *Rammer Jammer*, "Now Is the Time for All Good Men." A fictitious Alabama state senator named the Honorable F. B. MacGillacuddy, chairman of the Citizen's Committee to Eradicate the Black Plague, argues strenuously for the passage of a bill that is nothing more than a warmed-over post-Reconstruction gambit to disenfranchise blacks. It would require persons registering to vote to answer written questions about the U.S. Constitution to the satisfaction of the local registrar. The bill passes, but Senator MacGillacuddy is stunned when he fails the test, too. He appears before the U.S. Supreme Court, pleading, "I come to you on a matter of gravest importance. My civil liberties are being threatened. You boys all know me, I was in Congress with most of you. A diabolical group down in Alabama slipped one over on the honest, decent citizens of the state three years ago. . . . Whatta you going to do about it, boys?"[22] On the bench at the time was

Associate Justice Hugo Black, a graduate of the University of Alabama
Law School; when Justice Black was running for state office in the
1920s he was an outspoken member of the Ku Klux Klan.[23]

As senior year approached, Lee's activities related to creative writing
demanded as much time as law school. She was highly visible to the
campus at large too as columnist, satirist, and editor. So it's surprising
then she wasn't invited to join the fiction workshop run by her instructor Hudson Strode, who also taught Shakespeare. Strode was one of
the best-known creative writing teachers in the country and his
workshop was a forerunner of today's MFA programs. He recruited
Elise Sanguinetti, a "lowly person" on the *Rammer Jammer*, but not
Miss Lee. Why?

Born on Halloween in Cairo, Illinois, Hudson Strode grew up in
Demopolis, Alabama, and considered himself a Southerner. After
graduating from Columbia University, he had tried a career as an actor
but Sir Johnston Forbes-Robertson, one of the foremost British Shake-
speareans of the day, told him he was too short. Strode also had a high,
squeaky voice. Lessons from a voice teacher eventually dropped his
register two octaves into a rich, smooth baritone "that he used bril-
liantly in his famed class on Shakespeare's tragedies, making Hamlet's
voice boom through Morgan Hall."[24] To improve his carriage, Strode
walked the banks of the Black Warrior River on the edge of campus
balancing a book on his head. He wore ascots instead of ties and draped
a Burberry overcoat around his shoulders like a cape. He smoked a
pipe. He was a bit of a character.[25]

His workshop received an average of twelve hundred manuscripts
annually from students eager for one of fifteen to twenty-five spots
available. "If you were chosen," one of his students remembered, "he
made you feel as though you had already accomplished a writing feat;
you were among the few. At his table, you were sitting with the great."[26]
The workshop met two nights a week at a big table on the fourth floor
of the library. Helen Norris, who was to be Alabama's poet laureate
from 1999 to 2003, respected his judgment. "He was always right when
a story needed more development. He had a marvelous sense of what

he needed more of: 'Well, I need something *more* there.'"[27] Thomas Hal Phillips, later a novelist and screenwriter, revered him. "To me, he was *the* master. Once, as we were about to cross campus from his Shakespeare class to the library, I was going down the steps with three or four other people right behind him. I referred to him out loud as 'the master.' He stopped and dressed me down and said I shouldn't call him that. But I defended myself by saying I meant it, I *believed* it."[28] Consequently, if Lee, a future Pulitzer Prize winner, was in Strode's Shakespeare course and he was aware of the quality of her writing—in and out of class—then why wasn't she among the twenty-five students in his workshop?

The simple answer might be that she didn't make the cut. With submissions pouring in, she would have had about a one in forty-eight chance of being accepted, according to Phillips, who was also Strode's teaching assistant and reviewed many of the applications. Or perhaps she didn't have the requisite fifty sample pages of manuscript ready. Sanguinetti said that Lee didn't have time to write lengthy fiction; her output was limited to articles for the *Rammer Jammer*.[29]

There's one more possibility: that she didn't take Professor Strode seriously. He was a disappointed actor who declaimed passages from Shakespeare in class, probably thinking his students would enjoy seeing scenes performed; but Miss Lee, said Norris, dismissed him as "pompous. She would be almost rude to him."[30] One day, as he was holding forth in his mellifluous voice, she drew a caricature of him as Hamlet addressing Yorick's skull. It was so good that the class secretly passed it back and forth, sputtering with laughter.

Teachers, though, are not as obtuse as some students would like to think; and if Professor Strode was aware that Miss Lee ridiculed him, he would not have been inclined to recruit her for his little band of hopeful writers that met two nights a week. She couldn't have expected he would. Years later, she acted rather resentful when reporters asked her whether she'd taken Hudson Strode's famous workshop and she had to answer no.

Lee closed out the 1946–47 school year in June by severing her ties with the *Rammer Jammer*. One year as editor in chief was enough. Besides, her law school classes were all-consuming and she was forced to spend most evenings studying at the library until midnight. She still had a year to go after her senior year because law at Alabama was a five-year program. The stress must have been considerable, and her teetotaling father would not have been to pleased to learn that she was drinking hard liquor in an effort to relax.[31]

Classes ended in May, and she went home by train. An important family event was coming up: her brother, Edwin Coleman Lee, was marrying Sara Anne McCall, Nelle's friend and classmate since childhood.

Edwin was seven years older than Sara and, according to friends, hadn't given her a second look when they were growing up together, because she was still in elementary school when he enrolled as a freshman in industrial engineering at Alabama Polytechnic Institute.[32] Later, she went to Huntingdon College the same year as Nelle, but by then Edwin was serving with the Eighth Air Force. In June 1944, he participated in the Normandy invasion, flew support for General Patton's Third Army in Europe, and received the Purple Heart. In 1946, Captain Lee returned to Monroeville. He and Sara fell in love; the wedding was set for Saturday, June 28, 1947, in Monroeville.

The weather was hot, so the guests were relieved that the ceremony at the Methodist Episcopal Church was scheduled for six o'clock in the evening. Inside the church, garlands of southern smilax and tall baskets of Snow Queen gladioli decorated the aisle and altar. The bride wore a dress with a high collar, full skirt, and long train that was a modern adaptation of an antebellum wedding gown. The maid of honor was later to become the mayor of Monroeville; Nelle was a bridesmaid. The reception was held outside, at the bride's home. Frances Lee, by now quite overweight and needing to make regular visits to Vaughn Memorial Hospital in Selma, found it best to let well-wishers come to her where she was seated at the groom's table.

Everything would have been ideal for patriarch A. C. Lee, almost seventy, except that shortly after arriving home for the summer, his youngest daughter had broken some unwelcome news. She had only enrolled in law school because "it was the line of least resistance," meaning she knew how much her father wanted her to join Alice at the firm. But she didn't like law school; couldn't imagine pursuing law as a profession.[33]

The exact words she used aren't known; but to several of her female classmates (those who remember her), Nelle Harper Lee from Monroeville appeared to be lonely and frustrated. "She never made a great effort to get to know anybody; she had her mind on what she had her mind on."[34] In criminal law class, "she would not have been noticed except for the fact that she was in a large class of males. She was habitually dressed in a baggy pullover, with a skirt and loafers, her hair pulled behind her ears, and no makeup. To say that she was reclusive is an understatement. She was very quiet, spoke to no one—except when the instructor called on her to respond. Even then, she did so with as few words as possible."[35] Outside of class, she was discourteous. "Lawyers sort of have to conform, and she'd just as soon tell you to go to hell as to say something nice and turn around and walk away."[36]

Truman Capote claimed she had a secret sorrow, but omitted the details; only that "She had a great love affair with one of her professors at college, and it did something to her. It didn't end up well. It was a law professor. I don't know if [the pain] still exists now."[37] Capote was a gossip, though, and maybe his story should be discounted; except that a female law student who knew Lee heard the same rumor.[38]

Love affair or no, Lee's overriding desire was to quit law school before taking a degree and to become a writer instead: a starry-eyed plan it must have seemed to her father—someone who had never had anything handed to him in his career—and the end of his hopes for seeing "Lee & Daughters, Attorneys" become part of his legacy to Monroeville.

five

To New York City by Way of Oxford

"She got an itch to go to New York and write."

—ALICE LEE

A. C. Lee might have tried to persuade Nelle to return to Monroeville after graduation by pointing out that if writing was what she cared about, she could take over the *Monroe Journal* from him and Alice. She could do a service by her family, the town, and the county if she did. Moreover, becoming a lawyer wasn't necessary; although a law degree—a degree of any kind—was always good insurance.

But that plan didn't satisfy his headstrong daughter either, and an episode that summer, about the time of Edwin Lee's wedding, is worth mentioning. One day in the offices of the *Baldwin Times* in Bay Minette, Alabama, the paper's publisher, James Faulkner, received an unexpected visit from A. C. Lee. Lee got right to the point. "I understand you are interested in establishing a newspaper in Monroeville." Faulkner replied that he wasn't, because the town couldn't support two competing papers.

"Well, how would you like to buy one already in existence? I'll sell the *Monroe Journal* to you right now for fifteen thousand dollars." The

Journal was his to sell because of the four original partners in the enterprise, one had died and the Lees, father and daughter Alice, effectively owned most of the newspaper now.

Faulkner could hardly believe his ears: he had been dreaming about an opportunity like this. He even had a potential partner lined up: the *Baldwin Times* editor, William Stewart. Quickly, as if worried that Lee might change his mind, Stewart and Faulkner scrambled to put together the financing, shaking every money tree they could. Stewart borrowed three thousand dollars from his brother, and Faulkner sold a parcel of timberland he owned for another three thousand dollars. With six thousand dollars in hand, they borrowed another nine thousand dollars, partly from Lee's former law partner, J. B. Barnett, now president of the Monroe County Bank, and the rest from the First National Bank in Mobile. Alice Lee completed the legal paperwork transferring ownership of the *Journal* to Faulkner and Stewart.

Thus after eighteen years in the newspaper business, the Lees were officially out of it. (Ten years later, Faulkner sold his half interest to his partner for $115,000; in the mid-1990s, Stewart sold the paper for $2 million.)[1] On June 26, 1947, A. C. Lee published his final editorial. "As we are bowing out of the newspaper field it is but natural that we allow our thoughts to go back over the years of our service for the purpose of a critical review. And with the added experience of the years we are unable to recall any position we have previously taken on any important question that we would wish to change. Again we express our most profound appreciation for the splendid cooperation accorded us through the years by our good friends throughout the county."[2] He was letting go now of the small dynasty he had hoped to build in the town that had so richly rewarded his efforts. He wrung a concession at least from his daughter before she quit college altogether. In August, she boarded a train and rode it north to Tuscaloosa, for the sake of giving of giving law school another try.

It was no good, though. By spring 1948, it was clear she wasn't showing the same enthusiasm for practicing law that Alice had. Or perhaps Alice never was all that interested in becoming a lawyer in the first place but took up the challenge laid down by her father anyway. Her siblings Edwin and Louise had graduated from Auburn and were pursuing careers on their own: not the same dedication to family that Alice had shown. But only Nelle refused to go down the path of higher education followed by the older children.

So Mr. Lee agreed to provide an incentive—one that would acknowledge her love of literature. Perhaps, if she could have an experience that showed she was not making a Hobson's choice—law or nothing—she would see what a well-paid career such as law could provide, including the means to travel and write as an avocation. On April 29, 1948, an item in the *Monroe Journal* described what Miss Lee would be up to that summer: "Miss Nelle Lee, University of Alabama law student and daughter of Mr. and Mrs. A. C. Lee of Monroeville, has been accepted as an exchange student at Oxford University in England during the coming summer. She will sail from New York on June 16."[3]

It would be a pilgrimage to the land of her favorite writers—Austen, Stevenson, Lamb, Fielding, Butler—who until now had lived for her only between the covers of books. And perhaps it would break the spell of her unhappiness. It also suggests, however, that Mr. Lee indulged his youngest, which, if the Lee family ran true to the rest of the human race, Alice must have recognized. Maybe it inspired some jealousy. After all, it fell to Alice, the eldest, to fulfill her father's ambitions while Nelle was granted more latitude, more freedom. Somehow, she had become exempt from the fatherly expectations that her brother and two sisters had met.

Student exchanges with European countries—a new idea after World War II—were strongly supported by both Congress and religious and social service organizations. The purpose of the exchanges was to promote mutual understanding between the American people and other cultures; and "to correct misunderstandings about the United States abroad." In addition, exchanges appealed to organizations such as the American Friends Service Committee and the Future Farmers of America as opportunities to send young people abroad as a gesture of peace and goodwill. In April 1947, the State Department received two C-4 troopships, the *Marine Tiger* and the *Marine Jumper,* to ferry students to Southampton, Plymouth, Genoa, and Cherbourg.

Things got off to a rather slow start. When the *Marine Jumper* sailed out of New York harbor in June 1947, only 105 American students were aboard. (Adding poignancy to the idealism behind student exchanges was the arrival three weeks later of seven foreign vessels bringing 2,920 European refugees to the United States, all in one day.)[4] The following year, 1948, when Nelle was scheduled to leave, organizers were confident that ten thousand students would sail by August.

On the other side of the Atlantic, European universities responded eagerly to student exchanges. Summer-term courses, anywhere from three to six weeks long, included German-Austrian culture near Salzburg; classical and archaeological studies in Naples; art and music appreciation in France. Six British universities offered Shakespeare, Elizabethan drama, or European civilization. Harper Lee enrolled in Oxford University's Extramural Studies Summer School program, "European Civilization in the Twentieth Century."

On the morning she prepared to board the *Marine Jumper* in New York harbor, nearly six hundred young people were hugging their parents, posing for snapshots, and waving as they climbed the steep gangway. The ship, among the largest transports built during the war, was one and a half times the length of a football field, seventy-one feet wide, and still painted military olive-gray. The only indication that times had changed was a red, white, and blue band painted around the ship's smokestack. And the accommodations were rows of bunks with one shower room big enough for thirty-five people—"just like you'd expect in the army," commented one of the students.[5]

At last the hawsers were pulled in, and the *Marine Jumper* got under way, assisted by a tugboat or two to point the ship's bow toward the Atlantic. Then, after New York dipped below the horizon and they were well out to sea, coordinators on board assembled the students for the first of a series of orientation programs about the places they were going. A Harvard undergraduate said he met

Quakers, Youth Hostelers, Adventure Trailers, one delegate to the World Council of Churches, and huge numbers of young tourists going abroad ostensibly for study in London, Paris, Copenhagen, Geneva, and elsewhere. Their groups held orientation programs on the ship twenty-four hours a day, passed out reams of literature, held foreign language courses daily, and generally showed their eagerness to promote international understanding and prevent future war.[6]

Meals on board were filling but greasy, contributing to seasickness.[7] But once the youngsters got used to the motion of the ship, the main deck on starry nights was usually dotted with travelers lying on their backs, feeling the thrum of the ten-thousand-horsepower turbines underneath them as the ship rolled through the swells at fifteen knots.

On Friday, June 25, via the loudspeakers between decks, it was announced that passengers bound for England should prepare for landing soon at Plymouth. After hastily eating breakfast, Lee waited until 9:00 A.M. for a motor launch to pull alongside to ferry her group to customs. Over the hubbub of the milling crowd of students, officials loudly explained how to locate the luggage. After finding her bags, Lee went with the rest to the money-exchange counter and watched dollars become pounds, crowns, shillings, pennies, farthings. The money seemed byzantine. When it was her turn to purchase a ticket for the train to Oxford, she held out her hand and murmured like the others, "Take what you need."[8]

A four-hour train ride brought the spires of Oxford within sight, by which time the students were so hungry that they were bartering rolls and fruit saved from breakfast. As the train crossed the Isis River, on the west side of the university, Nelle could see Christ Church's octagonal Tom Tower, whose seven-ton bell has rung every night since the late 1600s to mark curfew. The welcoming dinner that evening was held in a centuries-old hall with stained-glass windows, carved beam ceilings fifty feet overhead, and wood-paneled walls.

She was enrolled in twentieth-century European civilization, but Lee was permitted to attend other lectures too, on philosophy, politics, economics, or general topics. There were three others every day to choose from, on topics such as free will, the nature of truth, political theories and moral beliefs, communism, modern painting, and the history of Oxford University. In all, there were seventy speakers taking a turn presenting, including the novelists Elizabeth Bowen and Joyce Cary; A.J.P. Taylor, one of the most controversial historians of the century; the pianist and music critic William Glock; Hugh Trevor-Roper, the historian of early modern Britain and Nazi Germany; and the pioneering geneticist J.B.S. Haldane.[9] For someone like Lee, a true Anglophile, it was a feast. She visited the Bodleian Library often, walking among rows and rows of centuries-old volumes—more than three million in all—including original manuscripts of Old English poetry and prose dating from *Beowulf,* and even earlier.

After that experience, Nelle lasted only one more semester in law school. She couldn't continue, because, as Alice said later, "She fell in love with England."[10] She had walked streets known to writers she admired and had imagined herself in their company. What she needed to do now was to write earnestly. Truman had just published his first novel, *Other Voices, Other Rooms*, to extravagant reviews comparing him to William Faulkner, Eudora Welty, Carson McCullers, and Flannery O'Connor. She couldn't hope to duplicate his success the first time out, but she had to make a start. At the end of the first semester, she withdrew from law school and prepared to follow in Capote's footsteps to New York.

For a while she lived at home and saved money, waitressing at the Monroeville golf club. But having "got an itch to go to New York and write," said Alice, twenty-three-year-old Nelle Lee did exactly that in 1949.[11] Her place was an unfurnished, cold-water flat in Manhattan, at 1539 York Avenue, two blocks from the East River, with an iron fire escape where she could sit and think on hot nights.

But breaking her ties with Monroeville was not as easy as that. Her mother's health was poor and continued to decline. One winter evening in early 1951 in Selma, Alabama, an alumna of Huntingdon College recognized Nelle walking along by herself, lost in thought. She pulled over and offered her a ride to wherever she was going. Nelle asked to be taken a few blocks to Vaughn Memorial Hospital—her mother was there. It was clear that she was preoccupied with worry and the two rode in silence the rest of the way.[12]

Mrs. Lee never left the hospital, and on June 2, 1951, she died. Nelle was twenty-five. Her mother had long been beset by a "nervous disorder," as the family preferred to call it, compounded by poor health in general. What Harper Lee understood about her mother, she poured into Aunt Alexandra's character in *To Kill a Mockingbird*, who closely resembles Frances Lee. "She was not fat, but solid, and she chose protective garments that drew her bosom up to giddy heights, pinched in her waist, flared out her rear, and managed to suggest that Aunt Alexandra's was once an hour-glass figure. From any angle it was formidable." Aunt Alexandra also had "boarding-school manners," as Mrs. Lee would have from attending Julia Tutwiler's School for Girls. If Aunt Alexandra shared another characteristic with Mrs. Lee too, it would be unfortunate for Nelle growing up: Scout says of her aunt, she was "analogous to Mount Everest: throughout my early life, she was cold and there."

Just six weeks after Frances's long-expected passing, the Lees suffered a second loss. The previous March, at the beginning of the Korean War, Edwin Lee had been recalled to duty in the Army Air Forces and assigned to Maxwell Air Force Base in Montgomery. On July 12, after a strenuous game of softball, Major Lee complained of not feeling well and went to the officers' quarters to lie down. He was found dead the following morning of a cerebral hemorrhage at age thirty.[13]

At the funeral in Monroeville, presided over by the Methodist Episcopal's new minister, Reverend Ray E. Whatley, several hundred mourners dressed in black surrounded the grave on all sides, including three ministers representing the major Protestant denominations in town. The July heat was suffocating, although the service had been delayed until 5:00 P.M. for that reason. Standing beneath the awning over the grave site was Edwin's widow, Sara, with the couple's three-year-old daughter, Mary, their nine-month-old son, Edwin, Jr., the Lee sisters—Nelle, Alice, and Louise, who was now Mrs. Herschel Conner—and the Conners' eleven-year-old son, Hank.[14] A. C. Lee, seventy-one years old and bent under the weight of a double load of grief in such a short space of time, bore up as best he could.

Reverend Whatley concluded the service about 6:30 P.M. The three other attending ministers complimented him on his handling of the funeral, one of his first in his new capacity. Though not a forceful man, Reverend Whatley always made a point of looking people in the eye and giving them a firm handshake. He remained by Edwin's grave for nearly an hour, receiving introductions to many of the people in his 376-member congregation.

Without Edwin, who had been living in Monroeville, the brunt of family affairs now fell squarely upon Alice. Harper Lee tweaked this reality only slightly in *Go Set a Watchman*. "Just about that time, Jean Louise's brother dropped dead in his tracks one day, and after the nightmare of that was over, Atticus, who had always thought of leaving his practice to his son, looked around for another young man." Louise Lee had family responsibilities more than two hours away by car in Eufaula; and A.C. was getting on in years.[15] Nelle, of course, was far away in New York, working on a book, she said.

six

Go Set a Watchman

I have a horrible feeling that this *will* be the making of me,
that it will be goodbye to the joys of messing about.

—HARPER LEE, writing to a friend (1956)

After the double loss in her family, Nelle returned to New York City
and continued juggling what would become another six years of work as
an airline reservationist with writing at night and on weekends. Meanwhile, the city had polished some of the rougher edges of her personality that had alienated her from people when she was younger. Becoming
independent had relieved her of the need to rebel against authority.
Her sense of humor, so cutting in college, had evolved into a more self-
deprecating wit.

It was through Truman that she finally made two close friends
who became a second family. The introduction occurred in autumn
1954 during rehearsals of the Broadway musical *House of Flowers* at
the Alvin Theatre on West Fifty-second Street. Nelle wouldn't normally have found herself in the wings of a theater examining the
mysteries of light boards, scrims, cables, and pulleys. But Truman had
brought her along because he had cowritten the show's book and lyrics
with Harold Arlen, composer of "Over the Rainbow" for *The Wizard of*

Oz.[1] As Truman's tagalong friend for the day, Nelle got to listen to run-throughs of songs and dance numbers for the show. The storyline was about a comic competition between the madams of two bordellos in the West Indies, in the midst of which a romance blossoms, defying the show's atmosphere of cynicism about love.

Helping to freshen up some of the lyrics was Michael Martin Brown, originally from Mexia, Texas. Michael was almost exactly the same age as Nelle's late brother, Edwin. After a stint of teaching, he had turned to composing and writing lyrics for a living. And in 1954 he was enjoying life at the top of his form. A novelty song of his, "Lizzie Borden (Fall River Hoedown)," had become a showstopper for the Broadway revue *New Faces of 1952.*[2] Brown and Nelle shared a tongue-in-cheek sense of humor, which tended to go unnoticed at the gabfests she attended in people's apartments. Michael, she said, was "brilliant and lively; his one defect of character was an inordinate love of puns. His audacity sometimes left his friends breathless—who in his circumstances would venture to buy a townhouse in Manhattan?"[3] Since she lived only a ten-minute subway ride north of them, Michael invited her over to meet his wife, Joy.

They lived in a two-story, seven-room, late-1800s townhouse at 417 East Fiftieth Street, with Michael's ebony grand piano dominating the living room. Joy Brown, taking care of the couple's two toddlers, was an "ethereal, utterly feminine creature," in Nelle's eyes.[4] She had trained with the School of American Ballet and danced with several companies, including the Ballet Russe de Monte Carlo and Les Ballets de Paris. But motherhood suited her too, and she had retired from dance. The three friends sang show tunes at Michael's piano or gorged on Joy's latest concoction in front of the fireplace. Joy loved chocolate; during one of Nelle's increasingly frequent visits, she whipped up a big batch of fudge. "Common interests as well as love drew me to them. An endless flow of reading material circulated amongst us; we took pleasure in the same theater, films, music; we laughed at the same things, and we laughed at so much in those days."[5] Michael and Joy listened as Nelle vouchsafed to them her hopes for becoming a writer, and they applauded the stories she read to them in a tremulously embarrassed voice: "The Land of Sweet Forever," "A Roomful of Kibble," "Snow-on-the-Mountain," "This Is Show Business," and "The Viewer and the Viewed."[6]

So it happened, in mid-November 1956, that Harper Lee found herself pacing back and forth outside the offices of Williams and Crain at 18 East Forty-first Street. Annie Laurie Williams was Michael Brown's agent, and specialized in handling film and dramatic rights for literary properties; her husband, Maurice Crain, a former journalist, represented authors. Michael had been encouraging Nelle to show some of her work to his agent—he had put in a word for her—but now that she was actually here outside the building, she couldn't get up the nerve to go in. Her fear of being rejected was such that she hadn't published anything since college. She decided to walk around the block once more—her third time.[7]

Annie Laurie Williams (she preferred to use all three names) came from Denison, Texas, a bleak cattle railhead near the Texas-Oklahoma border. She quit high school to go into show business, saving her money as an office secretary until she could take drama classes in Dallas. Touring with a vaudeville company brought her to New York in the 1920s, and she appeared in a few silent movies, but the industry was already going west to Hollywood. For six years she wrote feature stories and book reviews for the *New York Morning Telegraph* until she realized that some novels became films, and she knew something about both sides of the equation: show business and publishing.

Her first successful sale was Lloyd C. Douglas's *Magnificent Obsession,* which became a hit movie in 1935. "That took nerve," she said, "because no movie executive at the time wanted to buy a book by an unknown Lutheran minister."[8] In 1936, she convinced Margaret Mitchell that her first novel, *Gone With the Wind,* would sell in Hollywood, too. First, 20th Century–Fox made a substantial offer, which Williams turned down; then Warner Bros. almost doubled theirs, but Williams said no, leaving Mitchell shocked by her agent's audacity. Instead, Williams held out for the equivalent of a million dollars—and got it. In 1942, she sold John Steinbeck's *The Moon Is Down* for three times that amount, setting a record for screen rights. To a reporter's query about whether it was true that her Hollywood deals for Clarence

Day's *Life with Father,* John Hersey's *A Bell for Adano,* and Kathleen Winsor's *Forever Amber* had totaled $800,000 worth of literature sold in a single day, Williams deadpanned, "Frankly, I don't do that much business in a whole week."[9]

She and Maurice Crain had married in the mid-1930s, when he was a city editor for the *New York Daily News.* When war was declared in 1941, Cain enlisted, even though he was almost forty. "Pops," as the other Army Air Corps cadets called him, made staff sergeant on B-17s as a ball turret gunner. On June 23, 1943, while flying with the 401st Squadron of the Ninety-first Group out of East Anglia, his bomber, the *Mary Ruth,* was shot down over the Ruhr Valley. After eluding capture for five days, he was eventually shipped via boxcar with hundreds of other prisoners to a prisoner-of-war camp near Krems, Austria.

His war experiences left him with two nervous habits: He was extremely fastidious, always keeping his office immaculate and highly organized as if, for some reason, he might not be back. Second, he hated wasting time. He seemed to feel deprived of an adequate share of it. After a long day at the office, he chided Annie if they were late for a dinner at a restaurant: he liked to arrive on the stroke of eight o'clock. His brand of cigarette was Camels, and he smoked two packs a day. The women in the office, amused by his seriousness all the time, affectionately called him "Old Wooden Face."[10]

The office policy about submissions from unknown writers was "If it's good, we want it. If it isn't, but you show promise, we are still interested. At any rate, we usually try to offer some helpful comment."[11] Consequently, when the secretary brought in some stories by a young woman who had dropped them off, Maurice gave them a read. Not long afterward, he came dashing out of his office, telling everybody: "This girl is gifted. She's a real talent."[12] He called her and invited her to have dinner with him.

It's likely they met at Sardi's, one of Crain's favorite restaurants. During the small talk, Lee mentioned that she was a "very good friend of Truman Capote's,"[13] an innocent gaffe: Annie Laurie Williams had handled some of Truman's work and found him difficult to manage. He went off on long junkets to Europe without letting her know his itinerary, and he insisted on examining all financial statements himself: probably a reaction to his parents' spendthrift ways when he was a child. But Crain liked this nervous young woman with the soft southern accent. His mother went by "Nellie"—Helen Greene Nellie Berryman. Also, he and Annie Laurie considered themselves Southerners because they were both from Texas.[14]

Crain complimented Nelle on her ability to tell a good story. One of her submissions in particular, "Snow-on-the-Mountain," about a boy who avenges himself on an old scold in the neighborhood by ripping up her flowers was especially good. But the others needed more work. At this point, "Snow-on-the-Mountain" was the only story he thought he might be able to place.[15] The others he was returning to her with the caveat that short stories were hard to sell. Novels were easier—"Had she thought about writing one?"[16]

She had, of course—most writers do at some point—but the investment of time was daunting. She had already spent seven years on this batch of submissions. In addition, the demands of working full-time put free time to write at a premium. She told Crain she would think about it.

Her annual Christmas visit home to Monroeville was only a few weeks away, and now she would have some big news to share. After all, when she had dropped out of college intending to become a writer, her plan was received with more than a pinch of salt. She would arrive at the railroad station in Evergreen, Alabama, bearing gifts like a female magus from the East and be reunited with Alice and her father. Then she would take a few days to drive back and forth to Eufaula to visit her sister Louise and her family. A trip to the balmy South acted as a vaccination against the long, dark, slushy months of winter about to descend on the Northeast.

But this year, word came from BOAC management that only Christmas Eve and Christmas Day were vacation days; the rest of the time, she would be needed at the reservation counter to handle the holiday rush. Her disappointment brought on a sudden bout of homesickness. "New York streets shine wet with the same gentle farmer's rain that soaks Alabama's winter fields. . . . I missed Christmas away from home, I thought. . . . I missed the sound of hunting boots, the sudden open-door gusts of chilly air that cut through the aroma of pine needles and oyster dressing. I missed my brother's night-before-Christmas mask of rectitude and my father's bumblebee bass humming 'Joy to the World.' "[17]

When the Browns heard that she would be alone on Christmas Eve, they invited her over to stay the night and the following day too, as late as possible before returning to work.

So on Christmas morning, instead of waking up in her cold-water flat, Lee opened one eye to see a small early-riser in footie pajamas commanding her to rise and shine. Downstairs, everyone had already gathered at the foot of the tree and were preparing to distribute presents. Michael had built a crackling fire in the fireplace. The Browns were in an especially happy mood because Michael had received a financial windfall from his musical comedy special *He's for Me,* starring Roddy McDowell, slated to air on NBC in July. Things couldn't be better.

Knowing that she couldn't afford expensive gifts, the Browns had suggested that bargain-basement gifts should be all that was allowed. Lee was pleased with herself because she had purchased for Michael a handsome portrait of Sydney Smith, the eighteenth-century founder of the *Edinburgh Review,* for thirty-five cents; and for Joy, she'd rooted through used-book stores for a year until she found a complete set of the works of Lady Margot Asquith, an English wit. With pride, Nelle handed out her presents. And then there was a pregnant pause. The Browns, smiling, let her twist in the wind a little a bit.

Finally Joy said, "We haven't forgotten you. Look on the tree."

Tucked inside the boughs of the tree was a white envelope with "Nelle" written on it. She opened it. Inside a note read, "You have one year off from your job to write whatever you please. Merry Christmas."

"What does this mean?" she asked.

"What it says."

Several seconds passed before she found her voice. "It's a fantastic gamble. It's such a great risk."

"No, honey. It's not a risk. It's a sure thing."

She went to the window, "stunned by the day's miracle," she remembered later. Her friends had given her, she realized, "a full, fair chance for a new life." Not through "an act of generosity, but by an act of love. *Our faith in you* was really all I had heard them say."[18]

A few weeks later, she wrote rapturously to a friend about the Browns' offer: "The one stern string attached is that I will be subjected to a sort of 19th Century regimen of discipline: they don't care whether anything I write makes a nickel. They want to lick me into some kind of seriousness toward my talents, which of course will destroy anything amiable in my character, but will set me on the road to a career of sorts. . . . Aside from the et ceteras of gratefulness and astonishment I feel about this proposition, I have a horrible feeling that this *will* be the making of me, that it will be goodbye to the joys of messing about. So for the coming year I have laid in 3 pairs of Bermuda shorts, since I shall rarely emerge from 1539 York Avenue."[19]

She would have to carefully budget the Browns' gift of money, but it was enough to pay for rent, utilities, and canned groceries destined for the hot plate in her flat. She quit her job at BOAC, and soon her writing regimen fell into place: out of bed in the late morning, a dose of coffee, and then to work—all day long until midnight sometimes. All she needed was "paper, pen, and privacy."[20] Now that she'd been liberated from having to work nine to five, her output soared.

A novel requires a situation with heft: it must be large in scope, with important ideas and shifting alliances between characters. A theme, or several, should emerge. Until now, Lee had been writing short stories. But away in Monroeville, a small drama had ended recently involving her father and the Reverend Ray E. Whatley, the minister who had presided at Edwin's funeral in July 1951. There were issues connected with circumstances of the type she wanted to address in fiction. As she sat down to write her first novel, it's worth recounting what had happened because of the light it casts on the Monroeville she left behind.

To start with, her father did not believe that a church pulpit was the proper place for preaching about secular issues—politics and so forth. The mission of the Methodist church was to bring people to salvation, *not* to promote social justice. He was a gradualist when it came to change, and believed that Sunday service should not be turned into a debating society. On this point he was in agreement with Methodist pastor G. Stanley Frazier, an outspoken segregationist in Montgomery who believed that the church should bring souls to God, and not ensnare them in transient social problems.

Not long after Edwin Lee's funeral, the relationship between A. C. Lee and the Reverend Whatley began going downhill. For Labor Day, Whatley delivered a sermon titled "The Laborer." After pointing out that control of the church was often in the hands of the wealthy, he warned, "If we lose the common man from our church, it will spell doom for us, for there are always labor unions and other organizations to welcome him in."[21] There were whispers afterward that the sermon had "created some feeling."

Six months later, in February 1952, Whatley gave a sermon entitled "A Brotherhood of Love," about race relations. "There are many mistaken assumptions about Negroes in America," he told the congregation. He disputed impressions about Negroes' desiring to intermarry with whites and about Negroes being intellectually inferior, which tests had shown not to be true. He called for equal economic opportunity, saying that it was the purpose of the federal Fair Employment Practices Committee (FEPC), for example, to try to end discrimination in hiring practices.[22]

If Whatley had touched A. C. Lee with the frayed end of an electrical cord, he couldn't have sent a stronger jolt through him. Lee was adamantly opposed to the FEPC, as were many businessmen. Federal hiring guidelines, he had once declared in an editorial, would "take away from every employer in this United States the right to choose his employees."[23]

In any case, he'd heard enough—he was going to have to speak to Whatley privately after the service ended. The young reverend needed to be taken in hand, and firmly. Lee was chairman of the Official Church Board, a deacon, and a lay member of the Methodist Annual Conference; his influence had been felt in the church's decision to accept Whatley in the first place.

After the last of the congregants had exited, he told Reverend Whatley that he needed to see him. They walked to Lee's office at the back of the sanctuary, where his lifetime of involvement in the Methodist church was visible everywhere, from the pictures on the walls to the

books on the shelves. Soon after he and his family arrived in Monroeville, in 1912, he had volunteered to serve on the building committee for
a new church, the first in the area since 1835. But scarcely had the
debt been retired than the building caught fire, in 1929. The committee
reconvened and started again; so Lee had twice been instrumental in
administering a Methodist church in Monroeville.

Now, he barely waited for Whatley to close the door before getting
to the point.

"Get off the 'social justice' and get back on the gospel," he said
sharply.[24]

Shocked, Whatley explained that he believed it was within his
responsibilities as minister to speak about issues that touched on all
moral questions that Christians should be concerned about, especially
brotherhood.

A.C. cut him off. He wasn't interested in a theological debate: the
day's sermon was inappropriate and had upset people. They felt lec-
tured to, and that's not what they came to church for. If anything,
Whatley had alienated people. Was that his purpose?

Whatley admitted that it wasn't, of course. A.C. became more con-
ciliatory and urged the young man, in the future, to keep the church's
mission foremost in his mind. That was important.

A year passed until Whatley preached on the theme of brotherhood
again; his sermon, "My Brother's Keeper," took its title from Genesis
4:1–10, in which Cain asks God if he should be expected to take care of
his brother Abel. No offense could have been taken from his initial
observations about the challenges of interacting with people. But then
he turned to Alabama and the example it presented. Because of the
impact of mass communication, "no longer can we isolate ourselves and
our actions. They are heard and seen literally around the world. Any
act of injustice, unfair discrimination, or intimidation occurring in the
United States—whether in Alabama, New York, or any other state—
may make headlines all over America. But that is not all. These incidents make splendid propaganda materials on the other side of the
globe.

"Who then are our brothers?" Whatley continued. "Surely we would
not say that God does not love a yellow man, or a brown man, or a red

man, or a black man just as he does a white man. He is the God and Father of us all. If that is true, then we are all brothers."[25]

The remainder of the sermon was anecdotal, but the die was cast. The board of the church convened and in the spring of 1953 they informed Reverend Whatley that the members were seeking a "more evangelistic" preacher; they would be requesting that he be assigned to another post.

The vagueness of the reasons given was deliberate. "When they initially opposed you, they would try not to oppose you on the issue of race," said the former Methodist minister Donald Collins, author of *When the Church Bell Rang Racist: The Methodist Church and the Civil Rights Movement in Alabama* (1998). "They would always try to find something else, if they could. If they couldn't be successful at that, then they would attack you on race."[26] For years afterward, Whatley wondered why a minister couldn't be both evangelistic in the traditional sense and also preach a social gospel. But "concerns for racial justice and brotherhood were apparently part of my problem," he decided.[27]

Reassigned to the six-hundred-member St. Mark's United Methodist Church in Montgomery, Whatley became active in issues of race and equality. In 1955, he was elected president of the Montgomery chapter of the Alabama Council on Human Relations. His vice president was twenty-six-year-old Dr. Martin Luther King, Jr., the pastor of Dexter Avenue Baptist Church.

In January 1957, Harper Lee returned to Maurice Crain's office with a short story, "The Cat's Meow," and the first fifty pages of a novel, *Go Set a Watchman*, the title taken from the book of Isaiah in the King James translation, "For thus hath the Lord said unto me, Go, set a watchman, let him declare what he seeth" (Isaiah 21:6). A week later, she was back again, this time with one hundred more pages. From then on, she dropped off about fifty new pages with Crain every week through the end of February.[28] With the first draft of the novel in hand, Crain got out his red pencil and went to work editing it. The parent of *To Kill a Mockingbird*, he later said, "was about the most replanned and rewritten book I ever had a hand in, and it turned out finally that all the labor on it was well justified."[29]

In *Go Set a Watchman*, twenty-six-year-old Jean Louise Finch returns by train, the Crescent Limited, to Maycomb, Alabama, after an absence of five years in New York City to visit the town and the people that nurtured her. The novel's opening is one of its better-written passages:

> The countryside and the train had subsided to a gentle roll, and she could see nothing but pastureland and black cows from window to horizon. She wondered why she had never thought her country beautiful. . . . The train clacketed through pine forests and honked derisively at a gaily-painted bell-funneled museum piece sidetracked in a clearing. It bore the sign of a lumber concern, and the Crescent Limited could have swallowed it whole with room to spare. Greenville, Evergreen, Maycomb Junction.

As if reluctant to stop, the train overshoots the station by a quarter mile and Jean Louise steps off with her luggage, helped down by the conductor. Waiting for her a few pages into the novel are many of the characters who later appear in *To Kill a Mockingbird*: her father, Atticus; Aunt Alexandra; Uncle Jack Finch; Calpurnia. Dill is mentioned, too; but Jem has died in a manner similar to Edwin Lee's sudden, early death.

The place she's stepping into is the landscape of her childhood—a southern childhood, haunted by the past. As a former U.S. senator from Alabama, Maryon Pittman Allen, born in 1925, describes that lost world: "Southern children don't simply skip and play through their lives. Family affects them immensely: how the family lives, what it believes in every kind of way. We feel a need for a long time to mimic what our elders say, do, believe, and strongly feel. But some children eventually break out of the family mold and become their own persons and learn to have beliefs of their own, usually beginning in college."[30] It's precisely the moment of separation between parent and child, past and present, that Lee addresses in *Go Set a Watchman*; a sudden sense of unbelonging—the "apartness" that Lee felt as a child is amplified into a kind of vertigo that the returning twenty-eight-year-old Jean Louise experiences as nausea. "Go away, the old buildings said. There is no place for you here. You are not wanted. We have secrets."

The second most important character after Jean Louise is her father, Atticus Finch. Had *Go Set a Watchman* been published before *To Kill a Mockingbird*, readers would have been introduced to him as a gnarled old gentleman of seventy-two—about the same age as Harper Lee's beloved father in 1956—who is bent and ailing from rheumatoid arthritis. He is a courtly man, insightful, politically astute, and a good judge of people—characteristics Mr. Lee shared with his fictional likeness. He is, however, a man of his time, belonging to the generation that was born before the turn of the twentieth century.

Atticus at seventy-two cannot see any good coming of the changes being forced on the South by the federal government, the courts, and organizations such as the National Association for the Advancement of Colored People. Atticus warns Jean Louise that the NAACP will continue to litigate for equality "with its fantastic demands and shoddy ideas of government" and overturn everything that's been so carefully maintained. White Southerners of high and low station alike perceive a second Era of Reconstruction being visited on them, and they are rallying their forces to resist it.[31] The generation that experienced the social leveling of the Great Depression will fight against going back there.

Trying to see that period through the eyes of white adults—not from Scout's innocence as a child in *To Kill a Mockingbird*—is critical to understanding why Atticus Finch in *Go Set a Watchman* is a racist.

What nine-year-old Scout only glimpses in *To Kill a Mockingbird* is the economic collapse of southern society and the impact of the Great Depression. Atticus gives her a lesson. "The Cunninghams [who pay their bills with farm produce] are country folks, farmers, and the crash hit them hardest." Professional people are poor because farmers are poor: "nickels and dimes were hard to come by for doctors and dentists and lawyers." This was the hardscrabble life of poverty that had oppressed blacks for generations; but to whites, the loss of social status—loss of a sense of "better than"—felt humiliating.

In Dothan, Alabama, for example, a town not far from Monroeville, a desperate man in 1934 scraped together fifteen cents to send a telegram to Governor B. M. Miller: AM BLIND AND CANT WORK IN THE DITCHES AND UNEMPLOYED AGENCY WONT GIVE ME ANY GROCERIES THAT CAME IN TODAY SALVATION ARMY WONT HELP US WE NEED SOMETHING TO EAT PLEASE WIRE BY WESTERN UNION WHAT TO DO. Hunters took to the woods with such grimness that no deer or wild turkeys were left, only small game. One cold morning in the mid-1930s, Harper Lee's cousin R. B. "Dickie" Williams rose at dawn to hunt in the fields surrounding Finchburg. He was out all day with several other young men until the autumn sky grew dark. The count was six raccoons, twenty-nine squirrels, five ducks, and a rabbit. Nelle sometimes found bushel baskets of homegrown food left on the back steps in lieu of cash payment for her father's legal services, just as Scout does in *To Kill a Mockingbird*.

Faced with such a falling off in status, whites sought to keep themselves ascendant in ways large and small. Unscrupulous employers were known to "cook the books" to keep washerwomen, housekeepers, yardmen, sweepers, and nannies dependent on them, for instance. Schools for black children were poorly equipped and unfunded, making illiteracy another tool of oppression.[32] The "Black Codes" governing the relationship between whites and blacks had existed since Emancipation, but during hard times, blacks needed to be especially careful about not seeming to act "above" themselves.

"From Monday to Saturday," said the Rev. J. O. Malone of the African-American Bethany Baptist Church in Burnt Corn, "you weren't welcome in Monroeville, unless you were working with somebody. Even just a pleasure stroll uptown was taboo, and oftentimes the law enforcement would find a way to bother you about doing that." During the week, when blacks encountered white people in town, the protocol was "step aside, no eye contact, they didn't speak to you in public even if they knew you."[33] A young white girl recently arrived in Monroeville from Texas was surprised by the amount of deference expected. "My Mom, my sister and I were walking home from a movie in town, and there was a black man approaching on the sidewalk.

He took off his hat, and stepped off the sidewalk as we passed. I asked my mother why he did that, and she said 'That's just the way they do down here.'" Likewise, when the Finches' housekeeper and nanny, Calpurnia in *To Kill a Mockingbird*, brings Jem and Scout to her church on a Sunday, "the men stepped back and took off their hats; the women crossed their arms at their waists, weekday gestures of respectful attention. They parted and made a small pathway to the church door for us."

The South was a segregated society in law and custom; but in the eyes of whites, it worked—it was practical, so long as the cardinal belief was observed in every respect that black Americans were inferior.[34] Patiently, Atticus Finch in *Go Set a Watchman* explains to Jean Louise the paternalistic "white man's burden" notion—still accepted in the late 1950s—used to justify withholding black Americans' rights: "Honey, you do not seem to understand that the Negroes down here are still in their childhood as a people. You should know it, you've seen it all your life. They've made terrific progress in adapting themselves to white ways, but they're far from it yet." He's incredulous that his daughter would disagree. "Then let's put this on a practical basis right now," he says. "Do you want Negroes by the carload in our schools and churches and theaters? Do you want them in our world?"[35] To him, integration invites anarchy, and he is far from alone in thinking so. During a debate in Congress in 1957 over a civil rights bill, a conservative New York–based magazine, the *National Review*, asked whether white Southerners would continue to be able to maintain political control over black communities if the bill passed. "The sobering answer is Yes—the white community is so entitled because, for the time being, it is the advanced race."[36] Unquestionably, whites had the upper hand, and they would pull any levers, offer any argument that seemed feasible to maintain the status quo.

Harper Lee knew this, but the for the sake of exposing it in *Go Set a Watchman,* she has Jean Louise discover a racist tract among her father's papers, titled "The Black Plague." A few pages later, from her perch in the "blacks only" balcony of the county courthouse, she observes a meeting of the local, pro-segregation White Citizens' Council. A demagogue is railing about "mongrelization," and the audience includes not only her father, but also several other men—"men of substance and character, responsible men, good men"—from the town's professional class. This is a new kind of Klan, she thinks to herself, but essentially they are "the same people who were the Invisible Empire, who hated Catholics; ignorant, fear-ridden, red-faced, boorish, law-abiding, one hundred per cent red-blooded Anglo-Saxons, her fellow Americans—trash." The revelation disgusts her and she feels physically sick. "What was this blight that had come down over the people she loved?"

Is her shock at what she discovers persuasive? Not very. It's hard to accept that Jean Louise, having been raised in the South, would be unaware of upright citizens condoning racism; but it sets the stage for her accusing Atticus of being a hypocrite. "You double-dealing, ring-tailed old son of a bitch! You just sit there and say 'As you please' when you've knocked me down and stomped on me and spat on me, you just sit there and say 'As you please' when everything I ever loved in this world's—you just sit there and say 'As you please'—you love me! You son of a bitch!"

But then, *Go Set a Watchman* is Lee's first sustained effort at writing a novel. She struggles with point of view, vacillating between first and third person; the distance in scenes zooms in and out, from close up to far back; and sometimes it's hard to tell who is speaking. But as a cultural document about a time and place in America not so long ago, it's a valuable reading experience—especially because readers recoil from Atticus, just as Jean Louise does, now that they understand him through the eyes of an adult, and not from the perspective of nine-year-old Scout. Its best single scene demonstrates in breathtaking economy how racism makes strangers of people, even of those whom we love. Jean Louise realizes that she has never really known Calpurnia, the woman who raised her. " 'Tell me one thing, Cal,' she says, 'just one thing before I go—please, I've got to know. Did you hate us?' The old woman sat silent, bearing the burden of her years. Jean Louise waited. Finally, Calpurnia shook her head."[37]

In spring 1957, Crain judged that the novel was ready to go out to publishers, and an unsolicited manuscript bearing the title *Go Set a*

Watchman arrived at the offices of J. B. Lippincott in New York.[38] In the meantime, Harper Lee—not wanting to waste a day of her writing sabbatical—surprised Crain at the end of May with one hundred and eleven pages of a second novel, *The Long Goodbye*.[39] Days later, he phoned her with good news: Lippincott had requested to meet with her about her novel. Her pen froze.

seven

Tay Hohoff Edits *Go Set a Watchman*

Now for the story of a first novel where the genius of the
author was unmistakable from the outset.

—J. B. Lippincott corporate history,
privately published (1967)

The Lippincott editors who assembled to meet Nelle were all men
except one: the vice president, a woman in her early sixties dressed in a
business suit, with her steel-gray hair pulled tightly back. Her name
was Theresa von Hohoff—but she preferred the less Teutonic-sounding
"Tay Hohoff."[1] Her voice was raspy from too many cigarettes and her
eyesight was failing, but her associates knew her as "a powerful gray-
haired lady who knew her own mind" and spoke frankly.[2]

Hohoff had been raised a Quaker in a multigenerational home in
Brooklyn where "thee" and "thou" were used.[3] She attended the Brook-
lyn Friends School, and the Quakers' social consciousness had never
left her. Outside the office she was completing a book of her own,
A Ministry to Man (1959), a brief biography praising John Elliot
Lovejoy—her ideal of a social reformer.

Elliot was a descendent of Elijah Lovejoy, killed by a mob in Alton,
Illinois, because of his editorials condemning slavery. "Once in open
court," Hohoff wrote, "Lovejoy daringly cut a Negro's bonds before the

Fugitive Slave Law could be invoked, while his small daughter looked on shivering with pride and terror." John Lovejoy's goal was to work for the betterment of society by promoting the best life of others. In 1897, after receiving a doctorate in Germany, he founded the Hudson Guild, which became like Hull House in Chicago, one of New York's most successful settlements. Hohoff was deep into describing the zeal of this reformer when Harper Lee arrived for her appointment to discuss *Go Set a Watchman.*

Hohoff enjoyed working with young writers: some of the many she guided during her career included Zora Neale Hurston, Thomas Pynchon, and Nicholas Delbanco. As she studied the "dark-haired, dark-eyed young woman [who] walked shyly into our office on Fifth Avenue," Hohoff instinctively felt she would like her.[4]

To Lee, the meeting was excruciating. The Lippincott editors talked to her at length about *Go Set a Watchman,* explaining that, on the one hand, her "characters stood on their own two feet, they were three-dimensional." On the other, the manuscript had structural problems: it was "more a series of anecdotes than a fully conceived novel." (A first reader reported to Hohoff that the manuscript was "diffuse," "autobiographical," and much too long.)[5] Hohoff made suggestions about how Nelle could address their concerns. Turning her head back and forth to acknowledge the remarks from this round-table dissection, Nelle obediently nodded and replied politely in Alabama-accented monosyllables, "Yes, sir. Yes, ma'am." She assured them that she would try. Finally, they wished her luck on a revision and hoped to see her again. She left, taking her manuscript with her.

Hohoff hoped they hadn't discouraged her. (Someone in the office heard a rumor that she had arrived from Alabama with a trunkful of writing and "lived in a garret on macaroni.")[6] Even though Lee had never published anything, not even an essay or short story, her draft of a novel "was clearly not the work of an amateur or a tyro," Hohoff decided. In fact, it was hard to believe that Nelle was in her early thirties and had waited until now to approach a publisher. "But as I grew to know her better," Hohoff said later, "I came to believe the cause lay in an innate humility and a deep respect for the art of writing. To put it another way, what she wanted with all her being was to *write*—not merely to 'be a writer.'"[7]

By the end of the summer, Lee had resubmitted her manuscript. Hohoff found "it was better. It wasn't *right*. Obviously, a keen and witty and even wise mind had been at work; but was the mind that of a professional novelist? There were dangling threads of plot, there was a lack of unity—a beginning, a middle, an end that was inherent in the beginning."[8] But Lee's willingness to accept criticism, and how quickly she delivered a revision, convinced Hohoff to offer her a contract with an advance of a thousand dollars for an "untitled novel."[9]

As editor and writer got down to the business of working together, Hohoff discovered "a vivid and original personality hiding behind her intense reserve." The younger woman's speaking and writing voices were very similar—wry, subtle, and engaging, perfectly suited for the regional southern novel she wanted to write. Hohoff encouraged her to pursue that vein, digging into Monroeville and its people. Another of Hohoff's authors, who knew Lee, said the challenge was making "the pieces fit together nicely, because they weren't in novelistic order. Tay started her thinking about the arrangement of events. It's like a piece of iron sculpture. It starts out as pieces of metal, and then through arranging and rearranging becomes a melded work of art."[10]

What story could Lee tell, Hohoff wanted to know, that could pull everything else together?

In *Go Set a Watchman*, Lee hasn't yet developed the ability to let drama carry ideas. She's heavy on summary and exposition, to the detriment of the story unfolding. "Her father's office had always been a source of refuge for her. It was friendly. It was a place where, if troubles did not vanish, they were made bearable. She wondered if those were the same abstracts, files, and professional impedimenta on his desk that were there when she would run in, out of breath, desperate for an ice cream cone, and request a nickel. She could see him swing around in his swivel chair and stretch his legs. He would reach down deep into his pocket, pull out a handful of change, and from it select a very special nickel for her. His door was never closed to his children."[11]

But when she recreates scenes from childhood from the eye-level perspective of a child, another sensibility takes over. The reader is *there*, watching, belonging to the moment, as when Dill, Scout, and Jem are trying to decide how to spend the day:

> Lemonade in the middle of the morning was a daily occurrence in the summertime. They downed three glasses apiece and found the remainder of the morning lying emptily before them. "Want to go out in Dobbs Pasture?" asked Dill. No. "How about let's make a kite?" she said. "We can get some flour from Calpurnia . . ." "Can't fly a kite in the summertime," said Jem. "There's not a breath of air blowing." The thermometer on the back porch stood at ninety-two, the carhouse shimmered faintly in the distance, and the giant twin chinaberry trees were deadly still. "I know what," said Dill. "Let's have a revival."

Lee is at her best when she's not trying to craft a treatise and hammer it out as dialogue. In the passage just quoted, there's atmosphere, a mood, and an authenticity about the nature of childhood that becomes one of the best-loved aspects of *To Kill a Mockingbird*. Hohoff must have recognized these gems scattered throughout *Watchman*, the evidence being that the change in perspective from a twenty-eight-year-old Jean Louise to a nine-year-old Scout is what drives the second novel and creates its charm. The change also allows Atticus to become the moral agent, instead of Jean Louise, decrying like a modern Elijah all those who have sinned in Maycomb.

Second, a trial is mentioned in passing in *Go Set a Watchman*. "Atticus took his career in his hands, made good use of a careless indictment, took his stand before a jury, and accomplished what was never before or afterwards done in Maycomb County: he won an acquittal for a colored boy on a rape charge. The chief witness for the prosecution was a white girl. . . . [T]he defendant had only one arm. The other was chopped off in a sawmill accident." In miniature, it sounds like the Tom Robinson trial in *To Kill a Mockingbird*. And indeed a trial with similar elements had occurred when Lee was a child, and her father was editor and publisher of the *Monroe Journal*.

On Thursday, November 9, 1933, the *Monroe Journal* reported that a white woman named Naomi Lowery told authorities that Walter Lett, a factory worker near Monroeville, had raped her. According to the newspaper, Lett "was captured on Saturday afternoon and taken into custody. Fearing that an attempt would be made to lynch the Negro by a mob following the news of the attack, Sheriff Sawyer took the Negro to the jail in Greenville for safekeeping."[12] So far, the incident follows parallel incidents in *To Kill a Mockingbird* almost exactly.

After waiting six months in jail for the circuit court's spring term to begin, Lett was arraigned in the Monroeville County Courthouse on March 16, 1934, on a grand jury indictment for the crime of rape. He pleaded not guilty.[13] The case took an unusually long time to be decided because Lett had a strong alibi. It was not until 9:00 P.M. that the jury of twelve white men returned its verdict of guilty. "Those are twelve reasonable men in everyday life, Tom's jury," Atticus says in *To Kill a Mockingbird*, "but you saw something come between them and reason. . . . There's something in our world that makes men lose their heads—they couldn't be fair if they tried." Judge Hare set the date of Walter Lett's death by electrocution for May 11, 1934.[14]

The verdict, however, didn't sit well with some of the leading citizens of Monroeville and the county at large. Apparently, there was more to the matter than had come out at the trial. Objections reached the statehouse in Montgomery, and Governor B. M. Miller granted a stay of execution. A second reprieve moved the date again to July 20. The reason for the stays, Miller told the *Montgomery Advertiser,* was that "many leading citizens of Monroe County" had written to him stating, "there is much doubt as to the man being guilty."[15]

One of the petitioners may well have been A. C. Lee. He was the editor and publisher of the *Monroe Journal*, a director of the Monroe County Bank, an attorney, and the incumbent state representative from Monroeville. If his name hadn't been among the "many leading citizens of Monroe County" calling for clemency, Lett's cause might have suffered.

To dispose of the problem, Governor Miller split the baby, commuting Lett's sentence from death in the electric chair to life imprisonment. But it was too late. Lett had been incarcerated four miles north of

Montgomery on Kilby Prison's death row. Two months before his arrival, six prisoners had been electrocuted in the death chamber. The room had no soundproofing and inmates had heard nightmarish sounds of agony. While Lett waited his turn to die three different times, he suffered a mental breakdown. The prison physician wrote to the governor, "He now lies in an assumed state of catalepsy and demonstrates fairly definite features of schizophrenia."[16] Miller asked the state physician inspector to examine Lett personally. "It is my opinion that the above named prisoner," the inspector replied a few days later, "the man whose sentence you recently commuted, is insane."[17] At the end of July 1934, Lett arrived at Searcy Hopsital for the Insane in Mount Vernon, Alabama, and he remained there until he died of tuberculosis three years later. Then a truck carried his body to Atmore and delivered it to his mother.

The potential of Walter Lett's trial to inspire sympathy, and its power to cast light on a racist judicial system, makes it a likely choice as the basis for Tom Robinson's trial in *To Kill a Mockingbird*. Recommending it too is that the trial took place in the Monroe County Courthouse, which Harper Lee knew well.[18]

But the Lett case, while supplying everything necessary for a good plot, lacked a central character that would be meaningful to Harper Lee—her father in the role of defense attorney. And there had been such a case, in fact, with similar themes; it occurred very early in A. C. Lee's career, when he had been appointed to defend two men accused of murder.

In 1919, William Henderson Northrup of Lower Peach Tree, Alabama, owned a general store near the Alabama River. His riverfront location put him in an advantageous spot for doing business. When travelers shoved off from the eastern bank of the river at Davis Ferry and crossed the two-hundred-foot span of brown water via rope ferry, there was Northrup on the other side—in the catbird seat for securing the business of folks needing to purchase a few things. Customers knew sixty-nine-year-old Northrup as a friendly man who had lost one arm in a sawmill accident when he was a teenager. (Tom Robinson had a similar impairment—"His left arm was fully twelve inches shorter than his right"—which Lee used, along with the circumstances of the Walter Lett case, to create the circumstances of Maycomb's rape trial.)

On Saturday morning, September 14—a clear day that promised to be another late-summer scorcher in the upper nineties—Northrup was discovered by an early customer lying on the floor of his store, dying from a blow that had cracked his skull and crushed his shoulder. He was incoherent and incapable of giving a description of his assailant or assailants. The motive for the attack was obvious, though—the cash drawer didn't have a cent in it. By the time the Monroe County deputy sheriff arrived, Northrup was dead. Later that day, the deputy sheriff arrested Frank and Brown Ezell, father and son, and locked them in the Monroeville county jail. A lynch mob gathered, so the prisoners were removed to another county for safekeeping.

To defend two black men on charges of murdering a white man, Judge Murdock McCorvey Fountain (the same who remanded custody of Son Boulware to his father) appointed a young attorney with a promising future in Monroeville, but no criminal trial experience: Nelle Harper Lee's father, Amasa Coleman Lee. He would have less than two weeks to cobble together a defense.

He did his utmost—including objecting to the fact that one of Northrup's sons was on the jury—but he lost, as he was destined to, given the times.[19] When the foreman returned to read the verdict, Lee copied it down. His handwriting becomes agitated and irregular before regaining its usual composure with the last few words: "We the jury find the defendants, Frank Ezell and Brown Ezell guilty of murder in the first degree as charged in the indictment and we further find that they suffer death by hanging." The date of execution was set for December 19.

On the appointed day, a large crowd assembled outside the county jail across from the courthouse. Some of the curious had brought umbrellas to ward off the cold, steady rain, but many just stood waiting with their collars turned up. Inside the jail, Frank and Brown Ezell stood on an iron grating, anchored into the wall about ten feet above the first floor and reached by a ladder. In the middle of the grating was a trapdoor with a pair of leaves, each approximately two feet wide by four feet long. From a beam eight feet above the prisoners' heads hung a rope ending in a noose. The sheriff and his assistants positioned Frank Ezell over the trap door. The crowd outside strained to hear if he had anything to say. He said he was innocent and denied having anything to do with the crime. Then a hood was placed over his head and the noose snugged around his neck. His hands were tied behind his back.

On a signal, the doors divided and he dropped straight down and stopped with a neck-breaking jerk at knee level with the men standing below. A local physician stepped forward and listened to his heartbeat. Minutes passed until the doctor pronounced him dead. Then Brown Ezell, after asserting that he had acted alone and deserved his punishment, joined his father in death within the hour. The sheriff came out and announced to the crowd that both men had paid the penalty and were indeed dead.[20]

But that was not the end of it. Not long after the sentence was carried out, in New York City, Clyde McCall Northrup, the murdered man's eldest son, received a package postmarked Monroeville. Thinking perhaps that it was an early Christmas gift from relatives, he removed the wrapping and opened the box. Inside, wrapped in newspaper dotted with dried bloodstains, were two heavy hanks of hair— the scalps of Frank and Brown Ezell—and a note reading, "Justice has been done in Alabama."[21]

Attorney Lee never took another criminal case; he remained a title lawyer for the rest of his professional life. How deeply he felt about the almost perfunctory hangings of the Ezells was left to his daughter to allude to in what would become *To Kill a Mockingbird*. The hanging of Atticus Finch's first two clients "was probably the beginning of my father's profound distaste for the practice of criminal law." But through the character of Atticus, Harper Lee highlights her father's decency when he was a young, well-intentioned lawyer; and for plot, the Walter Lett case offered an incendiary issue: a sexual transgression against a white woman.

With the core components of her novel in place, she set to work revising again in the winter of 1957–58. Hohoff's role continued to be providing "professional help in organizing her material and developing a sound plot structure. After a couple of false starts, the story line, interplay of characters, and fall of emphasis grew clearer, and with each revision—there were many minor changes as the story grew in strength and in Nelle's own vision of it—the true stature of the novel became evident." The time frame became the middle of the Depression, between the summer of 1932 and Halloween night 1935, when Maycomb County is so poor that the energy of life itself seems to be on hold. Hohoff remembered:

> We talked it out, sometimes for hours. And sometimes she came around to my way of thinking, sometimes I to hers, sometimes the discussion would open up an entirely new line of country. . . .
>
> We saw a great deal of each other during this period, and, if conditions make it possible, I believe such close, frequent communication can be of enormous benefit to the author, the book, and incidentally to the editor. But of course writing is the loneliest of activities. Harper Lee literally spent her days and nights in the most intense efforts to set down what she wanted to say in the way which would best say it to the reader. . . . It's no secret that she was living on next to nothing and in considerable physical discomfort while she was writing *Mockingbird*. I don't think anyone, certainly not I, ever heard one small mutter of discontent throughout all those months of writing and tearing up, writing and tearing up.[22]

Colleagues of Hohoff's say she took nothing else on—no other manuscripts—for six months while she worked with Lee.

Capote later said that the first two-thirds of the book, the portion about Scout, Dill, and Jem (Nelle, Truman, and Nelle's brother, Edwin, probably) trying to coax Boo Radley out of his house, "are quite literal and true."[23] Supporting this is the way actual incidents reported by the *Monroe Journal* during those years became part of the fabric of the story. For instance, in February 1933, when Nelle was six years old, a Mr. Dees fired a shotgun at somebody prowling in his collard patch (a black man, and the shot killed him), a parallel to the episode in which Nathan Radley fires a load of buckshot in Jem Finch's direction while Jem is retrieving his pants from Boo Radley's backyard.[24] In May 1934, a rabid dog bit two adults and two children, prefiguring the scene in the novel of Atticus shooting a mad dog.[25] As Capote said, "Most of the people in Nelle's book are drawn from life."[26]

However, he had nothing to do with the actual writing of the book, although some Monroeville residents believe the legend: "I've heard they were up there at the old Hibbert place, which is right north of Monroeville—out there in the woods. They just went out there, there's an old farmhouse, and they went out there and wrote and wrote and wrote."[27] Tay Hohoff's son-in-law, Dr. Grady H. Nunn, said that such a deception wouldn't have occurred to Lee.

> I am satisfied that the relationship between Nelle and Tay over those three years while *Mockingbird* was in the making developed into a warmer and closer association than is usual between author and editor. I believe that special association came about at least in part because they worked, together, over every word in the manuscript. Tay and [her husband] Arthur became Nelle's close friends, sort of family, and that friendship continued beyond the publication of the book. I doubt that the special closeness could possibly have happened had there been an alien ghostwriter, Capote, involved.[28]

Also, given Capote's inability to keep anybody's secrets (as friends who read his posthumous novel *Answered Prayers* discovered to their horror), it's preposterous that he wouldn't have claimed right of authorship after the novel became famous. He did say, which Lee never denied, that he read the manuscript and recommended some changes because it was too long in places. "Yes, it is true that Nelle Lee is publishing a book. I did not see Nelle last winter," Capote wrote to his aunt Mary Ida Carter, "but the previous year, she showed me as much of the book as she'd written, and I liked it very much. She has real talent."[29]

For all her talent, Lee couldn't shake her difficulty with first and third person. Here's the adult Jean Louise speaking:

> When I was almost six and Jem was nearly ten, our summertime boundaries (within calling distance of Calpurnia) were Mrs. Henry

Lafayette Dubose's house two doors to the north of us, and the Radley Place three doors to the south. We were never tempted to break them. The Radley Place was inhabited by an entity the mere description of whom was enough to make us behave for days on end; Mrs. Dubose was plain hell.

That was the summer Dill came to us.

Then the child Scout describes the actual moment Dill appeared, and drama replaces exposition. In a cinematic sense, the narration provided by the adult Jean Louise is like a voice-over.

It might be that Lee floundered when she was trying to settle on a point of view, or was incapable of maintaining one. She rewrote the novel three times: the original draft was in the third person; then she changed to the first person and later rewrote what became the final draft, blending the two narrators, Janus-like, looking forward and back at the same time.[30]

She later called this a "hopeless period" of writing the novel over and over. She "spent her days and nights in the most intense efforts to set down what she wanted to say in the way which would best say it to the reader," said Hohoff.[31] The writing went at a glacial pace. Her deadline was May 1958 and she wasn't going to make it. She lived on pennies, still typing at the makeshift desk on York Avenue. No one "inquired too closely into what she ate," although now and then, a friend from Monroeville—another of Miss Gladys Watson's protégés— invited her over for dinner and the chance to talk about how the book was going.[32]

One winter night during her "hopeless period" she threw all of her work out the window and called Hohoff, upset. But her editor was never one to suffer fools gladly.[33] The novel was a collaborative effort— Hohoff's figurative fingerprints were all over the manuscript. There was also the matter of the advance, which would have to be paid back. Lee retrieved her still-gestating novel from the snow and kept working.

When the weather was better in the South than in New York City, she went home to Monroeville. A room at the golf course on the edge of town—now a country club her father belonged to—was a good place for writing uninterrupted. Also, just to get away, she would sometimes go to Truman's aunt Mary Ida Carter's house in the country, toting a bottle of scotch, and spend a long afternoon, reading and sipping. Her father and her sister Alice didn't approve of this, and not because they didn't drink. They objected to the amount she drank and the state she worked herself into. Capote's aunt Marie Rudisill claimed that Alice threatened to put her in a program for alcoholics if she didn't straighten up.[34]

Perhaps attempts to break through the "intense reserve" that Hohoff noticed about Lee contributed to her troubles with alcohol. Social situations made her uncomfortable, as Dr. Nunn happened to see one evening in 1958. "We were living in Tuscaloosa, and Tay visited us in connection with a Lippincott-sponsored search for promising authors in the writing program there. There were several such visits during our tenure there. As usual a New York–style cocktail party for Tay was included. Nelle was in Monroeville at the time and was invited up for the party. She arrived, was introduced around, and promptly disappeared. I discovered her later sitting on the back steps with our daughter, who was then five. They were there until Nelle left at the party's end. Definitely Nelle was no party lover."[35]

In any case, it was during one of her visits to Monroeville in the spring of 1959 that she completed a circle that had begun when she was still in high school. It was in Gladys Watson's English classes that she fell in love with British literature; and now at last, as her manuscript was in the final stages of preparation, she asked her teacher to critique it.

Miss Gladys Watson (now Mrs. Watson-Burkett) placed what would become one of the most popular novels of the twentieth century in a safe place: her sewing basket. In the evenings she would take it out, read it aloud to her new husband, and write notes in the margins.[36] One day after school, she asked one of her students, Cecil Ryland, to come up to her desk. She said she had finished proofreading a novel by a former student, and asked him to return it to her now. "And so, I gathered up the manuscript in an old stationery box, and took it and went knocking on her door. Nelle Harper Lee came to the door, and I said, 'Here's your book.' And she said 'Thank you.' Little did I realize that I held a little bit of history in my hands."[37]

Go Set a Watchman, renamed *To Kill a Mockingbird* in its third iteration (because "Mockingbird" suggested the South, and "kill" is always a good word to have in a title), had been "heavily edited" by Tay Hohoff and was slated for publication in May 1960.[38] Her role as midwife to the novel, she said, had been merely "an editorial call to duty."[39] Meanwhile, the manuscript of *Go Set a Watchman* was set aside as a draft, eventually coming to rest for safekeeping in the law offices of Barnett, Bugg & Lee.

That fall, in mid-November, while Lee was waiting for galleys of the book to arrive, Truman called about an article in the *New York Times*, headlined "Wealthy Farmer, 3 of Family Slain."

Holcomb, Kan., Nov. 15 (UPI)—A wealthy wheat farmer, his wife and their two young children were found shot to death today in their home. They had been killed by shotgun blasts at close range after being bound and gagged. The father, 48-year-old Herbert W. Clutter, was found in the basement with his son, Kenyon, 15. His wife Bonnie, 45, and a daughter, Nancy, 16, were in their beds. There were no signs of a struggle, and nothing had been stolen. The telephone lines had been cut. "This is apparently the case of a psychopathic killer," Sheriff Earl Robinson said.

William Shawn, the editor of the *New Yorker*, had assigned Truman to use the article as a springboard for writing about the impact of a quadruple murder on a small town. It was going to be a tough assignment. The Clutters' killer or killers were still on the loose. Truman, slight, blond, and bespectacled, was looking for someone to go with him.

To Lee, it sounded like an adventure. "He said it would be a tremendously involved job and would take two people. The crime intrigued him, and I'm intrigued with crime—and, boy, I wanted to go. It was deep calling to deep."[40]

eight

"See NL's Notes"

She had a down-home style, a friendly smile, and a knack for saying the right things. Once the ice was broken, I was told, Capote could get people to talking about the subject closest to their hearts, themselves.

—Kansas Bureau of Investigation detective
ALVIN DEWEY

They arrived at twilight in Garden City, a town of eleven thousand on the high western Kansas wheat plain, as the sky was turning a deep icy blue-green. The radio kept repeating the same bulletin at intervals: "Police authorities, continuing their investigation of the tragic Clutter slaying, have requested that anyone with pertinent information please contact the sheriff's office."[1] Driving down North Main Street, Truman and Nelle glanced expectantly left and right for the Warren Hotel. It was supposed to be the best and closest accommodation to the Clutter farm in Holcomb, a village of 270 residents seven miles west on US-50. Nelle noticed that street signs and even traffic lights were hard to see because everything was festooned with Christmas decorations—strings of lights, wreaths of evergreen, and red cardboard bells.[2]

The hotel was small but pleasant looking, nothing on the scale of the 1887 four-story Windsor, just down the street. Once called the "Waldorf of the Prairies," this edifice for rich cattlemen had been ruined by the dust bowl years in the 1930s and was teetering toward bankruptcy. At the Warren, they registered for adjoining rooms and then took the elevator upstairs to rest. The drive from Manhattan, Kansas, had taken eight hours, the last one hundred miles of it across country flat and featureless ("level," Kansans preferred to call it).

The next day, December 16, they walked a block to the Finney County Courthouse, the headquarters of the murder investigation. The courthouse, built to the same proportions as a gigantic lump of sugar and faced with whitish-gray limestone, was separated from the street by a half acre of lawn, in the middle of which was a bronze replica of the Statue of Liberty. The person they needed to see was Kansas Bureau of Investigation (KBI) detective Alvin Dewey, who had been appointed to coordinate the investigation by KBI chief Logan Sanford. Dewey was both a former Finney County sheriff and a former FBI agent. Chief Sanford had given him the additional responsibility of handling the press because he was not easily ruffled. In the field, a team of investigators was combing western Kansas for leads.

Nelle and Truman consulted a hand-painted directory on a dun-colored wall of the courthouse's first floor and took the stairs to the second. A secretary greeted them and escorted them to Mr. Dewey's office.

Alvin Dewey was "just plain handsome," Nelle decided on the spot, and made a point of saying so in her notes.[3] Dark-haired and dressed in a blue suit, he was seated at a large mahogany desk positioned catty-corner in a cramped room. His mission seemed defined by two prominent items in the room: a large Santa Fe Railroad map of the United States on the wall, and a thick criminal statute book on the desk. Dewey's brown eyes sized Nelle up—"a tall brunette, a good looker," he thought, an observation that suggests that Nelle had put aside the frumpiness of her college years to help Truman make a favorable impression.[4] Dewey invited them to sit down. His curiosity was piqued: he hadn't seen either of them among the reporters who had been hanging around during the past three weeks.

Truman, about five foot four and wearing a sheepskin coat, a long scarf that reached the floor, and moccasins—his version of Western wear, apparently—acted as if he thought he was pretty important. Nelle took her cue from Truman and waited for him to begin a carefully rehearsed introduction. The forty-seven-year-old Dewey concealed a smile behind a drag on his Winston cigarette when he heard the sound of his visitor's contralto voice.

"Mr. Dewey, I am Truman Capote and this is my friend, Nelle Harper Lee. She's a writer, too." The *New Yorker* magazine, he explained, had assigned him to write an article about the Clutter case. Miss Lee was his assistant. His friend, Bennett Cerf, the publisher of Random House books, had contacted Dr. James McCain, the president of Mr. Clutter's alma mater, Kansas State University, who had been very helpful. But now they needed to get down to *business*. They were here to find out the facts about the murder, the family, and how the town was reacting.

Dewey listened noncommittally. Except for the name-dropping, they sounded like your average reporters trying to get the inside scoop. "You're free to attend press conferences," he said. "I hold them about once a day."

"But I'm not a newspaperman," Capote insisted. "I need to talk to *you* in depth. . . . What I'm going to write will take months. What I am here for is to do a very special story on the family up to and including the murders."

Dewey indicated that he hadn't heard anything to make him change his original offer: they could attend press conferences with the rest of their kind.

"Look," Capote said, struggling to separate himself from newspaper men with daily deadlines, "it really doesn't make any difference to me if the case is ever solved or not."[5]

Dewey's face darkened, and Nelle suspected immediately that Truman had just torpedoed the mission. In fact, privately Dewey had been worrying for three weeks about the trail growing cold, and the dread of defeat was starting to gnaw at him: "In homicide, if you don't come up with some answers in twenty-four to forty-eight hours, you get a feeling in your gut that the thing may never be solved. . . . 'Anything new on the Clutter case?' folks would be asking me on the post office steps for months to come. And then it would be, 'Never did find out who killed the Clutters, did you?' for the rest of my life."[6]

Nelle Harper Lee's street in Monroeville, Alabama, when she was a child.
Her house was about where the car is parked.

A. C. Lee, the model for Atticus
Finch: civic leader, politician, and
title lawyer in the late 1930s.

Frances Cunningham Lee: a sensitive
woman whose "nervous disorder"
bewildered her youngest child, Nelle.

Edwin Coleman Lee, Harper Lee's brother and the model for Jem in *To Kill a Mockingbird.* *(Auburn University, 1940)*

The sophomore class of Monroe County High School. Nelle (second row from top, farthest right) adored her English teacher, Gladys Watson (top row, center).

Nelle (far right) poses stiffly with two classmates at Huntingdon College in Montgomery, Alabama, on a Sunday afternoon during her freshman year.

A happier Nelle (second from left) found her niche at the University of Alabama writing for campus publications. Here she appears in the 1948 yearbook as a "Campus Personality."

A snapshot of Nelle in downtown Garden City, Kansas, during the winter of 1959–60. *(Garden City Telegram)*

"Just plain handsome" is how Detective Alvin Dewey impressed Nelle the first time she met him while accompanying Truman Capote as his "assistant researchist" during the Clutter murders investigation in Kansas. *(AP Photo)*

An index card from the files of Harper Lee's agent indicating the retitling of *Go Set a Watchman* to *To Kill a Mockingbird* as Tay Hohoff edited the manuscript. *(Rare Book & Manuscript Library at Columbia University)*

Tay Hohoff "was a terrific editor," said one of her authors. "She would ask you questions. She would go through the manuscript and jot down little questions in the margins. From those questions, you would start questioning your own work." Only with the release of *Go Set a Watchman* has the extent of Hohoff's role in shaping *To Kill a Mockingbird* been appreciated. *(Therese Nunn Perry)*

Lee and producer Alan Pakula watch the filming of *To Kill a Mockingbird* in 1962. Nelle endured a punishing promotional tour after the film's release, using her teasing wit to charm reporters. (*AP Photo*)

Lee and Gregory Peck as Atticus Finch on the production set. Lee doubted his suitability for the role at first— she had Spencer Tracy in mind. (*Corbis*)

Alice Lee, Nelle's elder sister, an attorney and editor of the local newspaper like her father. Though petite, her nickname in the family was Bear.
(The United Methodist Church)

During a meeting of the National Council of the Arts in Tarrytown, New York, 1966, some of the members take a break. (Back to front) Nelle Lee; Roger Stevens, Broadway impresario; R. Philip Hanes, business executive; Agnes de Mille, dancer and choreographer.
(Photograph courtesy of R. Philip Hanes)

Nelle Lee attends Celebration of a Decade, a Los Angeles Public Library Awards Dinner held in her honor in 2005. *(Corbis)*

A worker prepares the earth in the Lee family burial plot, located in Monroeville's Old Methodist Cemetery, a few minutes' walk from the famous courthouse. *(AP Photo)*

Anger suddenly got the better of him. "I'd like to see your press card, Mr. Cappuchi," he snapped.[7]

Truman let the mispronunciation pass, seeing that they were off on the wrong foot. "I don't have one," he said mildly.

The get-to-know-you meeting had turned into a showdown. Exercising the better part of valor, Nelle rose. Both men got to their feet. Dewey bid them a stiff goodbye and, after they had gone, returned to his work.

The next day, Nelle and Truman appeared in Dewey's office again. "I just wanted to establish my identity," Truman said in a friendly voice, and presented his passport. Perhaps Nelle, witnessing the earlier confrontation, had reminded Truman that honey catches more flies than vinegar. The detective glanced at Capote's passport and repeated that they could attend press conferences. Truman thanked him as though they had been granted a special favor.

Dewey began seeing the two in the scrum of reporters as he delivered updates on the case. "They were quiet, attentive, asked few questions, and, as far as I could tell, caused no commotion. I did hear they were hard at work, interviewing everyone, people said . . . in Holcomb, up and down Garden City's Main Street, in farm homes, in the coffee-drinking places, in the schools, everywhere. The New Yorker was getting his story together." With his practiced eye, Dewey sized up the relationship between Capote and Lee and how important she was to him. "If Capote came on as something of a shocker, she was there to absorb the shock. She had a down-home style, a friendly smile, and a knack for saying the right things. Once the ice was broken, I was told, Capote could get people to talking about the subject closest to their hearts, themselves."[8]

She had accompanied Capote as his salaried "assistant researchist"—a term he invented for her. Their assignment was to take a six-inch news item in the *New York Times* about the murder of the farm family in Holcomb—just a pinprick on the map—and find the humanity buried beneath the crime. They would have to find out everything about the family—Herb and Bonnie Clutter, and their children, teenagers Nancy and Kenyon—so the Clutters would be real.

Capote wanted to accomplish this without the benefit of taking notes or tape-recording during interviews. He was convinced people were more guarded when they could see they were going on the record. He would just talk to people instead—conduct interviews as conversations. Her job was to listen and observe subtleties that Truman might be too busy to notice. Then they would return to the hotel and separately write down everything they could recall. Lee's gift for creating character sketches complemented Capote's ability to recall remarks. Many times over the next month, his telegraphic descriptions of a conversation would end with "See NL's notes" to remind him to use her insights later.

The hotel's Trail Room coffee shop became their unofficial office during the day for reviewing notes, or for keeping appointments with folks who could spare only enough time for a chat and a cup of coffee. If either Nelle or Truman drew a blank about a fact or a remark that had been made, they would prod each other's memories. In instances when key information was missing or unclear, they would have to go back and visit a person a second or a third time. "Together we would get it right," Nelle said.[9]

That was the plan. Unfortunately, obstacles existed everywhere, it seemed.

To begin with, residents in both Garden City and Holcomb were afraid. With the killer or killers still at large, interviews were hard to get. When Capote went alone to the home of Mrs. Hideo Ashida, a neighbor of the Clutters, she refused to open the door until he could provide her with the name of someone to verify his identity.[10] The Plains states were still reeling from the rampage the year before when two Nebraska teenagers, nineteen-year-old Charles Starkweather and his fourteen-year-old girlfriend, Caril Fugate, had killed ten people in five states. News of the Clutter murders had sent people in Garden City and Holcomb into a paranoid frenzy: farmers padlocked their gates and put combination locks on their sheds; homeowners installed deadbolt locks on doors; apartment dwellers added chain locks to their bedrooms. Some took the added precaution of fixing all the windows with ten-penny nails. Even though most folks said that the authorities should be looking for an outsider—a native would have known that

Herb Clutter never had any cash on hand—neighbors kept an eye on one another, and porch lights burned until dawn. The KBI received three hundred letters with tips from anonymous sources, many of them postmarked Garden City, accusing local people by name.[11]

But Nelle and Truman were determined to get this story, and Truman was notoriously persistent. Sometimes, a little cash would buy an interview. Mrs. Ashida's son Robert and other residents said that Capote willingly paid, if necessary.[12] In his list of expenses, written on the inside cover of a handsome gold-colored journal he had purchased in Italy, Truman itemized his Kansas expenses: car rental, meals on the train, and "farewell gifts," but left one amount unidentified: "spent cash $1400."[13]

Once invited into someone's home, however, he found a further stumbling block, a mundane problem that he and Nelle never anticipated, which was trying to keep the person's attention turned away from the TV. NBC had begun broadcasting from Garden City the year before, and the clear black-and-white picture on the screen seemed to hypnotize bored farming families trapped inside during the long winter. The nuisance of manic commercials in the background tested Nelle's and Truman's patience—neither of whom owned a television set—especially when the whole point of an interview was to try to talk intimately with someone.

Also interfering with getting good interviews was Truman himself—he just wasn't going over very well with people. "Nelle looked like normal folk. She was just a fantastic lady," said Harold Nye, one of the principal KBI detectives running down leads on the Clutter case, "but Truman was an absolute flake."[14] Nye, who went five days and nights without sleep during the week after the murders, had no patience for fancy Johnny-come-latelies showing up on the scene.

Neither did postmistress Myrtle T. Clare: "Capote came walking around here real uppity and superior-like and acting so strange that I think people was scared of him. He was real foreign-like, and nobody would open their doors for him, afraid he'd knock them in the head."[15]

"I thought Capote was queero," said Gerald Van Vleet, Clutter's business partner. "He was nosy as hell and very, very rude. He came out to my farm on a few occasions to talk to me, and I tried to avoid him."[16]

How they were going over was obvious to Nelle. "We were given the cold shoulder. Those people had never seen anyone like Truman—he was like someone coming off the moon."[17]

In the end, there were key people who refused to be interviewed under any circumstances; they'd had their fill of reporters snooping around, hoping to sniff out the gory details of a crime that had hit close to home in the tight-knit town. The first to find Nancy Clutter's body had been teenagers Nancy Ewalt and Sue Kidwell, who had run screaming from the Clutters' house. When Nelle and Truman approached Nancy Ewalt's father, Clarence, and asked for a moment of his time, he fixed them with his watery blue eyes, framed in a red weather-beaten face, and said evenly three times to their questions, "I'm a busy man," and finally turned away.[18]

Fortunately, one resource available to them—and to everyone else—was the legwork being done by Kansas journalists on the scene. The *Garden City Telegram,* the *Hutchinson News,* the *Kansas City Star,* and other papers were following the manhunt closely. Dr. McCain, the president of Kansas State University, had recommended to Nelle and Truman that when they arrived in Garden City they introduce themselves to Bill Brown, the managing editor of the *Garden City Telegram.* They tried, but he brushed them off. The crime had taken place in his backyard, and he wasn't dealing in out-of-towners. The lights in the newspaper office burned late most nights: "I was busy putting out a newspaper," he later said flatly.[19] In her notes, Nelle dismissed him as a "Catonahottinroof."[20]

Even if they had been able to enlist Brown's help, weaving a pastiche primarily from newspaper stories and secondhand reporting would have been unacceptable to the *New Yorker*'s editor, William Shawn. He was expecting art, not paraphrased remarks, hearsay, and canned statements from press conferences. Nelle and Capote understood that, of course, but after a week in Kansas the truth was their spadework hadn't turned up anything beyond what reporters on the scene had already unearthed. The dozen or so interviews they had conducted yielded predictable responses: people were shocked by the murders; congregation members at the church the Clutters attended eulogized them as a fine family; and so on. Herb Clutter, everyone said, was a go-getter, always smiling. Nelle knew enough about Bonnie Clutter, the mother, and daughter Nancy to form sympathetic composite portraits of them. Kenyon was a bit of a mystery—a loner, more absorbed by projects that would appeal to an engineer than to a farmer. But these were just sketches in the corner of a canvas that needed to be much larger and more original.

They didn't have much time to get the formula right. The Christmas and New Year's holidays were not far off, and then businesses would be closed and people would be occupied with family celebrations. No one would be interested in picking at the wound caused by the blow of the Clutter killings.

Capote began to believe that coming out to Kansas had been a mistake all around. "I cannot get any rapport with these people," he told Nelle. "I can't get a handle on them." Except for two high school English teachers who had read some of his work, no one knew him from the man in the moon. How many more times was he going to be called "Mr. Cappuchi" or "Ka-poat"?

"Hang on," Nelle said. "You *will* penetrate this place."[21] A few days later they got their big break.

On Sunday, December 20, Nelle and Truman were waiting to be picked up in the lobby of the Warren Hotel by Herb Clutter's former estate attorney, Cliff Hope. Hope was on Dr. McCain's list of people to get to know, and Truman had been pestering him for several days. Finally, he had agreed to drive the pair out to the Clutter farm. The KBI had placed the farm off-limits, but Hope agreed to intercede with the family's executor, Kenneth Lyon, explaining that Nelle and Truman were friends of Dr. McCain's. Lyon acquiesced, but insisted on being present, driving the two hundred miles from Wichita to meet them there.[22]

When Detective Nye found out later about the visit, he wasn't pleased: "I was in charge of securing the house. [Detective] Roy Church was helping me. We examined the entire house for evidence, during which all was secured. And how they got in later, I don't know."[23]

Cliff Hope turned out to be a lean, blond man who smoked a briar pipe; Kenneth Lyon was a "slim, dark" man and seemed to Nelle to have an "open honest face."[24] As Hope escorted them to the waiting car he mentioned that the trip out to the farm would take only about fifteen minutes. As they left downtown Garden City behind, the pavement ended with a thump and the road turned to gravel and gray dirt. Gray seemed to be the predominant color everywhere, bleeding into the sky, the leafless trees, and the frost-killed silvery grass. About a half mile south of Holcomb, they came to a lane leading off from the road. A "Road Closed" sign nailed to a sawhorse marked the entrance to the Clutters' River Valley Farm. Tacked to one end of the sawhorse, a limp red rag flapped disconsolately in the cold wind. Kenneth Lyon got out and turned the sawhorse aside to allow the car to pass.

The lane leading to the house was bordered on both sides by tall Chinese elms, their branches creating a spidery archway. The effect was graceful, but their aesthetic appeal was secondary to their practical purpose—they served as windbreaks for slowing the rate of dust or snow that whipped over the prairie during windy spells. Two years before, in 1957, a blizzard had buried Holcomb in snowdrifts twenty-seven feet deep in some places. A farmer lost in a snowstorm, or a motorist stopped on the road because the earth and sky were both a blur of white, could freeze to death within hailing distance of a house without a friendly landmark, such as a row of trees, to mark the way to shelter.

Isolation was always something to be on guard against in the vast, beguiling openness of the prairies. The night the Clutters were murdered, no one had heard the shots because the wind was blowing; not even employee Alfred Stoecklein, who lived with his wife and three children in a small house on the other side of the Clutters' enormous barn; and no one had seen anything suspicious in the utter darkness. The feeling of naked vulnerability translated into the dislike of strangers that had plagued Truman and Nelle thus far. As one old man had said in Mrs. Hartman's café on the day of the Clutter murders, "All we've got out here are our friends. There isn't anything else."[25]

Reaching the end of the quarter-mile lane, Cliff Hope parked near the front door. The yellow brick and white clapboard home with fourteen rooms, three baths, and two wood fireplaces had been built in the late 1940s, a time when many homes in the county went without running water. Surrounded by a lawn landscaped with pointed jade-green arborvitae, the big house had been the diadem of Herb's four-thousand-acre farm.

At forty-eight, Clutter had been justifiably proud of his twenty-year rise from 1939, when his financial records indicated he was worth "$1000 I hope," to his position as one of the wealthiest farmers in the state.[26] With the help of half a dozen employees, sometimes as many as twenty, he had raised sorghum, milo grain, and certified grass seed. That day on the Clutter farm, Nelle noticed that hundreds of red-and-white Hereford cattle were still grazing peacefully in the pasture.[27]

Even as his wealth expanded, Herb Clutter could be stubborn about taking advice concerning his financial affairs, and he had foot-dragged about estate planning, despite dogged reminders from Cliff Hope. "Herb would come into my office with some Saturday errands written on the back of an envelope. He gave me a few minutes, checked me off, and [went] on his way."[28] Clutter had died without a will to protect his Kansas fiefdom; and in a few months, River Valley Farm would be auctioned off by sheriff's order.

From around the barn, Alfred Stoecklein came out to meet the group. Stoecklein had been the Clutters' odd-job man ("spectacles and yellow rotting teeth," Capote noted; Nelle got the impression he drank, despite Herb Clutter's iron rule that he wouldn't abide drinkers).[29] Emerging from a car nearby was Gerald Van Vleet, Clutter's business partner. He was a big man in khaki work clothes and heavy boots who seemed more interested in twisting an engine belt in his rough hands than in making conversation. When Kenneth Lyon signaled from the house that he'd unlocked the front door, everyone started up the hedge-lined walk. The heat in the house was off, but the scent of lemon furniture polish hung in the chilly air. Van Vleet crossed the living room to Clutter's office and promptly sat down in his former partner's wooden swivel chair, rotating slowly back and forth. To every question Nelle put to him about the murder, he answered, "I wasn't here."[30]

Evidently, when it came to interpreting what this farm had to say about its former inhabitants, Nelle and Truman were on their own. They decided to examine the house separately: each would make maps of the floor plan and take notes on the contents of the rooms. In a sense, they would be interviewing the house the way they did people, and then, afterward, they could compare their impressions.

"Apparently [Hope] saw nothing evil in our explorations," Nelle noted, though he was "alert as a fox."[31] He and Lyon stepped away for a whispered conversation while Nelle and Truman oriented themselves to the layout of the house.

In a way, they had come full circle from their childhoods in Monroeville. They were figuratively once again on South Alabama Avenue, where they had lived next door to each other and fantasized that a madman lived down the street in the tumbledown house owned by the Boulware family. They had spied on that house, speculated about the goings-on inside, and dared each other to sneak inside that lair. Nelle had used the house, with some embellishments, as the home of Boo Radley in *To Kill a Mockingbird.* By contrast, this successful Kansas farmer's house, perched in a breezy, sunny spot, didn't have creaking hinges, broken shutters, and flickering shadows, or any of the lurid conventions associated with horror. But by exploring it, they were embarking once again on a hunt for something monstrous.

Nelle excused herself and walked past Van Vleet, who it seemed was permanently ensconced in his late partner's chair, to examine Herb Clutter's office.

Herb and his wife, Bonnie, forty-five, had been one of the most admired and active couples in Holcomb and Garden City. On the walls of Herb's dark veneer-paneled office were framed certificates and labeled notebooks covering his career. "If something happened in Holcomb, you pretty much knew Herb or Bonnie had something to do with it," said Merl Wilson, who, with his wife, Argybell, alternated with the Clutters in leading the local 4-H.[32] Herb had been president of the National Association of Wheat Growers and directed the Farm Credit Administration for the district covering Kansas, New Mexico, Oklahoma, and Colorado. The books in the floor-to-ceiling shelves in his office reflected his singular interests—*Crops in Peace and War, Beef Cattle in Kansas,* and *Farmers at the Crossroads.* In Garden City, Clutter had also served on half a dozen committees for the First Methodist Church. In many ways, he was to western Kansas what Nelle's father, A. C. Lee, was to southern Alabama: a pillar of the small-town community determined to preserve its sanctity.

Nelle headed upstairs next, out from under the quietly watchful eyes of Hope, Van Vleet, and Lyon. At the top of the stairs she looked briefly into a small bathroom with pink tile and towel rods before moving on to the bedrooms. Room by room, she began to take inventory in her notes, of everything she saw.

The first bedroom she came to had belonged to Eveanna, who was, by this time, married and living in Mt. Carroll, Illinois. (She was one of the two older daughters who no longer lived at home.) Bonnie Clutter had been sleeping in Eveanna's bedroom, and that was where her body had been discovered. Mrs. Clutter, a pretty wraith of a woman, taught Sunday school and belonged to the Women's Society of Christian Service. She was said to suffer from debilitating bouts of depression that kept her crying in bed for days. One night, she had been found wandering distractedly in Garden City and taken home. (Truman, rummaging downstairs in the basement bathroom, had found vials of prescription tranquilizers labeled "Bonnie Clutter, Wesley Hospital, take four a day.")[33]

Nelle glanced at the old-fashioned dresser of heavy oaklike wood with a big mirror, the throw rugs, and an "atrocious table lamp on the table beside the bed."[34] It was a stuffy room to be cooped up in. Then she moved on to Beverly's room, but since Beverly was away at Kansas University Medical Center studying nursing, and nothing about the crime involved her room, Nelle only took note of the dark, heavy furniture.

Around the corner was Kenyon Clutter's pale-gray-green bedroom. Solitary and studious, according to classmates, Kenyon had been fifteen when he died. His bedroom was the largest, stretching nearly half the length of the house, suggesting that he was the intended heir of River Valley Farm. On the bookshelf above his bed were titles of boys' books—the complete *Hardy Boys* series—and a handful of young adult bestsellers, including Junior Literary Guild selections. Framed pictures of his two eldest sisters, Eveanna and Beverly, held pride of place on one of the shelves above his desk. "Kenyon Always be Good," Nelle read in the corner of Eveanna's picture. There were also several completed plastic cars from model kits, three figurines of Kenyon's favorite breeds of dogs, two snapshots of his prize-winning sheep, and four horse figurines. Against the opposite wall stood an antique wind-up Victrola, a symbol of Kenyon's fascination with mechanical things.

Down the hall was the smaller bedroom belonging to Kenyon's sixteen-year-old sister, Nancy. Dark-eyed, creamy-complexioned, smart in school, active in school clubs, and the recent star of her school play, Nancy was any parent's ideal of a middle-class teenager. On the day before her death, she taught a neighbor girl how to bake cherry pie "her special way."[35] The walls of her bedroom were pink, and the ceiling painted light blue. She had created a vanity for herself by adding a skirt to an old table. On a cork bulletin board were photos of class-mates and clippings from the school newspaper. Near the window was a print of Jesus Christ; and above the bed where Nancy's body had been found were pictures of three kittens. In an overstuffed chair sat a button-eyed teddy bear that Nancy's steady, Bobby Rupp, had won for her at a county fair. Missing, though, and in the hands of the KBI as evidence, was a diary that Nancy had kept for three years with daily entries. "Damnation. We've got to see them," Nelle wrote in notes when she found out about the diary's existence.[36]

She returned downstairs where Lyon, Van Vleet, and Hope were making small talk. Truman was outside drawing a map of the property.

Having seen Herb Clutter's office already, Nelle walked around the living room. A light green sectional sofa matched the walls; the carpet was pink. Mounted above a console record player was another print of Jesus Christ. Christian books and magazines such as *A Man Called Peter* and *Guideposts* lay on shelves within reach of Herb's favorite easy chair—"modern religious crap," in Nelle's opinion.[37] Off the living room by an adjoining hallway was a large bathroom with pink tiles on the walls, white and chocolate-colored ones alternating on the floor, and a door to the master bedroom, where Herb slept alone. The walls of Herb's bedroom were light blue, the bed large enough for two; above it was a print of Jesus Christ, this time gazing down on biblical Jerusalem. (By now Nelle was beginning to see humor in the pronounced household themes; later she asked Truman if there was a print of Jesus by the washer and dryer she might have missed.)[38]

Going back out into the hallway, Nelle turned left toward the dining room, which was the same banal green as the living room. The dining table and chairs were blond and matched a breakfront. Continuing on through the dining room, she came to the white-and-blue kitchen Herb had designed with an eye toward good organization. The cabinets, featuring a built-in dishwasher and stove—unusual for the times— were all at a convenient height, and in a few places the kickboards turned down to provide steps for the children to reach things. There was an ingenious swinging door by the baseboard for sweeping refuse from the floor and sending it down a chute to a garbage can in the basement. One side of the kitchen was devoted to a breakfast nook with a table that would have been large enough to accommodate all six members of the family for a big farm-style breakfast.

Around the corner from the kitchen was a utility room. On the morning the murders were discovered, two boys doing chores on the farm had placed fresh milk inside the utility room at dawn and gone out again, unaware of why the Clutters weren't up and about.

That was all there was to see on the main and upper floors. Nelle went down into the basement.

At the bottom of the stairs was a third bathroom—very up-to-date, Nelle thought, and done in blue and white tile. The center room in the basement was the playroom, scene of church parties for the United Methodist Youth Fellowship. "They were typical 1950s church youth parties, probably on Sunday night, with refreshments, chatting and Ping-Pong. No dancing or music as I remember," said one of Eveanna's friends, Ted Hall. "Drinking, smoking and profanity was not a part of that crowd and most parents trusted their daughters with young men that they knew. Usually with good reason."[39] Kenyon's body had been found on the sofa, and Nelle made a dark blotch on her basement map to indicate that. She reached for the bookshelf and flipped through Nancy's 4-H notebook. The girl had written that her father had helped her decorate the basement by drilling holes over the fireplace for an eight-pointed star clock. In a corner of the playroom was a small vending machine that Kenyon had taken apart out of curiosity.

One room over, at the farthest end of the basement, was the furnace where Herb's body had been found lying on a cardboard mattress box. Nelle stood near a red stain on the wall and drew another gout of blood on her map to indicate the location of Herb Clutter's murder. She made no remark about the hellishness of the place, only listed what she saw: low ceiling, unfinished walls, cement floor, three water heaters. Then she went back upstairs to wait for Truman.

It had taken about an hour for Nelle and Truman to go through the house and walk around the property. They thanked Hope and Lyon for making the house available to them—especially in light of how far Mr. Lyon had driven—and bid taciturn Mr. Van Vleet goodbye. They had two more interviews scheduled that day: a second one with Mrs. Ashida, and one with Mrs. Clarence Katz, whose daughter Jolene was the girl Nancy taught to bake a pie on the last day of her life. Afterward, they returned to the Warren Hotel to go over their notes.

The inside of the house had been an eye-opener. For some time, Nelle had been wondering about the peculiar mix of behaviors in the Clutter family: Herb's hail-fellow-well-met conduct evident everywhere, Bonnie Clutter's debilitating emotional problems, Nancy's perkiness, and Kenyon's reputation as a loner. The interior of the big house provided a clue to the emotional atmosphere of River Valley Farm: it was cold and repressive. A small brass door knocker identified the occupant behind each bedroom door. It was as if the rooms were private offices belonging to individuals instead of one home embracing a family. Truman marveled at the implication: "quite impersonal," he jotted down.[40] But it suited Herb Clutter's need for control. Said a neighbor, Herb never did anything that didn't benefit Herb Clutter. He was a driven man—"spare, quick, and dynamic in appearance"—wrote a *New York Times* reporter sent to interview him in 1954 as a paradigm of the modern farmer.[41] The only way he'd permit a natural gas company to drill on his land, for instance, was if he received a one-eighth share of the profits. He used some of the gas money to pump underground water for the farm. Since his royalty receipts paid to run the water pump, he was getting both gas and water for nothing. His home operated along the same lines: tight, efficient, and well managed.

The two surviving Clutter daughters, Eveanna and Beverly, were the embodiments of women who grew up in such an environment. Arriving at the farm the day after the murders, they informed KBI investigators that they would like them to leave because there were things in the house they wanted. Detective Harold Nye, thinking about the shock they must have suffered, permitted them to enter certain rooms only. Once inside, they argued over furniture, knickknacks, kitchen utensils—everything in sight—like magpies. "I mean, good Lord," said Nye, "here we had the murder of the entire family, and we're working this thing up and they were in the house fighting over the merchandise that was there."[42] Once, he stopped to listen when they had fallen silent. They were taking a break to play the piano and sing.

Four days after the murders, neither young woman showed much emotion during the funeral. Nelle overheard a mourner speculate later whether they were under sedation.[43] (By contrast, Bobby Rupp, Nancy's steady, who had sneaked into the funeral home to hold his girlfriend's hand one last time, wept whenever he heard the song "Teen Angel" on the radio for months.)[44] After the service, Eveanna promptly went to the high school to collect Kenyon's and Nancy's belongings, completely cool and collected, said Nancy's English teacher, Mrs. Polly Stringer. Mrs. Stringer, fighting back tears because Eveanna looked so much like Nancy, was hoping Eveanna would let her keep the ribbon Nancy had worn in her hair the night she starred in the school play. But no, Nancy's sisters had to have that, too.[45] Hearing this, Nelle dubbed Eveanna "Miss Iceberg of 1959."[46]

The whole community was aghast when Beverly went ahead with her wedding the week after the murders. Invited guests who attended the ceremony at the First Methodist Church in Garden City were there out of a sense of loyalty to the family, but most had also been among the one thousand mourners at the four Clutters' memorial service. On the spot where just a few days earlier the caskets of her parents and brother and sister had been placed on biers, Beverly took her vows. The leftover funeral meats could truly have furnished the wedding feast. The sisters departed shortly thereafter with a vanload of furniture and clothing. In addition, they were each forty thousand dollars richer because Herb Clutter, by an eerie coincidence, had taken out a double-indemnity insurance policy on the day of his death.

For Nelle, it all added up with the material she had collected from the interviews—the house's interior, careful as a window display; the showy sanctimony of religious materials on view; and Mrs. Clutter, still an attractive woman in her midforties, sleeping apart from her husband and medicated for depression. Then there was Nancy, in her officelike bedroom, channeling sexual feelings into love objects such as stuffed toys appropriate for younger children. (The week of her death, her father had ordered her to break up with Bobby because Herb had caught the two petting, Nelle learned.)[47] And in the room next door to his sister's, Kenyon burrowed into his textbooks. No friends could link him to a girl. In school photographs, his face is completely without expression. In Herb Clutter's household, emotions were screwed down tight.

On one rare occasion Nancy had cracked. Mrs. Stringer told Nelle it had happened when she was giving the Clutter girl a ride home after school. As they were about to turn up the River Valley Farm's tree-lined lane, Nancy asked if they could please stop for a moment. Mrs. Stringer pulled over and waited. Groping for words, Nancy broke down: "If you only knew about Mother," she said, gasping between shuddering sobs.[48]

Nancy's mother was a casualty, but no one inside the family seemed to want to acknowledge it. "I can't worry about her," Herb snapped when someone in the community suggested they try the doctors at the Mayo Clinic.[49] Bonnie Clutter's emotional illness had left Nancy feeling utterly alone, deprived of female reassurance. Nelle spoke to a number of people who had known Nancy and her mother well, but she couldn't find "anything resembling a normal mother-daughter relationship. . . . Nancy was one of the lonely ones, not made any the less lonely by the fact that her days were spent in almost unceasing activity. . . ."[50]

Yet she was expected to carry on energetically, competently, like one of her father's employees. The normal concerns and feelings of a teenage girl had no place or outlet. She was a child, Nelle wrote sympathetically, "who had been trained by an expert to make every second and every penny count, bear her private sorrows in private and present a cheerful aspect to the public; she was taught early in life to take everything to God in prayer. . . . How did she maintain the outward semblance of a wholesome, extremely bright and popular sweet teenager without cracking at the seams? Her family life was ghastly."[51] In that light, Beverly and Eveanna's diamond-hard reserve offered its own explanation.

Bonnie Clutter was also a victim of the pressure that had caused Nancy to burst into tears, Nelle believed. But she suffered the additional pain of being tormented by guilt by what she saw as her failure to measure up to Herb's expectations on every count. As if arguing for the deceased, Nelle characterized Bonnie as "stomped into the ground by her husband's Christ-like efforts to regulate her existence. . . . She was probably one of the world's most wretched women: highly creative in instinct but with the creative will in her stifled over the years by a dominating husband. . . . She seems totally to lack a sense of achievement in any relationship; and truly so, for there's no indication that she was successful as a wife, a lover, a mother, a homemaker; or that she was successful as an effective personality in her own right or as Clutter's helpmate."[52]

The Clutters were an emotionally troubled family, and Lee wrote pages of notes providing evidence of it. But in the end, Capote barely used her insights in the final version of what would become *In Cold Blood*. One reason was simple: a harsh view of a murdered family would have been unacceptable. Feeling sympathy for the innocent was natural, and Capote, who wanted literary fame and a bestseller, knew better than to alienate readers. But another reason why it was necessary to paint the Clutters in flattering hues emerged later. Originally, Truman had arrived in Kansas to write about the impact of multiple murders on a small town. After he got to know the killers, however—two unexpectedly intelligent men but without moral restraint—Capote saw possibilities for a story about the nature of evil. To tell it in the strongest dramatic terms, he needed a foil for evil that was unblemished—an idealized Clutter family. He was aware, of course, that Herb Clutter, the "master of River Valley farm," could be a hard man and not always the benevolent neighbor and paterfamilias that Herb himself wanted to be seen as. Local authorities, in fact, seriously entertained the theory at first that Clutter's inflexible attitude might have led to the murders.

"Clutter prohibited hunters from hunting on his land," one deputy said. "Maybe one of them overrode Clutter's objections and ran into an argument that got out of hand."[53]

But to keep the Clutters consistent with his vision, Capote took the hunting scenario and turned it around. Early in *In Cold Blood*, he has Herb Clutter encounter some hunters trespassing on his land. In life, Herb would have sent them packing. The fictionalized Herb, on the other hand, is a model of Christian charity. When the trespassers "offered to hire hunting rights, Mr. Clutter was amused. 'I'm not as poor as I look. Go ahead, get all you can,' he said. Then, touching the brim of his cap, he headed for home and the day's work, unaware that it would be his last."[54]

It's a Hollywood fade-out by a writer with screenwriting experience who knew the importance of keeping the good guys separate from the bad guys.

The day following the visit to the farm, Monday, began the workweek leading up to Christmas on Friday, which would mean an enforced break in Nelle and Truman's research. The courthouse, library, and post office would be closed; even local law enforcement authorities would be hard to reach. To celebrate Christmas Day, the two would probably have to fall back on a holiday dinner special in the Warren Hotel coffee shop—turkey, gravy, instant potatoes, and canned cranberry sauce.

The holidays were unavoidable; but it was also isolation, the inimical feature of the prairies, that was still interfering with their making steady progress. Truman had arrived in Kansas with no friends, and still he hadn't made any. Like a child going to camp for the first time, he had boarded the train in New York with a suitcase loaded with food, afraid there wouldn't be any he liked where he was going. On the other hand, he was aware of Nelle's ability to get along with people and tolerate his need for attention. "She is a gifted woman, courageous, and with a warmth that instantly kindles most people, however suspicious or dour," he later told his friend George Plimpton, for a 1966 *New York Times* interview, "The Story Behind a Nonfiction Novel."[55] But under the terms of their partnership in Garden City, she was only following his lead. So far, they hadn't been in a friendly social situation where she could model, in a sense, how to take Truman "Cappuchi"—which was indulgently, and with a big grain of salt.

On Christmas Eve, Nelle spent part of the day assembling a description of the Clutters' last evening, based on several interviews with Nancy's boyfriend, Bobby Rupp, who had stayed at their house watching television until 10:00 P.M. on November 14. Sometime after that, police estimated, the killers had arrived.

The phone rang in Nelle's room. It was Cliff Hope. "You and Truman going to be in town tomorrow?" he asked.

Nelle said they were.

"Any plans?"

None that she knew of.

"How about coming over for Christmas dinner?" He mentioned that he and his wife, Dolores, were having another couple over: Detective Alvin Dewey and his wife, Marie.[56]

She and Truman accepted.

The Hopes lived in a cream-colored two-story house built in 1908 in Garden City—an old house by western standards—on Gillespie Place, a block-long street with a sign at either end announcing a private drive: "an attempt to establish a small-town aristocracy at one time, I suppose," remarked one of the Hopes' daughters, Holly.[57] There were eleven houses on Gillespie Place: eight across from the Hopes, and only three on their side. On Sundays, people tended to drive past slowly and stare.

Truman and Nelle arrived half an hour late because first he had to locate a gift bottle of J&B scotch, his favorite brand. During the introductions, Detective Al Dewey's wife, Marie, an attractive raven-haired woman, explained her southern accent by saying she was Kansan by marriage but Deep South by birth and upbringing—from New Orleans, in fact; to which Truman replied that he had been born in New Orleans and Nelle was from Alabama. "It was instant old home week," said Al Dewey.[58] Nelle, shaking hands, insisted everyone call her by her first name.

"Can I help in the kitchen?" she asked Dolores Hope.

"This way," Dolores replied happily. As the two women took twice-baked potatoes from the oven and put condiments in bowls to go with roast duck, the main course, Dolores found herself liking Nelle right away. "After you talked to her for three minutes, you felt like you'd known her for years. She was 'just folks'—interested in others, kind, and humorous."[59]

Dolores announced that dinner was ready, and the adults seated themselves in the dining room. The Hopes' four children—Christine, Nancy, Quentin, and Holly—sat at a smaller version of the grown-ups' table.

Looking around the scene, Truman realized it was a breakthrough in eliminating the town's suspicions about them, and he also knew Nelle deserved the thanks: "She was extremely helpful in the beginning when we weren't making much headway with the townspeople, by making friends with the wives of the people I wanted to meet," he later told Plimpton.[60] Here he was sharing a meal with Alvin Dewey, the coordinator of the Clutter investigation, who had completely stonewalled him just two weeks earlier. And as dinner got under way, Truman further learned that both couples, the Deweys and the Hopes, were bright, well-informed people, interested in him, Nelle, and books. "Reading was an unqualified good" in the Hope family, said Holly Hope, "a quiet pleasure, not requiring special equipment or adult supervision. The glass doors of the built-in china cabinet in the dining room were removed to make room for more books; magazines and newspapers accumulated on coffee tables and chairs until my mother took a stack to a neighbor or to a doctor's office. Even the rest of the household hesitated to interrupt a member of the family who was embarked on a story."[61] Al Dewey was a book lover, too; his ability to read deeply had helped him breeze through law enforcement training. Marie Dewey was secretary to Cliff Hope's father, former U.S. congressman Clifford R. Hope. Cliff, Jr., was a Harvard graduate; and Dolores wrote for the *Garden City Telegram*.

At last Truman was in his element with an audience; and the irrepressible raconteur leaned forward to signal that he was about to launch into one of his best tales. "Capote was the center," Al remembered. "What he had to say and the way he said it was usually intelligent and always interesting. His friend (she asked us to call her 'Nelle') was unaffected and charming. She joined everyone else in listening to Capote, never attempting to upstage or interrupt him. Capote talked about himself mostly . . . what he had written, who was suing him."[62]

Through it all, everyone took their cue from Nelle, who rocked back and forth with laughter at Truman's gossip and love of attention, and winked confidentially at the others when it was obvious Truman was stretching the truth. Dolores Hope said Nelle's motherly attitude was "almost like if you have a child who doesn't behave well" and begs people's indulgence.[63]

One of the Hopes' daughters, Holly, later author of *Garden City: Dreams in a Kansas Town*, said Christmas dinner that night brought together six people who became lifetime friends because they met on an intellectual level. "My experience in a small town is that there are always some people who have been involved in the arts and they like to keep up, but they might not have much opportunity. So when someone like Lee and Capote come through, it's a big deal. You just have to tap into it."[64]

By the end of the evening, Marie Dewey had invited Truman and Nelle to dinner at their house for red beans and rice—a real southern dinner. It was music to their ears. And Truman felt emboldened to ask a favor of Al. He and Nelle were going over to see Dr. Fenton, the coroner, the next day—would Al meet them there to smooth the way? Sure he would, Dewey said. Truman took to calling Al "Foxy"; and Dewey called him "pardner" in return.

"Harper Lee had a way of smiling as she explained in her soft drawl, 'Well, Truman is a genius, you know. He really is. He's a genius,'" said Dewey. "I don't know a lot about geniuses, but I could buy that."[65]

In retrospect, KBI detective Harold Nye, who by now was logging thousands of miles chasing down leads, saw the pattern developing. "Truman didn't fit in, and nobody was talking to him. But Nelle got out there and laid some foundations with people. She worked her way around and finally got some contacts with the locals and was able to bring Truman in."[66]

Dr. Robert M. Fenton, the Finney County coroner, stammered the next day during introductions. And because Detective Dewey's presence implied that the visit had some official importance, Fenton was anxious to impress his visitors. He produced a report he'd written, drawn from firsthand observations made at the Clutter crime scene, which he had dictated at the time into a Dictaphone. At first, he tried reading important sections of the report aloud, but his stammer grew worse. Nelle and Truman said they were really more interested in getting answers to specific questions. Fenton relaxed and, with the help of gestures to aid him in descriptions, such as forming a circle with his thumb to indicate the size and shape of a wound, the interview went more smoothly.

At one point, Nelle got up to admire photographs of Dr. Fenton's three children on a wall. He switched on the office light so she could get a better look.[67] As Nelle kept him busy, Truman slipped around the desk and read Fenton's Dictaphone transcript for himself. Hurriedly, he memorized as much as he could, and scribbled down a passage about Mrs. Clutter in particular: "The bed covers are thrown back as though the patient had been in bed and awakened, put the robe on; lying on a stool in front of the dresser is a heating pad and a small bottle of Vicks nose drops. No sign of struggle seen."[68] Returning to his seat, he joined Nelle in asking Fenton a few more questions; finally, they thanked him for his time.

During the whole cloak-and-dagger episode with the transcript, Detective Dewey said nothing.[69]

Nelle and Truman arrived at the Deweys' the following Wednesday night, December 30, at about 6:30 P.M. Marie Dewey had planned quite a spread: a shrimp-and-avocado salad (her mother had sent the avocados from New Orleans), red beans and rice cooked with bacon, cornbread, country-fried steak, and a bottle of sweet white wine. Al introduced the guests to the rest of the family: Alvin Dewey III, twelve; and Paul Dewey, nine.

Marie offered to get drinks for everyone—scotch and soda for Al, vodka and tonic for Nelle and Truman. Nelle invited little Alvin to sit beside her at the spinet piano and learn the bottom half of "Chopsticks," which he picked up immediately. Paul, not to be outdone, played "Auld Lang Syne" and "The Yellow Rose of Texas," one of his father's favorites.

For about an hour, the adults sat in the living room, getting better acquainted. (Two days earlier, Nelle and Marie had met for lunch at the Trail Room coffee shop and traded "girl talk" about how Marie and Al courted during World War II.) Al tried to play the role of good host, getting up from his easy chair to refresh drinks, but clearly the strain of seven weeks of relentless investigation was getting to him. His clothes hung loose; he drank three scotches, one right after the other. There was hardly a moment when a cigarette wasn't between his lips. Since the murders in mid-November, the KBI had received 700 tips; of those, he'd followed up on 205 on his own. Ninety-nine percent were worthless.

At about 8:00 P.M., dinner was ready. As everyone pulled up to the table, the phone rang for the sixth or seventh time since Nelle and Truman had arrived. Marie said it rang at all hours ever since the murders—always a call for Al about some aspect of the case. He got up to answer while they waited to begin eating. From his office down the hall, they could hear him talking louder and louder. When he returned a few minutes later, his voice crackled with excitement.

"Well, if you can keep a secret, this is *it*: our agent out in Las Vegas said they just nabbed those two guys . . . Smith and Hickock."

Marie started to cry. "Oh, honey . . . honey, I can't believe it."[70]

For Nelle and Truman, the news squared with what they had deduced on their own. A rumor had been percolating among the reporters at the Finney County Courthouse about a prisoner, Floyd Wells, in Lansing State Penitentiary, in Kansas, who read in the newspapers about the Clutter murders. Hoping to win a break from the prison authorities and claim the thousand-dollar reward offered by the *Hutchinson News*, Wells had told the warden about a former cellmate of his, Richard Hickock, who had planned to hook up with another guy, Perry Smith, and rob the Clutters. Hickock was convinced that

Clutter must have plenty of cash because Wells, a former farmhand on the Clutter place, had told him that there was a safe in the house. After Truman had found out as many details as he could about the rumor, he had written it up as incontrovertible fact, and carefully read a statement to Dewey one day at the courthouse to test his reaction. "Say, Dewey, I hear you've got a good lead going. . . . What do you think of this story out of the state prison?"[71] The bluff worked. Dewey shot Nelle a sharp look, lit a fresh cigarette, and refused to confirm or deny anything. But it was plain that they had hit the mark.

But now, in his euphoria, Dewey threw caution to the wind and put the pieces together for them. The call he had just received was from Detective Nye. The Las Vegas Police had taken into custody Smith, thirty-one, and Hickock, twenty-eight, for a minor traffic violation. Nye had been doing "setups" in several states, alerting the police to be on the lookout for them. As soon as Nye, Dewey, and a third KBI detective, Clarence Duntz, could get to Vegas, they would begin interrogating the suspects, who had been leaving a tantalizing trail of bad checks like bread crumbs all over the Southwest. Dewey got up from the table to retrieve photographs of Smith and Hickock taken during previous arrests.

"I've been carrying those faces around in my head for weeks," Marie said.[72] One night she dreamed she saw Hickock and Smith at a booth in the Trail Room coffee shop. But she was so frightened she couldn't move.

Al handed around the black-and-white jailhouse portraits—front and side views.

Nelle thought Richard Hickock had a "ghastly face," due to a disfiguration that made one eye off-center and larger than the other. He was tall and well built. Perry Smith's face, on the other hand, struck Nelle as having eyes that showed a "certain shrewdness and intelligent cunning."[73] The floor-to-ceiling ruler behind him indicated that he was five foot four—exactly Truman's height.

Once everyone had studied the pictures, Al laid out the next steps. Smith and Hickock had been arrested with pairs of boots that matched prints on the Clutters' basement floor—a "Cat's paw" sole and a diamond-tread heel—an early break in the investigation that had been

kept secret. (Marie opened a hall closet to retrieve a rubber boot belonging to one of the children to show what Al meant about tread patterns.)
The evidence of the boots, plus the Lansing State Penitentiary convict's
story, formed a pretty good circumstantial case. But the gold standard
in court was signed confessions; Al would have to get out to Las Vegas
as quickly as possible to assist in the interrogations. He got out a map
and estimated that it would take about a day and a half to drive to Las
Vegas if he, Clarence Duntz, and Roy Church left at 7:00 A.M. Nye had
said he could fly there.

"There's a lot of desert between here and Las Vegas," Dewey said,
tapping the map with his finger. "On the way back, I don't care if we
only make sixteen miles a day. We'll just drive around and around
until we've made them talk. One or the other, whichever's the weaker,
we'll kill him with kindness. We've already got them separated . . . it
shouldn't be long before we get them hating each other."

"Can I go with you?" Truman asked.

"Not this time, pardner."

From one of the pine cabinets in the kitchen, Dewey got out a bottle
of crème de menthe, Marie's "special treasure," he said, and poured
everyone a shot.[74]

Years later, Dewey insisted, "Capote got the official word on developments at the press conferences along with everyone else. Some people
thought then, and probably still do, that he got next to me and got in
on every move of the law. That was not so. He was on his own to get
the material for his story or book. . . . That's the way things were when
the good news finally came on December 30."[75]

Marie backed him up: "Alvin refused to talk about the case. We just
visited, that's all. Our friendship developed in that way, but the investigation wasn't talked about."[76]

But Nelle's notes about everything that was said and done that
night in the Deweys' home tell a different story.

The Associated Press and United Press International broke the news of
the arrests the next day. The KBI's director, Logan Sanford, had been
struggling to keep the investigation under wraps until the last possible
moment. A few days earlier, he had met privately with a reporter whose

hunches about the suspects' names and motives were correct. Sanford asked the reporter to hold his story until Smith and Hickock were in custody; otherwise, they would be tipped off before the KBI agents could nab them. In exchange for the favor, Sanford promised he would later share everything the bureau had on the case. The reporter said he would wait. When his gentlemen's agreement with Sanford came to light, his newspaper fired him.[77]

Nelle and Truman, however, continued to receive updates about the case through their friendship with the Deweys. Marie kept them posted on Al's progress as he crawled over the plains through heavy snowstorms, calling on New Year's Eve while she kept busy taking down the Christmas tree. The travel situation was precarious, she told Nelle—timing was everything. The KBI detectives had to reach Smith and Hickock before they read about themselves in newspapers. The plan was to blindside them about the Clutter murders, then ratchet up the tension by mentioning the existence of an unnamed "living witness"—actually the convict who had bunked with Hickock in the Lansing State Penitentiary. Under pressure, Smith and Hickock might confess to the murders, figuring there was no use holding out. The day after New Year's, Marie felt so stressed she told Nelle she'd driven to the post office, realized she had forgotten the special air mail stamp she needed, and then run out of gas returning to get it.

While they waited for more news from Al, relayed by Marie, Nelle and Truman followed a routine they'd developed that was a far cry from their shaky start a little more than three weeks earlier. Usually they started the day by walking two blocks to radio station KIUL. The news director, Tony Jewell, didn't mind them sifting through the AP or UPI wire services stories that spooled through the clattering teletype machines. Eavesdropping on informal messages between reporters in Garden City and editors on faraway city desks sometimes provided leads for interviews. "Dave," began one note, "Tell the New York Times man that the undertaker, whose name I'm no longer sure of but I rather believe it's Palmer, loves the sound of his own voice and obviously would like all the publicity he can get. I suggest he try to keep the undertaker's wife out of the picture—she tries to shush her husband all the time."[78] The loquacious mortician would end up on their list of people to see. Next, a stop at the courthouse was always mandatory, in case a press conference was scheduled. But as a result of their pipeline through the Deweys, they knew more than any of the reporters did. These preliminaries out of the way, they went out into the field like anthropologists to continue with their interviews.

By now, they could paint Garden City in broad strokes as a community, even its social hierarchy of respected old families ("determined by the amount of land their ancestors homesteaded," Nelle noted).[79] Next they needed to focus in particular on the Clutters' network of friends to re-create Herb, Bonnie, Nancy, and Kenyon, in order to flesh out the portraits Nelle had created after the visit to River Valley Farm. It was the only way to see them alive—through the eyes of those who had known them well.

On January 2, while Dewey, Duntz, and Church were still plowing their way through snowstorms and toward Las Vegas, Nelle and Truman interviewed Nancy Clutter's best friend, Susan Kidwell. Susan shared a tiny pink-and-yellow apartment with her mother, made more cramped by a huge Hammond organ against one wall.

As Nelle listened quietly to Susan and Truman talk, a vision of what Nancy Clutter valued in a friend became clear. Susan was "completely against the grain of the majority of her contemporaries and life in Holcomb and G. C. [Garden City]," Nelle realized. "Pathetically sensitive and lonely; stands out on landscape like a fine and well-wrought thumb. Girl of remarkable sensibility for 15. . . . Every cut, every pleasure, everything shows in her eyes. . . . Loved Nancy as she loved no other person."[80]

Truman used a more cinematic eye to describe Susan: "thin and extremely tall for her age." "[S]he has a broad-boned but thin and very expressive face, and a poor complection [*sic*]; nevertheless, she is an attractive girl with a good-speaking voice (low, and with rather elegant inflections) and a nice sense of humor. . . . She has long sensitive fingers; her hair is long, a sort of greenish/brownish blonde, and rolled up at the bottom. She has had an unhappy life; her father deserted Mrs. Kidwell some years ago etc. She and her mother live in a kind of genteel poverty

(Mrs. Kidwell, 'Of course, it's easy for you to see that we once had money')."[81]

Occasionally, Nelle and Truman went their separate ways in Garden City, particularly when Nelle wanted to act as a listening post. "She became friendly with all the churchgoers," Truman said.[82] The minutiae she heard from the gossipers in Garden City that he might not have heard contributed to the murmuring subtext that he later channeled into his narrative. "Nelle provided a number of insights and descriptions that Capote would have missed," said Dolores Hope.[83] For instance, Nelle found out that Nancy Clutter bit her nails when she was under stress; that the night of her starring role in the school play she held hands backstage with someone besides her boyfriend, Bobby Rupp (she liked to flirt, one of her teachers said); and afterward, she and Rupp went to a scary midnight movie because it was Friday the thirteenth. Truman later combined these details into a simulated phone conversation between Nancy and her best friend, Susan Kidwell:

"Tell," said Susan, who invariably launched a telephone session with this command. "And, to begin, tell why you were flirting with Jerry Roth." Like Bobby, Jerry Roth was a school basketball star.

"Last night? Good grief, I wasn't flirting. You mean because we were holding hands? He just came backstage during the show. And I was so nervous. So he held my hand. To give me courage."

"Very sweet. Then what?"

"Bobby took me to the spook movie. And *we* held hands."

"Was it scary? Not Bobby. The movie."

"He didn't think so; he just laughed. But you know me. Boo!—and I fall off the seat."

"What are you eating?"

"Nothing."

"I know—your fingernails," said Susan, guessing correctly.[84]

It was the synergy of two writers at work in Garden City that gave *In Cold Blood* such verisimilitude. George Steiner, a reviewer for the *Manchester Guardian,* called the book "uncanny" when it was published in 1965. "Looked at minutely enough, filtered through the lens of a highly professional recorder, caught by the tape recording ear in its every inflection and background noise, the most sordid, shapeless of incidents, take on a compelling truth."[85]

Nelle scoured the town for information that might be useful to Truman, applied the eye of a novelist to identify elements of drama, and opened doors of homes for him that otherwise might have remained closed. And now, in early January 1960, with the killers caught and soon to be returned to Garden City, Truman was about to come into a windfall of privileged information, as a result of the friendship that Nelle had nurtured with the Deweys. If KBI director Logan Sanford had known the extent of the clandestine breach in bureau protocol that was opening wider and wider, the entire investigation would have been compromised.

On Sunday morning, January 3, Marie Dewey phoned Nelle at the Warren Hotel to tell her, "Al made it."[86] Dewey had arrived in Las Vegas after midnight; Smith and Hickock had already signed waivers of extradition to Kansas, unaware that they were about to be questioned about the Clutter murders. Dewey expected to arrive back in Garden City late Tuesday or early Wednesday with both men in custody and, he hoped, a pair of confessions in hand.

The phantoms who had terrorized the community would be coming back. Until then, Nelle and Truman would just have to stay busy, biding their time. This being a Sunday just three days after New Year's Day, it was hard to overcome a feeling of lethargy. They spent most of the afternoon interviewing one person—the Clutters' housekeeper, Mrs. Helm—trying to get a better sense of how the family had lived. Despite his claims later that he never took notes, Truman either jotted down a few things in Mrs. Helm's presence or made notes afterward in a palm-size spiral pad he carried: "Mrs. Helm—did all laundry[.] Nancy did own housework. Saturday [the day of the murders]—had a large dinner. Steak—in sink soup bowls—3."[87]

That evening, while Nelle and Truman were having dinner at the Warren Hotel with a long-winded foreign correspondent, a waiter interrupted to say that there was a call at the front desk. It was Marie.

Hickock had confessed, she said—why didn't they come over right away for a celebration? Abruptly they extended apologies to their surprised dinner partner and made a quick getaway to the Deweys'.

Marie, Nelle, and Truman stayed up late discussing the case. Marie was feeling light as a feather and in the mood to talk about Al and his career in law enforcement. Around 10:45, Dewey called from Vegas to speak to Truman. Hickock's confession was Nancy Clutter's birthday present, Al said, she would have turned seventeen that day. Now Smith, hearing that Hickock had confessed, would likely crack, too. All four KBI detectives—Dewey, Nye, Church, and Duntz—were about to go out on the town and have some fun. Truman recommended the Sands Hotel Casino in the center of the Las Vegas Strip. Marie, proud to bursting about Al's work, brought out Christmas cards from convicts he had helped put away as proof that he cared about them.

The next day, Nelle filled three single-spaced, typewritten pages with everything she and Truman had heard. "Truman and Nelle were pretty damn good interrogators themselves," commented Nye later. "And they played Al and Marie both—it was obvious."[88]

On Monday morning, KBI director Logan Sanford, standing in for Al Dewey, held a press conference at the courthouse and announced to reporters that the suspects were on their way from Las Vegas and would get in sometime late Tuesday afternoon. Nelle met Marie at the Trail Room coffee shop for lunch after the press conference. A highway patrolman stopped by their table and asked Marie to call him when Al was about fifty miles away from Garden City, so his men could prepare for the big crowd expected outside the courthouse. After he left, Marie promised to call Nelle, too, the moment she heard anything.[89]

There was an anxious sense in the air of the curtain about to rise on the second act. Nelle and Truman, feeling too fidgety to start anything fresh, spent the rest of the afternoon just wandering around. With no particular purpose in mind, they walked the few blocks to the courthouse. In a hallway, they bumped into six-foot-four Duane West. West, twenty-eight, was just beginning a second two-year term as Finney County prosecutor, and was excited about the prospect of grilling Hickock and Smith in the courtroom. He was talkative in the glare of television lights, but when Nelle and Truman wanted a word with him, he wouldn't give them the time of day. From his suit pocket he produced an envelope, which, he showed them with a flourish, was addressed to "Mr. Duane (Sherlock Holmes) West." Nelle held her tongue, but jotted in her notes, "D.W. a slob."[90]

They climbed the stairs to Undersheriff Wendle Meier's office. Just deposited in the undersheriff's office as prime evidence was the shotgun used in the murders, which the KBI had found in plain sight at the home of Hickock's parents. The Savage 300 model twelve-gauge looked practically brand-new. Examining it, Nelle noticed someone had scratched *M* or maybe *H* near the trigger. It was an unexceptional weapon, the kind that any hunter, proud of his new purchase from a sporting goods store, might take into the fields on an autumn day.

With two hours of winter daylight remaining, the pair decided to drive the mile or so out on North Third Street to Valley View Cemetery, where the Clutters had been laid to rest. They hadn't visited the graves yet, but now, with the killers in custody, it seemed fitting that they should.

The sun was going down when they arrived, and it was cold. The cemetery was eighty-three acres, half of it unused. In the 1890s, a group of settler women had tried to beautify the prairie burial ground with trees and bushes, hauling barrels filled with water twice a day to nourish the plantings. But the long, brutal droughts of the dust bowl years in the 1930s had wiped out their efforts. Truman and Nelle walked the rows until finally—in Zone A, Lot 470, spaces 1–4—they came upon the mounded graves of Nancy, Kenyon, Herb, and Bonnie Clutter. The upturned earth was marked with the names of the interred, but there were no headstones yet or any signs of remembrance. Nelle found the scene "desolate and lonely in the extreme."[91]

Late that night, Al Dewey called Marie with a message for Truman: "I killed him with kindness." In the car during the ride across the desert, Smith had confessed.[92]

Hundreds of Garden City and Holcomb residents prepared to brave the blustery weather, with a temperature cold enough to bring on snow, on Tuesday, January 5, the day scheduled for Smith and Hickock's arrival. At the Deweys' house, Nelle and Truman had deposited a fresh bottle of J&B scotch with a note attached: Dear Foxy, After your long and heroic journey, we are certain you will appreciate a long swig of this. So: welcome home! From your ever faithful historians, Truman and Nelle.[93]

KBI chief Logan Sanford had said only that the suspects were due "late Tuesday afternoon," so Nelle and Truman showed up at the courthouse at around 3:00 P.M. to wait for word from Sheriff Earl Robinson's office. The hallway was filled with bored newsmen smoking and waiting. Nelle found a Coors beer ashtray to crush out her cigarette butts, and settled in. Out of the corner of her eye, she caught a glimpse of *Garden City Telegram* editor Bill Brown, who had figured out that she and Truman had some kind of pull with Dewey. He wasn't the only one, he said later. "I was busy talking to other KBI agents and local sheriff's officers who moaned about Dewey paying more attention to Truman than the case at hand."[94] A little after 4:00 P.M., the radio dispatcher announced to everyone that Finney County prosecutor Duane West would have to delay a press conference until five o'clock. A highway patrol captain appeared, champing on a cigar, and gave instructions to the press to keep the sidewalk clear. Lee assumed that a crowd must be gathering, and she went outside to see it. The overcast sky was cold enough to snow, but bystanders in twos and threes were beginning to fill the square. In her notes she wrote:

> The thermometer was dropping and T's ears (good barometer) were red; my feet numb. We had stood for perhaps twenty minutes when we were aware that a few teenagers grouped under a tree nearby was now a definite crowd. Two Holcomb High basketball jackets in the midst. As they waited, the teenagers squirmed, wriggled, fought mock battles; the girls giggled and flirted with the photographers—two ran over to the press line and asked to be photographed.[95]

A reporter asked a middle-aged man standing near the sidewalk if death would be sufficient punishment for the killers. "Like in the Bible," he replied. "An eye for an eye. And even then, we're two short." Capote overhead the comment and included it in *In Cold Blood*.[96] A photographer asked a gum-chewing little boy named Johnny Shobe to blow a big bubble, but the air was so cold that the trick worked only after several tries.

By 6:00 P.M., the crowd was four or five deep and had never stopped murmuring. Newsmen stamped their feet and blew on their hands. Then suddenly someone shouted, "They're coming!"

At the curb, two dark mud-splashed sedans rolled to a halt. Al Dewey got out of the backseat of the first car; then, quickly, a handful of other men exited both cars, as if on cue. The figures strode quickly up the sidewalk and toward the courthouse. It had grown so dark that the photographers' flashbulbs acted like strobe lights and caught them in midstep. There were no jeers, no catcalls from the crowd. Everyone seemed strangely struck dumb. Dewey had the arm of Perry Smith, who was a head shorter than Al and wearing dungarees and a black leather jacket. Hickock came next, also accompanied by a detective, but Nelle couldn't get a good look because a broad-backed policeman had stepped in front of her. When the platoon of suspects and detectives sprinted up the courthouse steps, Nelle, Truman, and the reporters surged after them.

They went up to the second floor where a large room had been set aside for a press conference. A few seats were still open in the front row before a table with four microphones. TV lights were switched on and lit up the place like day. Dewey sat down behind a mike and said, "Hello, Bill," to Bill Brown, and then smiled down at Nelle and Truman.

Questions came pell-mell from the reporters, but Dewey seemed to enjoy playing poker with everyone. Yes, the suspects had confessed, but no reporters would be allowed to listen to their taped interrogations or statements. Right now, Smith and Hickock were being held upstairs in the fourth-floor jail. They would be arraigned tomorrow morning.

"What time did you get in?" someone shouted.

"About five o'clock," Dewey said cryptically. It was 6:30 P.M. (The entourage had stopped to look unsuccessfully for evidence that Smith and Hickock claimed they had buried by a roadside.)

Duane West tried to direct some attention his way, but no one was interested. The press conference sputtered to an end.

Outside the courthouse, the crowd had dispersed, leaving a few pop bottles and candy wrappers in the grass. Truman was disgusted. He expected the return of the killers to be dramatic. Why had everyone just stood there gawking? And that press conference! The whole thing, he complained to Nelle as they walked back toward the hotel, was "a debacle."[97]

The next morning, the sound of a heavy iron door clanking shut overhead signaled that Smith and Hickock were coming down for their arraignment. Nelle, Truman, and about thirty-five members of the press had been waiting for an hour in the wood-paneled Finney County Courtroom since 10:00 A.M. Probate judge M. C. Schrader, a formal-looking, white-haired man in a dark suit, entered the courtroom and took his place behind the bench. ("Central casting judge," Nelle noted.)[98] She also noticed that the U.S. flag above him had forty-eight stars, although Alaska and Hawaii had become the forty-ninth and fiftieth states the previous year.

Hickock entered the courtroom first, without handcuffs, but flanked by sheriff's deputies, who directed him to sit in a chair at the very front. The glare of floodlights set up for television cameras enabled Nelle to see him as if he were an actor under stage lights. He was about five foot ten, she estimated, blue eyed and clean shaven with his dark blond hair in a crew cut. His clothes were drab: gray khaki trousers, blue denim prisoner's workshirt, brown shoes, and white socks. He rubbed his chin thoughtfully to reveal a large tattoo of a cat on his left hand. His face, misshapen as a result of a car accident, intrigued Nelle: "as if someone cut it down the middle, then put it back together not quite in place," a description Truman later changed to "It was as though his head had been halved like an apple, then put together a fraction off center."[99] As the judge read the charges against Hickock—four counts of first-degree murder—the defendant listened, eyes downcast and hands clasped. Nelle noticed that a muscle in his jaw twitched at the mention of Nancy Clutter's name.

"Would you like to have a preliminary hearing?" Judge Schrader asked.

"I'd like to waive a preliminary hearing," replied Hickock, in a Kansas rural-accented voice that most people would associate with the way cowboys talk. With that, and a few additional perfunctory remarks from the judge, Hickock returned upstairs.

Smith entered moments later. A short man with a ginger complexion and coal-black hair, indicating his heritage as the son of a Native American mother, he wore clothes similar to Hickock's, except that Smith's jeans were rolled at the cuffs, and his black shoes had a high polish. Heavy sideburns seemed to be an attempt to add seriousness to a face that was feminine and winsome. His dark brown eyes under long lashes glanced around at the reporters.

"Look," Truman whispered to Nelle as Smith sat back in the chair near the judge, "his feet don't touch the floor!"[100] It was an admiring remark that surprised her, but she understood its meaning: Truman was infatuated. Smith's size and demeanor seemed weirdly familiar. His dark coloring was a complement to Truman's fair skin and blond hair. Capote thought he was seeing his doppelgänger. "I think every time Truman looked at Perry he saw his own childhood," Nelle told *Newsweek* later.[101] The composer and author Ned Rorem went further. Over dinner in 1963, Truman talked about his progress on *In Cold Blood*. To Rorem, who was gay, he "seemed clearly in love" with Smith.[102]

Judge Schrader followed the same ponderous but necessary procedural reading of the charges against Smith. Nelle got the impression that Smith was pressing his lips together, trying not to cry. At the mention of Nancy Clutter's name, Hickock had reacted almost imperceptibly. Smith, on the other hand, sighed and squinted at the bright lights when the judge charged him with the murder of Herb Clutter. The last thing he had said to Clutter before killing him, Smith confessed to Dewey, was that "it wasn't long till morning, and how in the morning somebody would find them and then all of it, me and Dick and all, would seem like something they'd dreamed."[103]

"I wish to waive my rights to a preliminary hearing," Smith replied to Judge Schrader. Then, his appearance over, he pulled "himself up to his full minute height," in Nelle's words, and walked briskly from the room.[104] A reporter burst from his seat with the other newspeople and hurried after Smith, shooting photos. Prosecutor Duane West, watching the spectacle, angrily threw down a sheaf of papers.

Despite Al Dewey's announcement to the press that no one would be allowed to interview the suspects or listen to their tape-recorded confessions, all it took was a pair of fifty-dollar checks drawn on a New York bank and made out separately to Perry Smith and Richard Hickock for Nelle and Truman to talk to them on Monday, January 11. Dewey arranged for the meeting to take place in his office, with Smith's and Hickock's lawyers present.

Resting up at home the previous Saturday, Dewey had recounted for Nelle and Truman, step by step, what Smith had said during his interrogation. He "went into extraordinary detail about the crime," Dewey said, paraphrasing as much of Smith's confession as he could recall. Hickock was in another room, being questioned, but Smith's descriptions re-created the night of the murders so thoroughly that Hickock was nailed, too.[105] Thinking about what they would ask the killers, Nelle and Truman decided to skip over the crime, since that would become a matter of record anyway, and get them to talk about themselves instead.

On Monday morning, Dewey scooted a couple of extra chairs into his office. Smith came in first. Seeing that Nelle was standing, he waited for her to be seated. He acted as solemn as a "small deacon," Nelle thought, "feet together, back straight, hands together: could almost see a celluloid collar and black narrow tie, so prim he was."[106] Truman was ready with handwritten questions. Reflecting the fashionable interest in Freudian psychology at the time, he wanted to launch into a series of prepared questions about Smith's attitudes toward marriage, his father, and other introspective topics.[107]

Gently, Smith waved aside the questions after he heard the first few. His attorney hadn't briefed him about this meeting. "What's the purpose of your story?" he wanted to know. Nelle was taken aback by his condescending tone. Its purpose, they assured him, was to give him a chance to tell his side of the story. Nelle smiled at him several times, but his large eyes kept flicking away from hers.[108] He clearly felt "cornered and suspicious," Truman realized. To everything they asked over the next twenty minutes, Smith countered with "I decline," "I do not care to," or "I will think it over." Some kind of cat-and-mouse game was under way. After he returned to his cell, Nelle commented in her notes, "Rough going."[109]

Hickock, on the other hand, breezed in, ready for a good bull session. He plunked down in a chair before Nelle was seated. "Never seen anyone so poised, relaxed, free & easy in the face of four 1st-degree murder charges," Nelle marveled. "He gave the impression of being completely in the moment, with no concern about tomorrow's troubles."[110]

Nelle and Truman expressed admiration for Hickock's tattoos, which worked like a charm in unlocking his affability. Soon, he was talking about his favorite reading subject matter (motors or engineering); his vision of the good life (well-done steaks, gin rickeys, screwdrivers, dance music, and Camel cigarettes—he bummed five smokes from Nelle's pack); how often he liked to eat (three times a day, but in jail it was only two); how he'd like to get a good job in an auto shop and pay off the bad checks he'd written and live in the country. Then he segued to describing the high times he and Smith had had traveling around Mexico before they got caught in Las Vegas. It was practically more than Nelle and Truman could absorb. Truman said Hickock was "like someone you meet on a train, immensely garrulous, who starts up a conversation and is only too obliged to tell you *everything*."[111] Nelle tried to get questions in edgeways, to which Hickock would reply, "Yes, ma'am," and then commence spinning another yarn. "No trace of the Smith syndrome," Nelle commented dryly in her notes.[112]

Hickock would have extended his stay, except that Dewey had something he wanted to share with Nelle and Truman, so the suspect was shut off like a valve and taken back to his cell. After Hickock had gone, Dewey reassured Nelle and Truman, telling them not to worry if Smith wanted to play it cagey. Reaching into the Clutter case file in his desk, he produced for them the pièce de résistance: the transcripts of Smith's interrogations. Like dialogue from a play, the pages of transcribed conversation between Smith and the two KBI detectives, Dewey and Clarence Duntz, contained everything said in the nine-by-ten interrogation room during the three and a half hours that Smith was questioned in Las Vegas. The transcript couldn't leave the court-house and was too much for Nelle to copy, so she targeted key passages. As she worked, Dewey added visual descriptions that weren't evident on the tape.

AL: Perry, you have been lying to us, you haven't been telling the truth. We know where you were on that weekend—you were out at Holcomb, Kansas, seven miles west of Garden City, murdering the Clutter family.

(Perry white; swallowed a couple of times. Long pause.)

PERRY: I don't know anybody named Clutter, I don't know where Garden City or Holcomb is—

AL: You'd better get straightened out on this deal and tell us the truth—

PERRY: I don't know what you're talking about . . . I don't know what you're talking about.

(Al & Duntz rise to go.)

AL: We're talking to you sometime tomorrow. You'd better think this over tonight. Do you know what today is? Nancy Clutter's birthday. She would have been seventeen.[113]

When Nelle had finished copying as much as she could, Dewey let them see another piece of evidence: Nancy Clutter's diary, containing three years' worth of entries. Since the age of fourteen, Nancy had recorded, in three or four sentences every night, the day's events and her thoughts about family, friends, pets, and, later, her adolescent love affair with Bobby Rupp. Different colored ink identified the years. Nelle and Truman riffled through the pages. The final entry was made approximately an hour before Nancy's death. Nelle copied it down.[114]

With the seal on the KBI investigation broken, any pretense that Al Dewey was protecting the case from Nelle and Truman's prying eyes was dropped. They spent most of the rest of the week working out of his office. Harold Nye, shortly before his death in 2003, complained that Dewey was only supposed to "take care of the press, the news media, take our reports in, send them to the office, and be the office boy. But he was playing footsie with Truman and Nelle." Apparently, however, Nye, too, was brought into the loop. He later said, "Nelle and I would just stand in the corner or sit down on a chair and casually talk. But she was good, she was good."[115]

On Wednesday, January 13, Nye provided her with all the information he'd gleaned along the way while he pursued Hickock and Smith through the Plains and the Southwest, including his stop at the home of Smith's sister in San Francisco—disguised, he later wrote to Truman, as a local policeman pretending to be following up on Smith's parole violation. ("She was such a nice lady, and I always felt like a dirty dog for pulling that trick.")[116] In addition, he gave Nelle the inventory of items found in Smith and Hickock's stolen car; and finally, as Nelle copied Hickock's interrogation, or listened to a tape of it—it isn't clear which—Nye interrupted to add background or clarify the suspect's remarks. On Friday, Truman paid another fifty dollars each to Smith and Hickock to interview them, and this time Smith was much more forthcoming. He had decided, he said—once again exhibiting his strange sense of self-importance—to tell his story as a cautionary tale to others. Fortunately for those others, Nelle and Truman evidently resorted to hiding a tape recorder in the room, having been overwhelmed by Hickock's talkativeness. In her notes on Smith, Nelle says parenthetically, "I can hardly hear a word he says."[117]

No one else outside the investigation was granted anything close to the access Nelle and Truman had. The *Hutchinson News*, for example, was the first newspaper permitted to interview the killers, and that was more than a week after Nelle and Truman had talked to them. Had it not been for their friendship with Al Dewey—brought about by Nelle's making a favorable impression with people when Truman was perceived as "an absolute flake" and "uppity"—they would have been stopped cold.

In fairness, they were not like the journalists on the scene, either. As Bill Brown of the *Garden City Telegram* pointed out, "My deadline was immediate; Capote's was years away."[118] (Actually, at that time, Capote was still thinking in terms of a magazine article.) Capote may have given Dewey and Nye his word that he would be working on his article for months, at least—well beyond the date of a trial. There would be no leaks. And in those days of speedier justice, Smith and Hickock went to trial in late March, only three months after being captured. Still, the risk Dewey took was enormous. Looking back, Harold Nye, who became director of the KBI in 1969, thought better about the extent of his involvement, too. Dusting over his tracks, he said later, "I really get upset when I know that Al gave them a full set of the reports. That was like committing the largest sin there was, because the bureau absolutely would not stand for that at all. If it would have been found out, he would have been discharged immediately from the bureau."[119]

Dewey would never admit he'd let the cat out of the bag. "I never treated Truman any differently than I did any of the other news media after the case was solved. He kept coming back, and we naturally got better acquainted. But as far as showing him any favoritism or giving him any information, absolutely not. He went out on his own and dug it up. Of course, he got much of it when he bought the transcript of record, which was the whole court proceedings, and if you had that, you had the whole story."[120]

Loaded with notes from interviews, transcribed interrogations, newspaper clippings, some photos Truman had snapped, sketches of the Clutter farmhouse, and any copies Dewey had given them, Nelle and Truman boarded the luxury Santa Fe Super Chief on January 16 in Garden City. It was snowing hard, and they settled in for the forty-hour ride to Dearborn Street Station in Chicago. Over the course of approximately a month, they had gathered enough to lay the foundation of a solid magazine article for the *New Yorker*. They would have to return for Smith and Hickock's trial in March. If the two men were sentenced to death, should their execution be part of the story? It was a grisly thought. Before his ideas escaped him, Capote wrote some notes on a Santa Fe cocktail napkin.

Lee, of course, had plenty of other things to think about. As soon as she returned to New York, she would have to go over the galleys of *To Kill a Mockingbird*—a painstaking but nevertheless thrilling task for a first-time novelist. There was a small change she was thinking of making. The Kansas state motto, "Ad astra per aspera"—To the stars through difficulties—struck her as the right theme for the agricultural pageant that takes place in the fictional town of Maycomb at the end of the book. It sounded hopeful.

As she watched Truman in the seat opposite hers, musing out the window of the train, it probably seemed incredible that her novel would be in bookstores in a few months. Then she would have the right to call herself a writer, though not in Truman's league by any means. All she hoped for was a "quick and merciful death at the hands of reviewers."[121]

The Super Chief was delayed for six hours along the route, and when they arrived in Chicago, they had already missed their New York Central connection. They stayed in the city overnight and departed the next day, arriving in New York on Wednesday, January 20.

"Returned yesterday—after nearly 2 months in Kansas: an extraordinary experience, in many ways the most interesting thing that's ever happened to me," Truman wrote to his friend the photographer Cecil Beaton. "But I will let you read about it—it may amount to a small book."[122]

While she was waiting to return with Truman to Kansas, Lee had the bittersweet experience of reading the galleys of her first novel. This is how it would look, for better or worse. Although she was cautioned not to make significant changes, she kept seeing places she wanted to change.[123]

Also while she was home, she wrote a long feature story, which has only recently come to light, for the March 1960 issue of *Grapevine*, the magazine for members of the Society of Former Special Agents of the FBI. Headlined "Dewey Had Important Part in Solving Brutal Murders," the two-thousand-word article is an overview of how the case developed, step by step. It's the most comprehensive summary available of the investigation. As a piece of journalism, it's on a par with anything that might appear in a national newspaper: fact filled, tightly written, and in the voice of a reporter who isn't part of the story—the focus is entirely on Dewey. It demonstrates that although Lee needed quite a bit of editorial help with her fiction, she was a natural reporter.

However, it also creates a mystery of its own.

To begin with, why isn't it bylined? It was customary for the magazine to identify contributors; Lee must have requested that her name not be used. But for what reason? Probably it's another example of her not wanting to upstage Capote, who was on assignment for the *New Yorker*—the Clutter case was his story to tell. His "research assistant" is deferring to him, even though a *New Yorker* piece and a feature story for *Grapevine* would be miles apart in style.

Then why did she bother to write it at all?

As a kind of crib sheet for Capote—an outline of everything up until the trial—it's valuable. Weeks of detail-gathering are telescoped into an article that Truman could refer to without flipping through Lee's extensive typed notes. Its scope ranges from major events ("Dewey and his associates went into action. They discovered no alibi for the suspects from noon, November 14, to noon the next day. In Kansas City, warrants were out for the pair on bad check charges") to smaller human interest details that Capote could use ("Al Dewey, 12 pounds lighter from his exertions, looks forward to settling down again with his family at 602 North First Street in Garden City. Dewey's family consists of his wife, the former Marie Louise Bellocq, who was a secretary in the New Orleans FBI office, their sons, Alvin Dewey III, 13, and Paul David Dewey, 9, plus Courthouse Pete, the family Watch-cat. Pete, age 4, weighs 13 pounds, is tiger-striped and eats Cheerios for breakfast").

Ostensibly, the piece is about Dewey's legwork on the case. But it's quite flattering to Capote. The fourth paragraph includes a marquee announcement about how he has staked his claim to the story: "Truman Capote, well-known novelist, playwright, and reporter was sent by the *New Yorker* to do a three part piece of reportage on the crime, which will be later published in book form by Random House." This is stealing a march on another freelance journalist, Mack Nations, who was trying to sell his book proposal, too.

But as the subhead suggests—"Resident Agent for Kansas Bureau of Investigation Helped Bring to Justice Killers of his Neighbors"— the article's primary aim is to please Alvin Dewey. Capote would need his cooperation while *In Cold Blood* was being written. No other law enforcement personnel are mentioned in the article. Dewey, as Lee describes him, is a dedicated lawman—a modern Pat Garrett pursuing Billy the Kid. "Asked if he would pursue the case to its conclusion, Dewey said, 'I'll make a career of it if I have to.'"

Two months later, Harper Lee and Truman Capote were back in Kansas for the trial, scheduled to begin the third week of March. By coincidence, the Clutters' farm was going up for auction the same week.

They left behind a late snowy season in New York. A wet, warm spring had come to western Kansas. Nelle and Truman drove out to River Valley Farm on Sunday, March 21, to witness the sale. Bumper-to-bumper traffic met them at the entrance to the lane lined with elms, which were just beginning to cast a hint of shade. After crawling toward the house at a speed slower than a walk, they were waved into a muddy parking area strewn with hay. The sunny weather in the low seventies had brought out more than four thousand people for the largest farm auction in western Kansas history. There were cars and trucks from Colorado, Nebraska, and Oklahoma, and practically every county in Kansas west of Newton and Wichita. Auctioneer John Collins, his white shirt shining in the sun, sold everything of value to a swarm of men in coats and Stetsons—tools, tractors, and farm implements. "Herb had a lot of good stuff," Clutter's brother, Arthur, commented.[124] Two weeks earlier, the Clutter sisters, Eveanna and Beverly, had leased the land, the house, and all the buildings to a businessman from Oklahoma. Inside a big Quonset hut forty yards from the house, the Ladies Circle of Holcomb Community Church sold $500 worth of hamburgers, ham sandwiches, and pieces of pie.

On Tuesday, jury selection began. For the first time since the court-house was erected in 1929, the varnished church-type pews were slid to the sides and rear to leave room at the front for a special press table and thirteen chairs. Bill Brown of the *Garden City Telegram* handed out press passes, including one apiece for Truman and Nelle identifying them as representatives of the *New Yorker*. Truman had brought along the photographer Richard Avedon, who had to be content to sit on the side. The men at the press table, pleased to see Nelle back, had taken to calling her "Little Nelle."[125] Someone asked, tongue-in-cheek, whether Nelle and Truman would be coming back for the trial of the screwball that was poisoning dogs in Garden City—a total of twelve, according to the front page of the day's *Telegram*.

A little before ten o'clock, District Judge Roland Tate entered—a changed man, most folks noticed, since the death of his small son several years before—and took his seat on the bench. The courthouse custodian, Louis Mendoza, had spent most of Monday unsuccessfully trying to locate a U.S. flag with fifty stars on it, until Judge Tate instructed him to put the one with forty-eight back up. While Nelle and Truman had been out of town, Tate had weighed the youth and lack of experience of Finney County prosecutor Duane West and appointed a special prosecutor to assist him: Logan Green, who "looks like a mottled tough old piece of steak and has the voice to go with it," Nelle wrote. "He is going to be hell on the defense witnesses. Has a remarkable ease of delivery, of forming questions, of saying exactly what he wants to say exactly how he wants to say it."[126] The court-appointed counsel for Richard Hickock's defense, Arthur Fleming, nodded to Logan Green and said, "Cool morning." Perry Smith's attorney, Harrison Smith (no relation), also court appointed, pulled a chair up to the defense table, dressed like a "symphony in blue-gray," in Nelle's estimation.[127] Overhead, the telltale metallic clank of the jail door announced that Smith and Hickock were coming down.

The effects of sitting in jail for two months told on the two men. Nelle noticed Smith was softly rounder. "His thighs are like Lillian Russell's." Dick Hickock: "fatter, greener, and more gruesome."[128] Outwardly, the two men seemed bored, covering perhaps for being stared at by the forty-four prospective jurors who had assembled in the courtroom to be sworn in and questioned. District court clerk Mae Purdy called the jurors' names in a droning voice. Only four were women.

By day's end, the jury was composed entirely of men, including the reserve of alternates. Half were farmers. Smith, an amateur artist, had passed the time sketching on a legal pad. Hickock chomped relentlessly on a wad of gum, his chin resting on his hand now and then. The two men had implicated each other in their confessions, but there seemed to be no visible rupture in their relationship. Nelle saw Hickock glance at Perry Smith just once, "the briefest exchanges of glances, and the old eye rolled coldly.... Perry looked at him—gave Hickock one of his melting glances—really melting in its intensity—Hickcock felt eyes upon him, looked around and smiled the shadow of a smile."[129]

As expected, the turnout for the trial exceeded the courtroom's capacity of 160 persons. "Our trial was more like a circus than anything else," Dick Hickock complained to Mack Nations while they worked together on their book. "It took only one day to choose the jury.... The courtroom overflowed with spectators and the halls were lined with photographers and newspaper reporters. Every exit was covered by a pair of highway patrolmen. Extra deputy sheriffs were brought in from neighboring counties.... I never did think much of the Finney County Attorney and I sure liked him less after our first day in court. He kept pointing his finger at me and telling the jury how no good I was. I resented it."[130]

At the press table, Associated Press reporter Elon Torrence noticed that Truman, dressed in a blue sports jacket, khaki trousers, white shirt, and a bow tie, spent most of his time listening, while Nelle, bringing to bear her incomplete law school training, "took notes and did most of the work during the trial."[131]

There were no surprises. "How cheap!" exclaimed special prosecutor Logan Green in his closing argument to the jury. "The loot was only about eighty dollars, or twenty dollars a life." Harrison Smith and Arthur Fleming, attorneys for the accused, did not contest the state's evidence but pleaded for life imprisonment. Smith argued that capital punishment is "a miserable failure." The jury deliberated less than two hours.

On Tuesday, March 29, Judge Roland Tate sentenced both men to hang. As he thanked the jury, Hickock, with characteristic bravado, claimed he felt only contempt.

> I thought that these pompous old ginks were the lousiest looking specimens of manhood I had ever seen; old cronies that acted like they were God or somebody. Right then I wished every one of them had been at the Clutter house that night and that included the Judge. I would have

found out how much God they had in them! If they had been there and had any God in them I would have let it run out on the floor. I thought, boy, I'd like to do it right here. Now there was something that would have really stirred them up! When the jury filed out of the courtroom not one of them would look at me. I looked each one in the face and I kept thinking, Look at me, look at me, look at me![132]

This jury was no different from others in not looking at the defendants, Nelle wrote. "Why they never look at people they've sentenced to death, I'll never know, but they don't."[133]

Back in his cell, Perry Smith slipped a note with his signature on it between two bricks in the wall: "To the gallows . . . May 13, 1960."[134]

nine

Mockingbird Takes Off

A hundred pounds of sermons on tolerance, or an equal
measure of invective deploring the lack of it, will weigh far
less in the scale of enlightenment than a mere 18 ounces of
new fiction bearing the title *To Kill a Mockingbird.*

—*The Washington Post*, July 3, 1960

Harper Lee presented Capote with one hundred fifty pages of typed
notes, organized by topics such as the Landscape, the Crime, Other
Members of the Clutter Family, and so on. Truman, feeling expansive
as he rested in Spain after several months of working on the outline
for *In Cold Blood,* was suddenly in the mood to make one of his gossipy
pronouncements, for it was immensely satisfying to him that his
protégée—which is how he now regarded her—had written a publishable novel in which he was an important character. He urged his friends,
film producer David O. Selznick and Selznick's wife Jennifer Jones, to
watch for it. "On July 11th [1960], Lippincott is publishing a delightful
book: TO KILL A MOCKINGBIRD by Harper Lee. Get it. It's going
to be a great success. In it, I am the character called 'Dill'—the author
being a childhood friend."[1]

In the meantime, in Manhattan, the freezing air rang with the cries of
snowball fights between children. From the window of her apartment,

Lee could see ambushes about to be sprung from behind doorway stoops, and retreats made to the safety of parked cars. During her eleven years in New York, she had never witnessed such deep snow accumulating over a single night.

Somehow, though, a surprising spring snowstorm seemed in keeping with the dramatic, absolutely unexpected events that were turning the thirty-three-year-old woman's life around. Reader's Digest Condensed Books and the Literary Guild had chosen *To Kill a Mockingbird* as a selection for subscribers, meaning thousands of instant sales. Maurice Crain called and read to her over the phone the introduction written by the editor of the Literary Guild, John Beechcroft.

> This month we offer our members another discovery—*To Kill a Mockingbird* by Harper Lee. It is a first novel and shows the sincerity and intensity that so often marks an author's first book. The author calls it 'a love story pure and simple,' and it is the story of a small town and of a way of life that were close to the author's heart. Harper Lee was born in a small town in Alabama, and as she writes, the reader feels she is writing about people and places at once dear to her and unforgettable.[2]

After putting down the phone, Nelle hadn't been able to sit still. Torpor would have been a sign of ingratitude—the only thing that would do was for her to take the Lexington Avenue express subway down to Crain's office and share her happiness. "I sort of hoped that maybe someone would like it enough to give me encouragement. Public encouragement. I hoped for a little."[3]

The temperature was in the upper twenties, and she had a five-block walk to Lexington Avenue. She turned north to get the Eighty-sixth Street express stop, startled by a police officer blowing his whistle and pointing at her. She glanced around uncertainly.

"Yes, sir?" she said reflexively, her southern manners coming to the fore.

"You walked against the light. Couldn't you hear the cars?"

"Cars?"

He made her recite her name and address, then ripped off a ticket from his pad and handed it to her with a peremptory "Be careful."[4]

The incident rankled for a few minutes, but by the time she was standing on the subway platform with the train swooshing in front of her like a grimy silver dragon, the effect had worn off.

Five months before, in November when she had turned in the final version of her manuscript to Hohoff, there had been no indication that she should expect to be so happy. Lippincott's publicity department had slipped a note inside advance copies sent to reviewers. "Please set aside an evening or two real soon to read *To Kill a Mockingbird*. I'd be very happy to know your reaction. . . . We are rushing this paperbound copy to you so that you may share with us the rare fun and lift in the discovery of a new, fresh talent." Capote had contributed a blurb for the review copy. "Someone rare has written this very fine first novel, a writer with the liveliest sense of life, and the warmest, most authentic humor. A touching book, and so funny, so likeable."

Hohoff, while confident, had some reservations. A novel set in the South at the center of which was a rape trial might not send readers rushing to bookstores. "Don't be surprised, Nelle, if you sell only two thousand copies—or less. Most books by first-time novelists do."[5]

But now, suddenly, *To Kill a Mockingbird* was in impressive company: some of *Reader's Digest*'s recent picks had included Fred Gipson's *Old Yeller*, John Hersey's *A Single Pebble,* and *A Rockefeller Family Portrait*, by William Manchester. Being selected by the Literary Guild, Crain said, practically guaranteed that her novel would be a commercial success. At the prepublication party he and Annie Laurie threw for her, she expressed her gratitude in a presentation copy especially for them. "Maurice and A.L.: this is the charming result of your encouragement, faith and love—Nelle."[6] Then guests gathered around a cake in the dining room, frosted to look like the novel's cover—a leafy tree stood against a light brown background; the title in white letters in a black band across the top. As Nelle cut the first piece, everyone toasted her and the book, which already felt like a success.[7]

In Monroeville, the news of a local girl making good led to an exuberant item in the *Monroe Journal*: "Everybody, but everybody, is looking forward to publication . . . of Nelle Harper Lee's book, *To Kill a Mockingbird. . . .* It's wonderful. The characters are so well defined, it's crammed and jammed with chuckles, and then there are some scenes that will really choke you up."[8] Ernestine's Gift Shop, on the town square, scored a coup when the owner announced that Nelle would be holding a book signing there just as soon as she was back in town.

Within a few weeks after the publication party in New York, *To Kill a Mockingbird* hit both the *New York Times* and the *Chicago Tribune* lists of top ten bestsellers in July 1960. Reviewers for major publications—who would generally cast a skeptical eye on tales about virtue standing up to evil and peppered with homespun verities about life—found themselves enchanted by *To Kill a Mockingbird*.

"It is pleasing to recommend a book that shows what a novelist can do with familiar situations," wrote Herbert Mitgang in the *New York Times*. "Here is a storyteller justifying the novel as a form that transcends time and place." Frank Lyell, in another *New York Times* piece, breathed a sigh of relief that "Maycomb has its share of eccentrics and evil-doers, but Miss Lee has not tried to satisfy the current lust for morbid, grotesque tales of Southern depravity." The *New York World Telegram* predicted "a bright future beckoning" the author, and the *Tennessee Commercial Appeal* announced the addition of "another new writer to the growing galaxy of Southern novelists." The *Washington Post* began its review by praising the novel's power to carry a moral theme: "A hundred pounds of sermons on tolerance, or an equal measure of invective deploring the lack of it, will weigh far less in the scale of enlightenment than a mere 18 ounces of new fiction bearing the title *To Kill a Mockingbird*."[9] Annie Laurie Williams, who had been dumped by Capote as his agent for film and drama rights, couldn't resist gloating to him, "We are so *proud* of Nelle and what is happening to her book is thrilling."[10] Alden Todd, another one of Williams's young author-clients, strolled into the Francis Scott Key Book Shop in Washington, D.C., and learned that the owner had hand-sold two hundred copies of *Mockingbird* in less than a week.[11]

A few critics later found fault with the double-narrator technique whereby Scout and Jean Louise Finch—Scout as an adult—both tell the story. Phoebe Adams in the *Atlantic* dismissed the story as "frankly and completely impossible, being told in the first person by a six-year-old girl with the prose style of a well-educated adult." Granville Hicks wrote in the *Saturday Review* that "Lee's problem has been to tell the story she wants to tell and yet to stay within the consciousness of a child, and she hasn't consistently solved it." W. J. Stuckey, in *The Pulitzer Prize Novels: A Critical Backward Look*, attributed Lee's "rhetorical trick" to a failure to solve "the technical problems raised by her story and whenever she gets into difficulties with one point of view, she switches to the other." (On the other hand, the reader wonders how it will all turn out; there's a feeling of suspense, of "continual mystery" since Jean Louise is recalling the past with fondness.)[12]

In hindsight, reviews of the novel when it was published say a great deal about American culture then, especially prevailing attitudes about race. What was not discussed about the novel is more revealing than what was.

To begin with, *To Kill a Mockingbird* divides people and behavior into good or bad. Democracy, justice, and courage are good; racism, incest, and false allegations of rape are bad. Good white people like Atticus get respect from blacks who get to their feet in the colored gallery when he passes below, and the implications of this aren't questioned. Bad white people get what they deserve and die or disappear. There are no bad black people at all, which is simultaneously a stereotype and a subtle endorsement of racism. Black characters are one-dimensional, leaving readers feeling that they understand Calpurnia, Helen Robinson, Zeebo—for that matter, all blacks.

Racism receives tacit endorsement from Atticus, too. He overlooks the racism of characters such as Mrs. Dubose, while praising the "courage" she shows in breaking her drug addiction. Lynch mobs, such as the one that confronts Atticus outside the jail, are made up of decent people who can be shamed by a child out of their desire to torture and mutilate. Mr. Cunningham, Atticus says, is "basically a good man . . . he just has his blind spots along with the rest of us." And he assures Scout that the Ku Klux Klan was "a political organization more than anything" that briefly emerged "way back about nineteen-twenty" but "they couldn't find anybody to scare."

He's resigned to certain things as a wise man because good or bad behavior is often the fault of "breeding." The poor white-trash Ewells are irredeemable, because their kind are dirty, incestuous, and drunken; they belong at the dump. Bob Ewell has raped Mayella all her life but "what my pappa do don't count," and no one in court finds that abhorrent—that's just white trash for you. In the same way, nothing can be done about Boo Radley, held prisoner by his father for years, except to leave him alone, says Atticus.

Folks in Maycomb County get along because people have sense enough to stay in their lane, so to speak; by this logic, racism and segregation sound like a civic duty. The real problem in the South, according to the novel, is a mystery disease; just as rabies can produce a dog who's out of his mind, so racism is a form of confusion, or a result of being raised poorly, or a matter of not having any manners. Scout sails into her cousin Francis for calling her father "a nigger-lover"; she doesn't quite know what he means—it's how he said it, she explains. It was rude.

As Francine Prose wrote, albeit almost forty years later, "To read the novel is, for most, an exercise in wish-fulfillment and self-congratulation, a chance to consider thorny issues of race and prejudice from a safe distance and with the comfortable certainty that the reader would *never* harbor the racist attitudes espoused by the lowlifes in the novel."[13] Yet had *To Kill a Mockingbird not* reflected the political and social sensibility of the 1950s, even though it's set much earlier in the 1930s, it wouldn't have been as popular or talked about.[14]

Americans wanted to see themselves as justice-loving and believing in freedom, for example, especially in the face of communism, but the Emmett Till trial of 1955 in Mississippi was a notorious example of the opposite. An all-white, all-male jury deliberated sixty-seven minutes before acquitting two white defendants of murdering fourteen-year-old Till for whistling at a white woman. Hence the injustice of Tom Robinson's trial was greatly amplified in reader's minds in 1960 because it seemed much nearer in time, not an event from an earlier, benighted age in American history.[15]

Also, sexual intimacy between blacks and whites had always been an incendiary issue; but it was never was more violently opposed than after the U.S. Supreme Court's 1954 decision in *Brown v. Board of Education* threatened to violate sexual taboos by mixing black and white schoolchildren. An exhaustive 1947 study of southern culture by Gunnar Myrdal asked whites to choose among six categories in gauging what they believed blacks most desired by asserting their civil rights. First in ranking came "intermarriage and sex intercourse with whites."[16] From his research, Myrdal concluded that "sex was the principle around which the whole structure of segregation . . . was organized. And it was because of sex that racial segregation . . . was intended to permeate every aspect of society." By putting interracial sex and injustice at the center of her fictional trial, Lee made the adult concerns of the novel simultaneously present-day and enduring, too.

And perhaps that's why Atticus Finch had to lose in court; because had the law triumphed over "the secret courts of men's hearts," in Scout's phrase, meaning their fears and prejudices, the verdict would have been abhorrent to segregationists. What the law threatened to make them do, they could resist so long as they stood their ground. But the novel provides hope. Atticus and Sheriff Heck Tate choose not to have Boo Radley arrested—a subversive ending, an act of justice in spite of what the jury decides in the Tom Robinson case. It gives strength to the belief that people of good conscience can change society.[17]

In American culture, *To Kill a Mockingbird* would become like *Catch-22, One Flew Over the Cuckoo's Nest, Portnoy's Complaint, On the Road, The Bell Jar, Soul on Ice,* and *The Feminine Mystique*— books that seized the imagination of the post–World War II generation. A novel that played a part in questioning the "system."

A torrent of requests for interviews and book signings left Nelle breathless. Sacks of fan mail arrived at Lippincott. Capote wrote to friends: "Poor thing—she is nearly demented: says she gave up trying to answer her 'fan mail' when she received sixty-two letters in one day. I wish she could relax and enjoy it more: in this profession it's a long walk between drinks."[18] Most of the letters lauded the book, but a few were angry. "In this day of mass rape of white women who are not morons, why is it that you young Jewish authors seek to whitewash the situation?" complained a reader. Lee was tempted to reply, "Dear Sir or Madam, somebody is

using your name to write dirty letters. You should notify the F.B.I."
And she planned to sign it, "Harper Levy."[19] Another outraged letter
read:

> Regarding your successful book, *To Kill a Mockingbird,* you picked the
> kind of plot the Yankee element literally read. . . . You picked the same
> counterpart of Uncle Tom—the kind, harmless Negro accused/abused
> falsely by the arrogant whites. . . . You could write a book describing
> Southern whites killing Negroes and stacking them up like cordwood.
> It would make you another bestseller. . . . I've lived in the North five
> years. There are many good ones who mind their own business. When-
> ever you find the wiseacre who is going to remake the South—and
> never been here, they are filth and poison.[20]

As sales of the book rose into the hundreds of thousands during the
fall of 1960, Lee had the singular pleasure of a congratulatory letter
from Hudson Strode, her former Shakespeare professor and director of
the writing workshop at the University of Alabama. "I enjoyed the
book very much indeed. It is fresh, and skillfully done, with delightful
characters and the best possible ending. . . . I think part of your success
lies in the shock of recognition—or as the Japanese might say, 'the
unexpected recognition of the faithful "suchness" of very ordinary
things.' You have a wide, warm audience waiting for Number Two."[21]
(Privately, Strode wished she had been enrolled in his creative writing
seminar, telling his students, she learned a lot from him through Shakespeare.")[22]

One day, to escape the attention for a few hours, Nelle used the
excuse that Tay Hohoff was mad about cats to deliver to her an abandoned kitten with six toes on its forefeet. Nelle had found the kitten in
the basement of her building, cuddled up to the furnace. She named it
Shadrach, after the biblical character who endured Nebuchadnezzar's
fiery furnace. After delivering it safely to the Hohoff sanctuary, a "bee-
hive of books" scented with aromas of good tobacco and whiskey, Nelle
sank into a big comfortable chair and muttered, despite the early morning hour, "I *need* a drink. I'm supposed to be at an interview right
now." After she left, Hohoff and her husband, Arthur, had a good laugh

about how their young friend was finding out that literary success was not all it was cracked up to be.

For someone like Lee, who preferred solitude over parties, observing instead of participating, the onrush of instant celebrity resulting from *To Kill a Mockingbird* imposed a tremendous strain she hadn't expected. Capote, hearing of the effects of celebrity overtaking his friend, remarked: "Poor darling, she seems to be having some sort of happy nervous-breakdown."[23] Somehow, in the space of a very short time, just a few months, Nelle had gone from having a private self that she could control, to a public persona that she could not. Unlike Capote, for instance, who said, "I always knew that I wanted to be a writer and that I wanted to be rich and famous," Nelle didn't regard herself as an important person, and the attention being paid to her almost seemed to be happening to someone else. A revealing moment about her self-perception occurred during an interview with *Newsweek* in the lounge of New York's Algonquin Hotel. Catching sight of the Irish playwright Brendan Behan walking by, she confessed, "I've always wanted to meet an author."[24]

Just as long as the intense attention stayed primarily on the book, she could cope with it. Usually, her quick, folksy wit stood her in good stead during interviews. She was the first to poke fun at her heavy Alabama accent. ("If I hear a consonant, I look around.") She deflected seriousness by claiming to be a Whig and believing "in Catholic emancipation and repeal of the Corn Laws." Asked about how she wrote, she cracked, "I sit down before a typewriter with my feet fixed firmly on the floor." Not even her appearance was off-limits, within reason; she admitted to being a little heavier than she would like to be (according to a friend, she put herself on a thousand-calorie-a-day diet of "unpalatable goop").[25] Generally, interviewers, such as Joseph Deitch for the *Christian Science Monitor,* found her "instantly good company . . . a tall, robust woman with a winsome manner, a neighborly handshake, and a liking for good, sensitive talk about people and books and places like Monroeville, Alabama, her home town."

Monroeville offered the safest harbor for getting away from the attention. (This although the Boulware family was making noises about suing over the likeness between Son Boulware and Boo Radley. The

Lee sisters adopted a policy of brushing aside comparisons between characters in the novel and Monroeville residents. "They come right up to me and stuck their noses right in my face and declared there's nobody in the book that's real," said Capote's aunt Mary Ida Carter.)[26]

Not too many years earlier, the town's remoteness had been one of Nelle's chief reasons for wanting to stay in New York; now it guaranteed some peace of mind. Reporters and interviewers, after studying maps of Alabama where two-lane roads meandered like blue and black threads, opted to telephone the Lee residence instead of stopping by. When the phone rang, it was Alice who answered, refusing to allow her sister to take the call if it was about the novel.[27] The world and its demands could wait on the Lees' doorstep. Inside, Nelle liked to curl up with a book. Alice wouldn't even permit a television in the house, lest it disturb the quiet.

When word went round in Eufaula, however, that Nelle Harper Lee was coming to visit her sister Louise, a line of dessert-bearing ladies got busy. One woman, Solita Parker, with a reputation in the neighborhood for being a wit, pretended to be jealous that Monroeville had been chosen for the novel's setting. She firmly announced that Eufaula ought to chip in and rent Nelle an apartment, because there were so many peculiar characters in Eufaula to write about.

"Oh, you want a kick-back on stock in the publishing company," Nelle teased back.

"No," said the woman, "I just want to *read* the book."[28]

That kind of pleasantry and the feelings of gratification it inspired were exactly what Nelle had expected from publishing a novel. Here in these familiar surroundings, with people who spoke, thought, and joked as she did, she could be what she wanted—a Southerner satisfied with joining the tradition of regionalist writers south of the Mason-Dixon Line. Here she could give free rein to her personality. To a cookbook editor's request for a recipe that would "demonstrate food as a mean of communication," Nelle provided one for crackling bread—a backwoods staple—couched in the style of tongue-in-cheek southern humor that mixed formal talk with nonsense.

"First, catch your pig," she instructed. "Then ship him to the abattoir nearest you. Bake what they send you back. Remove the solid fat and throw the rest away." Having wasted most of the pig, the cook was then supposed to add the fat to meal, milk, baking powder, and an egg, and bake the dough in a "very hot oven." The result, Nelle promised, would be an authentic dish: "one pan crackling bread serving six. Total cost: about $250, depending upon size of pig. Some historians say by this recipe alone fell the Confederacy." To the editor, she concluded, "I trust that you will find the above of sufficient artistic and social significance to include in the cookbook."[29]

It was a response that friends would recognize as "typical Nelle"— offbeat, skeptical, thought-provoking. Friends from her days at the University of Alabama described her to the *Montgomery Advertiser* as "a warm though independent-minded girl who took great delight in deflating phoniness wherever it appeared."

To requests for more information about herself, she responded coyly. At Huntingdon College, the librarian Leo R. Roberts tried to compile a profile of the former freshman in response to journalists, alumnae, and Nelle's admirers who were clamoring to know more about the author whose book had sold more than half a million copies in six months. Roberts, probably a little nonplussed by the lack of information about Nelle in Huntingdon's archives, finally wrote to her in January 1961 requesting some facts about her background.

"I'm afraid a biographical sketch of me will be sketchy indeed; with the exception of M'bird, nothing of any particular interest to anyone has happened to me in my thirty-four years," she replied. After supplying a few details about her family, she deadpanned, "I was exposed to seventeen years of formal education in Monroeville schools, Huntingdon College, and the University of Alabama. If I ever learned anything, I've forgotten it."[30]

In September 1960, she agreed to a book signing at Capitol Book and News Company in Montgomery. Seated at a table next to a vase of white carnations and wearing a fresh-cut corsage pinned to her dress, she was the center of attention. Less a literary event than a combination celebration and reunion, the book signing was an occasion where people "crowded into the bookstore because they saw her picture in the paper, wondered if she were kin to so and so, heard that her book was good, knew her at the University of Alabama, knew someone who used to know her somewhere or had read the book and enjoyed it and came to say so."[31]

Nearby was her father, eighty-two-year-old A. C. Lee, looking very old as he watched quietly with his large owlish eyes through big glasses. His wife, Nelle's mother, Frances, had been dead for almost a decade. (A.C. himself would die in two years, still in the harness at the law office.) His suit vests, once buttoned tightly over a healthy paunch, now hung loose. The knuckles of his right hand turned white when he pressed hard on the crook of his cane to rise from his chair and shake someone's hand, perhaps an old acquaintance from his days as a state legislator. "I never dreamed of what was going to happen. It was somewhat of a surprise and it's very rare indeed when a thing like this happens to a country girl going to New York. She will have to do a good job next time if she goes on up." And then—still marveling, apparently, that Nelle had strayed from the narrow but dependable path of a nine-to-five job—he added, "I feel what I think is a justifiable measure of pride in her accomplishment, and I must say she has displayed much determination, confidence and ambition to give up a good job in New York and take a chance at writing a book."[32]

And because of the influence of his two daughters, and the passage of time, A. C. Lee had changed his views about race relations, too. Formerly a conservative on matters of race and social progress, he became an advocate for voting rights in his final years.

Part of the reason for his change of mind was the influence of events that no thoughtful American in the 1950s could ignore. Autherine Lucy, a black student, attempted to enroll at Harper Lee's alma mater, the University of Alabama, but violence on the campus for three days forced her to flee. Despite a court order to readmit her, the Board of Trustees barred her from campus. The former Alabama state senator J. M. Bonner, whom A. C. Lee probably knew from his own career in the statehouse, wrote to the *Tuscaloosa News,* "I call now on every Southern White man to join in this fight. I proudly take my stand with those students who resisted, and who will continue to resist the admission of a Negress named Lucy."

A contest of principles was gearing up in the South, and a civic-minded man like A. C. Lee could not fail to recognize it happening in his own backyard. In 1959, the Ku Klux Klan forced the cancellation of the annual Monroeville Christmas parade by threatening to kill any members of the all-Negro Union High School band who participated. Influencing A.C., too, was Alice, more progressive than he in matters concerning race. At a critical moment in the reorganization of the United Methodist Church, her beliefs about integration, honed over the decades, electrified an audience of hundreds of fellow worshippers.

During a meeting in 1964 at Huntingdon College of the Alabama–West Florida Conference, one of the few regional holdouts against integrating black Methodists with whites, a committee report concerning the "problems of our racially divided church" and society came to the floor. "A Call to Christian Thought and Conduct" called upon "Christians to uphold the law, repudiate racial hatred and violence, support freedom and equality for all, and apply compassion and understanding to those with whom we differ."[33] A motion to amend the church bylaws in favor of integrating congregations had been made, and the question was open for discussion. Those who were against were prepared with countermeasures—perhaps even a walkout, if necessary, depriving the meeting of a quorum.

For years, Alice had been impatiently waiting for such a moment.[34] Taking the floor microphone, she said: 'I move the previous question,' and sat down. The conference applauded enthusiastically and voted overwhelmingly to support her motion, voted to close discussion, and then proceeded to adopt the committee report without further debate. The advocates of racism were left holding their long-prepared speeches. "Miss Alice became the hero of the conference and from that day the enemy of the racists."[35]

By the time To Kill a Mockingbird was published, A. C. Lee was involved in redrawing congressional district lines. In 1962, while a reporter from the Montgomery Advertiser was interviewing Nelle at her home in Monroeville, Alice and A.C. stopped by on their way to the offices of Barnett, Bugg & Lee. The elderly lawyer interrupted to speak earnestly to the reporter about the importance of reapportioning voting districts to provide fairer representation for black voters. "It's got to be done," he said.[36] And then he continued on his way. It's interesting to speculate what he might have accomplished had he lived longer. When Monroeville residents politely stopped him on the street to ask him to sign his daughter's book, they often said, "But please don't sign it 'Mr. Lee'—sign it '*Atticus.*'"

The success of *To Kill a Mockingbird* caught Hollywood's attention almost immediately, and Annie Laurie Williams, as Nelle's agent for dramatic rights, had been reviewing proposals from filmmakers. She was in her element brokering deals between studios or production companies hunting for literary properties. Sifting through the proposals on her desk, however, she found too much of the usual overheated language about turning the book into a Hollywood hit.

The producer Robert P. Richards, for instance, wrote on behalf of himself and his partner, James Yarbrough. Yarbrough's credits included television dramas such as *Robert Montgomery Presents* and two western series, *Rawhide* and *Bonanza*. Richards felt strongly about the need to shoot on location and use "as many natives as possible for extras and bits." For the roles of Aunt Alexandra and Miss Maudie, he suggested Bette Davis and Ann Sheridan. "Atticus is a problem," Richards admitted; among the biggest leading men of the day—Marlon Brando, John Wayne, Burt Lancaster, Gregory Peck, and a few others—"the only one who might be right is Gary Cooper, but I'm afraid that his public image is wrong. The public is unwilling to think of Cooper as an intellectual." Yarbrough had an idea, though: "to ask John Huston to play the part, he is Atticus, in thought, body and personality, a little wilder, a little crazier."[37] Williams politely turned down their offer.

Most offers were from small outfits and partnerships. Major studios were conspicuously absent because *To Kill a Mockingbird* lacked the tried-and-true ingredients that attracted movie audiences: shoot-'em-up action, a love story, danger, or a clear-cut "bad guy." In addition, the press had likened *To Kill a Mockingbird*'s nine-year-old narrator Scout to preadolescent Frankie in Carson McCullers's *The Member of the Wedding,* and the film version of McCullers's novel had flopped. (The surface similarities of the two novels were not lost on McCullers, either, who commented acidly about Lee to a cousin, "Well, honey, one thing we know is that she's been poaching on my literary preserves.")[38]

It was just as well that the big studios weren't sniffing around, anyway. In thirty years of working with Hollywood, Williams had learned to adhere to a basic principle: try to get for authors and playwrights what they need to feel appreciated or satisfied. Some required top-dollar deals to feel validated; others would work only with directors or playwrights they admired. In Lee's case, Williams had an author who did not put emphasis on conventional marks of prestige. But she would be reluctant to let go of the story unless she could be assured that a film version would not be undignified or hurt people she loved. That was her price; and other considerations—the money paid for screen rights, percentage agreements, and so on—were of much less concern to her.

A second reality about doing business with Harper Lee was that the locus of control over the book was slipping from her hands alone and into Alice's. Williams knew she could close a film deal for the novel only if Alice approved of the people involved as much as Nelle did. Whoever was chosen to turn the novel into a film had to come across as decent and trustworthy.

The Lee family had come to the *To Kill a Mockingbird* party late, so to speak, but once it was clear that Nelle had achieved something grand, Alice began taking over her affairs. Previously, when Nelle was working full-time in New York as an airline reservationist and was down-at-the-heels, the Lees had allowed her to scrape along, probably figuring she would come to her senses eventually. Then, against all odds, this long run-up to what should have ended in a sorry admission that A.C. had been right all along instead resulted in Nelle's producing a novel that was becoming famous. Suddenly, the family was receiving calls from reporters, and with no choice except to acquit themselves well, they were undertaking the responsibility of managing their prodigy.

So it was that when Williams sent a follow-up letter to the Lee home about selling the motion picture rights to Alan Pakula and Robert Mulligan, she acknowledged that Alice, as family spokesperson and

Nelle's self-appointed manager, would have to be reckoned with every step of the way. "Dear Alice and Nelle," the letter began,

> [I tried] to keep in mind everything you said[,] Alice[,] about not getting any *cash* money for Nelle this year and not too much each succeeding year.... The sale is to Alan Pakula and Robert Mulligan, who are forming their own company to produce together, with Bob Mulligan also directing. This is the real "prize" having him direct the Mockingbird picture. Alan is a good producer but he knew when he first talked to Nelle in our office, that he must have a sensitive director to work with him. We think that Bob Mulligan is just right for this picture.[39]

She was not overstating their good luck in closing with Pakula and Mulligan, and she had held off a major studio until the pair could make their bid. As filmmakers, they were drawn to stories about character, life's tragic quality, and situations that were ripe for strong dramatization.

At first glance, Pakula would not give the impression of being the right man for the job of making a film about racial prejudice in a small southern town in the 1930s. Darkly handsome, the son of Polish immigrants, and a Yale graduate who dressed like a 1960s IBM salesman, Pakula was fastidious in ways that extended even to his film crews, insisting they pick up their cigarette butts after shooting on location. But he was also personable, warm, and conscientious. At twenty-two, he had turned away from the family printing business in New York, and become a production assistant at Paramount. His father underwrote his first film as producer, *Fear Strikes Out* (1957), the story of baseball player Jimmy Piersall's mental illness caused by his obsessively critical father, for which Pakula teamed with Robert Mulligan as director. The film was well received, and it not only launched Mulligan and Pakula's careers but also earned praise for newcomer Anthony Perkins in the role of Piersall. A publicist at Lippincott had urged Pakula to read *To Kill a Mockingbird*, and Pakula in turn had made Mulligan read it.

Bob Mulligan did not have Pakula's exterior polish, nor was he as reserved. Sandy-haired, informal, and impulsive, Mulligan was born in the Bronx and studied briefly for the priesthood before enrolling at Fordham University, where he majored in radio communications, receiving training that made him a specialist in the Marines during World War II. After the war, he started at the bottom at CBS as a messenger, but rose during the popularly nicknamed Golden Age of Television to become a director of live dramas aired on *The Philco Television Playhouse*, *Studio One*, and *Suspense*. Mulligan was part of a new wave of postwar directors learning their craft on television—men such as John Frankenheimer, Sidney Lumet, Arthur Penn, George Roy Hill, and Martin Ritt. Unlike Pakula, however, who later moved into directing films with a social-political agenda such as *Klute* (1971), *The Parallax View* (1974), and *All the President's Men* (1976), Mulligan would remain attracted to telling human interest stories: *Love with a Proper Stranger* (1963), *Up the Down Staircase* (1967), *Summer of '42* (1971), and *The Man in the Moon* (1991).

Overall, the fit was good between the content of *To Kill a Mockingbird* and what Pakula and Mulligan wanted to do artistically. Even better, the relationship between Nelle and Pakula had gotten off to a good start in Williams's office the previous autumn, during a meeting that Williams had presided over like an old-fashioned matchmaker. Well before the deal was closed, in January 1961, she had sent Pakula a letter lecturing him about not trifling with Nelle or her book: "From the very beginning, everybody who had anything to do with the book has felt that it was *special,* deserving the most thoughtful handling. Now if you can find exactly the right Atticus and exactly the right children, especially the little girl to play Scout, we will feel confident that you can produce the kind of picture you promised Harper Lee you would make when you first met her in our office."[40]

In the meantime, because Mulligan was still working on *The Spiral Road* (1962), a big-picture drama with Rock Hudson and Burl Ives about colonialism in the tropics, Pakula made arrangements to visit Monroeville and "see Nelle about the 'creative side,'" as Williams put it—though he knew in advance he was auditioning for Alice and A.C.'s approval, too. When he arrived in Monroeville in February 1961, the weather was overcast and rainy. But even if he had seen the town under the best conditions, it wouldn't have changed his mind about using it as a possible location: "There is no Monroeville," Pakula wrote glumly to Mulligan, meaning that modernization over the last thirty years had rendered the town characterless. Except for the courthouse, which the citizenry was considering tearing down because a new, flat-roof, cinder-block version was on the drawing board, Monroeville was a mishmash of old and new. A façade for Scout's neighborhood would have to be built on a studio back lot, and the interior of the old courthouse, which was not in good repair, would have to be measured and reconstructed on a Hollywood soundstage.

After spending several days getting to know the Lees, Pakula left for California, apparently having secured their approval about the ideas he and Mulligan had in mind for the film: "They want to give the movie the same approach that the book had," Alice said approvingly. Nelle, trying to assuage Pakula's disappointment about Monroeville with a dose of lightheartedness, sent him a few photographs with a note: "Here is the courthouse, some rain-rotted lumber, and two sprigs of Spanish moss to keep you company. If you'll believe me, that's the sun, not a flashbulb, shining on the side of the house."[41] He thanked her for the pictures, betraying no sense of concern about the crimp in his plans, and saying he was looking forward to meeting up with her in New York soon to introduce her to Bob Mulligan—"Affectionately, Alan."

The setting for fictional Maycomb that Pakula had expected to find had seemingly vanished. Where Capote's house had stood—the one belonging to Dill's aunt in the novel—was an empty lot. The streets that had emanated sour red dust on a hot day in the 1930s were smooth with blacktop. Now, teenagers crowded into the Wee Diner for Cokes and hamburgers, a hot spot for dates made from two buses joined together, with flower boxes and brightly painted booths. A visitor resting on one of the benches on the courthouse square might conclude, just looking around, that a film with a story like *To Kill a Mockingbird* was passé. How different times seemed from the days of lynch mobs and racist trials. On the other hand, blacks were not allowed to use the park or recreation facilities owned by the Vanity Fair underwear factory, the largest industry in town, and there were separate water fountains marked "White" and "Colored."

A few days after newspapers announced the sale of the movie rights to the novel in February 1961, an unsigned squib headed "Spreading Poison" appeared on the letters-to-the-editor page of the *Atlanta Journal-Constitution*: "That book 'To Kill a Mockingbird' is to be filmed. Thus another cruel, untrue libel upon the South is to be spread all over the nation. Another Alabama writer joins the ranks of traducers of their homeland for pelf and infamous fame."

In late spring 1961, planning for the movie entered a lull. Pakula and Mulligan were anxious to, in casting parlance, "set the star"—get a commitment for the leading man—so they could move on to making a distribution deal. The previous fall, Nelle had engaged in some star hunting on her own, thinking that a direct approach might entice an actor with a reputation for integrity that made him suitable for the role of Atticus. Through the William Morris Agency, she sent a note to Spencer Tracy. "Frankly, I can't see anybody but Spencer Tracy in the part of Atticus."[42] The actor replied via an agent, George Wood, that he "could not read the book till he has finished his picture 'The Devil at Four O'clock.' He must study and concentrate at present." Instead, Wood suggested Robert Wagner who "would love to hear from you and any ideas that you might have for him." In March 1961, Maurice Crain wrote to Alice: "The latest development is that Bing Crosby very much wants to play Atticus. . . . He should be made to promise not to reverse his collar, not to mumble a single Latin prayer, not to burble a single note."[43]

Aside from the movie, things were continuing to percolate on the literary front. By mid-April, *To Kill a Mockingbird* was approaching its thirty-fifth week on the bestseller lists. Yet Lee apparently couldn't shake the feeling that she was still an amateur who could learn from her betters. After having lunch with Crain, she went back to his office and happened to see the manuscript for a new novel by Fred Gipson, author of *Old Yeller*. "She picked up the first page, just to see how Fred Gipson began a story," Crain wrote to Gipson. "Under protest she was dragged away from it 111 pages later to keep another date, but took a copy of *Old Yeller* with her. You have another fan."[44]

Back home in Monroeville by the end of the month, Nelle was

invited to attend a luncheon of the Alabama Library Association. At the table of honored guests was her former professor Hudson Strode, with one of his former creative writing students, Mississippi regionalist writer Borden Deal, who had just published his sixth novel, *Dragon's Wine*. At the conclusion of the luncheon, Nelle received the association's literary award.

On Monday, May 2, when *To Kill a Mockingbird* was in its forty-first week as a bestseller and had sold nearly half a million copies, the phone rang in Annie Laurie Williams and Maurice Crain's offices. It was a friend of Williams's at a publishing house who wanted to speak to Nelle about hearsay from a reporter.

In California, Pakula had already heard the same rumor and was excitedly calling his partner, Bob Mulligan.

When Mulligan answered, Pakula shouted, "We got it! We got it!"

"We got what?" asked Mulligan.

"The Pulitzer Prize. Our book won it!"[45]

Nelle hardly dared believe it until she received an official call: "A friend from a publishing company called and had gotten the word from a newspaper. I haven't heard from the Pulitzer committee yet, but I haven't been back to my apartment since I heard the news."[46] When she finally did hear from a spokesperson for the Pulitzer Prize Committee, she called Alice several times, who by now was becoming adept in the role of her sister's spokesperson and at fielding phone calls from reporters. "Nelle was anxious to find out the local reaction," she said in response to questions. "She still claims Monroeville as her home, and when she leaves, it is usually for business purposes" (a hint that Alice was not reconciled to Nelle's living months at a time in New York). "The whole town of Monroeville is amazed about the Pulitzer prize."[47]

The annual Pulitzer Prizes in drama, letters, and music, created by the newspaper publisher Joseph Pulitzer in a bequest to Columbia University, were worth only five hundred dollars each at that time, but their cachet, in terms of bringing artists' names to the public, was enormous. Hudson Strode immediately tapped out a letter of congratulations to Nelle: "I announced the good news to my writing class last night and there was a response of cheers. The University and the State, and the whole South are proud of you. But no one more than myself."[48]

Besieged by phone interviews that kept her pinned inside Williams's office for hours, Nelle resorted to modesty and humor in responding to questions about herself. "I am as lucky as I can be. I don't know anyone who has been luckier."[49] She claimed that the effort to write the book had worn out three pairs of dungarees. And about whether a movie was forthcoming, all she would say was that production was slated to begin in the fall.

Almost immediately, a second avalanche of fan letters began. "Snowed under with fan letters," wrote *Newsweek*, "Harper Lee is stealing time from a new novel-in-progress to write careful answers."

It was the proverbial Cinderella story: from nowhere comes a young writer, without benefit of grants, fellowships, or even an apprenticeship at a major newspaper or magazine, who produces, on her first try, a novel snapped up by three American book clubs: Reader's Digest Condensed Books, the Literary Guild, and the Book-of-the-Month Club. In addition, the British Book Society had selected *Mockingbird* for its readers, and by the spring of 1961, translations were under way in France, Germany, Italy, Spain, Holland, Denmark, Norway, Sweden, Finland, and Czechoslovakia.

Truman Capote, who craved winning the Pulitzer or the National Book Award, and hoped he would with *In Cold Blood*, wrote to friends in Kansas: "Well, and wasn't it fine about our dear little Nelle winning the Pulitzer Prize? She has swept the boards."[50]

Despite Capote's casual tone, he no doubt resented this turn of fortune in his friend's life. After all, when they were children, he had been the one to urge her to write stories (he later revised the nature of their partnership, telling the *Washington Post,* "I got Harper interested in writing because she typed my manuscripts on my typewriter. It was a nice gesture for her, and highly convenient for me"). Moreover, Lee tended not to put the emphasis on winning the Pulitzer Prize that Capote would have. "The Pulitzer is one thing; the approval of my own people is the only literary reward I covet," she wrote to a friend.[51] It was gall that Truman had to swallow, as gracefully as he could, but his cousin Jennings Faulk Carter recalled, "The only time I've ever heard him say anything about Nelle's book was that he remarked, 'She got the Pulitzer, and I've never, never done that.' I forget how he put it, but you could tell he was hurt badly. That as much writing as he had done, he had never won it, but Nelle had."[52]

In mid-May, the Alabama legislature attempted to pass a resolution honoring Nelle, but a segregationist senator named E. O. Eddins stepped in to stop it. The senator had been at the head of the charge to ban Garth Williams's 1958 book *The Rabbits' Wedding*, which featured the wedding of two rabbits, one black and one white. The White Citizens' Council in Alabama, with Eddins's support, had attacked the Williams book as "communistic" and promoting racial integration. Eddins and other legislators tried but failed to remove the state's director of the Alabama Public Library Service, Emily Wheelock Reed, for refusing to remove the book from library shelves. But this time, Eddins sensed that a similar backlash might build if he lambasted Lee and *To Kill a Mockingbird*, so he finally withdrew his protest "lest it make a martyr of the author."[53] A joint resolution passed on May 26 offering "homage and special praise to this outstanding Alabamian who has gained such prominence for herself and so much prestige for her native state."

And there was surely more to come from an author so promising. She had written an essay, "Love—In Other Words," which appeared in the April issue of *Vogue* magazine. She told reporters that she had several short stories under way. She seemed to have talent and a work ethic that indicated that a long career was just beginning.

In its first year, *To Kill a Mockingbird* sold more than 2.5 million copies. W. S. Hoole, director of the University of Alabama libraries, "nearly fell over his size thirteens asking for the manuscript!" Nelle wrote to friends in Mobile, but she thought better of giving it to him.[54]

Maurice Crain, Annie Laurie Williams, and certainly Tay Hohoff, couldn't wait for Nelle's second novel. In July 1961, a teasing note arrived at Nelle's apartment on the Upper East Side, where she had just moved with a friend, Marcia Van Meter: "Dear Nelle: tomorrow is my first birthday and my agents think there should be another book written soon to keep me company. do you think you can start one before i am another year old? We would be so happy if you would. (signed) the mockingbird and annie laurie and maurice crain."[55]

To reporters asking the same question—What are your plans for a second book?—Nelle replied, "I guess I will have to quote Scarlett O'Hara on that. I'll think about that tomorrow."[56]

The remark was more than apt. As for Scarlett O'Hara, unpleasantness and hard decisions could always be put off until an eternal tomorrow, so "tomorrow" would never come for Nelle Harper Lee as an author. With her first novel, which became the most popular novel in American literature in the twentieth century, and which readers rank in surveys as the most influential in their lives after the Bible, Lee seemed poised to begin a writing career that would launch her into the annals of illustrious American writers. Instead, almost from the day of its publication, *To Kill a Mockingbird* took off, but gradually left its author behind.

ten

"Oh, Mr. Peck!"

"He's got a little pot belly just like my Daddy!"

—HARPER LEE

One cold night in early January 1962, Wednesday night services had just ended at the imposing First Baptist Church on Monroeville's town square when a stranger made his way up the front steps through the trickle of worshippers exiting the sanctuary. By his downcast and rough appearance, he appeared to be homeless.[1]

"May we help you?" asked one of the ushers.

"I'd like to see the reverend," came the gruff reply.

The usher assured the man that if he needed a meal or a place to stay, then that could be taken care of. No, that wasn't the problem, said the stranger. He needed to see the reverend. The usher, beckoning over a couple of gentleman who were busy returning hymnals to the backs of pews, explained the situation. They agreed to accompany the visitor to Dr. L. Reed Polk's office.

Reverend Polk was just hanging up his vestments when the little group appeared on the threshold of his office. He thanked the ushers, invited the tall and rather well built man in, and shut the door so they could have some privacy.

"What can I do for you?" asked Reverend Polk.

Looking up suddenly and extending his hand, the stranger said, "How do you do, sir—I'm Gregory Peck."

Peck was in town to meet the Lee family and to soak up some of the setting for the character he was going to play in the film version of *To Kill a Mockingbird*. The reason he had stopped at the First Baptist Church, he told Dr. Polk, was that he wanted to speak to someone who knew the town and its people. Polk had been the minister at First Baptist for more than fifteen years. Peck apologized for the disguise, but he didn't want word to get around that he was visiting before he'd gotten a chance to get his bearings and meet the reverend. Dr. Polk was amused and flattered that Peck had come directly to him.

For the next hour, the two men talked about the town and about the man Peck was going to play. The actor asked for particulars about Mr. Lee's standing in the community, his thoughts and behaviors— anything that "set Mr. Lee apart" would be helpful. Polk stood up and demonstrated how Lee had a tendency to fumble with his pocket watch as he talked and how he paced back and forth. Peck watched intently, making mental notes about how he was going to embody Atticus Finch on the screen.

Gregory Peck had not been Universal Studios' first choice for the role. Rock Hudson was offered the part, and he was prepared to do it when the project entered what is now sometimes called "development hell" in Hollywood—the period of massaging the screenplay and wrangling over creative control. But, in a nutshell, Pakula didn't want Hudson for the part; he wanted Peck. The studio agreed that if the latter would sign on, then they would provide the financing. Pakula sent the actor a copy of the novel. "I got started on it," said Peck, "and of course I sat up all night and read straight through it. I understood that they wanted me to play Atticus and I called them at about eight o'clock in the morning and said, 'If you want me to play Atticus, when do I start? I'd love to play it.'"[2] Peck formed a production company called Brentwood

Productions, which would be a three-way partnership with Pakula and Nelle Lee, who, with the assistance of Alice and Annie Laurie Williams, had formed her own company, Atticus Productions, as a tax shelter. Peck, however, would have input into the film's casting, the development of the screenplay, and other creative decisions.

With Peck on board, the next piece of business was turning the novel into a screenplay. Pakula deferred to Nelle before approaching anyone else, but she wasn't interested in the difficult work of adaptation. First, she was busy with a new novel, also set in the South. Working on it, she told a journalist, was like "building a house with matches."[3] The second reason was that she didn't mind if someone else pruned the book to fit a feature-length movie. She felt "indifference. After all, I don't write deathless prose." So Pakula turned to the playwright Horton Foote instead. "I was asked to write the script," said Foote, "because the actor, producer, and Miss Lee were familiar with my writings."[4]

A stocky, soft-spoken Texan with blue eyes, Foote actually had very little experience as a film writer. The only other screenplay he'd written was a film noir piece, *Storm Fear* (1955), the adaptation of a novel by Clinton Seeley, starring Cornel Wilde. A former actor, Foote had begun his career with the American Actors Theater, a small repertory group founded in the early 1940s. The theater's members at that time included Agnes de Mille, Jerome Robbins, and Mildred Dunnock. But he soon realized he was a so-so actor and started listening to friends who advised him to write plays about the town of Wharton, in southeast Texas, where he was raised.

When he was given the job of adapting *To Kill a Mockingbird*, he recognized a historical kinship with Nelle. His forebears had come from Alabama and Georgia in the early 1800s. Nevertheless, he worried about "despoiling the quality of the story" because "it's agonizing to try to get into someone else's psyche and to catch the essence of the work, yet knowing you can't be just literal about it. There has to be a point where you say, 'Well, the hell with it—I've got to do this job for another medium, and I've got to cut out this over-responsible feeling and roll my sleeves up and get to work.' "[5]

At Pakula's urging, Foote ratcheted up the drama by compressing the novel's three years into one. He added a touch of backstory, too.

"Harper never mentions the mother, and I was wondering how I could sneak in that emotional element. I remember as a boy my bedroom was right off the gallery on the porch and when I was supposed to be asleep I would hear things I was not supposed to hear from the adults. This was something I invented for the two children."[6]

Most important, he heightened the intensity of the novel's social criticism. Social protest, particularly about racial conditions in the South, receives more emphasis in Foote's screenplay than it does in Nelle's novel, a reflection of the civil rights movement's gaining momentum. To underscore this theme's seriousness, Foote removed some of Nelle's satire, probably thinking that too many caricatures of southern types would diminish the courageousness of Atticus's moral stance against the town. Gone are Aunt Alexandra and her racist church ladies; Colonel Maycomb, admirer of Stonewall Jackson; Miss Fisher, the barely competent first-grade teacher from northern Alabama who behaves like a carpetbagger of education; and Mrs. Meriwether, the long-winded speaker at the Halloween pageant. Foote added a dab of love interest to the story by having Miss Maudie from across the street appear at Atticus's breakfast table one morning, hinting that a relationship might be in the offing. Nelle, on the other hand, preferred her hero to be absolutely asexual—deaf, in fact, according to a political cartoon described in the novel, to the siren call of ladies in Montgomery who find the eligible attorney-legislator attractive.

In spite of the significant changes, Nelle later hailed Foote's screenplay: "If the integrity of a film adaptation is measured by the degree to which the novelist's intent is preserved, Mr. Foote's screenplay should be studied as a classic."[7]

Director Bob Mulligan wasn't so sure. "You know what your problem is," he told Pakula, after reading Foote's work, "too often you lose the point of the view of the children."[8] It was true, but Foote had chosen to thrust Atticus onto center stage at the expense of the children's coming-of-age story, believing the adult character could carry drama that would appeal to moviegoers.

A still more drastic change was contemplated. Before Peck had even read the screenplay, he wanted to drop the title *To Kill a Mockingbird*.

Annie Laurie Williams, who had assured Nelle that the novel's artistic integrity would be respected, was furious. "Don't believe any items you may see in the newspapers saying that Gregory Peck wants to change the title of *To Kill a Mockingbird*," she wrote to George Stevens, managing editor at J. B. Lippincott. "He has been signed to play the part of Atticus, but has no right to say what the title of the picture will be. The change of title has been denied by Mulligan and Pakula in a column story in the *New York Times*."[9]

Nevertheless, Peck was the star of the film, and had a considerable financial stake in it. Moreover, he had the support of Universal Studios in his back pocket. In ways that mattered, the film was more his than anybody else's.

After speaking to the Reverend Polk in his church office, Peck and his wife, Veronique Passani, checked in at the ranch-style LaSalle Hotel in Monroeville. Working the hotel desk that night was Miriam Katz. Not recognizing the stranger signing the register, she quietly repeated, "Gregory P-e-c-k . . . Oh, Mr. Peck!" Startled, she turned to the hotel's only bellhop and mustered all the decorum she could. "'D.J.! This is Mr. Peck. See that he gets anything he wants.'

"Peck smiled. 'Thank you very kindly, Mrs. Katz, but I don't want any special favors.'"[10]

Accompanying Peck was a small production crew, sent to photograph period details, and director Bob Mulligan and his wife. But Monroeville only cared that Gregory Peck was in town. The next day, when the word spread—broadcast by the fact that the actor drove around in a convertible—a legion of dessert-bearing ladies got busy. The presence of a movie star led to some strange contretemps. Peck strolled into the Western Auto Store owned by A. B. Blass and asked for a soft drink from the cooler. When Blass presented him with a Dr. Pepper, Peck fished around in his pockets and then sheepishly admitted he didn't have any money with him. Blass gallantly replied that the drink was on him so that he could tell his grandchildren that Gregory Peck owed him six cents. Peck thanked Blass for his largesse, but next he went to the Monroe County Bank for some cash. The girl in the teller window primly informed him that she needed to see some ID.

Behind her, the manager, feeling mortified, said evenly, "I think we can take Mr. Peck's check." Finally, it was time to attend to the primary reason Peck was in town: to meet the Lees and study, as unobtrusively as possible, the gentleman he was going to play.

The Lees no longer lived on South Alabama Avenue, having moved to a brick ranch house across from the elementary school not long after the deaths of Mrs. Lee and Edwin in 1951. Alice, no doubt, had felt her father needed a small change of scene, away from painful memories. Mr. Lee was looking forward to meeting Gregory Peck, although he was feeling tired as a result of a mild heart attack. He'd never met a film star. For that matter, he'd never seen Gregory Peck in a movie. The two men sat in the living room getting to know each other, while Nelle and Alice shooed away neighbors trying to peek in through the picture window. Peck got the impression that the elderly lawyer "was much amused by the invasion of these Hollywood types. He looked on us with benign amusement." For his part, the actor found Mr. Lee "a fine old gentleman of eighty-two, and truly sophisticated although he had never traveled farther than a few miles from that small Southern town."[11] They got along together well.

After an hour or so of conversation, Nelle offered to take Peck on a short tour of the square with a stop-off for lunch. The weather was brisk and overcast, but Peck, dressed only in a lightweight suit, gamely followed Nelle, who was wearing a parka, jeans, white socks, and sneakers, around town until they arrived at the Wee Diner.

The Wee Diner was built from two Montgomery buses joined at a forty-five-degree angle, creating a triangular courtyard effect. The intersection served as the entrance. To rustle up customers, owner Frank Meigs put a chopped onion on the grill and turned on the exhaust fan, a welcome smell to Lee and Peck on such a chilly January day. They slid into one of the booths and ordered.

Then, suddenly, through the door came Wanda Biggs, the official hostess for the Welcome Wagon. She had been tracking them all over town, she said, out of breath. On behalf of the Chamber of Commerce, she presented Gregory Peck with a basket of gifts and coupons for new-comers. "He was as polite and kind a man as I had ever met," Biggs later told everyone. "He asked if I would mind taking [the basket] to his wife across the street at the hotel. That he would like for me to meet her. I did and found her to be equally as warm and friendly. They were just our kind of folks."[12]

Nelle and Peck's final stop after the Wee Diner was the home of a local resident. The production crew had arranged to meet them there because they wanted to photograph what servants' quarters looked like in a grand old home. While flashbulbs popped, Peck made small talk with the owner about his spacious kitchen, including how he'd never had a real down-home southern meal, being from California.

Probably as a result of that remark, by seven thirty that evening, the lobby of the LaSalle Hotel was jammed with not only dessert-bearing ladies but also other well-wishers bringing covered dishes. Peck left a message at the front desk expressing his thanks and asked that the items be left for him to pick up. Not to be denied, teenager Martha Jones and a friend pushed through to the receptionist and asked which room Mr. and Mrs. Peck were staying in. They were informed huffily that the Pecks were not in at present. The two girls got in their car and drove around town on a scavenger hunt until they spotted Nelle's car outside the Monroe Motor Court. They went door by door, listening. Finally, hearing voices, they knocked, and were confronted by Nelle opening the door, who was obviously not amused.

"Martha Louise Jones, what are you doing here?"

"I was just hoping I could get Mr. Peck's autograph."

Behind Nelle in the room, intrepid Martha could see Peck, Mr. Lee, and Peck's wife, Veronique.

"Well, we're busy now. You just go on home."

"Hold on, Nelle," Peck said. "I'll be glad to give the young ladies my autograph." Star-struck, the two adolescents offered Peck damp scraps of paper. He signed both and then bid the girls a gracious good night.[13]

The following morning, the Pecks didn't venture outside the LaSalle Hotel lest they send the town into a second uproar. From the Wee Diner, Frank Meigs sent over breakfast on trays, and later the star sent him a handwritten note expressing his gratitude.

Production on the film was scheduled to begin in early February in Hollywood, and Nelle had been invited to attend. But she had also promised Truman that she would go with him to Kansas again after Christmas. So the middle of January—two weeks after Peck had left Monroeville—found her back in Garden City, Kansas, once again as Capote's "assistant researchist," though by now her profile in the town was higher than his. "It was pretty dicey for Nelle, as she was known by local people who had come to like her very much," said Dolores Hope.

> She was always very protective of Capote and made sure the limelight was on him most of the time. She was quick to divert mention of the Pulitzer prize back to Capote. She also gave him credit for his help and encouragement. My impression of the Pulitzer time is that people who had come to know Truman here in Kansas just had a gut feeling that he would have his nose out of joint about it. Nelle knew him so well and she was anything but an attention-getter herself. In fact, she shunned it. She was the exact opposite of Truman, being more interested in others than she was in herself.[14]

As gifts for her Kansas friends, she brought an armload of auto-graphed copies of *To Kill a Mockingbird.* Her stay was necessarily brief, however, because filming was slated to begin in a few weeks. (Her notes for Truman don't mention this second trip to Kansas, or a third one she made a year later. But indications are that she forged a closer relationship with Perry Smith and Dick Hickock while they were on death row because Truman let them know to expect a letter from her now and then.) Consequently, at the end of the first week of February, she boarded the Super Chief in Garden City, having finished helping Truman, and continued on to Los Angeles. Total sales of her book, hardback and paperback, were approaching 4.5 million. In an unusual move at the time for a publisher, J. B. Lippincott took out eighteen radio ads in major markets to announce that production was beginning on *To Kill a Mockingbird,* starring Gregory Peck.

Casting had been completed just in the nick of time, with some of the roles being settled on just weeks before shooting began. Pakula and Mulligan preferred faces audiences wouldn't recognize "to retain the sense of discovery, which is so important in the novel," Pakula said.[15] They turned to character actors from films, Broadway professionals— unfamiliar then to most film-going audiences—and, for the roles of the children, complete unknowns.

Frank Overton, as Sheriff Heck Tate; Paul Fix, as the judge; Richard Hale, as Mr. Nathan Radley; and Crahan Denton as Walter Cunningham, Sr.—all four were fixtures in Westerns, playing ordinary folk, and could be depended on to render solid performances. Alice Ghostley, who played Dill's aunt Stephanie Crawford; William Windom, who became prosecutor Horace Gilmer; Estelle Evans, who transformed herself into the Finches' housekeeper, Calpurnia; and Rosemary Murphy, who took the role of Miss Maudie Atkinson—all were stage and Broadway performers. Newcomers to film were Collin Wilcox Paxton as Mayella Violet Ewell, and Robert Duvall as Boo Radley, who had impressed Horton Foote when he gave a first-rate performance in Foote's drama *The Midnight Caller* at the Neighborhood Playhouse in New York. To prepare for the role of Boo Radley, Duvall stayed out of the sun for six weeks and dyed his hair blond, thinking it would give him an angelic look.

The competition for the role of Tom Robinson was down to two actors: Brock Peters and James Earl Jones. Peters badly wanted the part because his career seemed to be slipping into a rut of playing heavies and villains. "Well, of course, I was scared out of my wits," he remembered. "I didn't know how to present myself in order to get this coveted prize. I went into the meeting—it was in a building at Park Avenue and 57th Street and I tried not to appear frightened but I wanted to look cool and calm and still suggest the character of Tom Robinson, and do that dressed in a suit."[16] He got the part, and a few days before filming began, Peck called to congratulate him. Peters was so surprised, he didn't know what to say at first. "I worked over the years in many, many productions, but no one ever again called me to welcome me aboard, except perhaps the director and the producer, but not my fellow actor-to-be."[17]

The part of Bob Ewell, the impoverished white man who accuses Tom Robinson of having raped his daughter, was still open when actor James Anderson met with Mulligan. Raised in Alabama, Anderson told Mulligan with conviction, "I know this man." Mulligan believed he did, but he also had to confront Anderson with his reputation for drinking, fighting, and not showing up on sets. He told Anderson to come back in three days (probably to see whether he would be on time and sober). When Anderson arrived, Mulligan laid it on the line. "I want you to be in this movie but you and I are going to have to have a clear understanding. And you're going to have to take my hand and shake it. If you do, you have to promise me that you will be sober, that you will be on time, that you will not cause trouble for me or for anyone. And that you will do honor to this script. He said, 'I understand.' He put out his hand and shook mine, and he kept his word. Boy, did he know that man."[18]

The role of Jem went to thirteen-year-old Philip Alford, a child with practically no acting experience who auditioned only because his parents promised him a day off from school. Hundreds of children competed for the roles of the Finch children, including nine-year-old Mary Badham, who was selected for the part of Scout. A year later, she appeared in a *Twilight Zone* episode. She was feisty and frank, a good match for her character. When a reporter commented, "You're a very little girl for your age," she replied, "You'd be little, too, if you drank as much coffee as I do."[19] By coincidence, Alford and Badham were Birmingham natives who lived four blocks apart. Alford's parents were, however, working-class people, while Badham's could afford a black nanny to help raise her. The part of the Finches' next-door neighbor Dill went to nine-year-old John Megna, brother of actress Connie Stevens, who had recently appeared in the Broadway hit *All the Way Home,* based on James Agee's Pulitzer Prize–winning novel, *A Death in the Family.* "John looked up to me like a big brother," Alford said, and the two boys formed a childish pact to hate Badham.[20] (The threesome banded together when they were bored, however. One day, Alan Pakula was handed a note from studio security saying that they must stop fishing in the pond on a back lot. It was a freshwater reservoir and placed off-limits by the California Fish and Game Commission.)

Pakula and Mulligan had already arranged to shoot many of the scenes on soundstages at the Revue Studios, but that still left the question of what do to for exterior scenes, since Monroeville no longer resembled a Depression-era southern town. Alexander Golitzen, a former architect and the film's co-art director, studied sketches and photographs of Monroeville until he came up with an idea. Some of the houses in old Monroeville resembled clapboard cottages that were disappearing from the outskirts of Los Angeles. Golitzen suggested to his colleague, Henry Bumstead, that they get tips from wrecking companies on houses slated for demolition. Near Chavez Ravine, where a new baseball park for the Los Angeles Dodgers was nearing completion, they found a dozen condemned cottage-style houses. For a total of five thousand dollars, they hauled the frames to the set. Sometimes known as "shotgun hall" houses because they have a center hall with all the rooms off to the left or right, the houses were popular everywhere in the United States during the first thirty years or so of the twentieth century. For a quarter of the cost of building them from scratch on the set, the relocated houses were placed on either side of a re-created Alabama street, with porches, shutters, and gliders (seat swings) added for a touch of southern flair.[21]

When Nelle arrived on the set, she was dazzled not only by the illusion—the set "looked so real that I wanted to sit down in a rocking chair and fan myself"—but also by the attitude of the crew making the film. "I know that authors are supposed to knock Hollywood and complain about how their works are treated here," she said, "but I just can't manage it. Everybody has been so darn nice to me and everything is being done with such care that I can't find anything to complain about."[22]

On February 12, principal photography began. Until now, Nelle had been harboring some doubts about Peck's suitability for the role. "The first time I met him was at my home in Alabama. . . . I'd never seen Mr. Peck, except in films, and when I saw him at my home I wondered if he'd be quite right for the part." But that was without seeing him in character. "[T]he first glimpse I had of him was when he came out of his dressing room in his Atticus suit. It was the most amazing transformation I had ever seen. A middle-aged man came out. He looked bigger, he looked thicker through the middle. He didn't have an ounce of makeup, just a 1933-type suit with a collar and a vest and a watch and chain."[23] According to Michael Freedland, the author of *Gregory Peck*, "The day Harper Lee saw him for the first time walk out of his dressing room in his Panama hat and three-piece white linen suit she burst into tears and called, "He's got a little pot belly just like my Daddy!" "That's no pot belly, Harper," said Peck, "that's great acting."

Since her arrival in Los Angeles, Nelle had been "getting the royal treatment from the studios," according to novelist Fred Gipson's wife, Tommie, who kept Maurice Crain informed of his favorite client's activities. "I saw Nelle Lee's picture in the *L.A. Times* the other day. The story said she was visiting the Universal International lot. I was hoping we could buy her a dinner or a drink or something. She was only here for the weekend, it turned out, and was booked solid."[24]

The reason Nelle had to leave so abruptly was that her family needed her. Crain replied to Tommie, "She has a nephew in the Air Force, stationed at Lowry Field, Denver. His little pregnant wife developed pneumonia and landed in a hospital soon after she arrived in California. He couldn't get off the base often, and was worried sick. Nelle was the only member of his or her family within a thousand miles, so she went to Denver and took charge until the girl was out of danger. She finally made it home yesterday [February 19] and called us."[25]

It was too bad she couldn't have stayed to see the courtroom scenes. To film them, set designers constructed a soundstage set built to look exactly like the interior of the courthouse in Monroeville, based on painstaking measurements. Ironically, one of the novel's major themes is tolerance, but a production assistant kept reassembling the extras for the trial by shouting, "All the colored atmosphere upstairs; all the white atmosphere downstairs." Brock Peters, the film's Tom Robinson, had a word with him, and the call was changed to, "Downstairs atmosphere in, please; balcony atmosphere upstairs, please." Because of the mores of the times, Alford, Badham, and Megna were not allowed to attend the filming of the courtroom scenes, even though they appear to be watching from the courtroom gallery. For children that age, listening to a trial about rape and incest, even a fictional one, was deemed inappropriate.

During the trial, Brock Peters delivered one of the most memorable performances in the entire film. For two weeks of rehearsals and filming,

Peters was required to break down on the stand, begin to weep, and then make a dignified attempt to try to stifle his sobs. By the end of this slow disintegration, his self-respect has to gain hold again and turn into barely suppressed rage at being falsely accused. Mulligan coached him until, as Peters said, "Once we were on track I needed to go only to the places of pain, remembered pain, experienced pain and the tears would come, really at will." Peters later called those two intense weeks "my veil of tears."[26] Peck found it difficult to watch Peters because the actor's performance was so affecting.

Between Peck and James Anderson, the actor playing Bob Ewell, however, there was no love lost. To begin with, for some reason Anderson would only speak to Mulligan. Peck tried to make a suggestion about one of their scenes, and Anderson snarled back, "You don't show me *shit!*"[27] Second, he was a Method actor, meaning that he tried to remain in character at all times, which in this case was a violent man. In the struggle with Jem Finch, near the end of the film, Anderson yanked Philip Alford out of the frame by his hair.[28]

In April, after a month of filming, word reached the set that Harper Lee had returned to Monroeville because her family needed her again. At age eighty-two, A. C. Lee had died early in the morning on April 15, 1962.

Of his daughter, A.C. had said, "It was my plan for her to become a member of our law firm—but it just wasn't meant to be. She went to New York to become a writer."[29] It was typical of him that he tended to think the best of others, including his headstrong daughter who had proven him wrong about her choice to drop out of law school and write fiction instead. He believed that people are basically good, capable of improving, and as eager as the next person for a better future. Change was necessary.

It was true that in his private life, rigorous and traditional Methodism confined his reading of the Bible to questions of faith and salvation. But when, toward the end of his life, it became increasingly clear to him that issues of race and fairness overlapped with Christian morality, he enlarged his view of his responsibilities as a religious man. Also, political realities connected with the Civil Rights movement indicated that the law would eventually accomplish in secular ways what people of conscience had so far failed to do, or resisted.

On Easter Sunday, a week after his death, the *Montgomery Advertiser* wished for more men like Lee to come to the aid of the South, and help pour oil on the roiling waters.

Harper Lee, as is the case with most writers of fiction, says that the father in her book, Atticus Finch, isn't exactly *her* father. But she told John K. Hutchens of the *New York Herald Tribune* book section the other day that Atticus Finch was very like her father "in character and—the South has a good word for this—in 'disposition.'"

What makes Atticus Finch or Amasa Coleman Lee, thus a remarkable man? He was a teacher of his own children, a small-town citizen who thought about things and tried to be a decent Christian human being. He succeeded.

... Many Southern individuals and families with the Lee-Finch family principles have not asserted themselves and offset another image of the Deep South.

This may be an appropriate thought for this Easter Day. But if it is appropriate, let the individual say. The Lee family, and the Finch, is one of great independence. Amasa Coleman Lee, so evidently a great man, voted Democratic until the mid-30s, then independently. Said a daughter, "We have a great tendency to vote for individuals, instead of parties. We got it from him."

Indeed, was and is the Lee-Finch family so unusual? Could Amasa Coleman Lee, in his care, responsibility and sense of justice, have been so unusual and served so long in the Alabama Legislature, or so long edited a county newspaper in the deep south of this Deep South state?

There are many "likenesses" of Atticus Finch. They are far too silent.[30]

After her father's death, Nelle buried herself in writing. "Not a word from Nelle," Capote wrote to Alvin and Marie Dewey on May 5, "though I read in a magazine that she'd 'gone into hiding; and was hard at work on her second novel.'"[31] To her friend Dolores Hope in Garden City, Lee confided that the work was "rough going," because of demands on her time connected with both *To Kill a Mockingbird* and the film. Worrying her more, though, was the strain involved in writing anything that must follow an all-out success. "The book reviewers wait with axes sharpened. They'll be like vultures." She had been lucky the first time; but this was different.

She may have retreated to Maurice Crain and Annie Laurie Williams's Old Stone House in Riverton, Connecticut, which was becoming one of her favorite places to work. Located on a winding black tar road surrounded by woods and constructed in 1749 from stones and hand-hewn timbers, the original was as solid as a colonial outpost and ideal for solitude. In the backyard, Crain had planted gardens and built two pools for his nieces, Penny and Joy Hafner. "He wasn't afraid of work. He was often out there in a pair of overalls and mixing cement or laying stones and so forth," said Douglas Roberts, who dated one of the Hafner girls. Near to Crain and Williams lived fellow Texan Ruth Cross, author of *The Golden Cocoon*, who labored with her husband to restore forty run-down acres and a crumbling house. When they were finished, they dubbed it Edendale. Because the Old Stone House was conducive to writing without distractions, Williams and Crain regularly offered it to authors, among them Kathleen Winsor and Alan Paton.

Lee found the Old Stone House congenial, and not just because she was so fond of Crain, Williams, and their relatives Fern and "Dutch" Hafner, who were frequent guests. Nelle didn't own a car, but many times she drove her hosts in a rented car, and the threesome enjoyed the ride up to Connecticut, bringing them to the Old Stone House before nine o'clock on a Friday night for a late dinner. If the Hafners or other in-laws were there, a few hands of bridge or games of Scrabble by the fireplace were favorite ways to spend an evening. "You had to be careful playing against Nelle or Maurice, they were both so bright—minds like cameras."[32] Sometimes, Lee stayed behind on Sunday, when the others had left, and worked the entire week alone. A neighbor, Roy Law, brought groceries from town, took care of the property, and delivered wood for the fire when the weather was cold.

It was an idyllic setting, but even there she found no magic charm for turning out publishable material. In fact, the previous November she had received what probably was her first rejection letter—from *Esquire* magazine. Commissioned to write a short nonfiction piece on the South—an easy assignment it would seem for the winner of the Pulitzer Prize—she submitted an article so far off the mark that editor Harold Hayes was a little embarrassed about how to respond.

> I feel lousy about returning this to you. . . . What seemed to go wrong—from our point of view—is that the piece is working too hard to carry a lot of weight—humor, characterization, the barbarity of the Klan, the goodness of a brave man and so on. A novel's worth, in fact, with the result that it never quite makes it on either of these levels as a short feature. I'm sympathetic to your decision to change it to a fictional form, and I really don't think that is a factor against it.

Hayes paid her two hundred dollars for her "willingness to be pursued relentlessly by us for a piece that was our idea for you to do."[33] The fact that she had submitted a piece of fiction with *To Kill a Mockingbird* overtones again, when a nonfiction piece was requested, suggests a certain lack of versatility.

Principal shooting on *To Kill a Mockingbird* had ended May 3, and the picture wrapped in early June 1962. During the five months of production, Alford had grown from four foot eleven to five foot three, and his costumes had to be altered several times. Also, his voice was beginning to change. The final scene to be filmed was outside the jail, when Atticus is protecting his client from a lynch mob and the children unexpectedly intervene. Badham, who didn't want the film to end, kept deliberately flubbing her lines over and over, until her mother pulled her aside and told her that L.A. traffic would be a nightmare if she made everybody stay any longer. Chastened, she said her lines correctly, then Peck, whom the children loved to spray with squirt guns, stepped back. From overhead, the lighting crew poured buckets of water on them.

Peck said he felt good about how the shooting went. "It seemed to just fall into place without stress or strain."[34] He was not pleased, however, when he saw the rough cut of the picture. In a memo to his agent, George Chasin, and Universal executive Mel Tucker dated June 18, 1962, he itemized forty-four objections to the way his character was presented. In sum, the children appeared too often, in his opinion, and their point of view diminished the importance of Atticus. "Atticus has no chance to emerge as courageous or strong. Cutting generally seems completely antiheroic where Atticus is concerned, to the point where he is made to be wishy-washy. Don't understand this approach."[35] But Pakula and Mulligan had taken the precaution of stipulating that they would make the final cut, which kept them, and not the studio, in control of the editing. "Universal did not like the picture very much," said Foote, "and if they had got their hands on it, God knows what they would have done, but they couldn't."[36]

After reviewing Peck's memo, Mulligan and Pakula made another pass at reediting the film, but the star still wasn't satisfied. In a second memo to Universal's Tucker, on July 6, Peck wrote, "I believe we have a good character in Atticus, with some humor and warmth in the early stages, and some good emotion and conflict in the trial and later on. . . . In my opinion, the picture will begin to look better as Atticus' story line emerges, and the children's scenes are cut down to proportion."[37] More footage fell to the cutting room floor, including whole scenes of the children. Pakula said later, "It just tore my heart out to lose the sequence [where Jem reads aloud to Mrs. Dubose, who is dying]."[38]

In the end, Peck positioned himself firmly and prominently at the center of the film. Only about 15 percent of the novel is devoted to Robinson's rape trial, whereas in the film, the trial scenes add up to more than 30 percent of the two-hour running time.

Meanwhile, Nelle continued to work on her follow-up to *To Kill a Mockingbird*; the pressure was on her for a repeat performance. In August, Capote wrote to the Deweys, "As for Nelle—what a rascal! Actually, I know she is trying very hard to get a new book going. But she loves you dearly, so I'm sure you will be the first to hear from her when she *does* reappear."[39]

The success of her first novel had given her something like the corner on the market for popular fiction about growing up in the Deep

South. Other authors who wrote about the same region discovered that reviewers held up *To Kill a Mockingbird* as the standard. Elise Sanguinetti, Nelle's friend from the *Rammer Jammer* days, complained about comparison because her novel *The Last of the Whitfields* (1962) seemed to be getting scant attention. A coming-of-age novel told from the perspective of an adolescent, it describes how two upper-middle-class white children in Georgia cope with the new social order welling up around them. "The book is running into some difficulties with this Mockingbird rage that is going about," Sanguinetti wrote to her mentor, Hudson Strode. "The early reviewers seem to think they are very similar. I didn't think so, and ironically I wasn't very taken with that book. The Negro-white situation there was much too melodramatic for my taste and somewhat unbelievable (as was a nine-year-old daughter of a lawyer going around saying 'ain't' all the time etc.). But one can't argue with success, can you?"[40]

Success was an understatement. By now, Nelle's novel had completed an eighty-eight-week run on bestseller lists, and she was wealthy. In September 1962, the Methodist Episcopal Church of Monroeville broke ground on a new educational building and chapel, helped by an annual percentage of royalties which Nelle had earmarked for it. In addition, she purchased furnishings for the chapel in memory of her parents and her brother, and commissioned a statue of Methodist founder John Wesley. Nevertheless, she was uncomfortable with the assumption that she was rich, which she tried to undercut with rough humor. On the day of the dedication ceremony for the chapel, Nelle rose to use the ladies' room before events got under way. Reverend A. F. Howington cautioned her not to leave her purse on the pew. "Goodness, don't do that—someone might take something," he said.

"Take something!" Nelle replied. "I spent my damn money on this church. There's nothing in it."[41]

Although *To Kill a Mockingbird* was no longer on the bestseller lists, it continued to sell thousands of copies weekly, both in the United States and abroad, buoyed along not only by its appeal to readers but by a wave of concern about race and justice that was gaining strength.

On September 25, 1962, James Meredith, a twenty-eight-year-old black Air Force veteran, attempted to enroll at the University of Mississippi, at Oxford, where he had been accepted. Surrounded by white United States marshals, Meredith approached the offices of the Board of Trustees. Blocking the doorway was Governor Ross Barnett.

"Which one of you is Meredith?" asked Barnett. The fifty state legislators flanking the governor erupted in laughter. Barnett then read a prepared statement: "I, Ross R. Barnett, governor of the State of Mississippi, having heretofore by proclamation, acting under the police powers of the state of Mississippi . . . do hereby deny you admission to the University of Mississippi."

Five days later, on a Sunday afternoon, Meredith, this time accompanied by 536 deputy U.S. marshals wearing white helmets and carrying billy clubs, arrived at his assigned dormitory and was placed under protective guard. Then a contingent of marshals walked a half mile to the Lyceum building to prepare the way for Meredith to register for classes. But the registrar was nowhere to be found. Outside the Lyceum building, students tore down the United States flag and ran up the Confederate Stars and Bars. By nightfall, thousands of students and townspeople were battling with the marshals. Rocks, Molotov cocktails, and occasionally bullets spattered the streets. President John F. Kennedy went on national television to announce the federalizing of fifteen thousand National Guard troops to maintain law and order in Mississippi. During the riot in Oxford, two men were killed and hundreds injured. Of the 536 marshals, 166 were injured, and 30 suffered gunshot wounds. Said one military police officer, "I can't believe this is America."

On October 1, Meredith walked to his first class, a seminar on colonial American history, again escorted by U.S. marshals past a crowd of hundreds of jeering students.

Against this backdrop, in November, Nelle received her first honorary doctorate of letters, from Mount Holyoke College in Massachusetts. Along with Senator Margaret Chase Smith from Maine, she had been chosen, said Mount Holyoke authorities, because the two women had "won the kind of recognition in their own fields that is customarily accorded to men." At the Founder's Day ceremony, college president

Richard Glenn Gettell said, *To Kill a Mockingbird* had "made possible in us a deeper perception of the forces at work in our society. Without sensationalism, without cynicism, without bitterness, but with delicacy and strength, compassion and sternness, you have humanly treated the great themes of justice and suffering and the growth of understanding, and have formed them into a memorable work of art."[42]

Her appearance at Mount Holyoke was the start of a long period of standing before audiences. The film *To Kill a Mockingbird* was slated for release at Christmas in order for it to qualify for the 1962 Academy Awards, and Nelle had agreed to pitch in with publicity. Alice claimed that her sister "would be terrified to speak" to groups, but it was not so, judging from how cleverly she handled herself before a roomful of newsmen in Chicago shortly after the film's release. After a local press agent muffed her introduction by calling her "Miss Hunter," Nelle stepped up to take questions. "She is 36-years-old, tall, and a few pounds on the wrong side of Metrecal [a diet drink]," wrote a reporter for the Chicago Press Club's newsletter, *Overpress*. "She has dark, short-cut, uncurled hair; bright, twinkling eyes; a gracious manner; and Mint Julep diction." Lee's repartee with the reporter was keen.[43]

REPORTER: Have you seen the movie?

LEE: Yes. Six times. (It was soon learned that she feels the film did justice to the book, and though she did not have script approval, she enjoyed the celluloid treatment with "unbridled pleasure.")

REPORTER: What's going to happen when it's shown in the South?

LEE: I don't know. But I wondered the same thing when the book was published. But the publisher said not to worry, because no one can read down there. . . .

REPORTER: One of your sisters is a lawyer. Is she a criminal lawyer?

LEE (DEADPAN): She's not a criminal, no.

REPORTER: You studied law, too, didn't you?

LEE: Yes. For three years. I had to study something in college, and I grew up in a legal household. (Her father, like the hero of *Mockingbird,* is also a lawyer—ed.) The minute, though, that I started to study law, I loathed it. I always wanted to be a writer.

REPORTER: How did the lawyers you know like the book?

LEE: Southern lawyers don't read novels much.

REPORTER: I understand that Gregory Peck, after seeing his straight dramatic performance in *Mockingbird*, says he will no longer do romantic leads.

LEE: Maybe he liked himself in glasses.

REPORTER: When you wrote the book, did you hold yourself back?

LEE (PATIENTLY): Well, sir, in the book I tried to give a sense of proportion to life in the South, that there isn't a lynching before every breakfast. I think that Southerners react with the same kind of horror as other people do about the injustice in their land. In Mississippi, people were so revolted by what happened, they were so stunned, I don't think it will happen again.

REPORTER: If you wanted to be a writer, why did you study law?

LEE: I think you should always do the opposite thing from what you want to do. If you have a job writing during the day, I think it's too hard to try and write four hours when you go home. So dig ditches for a living, anything. A change of pace is good.

REPORTER: Do you find it difficult to write?

LEE: I've found it difficult in terms of time. A lot of people like to drop around and visit now. I'm drinking more coffee than ever.

REPORTER: Do you find your second novel coming slow?

LEE: Well, I hope to live to see it published.

REPORTER: How long have you been working on it?

Lee: I've spent one and a half years on it now. *Mockingbird* took two and a half years of writing. . . .

Reporter: What do you think of the Freedom Riders?

Lee: I don't think this business of getting on buses and flouting state laws does much of anything. Except getting a lot of publicity, and violence. I think Reverend King and the NAACP are going about it in exactly the right way. The people in the South may not like it, but they respect it.

Reporter (cub variety): I came in late, so maybe you've already been asked this question, but I'd like to know if your book is an indictment against a group in society.

Lee (nonplussed): The book is not an indictment so much as a plea for something, a reminder to people at home. . . .

Reporter: Were the characters in the book based on real people?

Lee: No, but the people at home think so. The beauty of it, though, is that no two people come up with the same identification. They never think of themselves as being portrayed in the book. They try to identify others whom they know as characters.

Reporter (grinning slyly): What with royalties and a sale to the movies, you must be getting awfully rich.

Lee: No, not rich. You know that program we have at Cape Canaveral? I'm paying for it. Ninety-five percent of the earnings disappeared in taxes.

Reporter: Will success spoil Harper Lee?

Lee: She's too old.

Reporter: How do you feel about your second novel?

Lee: I'm scared.

Reporter: Don't some people presume the name "Harper Lee" belongs to a man?

LEE: Yes. Recently I received an invitation to speak at Yale University, and was told I could stay in the men's dormitory. But I declined that part of the invitation. (She smiled.) With reluctance.

Truman intimated to others that he knew how Nelle was coming along with her new book, but apparently she didn't confide in him about it. "I can't tell you much about Nelle's new book," he wrote to Donald Cullivan, a former Army buddy of Perry Smith's. "It's a novel, and quite short. But she is *so* secretive."[44] In any case, she couldn't have been devoting much time to it, because publicity demands having to do with the upcoming release of the film were keeping her busy.

For instance, amid all the other scheduled appearances, she received an invitation to visit the Texas home of Vice President Lyndon Baines Johnson and his wife, Lady Bird. Lee and novelist Allen Drury (*Advise and Consent*, 1959) were called on to speak to students. They answered questions ranging from "How can you prepare yourself to become a novelist?" ("Read your head off," Lee recommended) to "Do novelists make exceptional grades in high school English?" ("Those were the only good grades I ever did get," she said).[45] But don't think, she added, that writing a novel will make you automatically beloved. One afternoon she was leaving a country school near Monroeville when a boy of ten or twelve followed her out from the building with his teacher.

"Herbert," said the teacher, "do you know who she is?"

"No, ma'am."

"She has written a very famous book," the teacher hinted.

"She has," Herbert said flatly.

"This is our own Miss Harper Lee, who has written a wonderful book," explained the teacher. "If I hadn't kept you in after school, you would have missed seeing her. Aren't you glad, Herbert?"

"No, ma'am."[46]

On Christmas Day, 1962, two days after J. B. Lippincott had donated three hundred books in A. C. Lee's memory to the Monroe County Library, *To Kill a Mockingbird* premiered in Hollywood. Lee endorsed the film, beginning to end. "It's a fantastically good motion picture. And it remained faithful to the spirit of the book. It is unpretentious. Nothing phony about it."[47] Annie Laurie Williams wrote to Capote: "You will be happy to know that Nelle's picture *To Kill a Mockingbird* is getting rave reactions from everyone who has seen the previews."

Alabama cities and towns vied to be the first to premiere the film in the state. The prize had gone to Mobile for the third week of March; Monroeville, which had submitted a petition of citizens' signatures, would get it at the end of March, even before Birmingham—a plum for a small town. In the meantime, First Lady Jackie Kennedy arranged for a private showing in Washington, D.C., in early January for one of her charities. Alan Pakula proudly showed the film to several senators and Supreme Court justices, but he ended up with the wrong print, "a study in grays—no black and white resonance. It was one of the worst nights of my life."[48]

On Valentine's Day, 1963, the film opened in New York City. Nelle soldiered on through another public appearance, having given her word that she would. "I must quote to you from a letter I received from a Mr. John Casey, the man who is in charge of the preview room at Universal-International at 445 Park Avenue," Williams wrote to Alice Lee. "Harper Lee is such a wonderfully warm and friendly woman that I have had all I could do to keep from giving her a big hug right in public. 'Oh Susanna, do not cry for me, 'cause I met a real fine woman and her name is Harper Lee.'"[49]

Audiences for the New York premiere lined up around the block.

Despite the film's subject matter, racism and intolerance, the first few minutes of the movie run against audiences' expectations by showing images of innocence. Credits appear over a child's collection of miniature toys contained in an old cigar box. An unseen child hums, picks up small objects, and draws with crayons on construction paper, a sequence that title designer Stephen Frankfurt shot on his kitchen table on East Fifty-eighth Street in New York. Frankfurt enlisted a neighbor girl to play at the table. Each of the objects in the box has a real or symbolic meaning, including a white marble, which starts to roll via a concealed magnet until it gently bumps into a black one. The *click!*, when the marbles touch, cues the music, a simple melody played on a piano with one hand, as if a child were picking out a tune. Composer Elmer Bernstein, a former concert pianist who had studied under Aaron Copland, suggested the theme music for Mulligan by placing the phone next to his piano one morning and playing it for him. Mulligan was delighted. The effect of the plaintive but sentimental music, which swells into an orchestral treatment, combined with the tiny world inside the cigar box, is charming and, as Mulligan said, "put us directly into the movie."[50]

At the time, the film was considered politically liberal because of the attention paid in the screenplay to social justice. Looking back, however, Peck's insistence that Atticus's character occupy more of the film's center injects a heavy dose of white patriarchal values. In a word, Atticus, an educated white male, appears to be the most important person in the film. Everyone else defers to him, humors him, reacts to him, or disagrees with him. As one critic noted, the elimination of Scout's voice-over from most of the film means that the viewer doesn't see small-town southern society from the perspective of a young female growing up in it.[51] Instead, *To Kill a Mockingbird* is largely Atticus's story, even to the point that Tom's fate, which means death, seems less important than Atticus's losing the case—a critical failure in making the audience "walk in Tom's shoes," as Atticus would have put it.

After the New York premiere, reviewers by and large praised the film as entertainment, though some of the more perceptive identified aesthetic problems.

"The trial weighed upon the novel, and in the film, where it is heavier, it is unsupportable. The narrator's voice returns at the end, full of warmth and love . . . but we do not pay her the same kind of attention anymore. We have seen that outrageous trial, and we can no longer share the warmth of her love," wrote *Newsweek*.[52] Bosley Crowther in the *New York Times* pointed out, "It is, in short, on the level of adult awareness of right and wrong, of good and evil, that most of the action in the picture occurs. And this detracts from the camera's observation of the point of view of the child. . . . [I]t leaves the viewer wondering precisely how the children feel. How have they really reacted to the things that affect our grown-up minds?"[53]

Brendan Gill, writing for the *New Yorker*, disliked that the film's resolution, Bob Ewell's death, was no more defensible than it was in the novel: "In the last few minutes of the picture, whatever intellectual and moral content it may be said to have contained is crudely tossed away in order to provide a 'happy' ending. . . . The moral of this can only be that while ignorant rednecks mustn't take the law into their own hands, it's all right for *nice* people to do so."[54]

Andrew Sarris for the *Village Voice* wrote the most critical review of all: " 'To Kill a Mockingbird' relates the Cult of Childhood to the Negro Problem with disastrous results. Before the intellectual confusion of the project is considered, it should be noted that this is not much of a movie even by purely formal standards."[55]

Nelle was unfazed. "For me, Maycomb is there, its people are there: in two short hours one lives a childhood and lives it with Atticus Finch, whose view of life was the heart of the novel."[56]

The juggernaut of publicity rolled on into the early winter of 1963. Nelle had promised Truman she would accompany him to Garden City again, but he was clearly becoming peeved at having to play second fiddle to her success. "I think our friend Nelle will meet me in G.C.," Capote wrote to the Deweys in February. "However, she is so involved in the publicity for her film (she owns a percentage, that's why; even so, I think it very undignified for any serious artist to allow themselves to be exploited in this fashion)."[57]

Williams, on the other hand, couldn't have been more pleased with Nelle. Writing to Alice Lee on February 16, she lavished praise on her:

When Nelle came in yesterday with the enclosed clippings, she was so tired she could hardly sit. She had been with the Universal people being interviewed by Hal Boyle of the Associated Press and the hours on hours of public appearances, plus sitting and being asked questions, was about all she could take. . . . [S]he talks so well before little or big audiences and never stops or is halting in what she is saying but "performs" like a real professional lecturer, but when she gets through, she always thinks she didn't do so well and gets real surprised when you tell her how good she is.

I have never seen a picture receive so much love and tender affection as *To Kill a Mockingbird*."[58]

Nelle had opened up with Hal Boyle more than she had with most interviewers, or perhaps she was becoming more relaxed. She admitted, tongue in cheek, "Success has had a very bad effect on me. I've gotten fat—but extremely uncomplacent. I'm running just as scared as before." Perhaps speaking of herself and the pressures on her, she said, "Self-pity is a sin. It is a form of living suicide. . . ."[59] Williams wrote to Alice, "It was a good interview and I'm glad Nelle 'spoke her mind.' "[60]

The Alabama premiere took place on March 15, with many shows sold out in advance. Two weeks later, the film arrived in Monroeville, and Nelle was in town to witness the reaction. A full-page ad in the *Monroe Journal*, paid for by businesses, trumpeted, "We Are Proud of Harper Lee . . . and Her Masterpiece! We Would Like to Share with Her These Moments of Artistic Triumph!" Reserved-seat tickets were on sale by March 17 at the theater box office or by mail order: one dollar for adults and fifty cents for children. The first five customers who brought in a live mockingbird would receive ten dollars apiece.

Dorothy and Taylor Faircloth drove over from Atmore on a starry, cool night to see the movie: "You were really fortunate to get tickets. It was a fantastic event for a small town like Monroeville."[61] Also in the audience was Joseph Blass who, as a teenager, had caddied for Mr. Lee. "Mr. Lee did not look much like Peck in the movie, although Peck, who had spent time with Mr. Lee, copied some of his mannerisms in a way that was almost eerie to those of us who knew him."[62]

When the film ended, remembered Taylor, there was no applause. Few people said anything until they reached the lobby. "At that time in the South, everybody seemed to be divided. You were either a liberal or a racist. And when the movie ended, the discussion afterwards went along those lines."[63] The film was held over a week. Nelle posed for a photo under the marquee with some Monroeville dignitaries, squinting in the springtime daylight, but obviously beaming.

The film was the object of enjoyment and praise, but judging from its premiere in Birmingham at least, it didn't seem to prick people's consciences. When the film opened in Birmingham, on April 3 at the

Melba Theater, "huge crowds jammed the street . . . to catch a glimpse of the movie's two child stars: Birmingham natives Mary Badham and Philip Alford," writes S. Jonathan Bass in *Blessed Are the Peacemakers*. "Ironically, the story line depicted white bigotry and black injustice in Alabama during the 1930s and illustrated the meaningful role a paternalistic, decent, and moderate white southerner could play during a racial crisis. Regardless, the movie apparently had little impact on the racial outlook of Birmingham's white community during the spring of 1963."[64]

At the same time that the Melba Theater was filled with appreciative audiences, the Southern Christian Leadership Conference had organized thousands of black children to march in Birmingham. Police carried them off in buses to jail. When there was no more room, "Bull" Connor ordered that police dogs and fire hoses be turned on the demonstrators. The pressurized water was powerful enough to rip the bark off trees and sent children skidding down the pavement. After weeks of violent acts by the Birmingham police, Attorney General Robert Kennedy successfully lobbied white business leaders to desegregate public facilities. The whole country, he pointed out to them, even parts of the western world, was watching the city of Birmingham become a spectacle of brutality.

By spring of 1963, *To Kill a Mockingbird* had been nominated for eight Academy Awards, including Best Picture, Best Director, Best Supporting Actress (Mary Badham), Best Black-and-White Cinematography, and Best Music Score—Substantially Original.

As a year in film history, 1962 had been remarkable for the number of high-quality films released, many of which became classics. John Frankenheimer had directed three of those films: *All Fall Down*, adapted from James Leo Herlihy's novel about a dysfunctional family, starring Warren Beatty, Eva Marie Saint, Karl Malden, Angela Lansbury, and Brandon De Wilde; *Birdman of Alcatraz*, with Burt Lancaster, making a plea for prison reform; and *The Manchurian Candidate*, a political thriller about right-wing zealots taking over the government. Blake Edwards released two: a stylish thriller, *Experiment in Terror*, and an uncompromising look at alcoholism, *The Days of Wine and Roses*, which was Jack Lemmon's breakout role as a dramatic actor.

Arthur Penn directed the film version of his Broadway hit *The Miracle Worker*, starring Anne Bancroft and Patty Duke. Also from Broadway came the screen version of *The Music Man*, starring Robert Preston. Stanley Kubrick adapted Vladimir Nabokov's *Lolita*.

In the Western genre, Sam Peckinpah's *Ride the High Country* put a rousing moral dilemma in the hands of two cowpokes, veteran actors Joel McCrea and Randolph Scott, each in one of his best roles. John Ford directed *The Man Who Shot Liberty Valance*, and Kirk Douglas starred in *Lonely Are the Brave*, a modern-day Western.

Two horror films that year depended on psychological twists: *Whatever Happened to Baby Jane?* featured Bette Davis and Joan Crawford in roles that destroyed their images as femme fatales; and Robert Mitchum was alternately charming and frightening as he stalked a family in *Cape Fear*. For the epic re-creation of D-day, *The Longest Day*, Darryl F. Zanuck engaged the talents of so many actors that audiences became preoccupied with whom they could recognize.

From abroad came two François Truffaut masterpieces, *Shoot the Piano Player* and *Jules and Jim*. David Lean's epic *Lawrence of Arabia* probed the masochism and megalomania of its hero, T. E. Lawrence, played by Peter O'Toole in his first major role. Marcello Mastroianni was nominated for an Oscar in Pietro Germi's satire of infidelity and male arrogance, *Divorce Italian Style*. Tony Richardson released *The Loneliness of the Long-Distance Runner*. Finally, Alain Resnais puzzled audiences with his enigmatic *Last Year at Marienbad*.

On awards night, April 8, Nelle went to a friend's house in Monroeville to watch the presentations. She didn't own a television because "it interferes with my work." Horton Foote won the Best Adapted Screenplay Oscar, and the team of Art Directors/Set Decorators for *To Kill a Mockingbird* also received the top honor. Some days before the ceremony, Nelle had sent Gregory Peck her father's pocket watch, engraved, "To Gregory from Harper." Now, as he sat in the Hollywood audience waiting for the envelope to be opened and the announcement made of who had been voted Best Actor, Peck clutched the watch. When Sophia Loren read his name as the winner, he strode onto the stage with A.C.'s watch still in his hand. One of the first people he thanked was Harper Lee.

She cried "tears of joy."[65]

A few days later, Truman returned to Monroeville from Switzerland to visit his aunt Ida Carter. About forty people attended a little party at the Carter home for both Truman and Nelle. But most of the attention, Truman couldn't help but notice, went to Nelle.[66]

eleven

Unfinished Business

"All I want to be is the Jane Austen of south Alabama."

—HARPER LEE

After the end of the publicity connected with the film *To Kill a Mockingbird*, Lee was free to work as much as she liked on her next novel. Alice was handling her finances, and income from *To Kill a Mockingbird* and the Academy Award–winning film adaptation were like two tributaries of a stream flowing to Monroeville. "My advice would be for you to work out just how much money Nelle can take in the coming years," Williams suggested to Alice, "without causing too much to be paid to the Government, and then when we know what her tax situation is, we can then make arrangement with the Atticus Company to let her have so much a year."[1]

Williams, Crain, and Lee were practically inseparable; when Nelle was in New York, they saw each other almost daily during the summer of 1963. On weekends, she often went up to their home in Connecticut. "Nelle is looking fine again, we are glad to report," Williams reassured Alice, referring to the young author's fatigued state after the grind of her public appearances earlier that year."[2]

Williams, no doubt, recognized the importance of staying in Alice's good graces. Nelle discussed everything with her older sister. Alice scrutinized contracts and percentages, and weighed in on negotiations that affected Williams's bottom line. So keeping on the best of terms with the Lee clan was good business. In addition, Alice seemed able to snap her fingers and make Nelle scamper back to Monroeville, interrupting her sister's work and potentially delaying the second novel still more—another financial consideration from an agent's point of view. As it turned out, Alice jumped at an invitation and made arrangements for both herself and middle sister Louise Conner to visit in the fall and get to know these important friends of Nelle's.

Meanwhile, the civil rights movement reached a watershed that summer. In June, George Wallace, the governor of Alabama, stood in front of a schoolhouse door at Nelle's alma mater, the University of Alabama, in a symbolic attempt to oppose the enrollment of Vivian Malone and James Hood. When federal marshals confronted Wallace, he stepped aside, but segregationists cheered his protest. At her home near the campus of the University of Alabama, Hudson Strode's wife, Therese, not sympathetic to the civil rights cause, felt dread about the course of events and voiced the sentiments of many white Southerners. "I have given up completely," she wrote to a friend.

> The white race is lost. The U.S. has become not only the champion but leader of the colored races. Now I understand why Plato rejected democracy, regarding it as little more than rule by the mob. And Greek mobs were neither black nor "mixed."
>
> Hudson walks in and out among it all like Daniel in the lion's den. We pay as little attention to it as possible. . . . Do not worry about us, darling Peggy. We live five miles from town in the midst of twenty acres of trees. Negroes are urban people. If these green, gentle woods were the Wilds of Africa, they could not regard them with more terror.[3]

In August, a quarter of a million people participated in the March on Washington, which was climaxed by Reverend Martin Luther King, Jr.'s "I have a dream" speech, delivered from the steps of the Lincoln Memorial.

But privately Nelle was wary of forcing too much, too soon. As she had said to reporters in Chicago during her promotional tour for the film, in answer to a question regarding the Freedom Riders, "I don't think this business of getting on buses and flouting state laws does much of anything. Except getting a lot of publicity, and violence."[4] She was right about the white South having a culture that was sensitive to northern coercion. According to Alabama historian Virginia Van der Veer Hamilton,

> Plain folk sensed that it was *they,* not the most prosperous whites, who were to ride buses, live in neighborhoods, and compete for jobs with blacks; *their* children who were to be seated alongside black children in schools. But the sight of white demonstrators from the North goaded them to even greater fury. Here came another wave of outsiders retracing the steps of all those old abolitionists, Yankee soldiers, school teachers, missionaries, and federal judges who had meddled in the affairs of their state. They were concerned that they would count for even less.[5]

"Nelle didn't agree with the tactics being used to integrate the South," said Kay Wells, a friend from Kansas who visited Nelle in New York. "She thought sending troops was only going to cause more trouble and anger people."[6]

In her private opinion, Lee was not speaking as the author of a "novel of man's conscience," as she described it, "universal in the sense it could have happened to anybody, anywhere people live together."[7] But as a Southerner, hers was "not an uncommon position for even progressive people to take," according to Donald Collins, author of *When the Church Bells Rang Racist*, a history of segregation in the Methodist church. "They didn't object to the goals being sought, but rather the methodology that was being used. It was a way of not fighting the real issue."[8]

Meanwhile, national concern over law and order and civil rights was adding to *To Kill a Mockingbird*'s foothold in public schools. Eight percent of public junior high schools and high schools nationwide had added the novel to their reading lists only three years after its publication.[9] Nelle marveled at the book's appeal to youngsters: "I find that hard to understand. The novel is about a former generation, and I don't see how this younger generation can like it." Informed that she had done a wonderful job of writing for children, she replied, tongue in cheek, "But I hate children. I can't stand them."[10]

In September, the exchange of letters between Williams and Alice Lee became more animated with excitement over their getting together at the Old Stone House. "It will soon be time for you and Louise to start on your trip," Williams wrote to Alice. "We are all standing on tiptoe waiting to see you."[11] Alice replied, "I do hope that the leaves are beginning to turn so they will put on a spectacle for us in October. . . . Don't worry about feeding us, just being at the farm with you is going to be exciting enough to keep us going, and we will start N.H. [Nelle Harper] on a reducing diet when we arrive!"[12]

If Williams felt any trepidation about meeting Alice, now the head of the Lee family, and Louise, her anxieties were put to rest only moments after the sisters arrived. Alice presented Williams with a gift: a handmade apron sewn by her aunt Alice McKinley, her mother's sister in Atmore, Alabama. Williams wore it every moment she was in the kitchen. The New England weather was perfect for autumn, and the trees surrounded the colonial Old Stone House with a panorama of fall colors. The sisters stayed for a week and then attended to some business in Manhattan. In the city, they lunched with Jonas Silverstone, an attorney whom Williams had retained to handle the income from films and plays. He informed Alice to expect a check for Nelle in the neighborhood of fifty-eight thousand dollars—the equivalent of ten times the average annual salary of a wage earner in 1963.[13]

Finally, though, it was time for the Lee sisters, including Nelle, to head back to Alabama. She was eager to get back to her new book. "You know that we always talk on the phone on Sunday night just to report on our weekend and find out 'how you feel,'" Williams wrote to Nelle, "and this letter is just to say we are glad you are with Bear [Alice] but we sure *do miss you.*"[14]

Alice by now was a single woman living on her own with a well-established career in the offices of Barnett, Bugg & Lee; but she still gave a tug to her youngest sister, when it was time, in Alice's judgment, for Nelle to come home. To an interviewer, Nelle said with a hint of defeat, "Well, I don't live here, actually. I see it about two months out of every year. I enjoy New York—theaters, movies, concerts, all that—and I have many friends here. But I always go home again."[15] She was rich, almost forty, and had been a regular Manhattanite for fifteen years, but she had to return to a town without so much as a bookstore for stretches of six months or longer every year. Both her parents were dead; her former sister-in-law, Sara, had remarried and moved away after Edwin Lee's death; and Louise lived two hours from Monroeville, yet Alice insisted that Nelle "come home."

Back in Monroeville, Nelle bent to the task of trying to write regularly. Requests for personal appearances and speeches were still pouring in, but she decided that since "I'm in no way a lecturer or philosopher, my usefulness there is limited." At a dinner given in her honor at the University of Alabama, she warned her hosts to expect a "two-word speech," and that if she felt talkative, she might add "very much."[16]

Even in a small town, however, demands on her time were hard to escape. "I've found I can't write on my home grounds. I have about 300 personal friends who keep dropping in for a cup of coffee. I've tried getting up at 6, but then all the 6 o'clock risers congregate."[17] To get away by herself, she went to the golf course, forgiving her neighbors for their trespasses on her privacy. "Well, they're Southern people, and if they know you are working at home they think nothing of walking right in for a cup of coffee. But they wouldn't dream of interrupting you at golf."[18] She liked to spend the hours on the golf course thinking about her novel. "Playing golf is the best way I know to be alone and still be doing something. You hit a ball, think, take a walk. I do my best thinking walking. I do my dialog, talking it out to myself."[19]

She had to know at least two chapters ahead what characters were going to do and say before she could make any progress. Even so, she was a slow writer. Her method was to "finish a page or two, put them aside, look at them with a fresh eye, work on them some more, then rewrite them all over again."[20]

As 1963 neared an end, Alice did a rough estimate of her sister's income and taxes. Nelle "nearly flipped," Alice wrote Williams, about the tax implications of her income, "and she worried terribly for a short while, then she took off to the golf course and had a good time."[21] Worrying about money, her second novel, and dieting—Williams congratulated her "on losing all those pounds"—was making her a little snappish. Truman wrote soothingly to Marie Dewey after Nelle groused that she was too busy to get together with her. "Don't be upset about Nelle. That's just the way she is. And always will be. It doesn't mean a thing. She *adores* you both."[22]

Before she had published anything, Nelle imagined the writer's life as the best possible for someone like her who loved independence and shunned conformity. Now she was discovering that expectations of success could be a ball and chain.

Come spring, Nelle returned to New York. She was eager to continue her stays at the Old Stone House, where she could be with friends but also left alone when she needed to work. "I have a place where I don't know anybody and nobody knows me. I'm not going to tell, because somebody would know."[23] In Connecticut, her pattern was to write steadily for six days, then stop and take a break for two, which suggests that she worked approximately Monday through Friday, then let her pen rest when Crain, Williams, and a few of their in-laws arrived on weekends. Although writing "has its own rhythm," she said, it was "the loneliest work there is."[24]

She also had to be back in New York because Truman needed her help with the final phases of *In Cold Blood*. For more than four years, he had been laboring on the manuscript. His childish handwriting filled more than a dozen school notebooks, every paragraph double-spaced and written in pencil. To keep from looking back at what he'd finished, he turned the notebook upside down for the next blank page. The work continued while he made return trips to Garden City, sometimes accompanied by Nelle, and to the Kansas State Penitentiary to interview Perry Smith and Dick Hickock on Death Row. Most of the book was finished by 1964, but appeals by the killers' attorneys forced the case upward through the legal system, even to the U.S. Supreme Court. Capote wrote to Bennett Cerf at Random House, "please bear in mind that I *cannot* really finish the book until the case has reached its legal termination, either with the execution of Perry and Dick (the probable ending) or a commutation of sentence (highly *un*likely). . . . Nevertheless, it is the most difficult writing I've ever done (my God!) and an excruciating thing to live with day in and day out on and on—but it *will* be worth it: I *know*."[25]

Of the two possible outcomes, Capote knew that the most satisfactory dramatic denouement would be execution. KBI detective Harold Nye, who had pursued Hickock and Smith all over the West, wouldn't settle for anything less. "I'm not really bloodthirsty," he wrote to Truman, "but I will never feel the case is closed until I see that pair drip [*sic*] through the hole."[26] Capote was not so blunt, but he had taken the precaution to ask permission to attend Smith and Hickock's hanging. On Truman's behalf, Cliff Hope wrote to Robert J. Kaiser, director of Penal Institutions, requesting that Capote be allowed to serve as a witness. Kaiser replied, "I can tell you quite frankly that I would not recommend to the Warden such permission. Numerous people have made a similar request, and I can anticipate many more in the event an execution date becomes imminent."[27]

Until the book was in print, it was important that Truman remain in good standing with the folks of Garden City and Holcomb. He would need some of them to sign legal agreements. In the spirit of reciprocating their hospitality, for instance, Truman let it be known that he would welcome a visit from anyone who happened to be in New York. But he was surprised when Duane West, the Finney County prosecutor, took him up on the offer. West had never acted friendly to Truman and Nelle, and Capote had already whittled down his role in the book to a nub. West wrote to say that he and his wife would be attending a Red Cross convention in Manhattan in May 1964. Inwardly, Truman groaned. He called Nelle and asked her to please help him by playing hostess. She agreed, which meant getting gussied up, one of her least favorite things to do.

They fêted the out-of-towners by pulling out all the stops. First, they escorted them to a performance of *Hello, Dolly!*. Then, after the curtain, Truman played his trump card by escorting everyone backstage to meet the show's star, Carol Channing. Next it was off to Sardi's for a late dinner, during which the author pointed out a caricature of himself hanging on the restaurant's wall of celebrities. When the two couples finally parted, Truman breathed a sigh of relief. "I spent all of last week in the city—where [I] was caught by Mr. Duane West," Truman wrote to the Deweys. "Nelle and I (for our sins) took them to see 'Hello, Dolly'—ugh. I thought he was bad, but *the wife is worse!* The End. What a pair! Never again."[28] A few weeks later, he followed up with a letter to West, recounting their good time together and asking him to sign a release. The release stated that West would never write about the Clutter murders.

But West was a "good ol' boy" who could tell when he was being had, Nye said, and he didn't take the bait. "Now I know why we were treated so royally in New York," West said later, apparently convinced Nelle was in on it, too. Capote was angry, but tried to conceal his frustration in a chilly reply. "If you do not care to sign the release, that is of course your privelege [*sic*]. But please do not think, as I am told you do, that this matter of the release was why I tried to be hospitable during your New York visit. My motive was much simpler: I liked and respected you—and because you wrote to advise me of your impending trip, assumed you have some regard for me."[29]

Things went better a few months later when Harrison Smith, Perry Smith's attorney, arrived with his children for a visit. Again, Nelle and Truman rolled out the red carpet. They guided the Smith family to the 21 Club for dinner, where Bennett Cerf and his wife were waiting. (The attorney recognized Cerf as the "guy from 'What's My Line?.'") And the top-drawer treatment had its intended effect. "It was the thrill of a lifetime for my kids," said Smith. Capote also mentioned that his apartment was available for months at a time—why didn't Harrison keep that in mind for the family's next trip? "You know," said Smith, "he must have thought I was somewhat of a good Joe if he'd invite me to use his apartment."[30]

Whether Lee had any second thoughts about helping Capote manipulate the people he needed for his book isn't clear. All she would say about her role in assisting him was, "It was the sort of obligation I was proud to pay back."[31] The irony is Capote was using her, too. It seemed as if the process of reporting and writing the book had transformed him into a person who was, more than ever, completely self-centered and willing to exploit any of his friends in his own self-aggrandizing quest for fame and fortune. About the time he had written all but the final chapter of *In Cold Blood*, Capote stopped off in Topeka to see KBI detective Harold Nye at his home. While they were talking about the case and the final stages of the book, Nye remarked. "Well, Nelle will certainly play a part in all this."

"*No*," Capote said emphatically, "she was just there."

That response never sat well with Nye. "As well as they knew each other," he said, looking back, "there is no reason not to give some credit to her."[32]

Shortly before the visits of the Wests and Smiths to New York, Nelle gave one of her last interviews, in March 1964, which also happened to be her best. She appeared on Roy Newquist's evening radio show, *Counterpoint,* on WQXR in New York. Newquist, a Midwesterner, loved everything about books and writers. He had studied creative writing under Sinclair Lewis and Mari Sandoz; then, bowing to the exigencies of having to make a living, he went into advertising. But his syndicated book reviews and radio program eventually became a second career. Once a month, he commuted from his Chicago-area home for his broadcast in New York. A genial and engaging man, he had the ability to put people at ease. And Nelle, normally given to bantering with reporters and deflecting personal questions, opened up as she never had about her work and her aims as a writer.

She described herself to Newquist as someone who "*must* write. . . . I like to write. Sometimes I'm afraid that I like it too much because when I get into work I don't want to leave it. As a result I'll go for days and days without leaving the house or wherever I happen to be. I'll go out long enough to get papers and pick up some food and that's it. It's strange, but instead of hating writing I love it too much." Newquist asked her to name the contemporary writers she admired most. At the top of her list she put her friend Capote.

"There's probably no better writer in this country today than Truman Capote. He is growing all the time. The next thing coming from Capote is not a novel—it's a long piece of reportage, and I think it is going to make him bust loose as a novelist. He's going to have even deeper dimension to his work. Capote, I think, is the greatest crafts-man we have going."

About her own ambition as a writer, she expressed a desire to write more and better novels in the vein of *To Kill a Mockingbird.*

> I hope to goodness that every novel I do gets better and better, not worse and worse. I would like, however, to do one thing, and I've never spoken much about it because it's such a personal thing. I would like to leave some record of the kind of life that existed in a very small world. I hope to do this in several novels—to chronicle something that seems to be very quickly going down the drain. This is small-town middle-class southern life as opposed to the Gothic, as opposed to *Tobacco Road,* as opposed to plantation life.
>
> As you know, the South is still made up of thousands of tiny towns. There is a very definite social pattern in these towns that fascinates me. I think it is a rich social pattern. I would simply like to put down all I know about this because I believe that there is something univer-sal in this little world, something decent to be said for it, and something to lament in its passing.

And then she added a remark that set the bar high for herself—perhaps too high, in hindsight—but one that seemed plausible for a writer who had already written one of the most popular books since World War II.

"In other words," she said, "all I want to be is the Jane Austen of south Alabama."[33]

In the summer of 1964, with her novel still unfinished, she opted for a vacation on Fire Island, hoping for a salutary effect on her imagination by combining work and play. The Browns were staying on the island for several months and invited her as their guest. Michael had written and produced a musical revue called the *Wonderful World of Chemis-try* for the Du Pont pavilion at the 1964 New York World's Fair. A dozen times a day, performers clad in space-age tights of white and orange, and white bowlers with sprays of Styrofoam molecules, sang and danced the story of chemistry from ancient Greece to modern times. The show would run for a year, and as Michael and Joy liked to do with financial windfalls, they were celebrating.

Nelle's accumulating fortune, on the other hand, continued to worry her, because her income had catapulted her into a tax bracket associated with the rich. The situation was at odds with the simple lifestyle she preferred. "We know that Nelle Harper wishes these checks would not come in every few months, but I'm sure we understand that there's no way of stopping them," Williams wrote to Alice in August, enclosing another check.[34] The original J. B. Lippincott edition of *To Kill a Mockingbird* was still selling, and the Popular Library paperback had sold about five million copies. *Reader's Digest* magazine continued to distribute two million copies of the novel's abridged version. There were six hardbound editions in German, an Italian version, and the Swiss book club Ex Libris had chosen it as a selection. The novel continued to sell vigorously in England, in both the Heinemann and Penguin editions. British Reader's Digest Condensed Books and its branches in Australia, New Zealand, and South Africa distributed the novel as a bonus to new members. During the summer Nelle was on the island, translations in Hungary, Romania, and Greece appeared. The U.S. Information Agency was looking into publishing translated editions in the Middle East. Nelle had received invitations to speak all over the world. Even in the Soviet Union, beyond the reach of copyright, audiences packed a playhouse to see an unauthorized adaptation of the novel for the stage.

To check in with his bestselling client, Maurice Crain took the thirty-minute ferry ride to Fire Island. It was obvious to him from a glance that Lee wasn't going to get much done on her new book. Joy Brown was nine months pregnant, and the couple's two little boys were at the age when they raced between the cottage and the beach all day. Not long after Crain departed for the mainland, Joy ignored her doctor's advice to go home to Manhattan because she was due. One night, after the last ferry from the island had left, "Mike had to get a patrol boat and hire an ambulance to rush her to the hospital," Williams wrote Alice Lee. "She got there just in time as the baby was born only fifteen minutes after she got there."[35] In circumstances suitable for a romantic comedy, Nelle pitched in, putting her work aside, and helping the Browns get a handle on the pandemonium.

She stayed on all through September, being a good sport, while Crain and Williams went up to the Old Stone House without her. Perhaps in a bid to induce Nelle to return to Connecticut, where she could enjoy peace and quiet, Williams wrote Alice, "We talk to Harper Lee on the phone almost every day, but we go to Connecticut on the weekends, so do not get to see her. I have not been out to Fire Island yet, and feel sure that I won't get around to making the trip this season. . . . Wish we were greeting the Lee sisters. I can realize [sic] it has been a year since you all were here."[36]

Nelle stopped off only briefly in the city before taking the train to Monroeville for the holidays. But then, the third week of January 1965, she was involved in a terrible kitchen accident. She "burned herself very badly, especially her right hand. It seems some sort of pan caught fire and exploded," Capote wrote to Perry Smith. Friends called and sent cards from New York and Kansas as word spread that the accident was serious and Nelle was in the hospital.

With her hand wrapped in white gauze from her fingers to her forearm, she was limited to reading and answering correspondence with Alice's help. It would be months before doctors would know whether she needed plastic surgery. Perhaps because she was out of action at the typewriter, Nelle accepted an invitation of the sort that she would normally have refused on the grounds that she was "in no way a lecturer or philosopher."

Colonel Jack Capp, course director of English 102 at the U.S. Military Academy at West Point, had added *To Kill a Mockingbird* to the freshman syllabus. With the concurrence of the department head, he ventured to invite Lee to address the freshman class of cadets. There was a precedent: three years earlier, William Faulkner had accepted a token honorarium of $100 for speaking. "She was interested," recalled Colonel Capp, "but deferred acceptance until we could meet her in New York to discuss details. Midmorning on the appointed day, Mike Cousland, a well-featured, mannerly bachelor major and I went to Harper's pied-à-terre in Manhanttan, a small apartment on the upper East

Side." It was only 10:30, but Lee insisted on pouring mixed drinks. After a nice get-to-know-you chat, a date was suggested and Nelle agreed. Then she insisted they go to Sardi's for lunch. More drinks followed, after which "Mike and I floated happily back up the Hudson" behind the driver of an Army sedan to West Point.[37]

In March, the thirty-nine-year-old writer arrived on the campus, located fifty miles north of New York City on a promontory overlooking the Hudson River. The talk was scheduled for the auditorium, and until Nelle took her seat on the stage, the seven hundred young men in gray uniforms remained standing. "After the introduction formalities, she began lighting a cigarette," said Capps, "but, turning to Major Cousland and referring to the cadet on her left, asked, 'Can he smoke?' 'No,' said Mike, 'he can't.' 'Then I can't either,' she replied and stubbed out her cigarette in the nearest ashtray. Once the cadets were seated, they studied their speaker. She was "conservatively garbed in a simple dark dress," according to Gus Lee, who later wrote *Honor and Duty* about his experiences at West Point, "her hair wrapped in a conservative bun atop her head. Her voice was softly Southern, with high musical notes, and crystal clear in a hall that was utterly silent."[38]

"This is very exciting," she said slowly, "because I do not speak at colleges. The prospect of it is too intimidating. Surely, it's obvious—rows of bright, intense, focused students, some even of the sciences, all of them analyzing my every word and staring fixedly at me—this would terrify a person such as myself. So I wisely agreed to come here, where the atmosphere would be far more relaxing and welcoming than on a rigid, strict, rule-bound, and severely disciplined college campus."

For the first time since becoming a class, the young men laughed together, and followed their laughter with a roar of applause.

Knowing that the young men were away from home, many for the first time, she made a subtle comparison between aspects of *To Kill a Mockingbird* and the cadets' future mission as soldiers:

When we seek to replace family in new environs, we seek to reestablish trust, and love, and comfort. But too often we end up establishing difference instead of love. We like to have all our comforts and familiars about us, and tend to push away that which is different, and worrisome.

That is what happened to Boo Radley, and to Tom Robinson. They were not set apart by evil men, or evil women, or evil thoughts. They were set apart by an evil past, which good people in the present were ill equipped to change. The irony is, if we divide ourselves for our own comfort, *no one* will have comfort. It means we must bury our pasts by seeing them, and destroy our differences through learning another way.

Regarding people who were difficult to accept or respect, Nelle said, "Our response to these people represents our earthly test. And I think, that these people enrich the wonder of our lives. It is they who most need our kindness, *because* they seem less deserving. After all, *anyone* can love people who are lovely."

Then she reflected on how writing *To Kill a Mockingbird* had influenced her life. "People in the press have asked me if this book is descriptive of my own childhood, or of my own family. Is this very important? I am simply one who had time and chance to write. I was that person before, and no one in the press much cared about the details of my life. I am yet that same person now, who only misses her former anonymity."[39]

A few weeks after speaking at West Point, Nelle received another request for her presence, one that couldn't be further away in spirit from speaking to an audience of hopeful, forward-looking young men. Perry Smith and Dick Hickock asked her to attend their executions. They had the right to choose witnesses and they had both named Nelle and Truman.

"Truman tracked down Nelle to the Old Stone House and called her there," Joy Hafner-Bailey, Maurice's niece, remembered. "He said the killers had asked for her and he needed her besides for this final episode that would close the book. But she didn't want to go. She refused." Nelle formally replied to Warden Charles McAtee that she would not attend.[40]

The killers' appeals had been heard and denied, twice, by the U.S. Supreme Court. Finally, five years after their conviction in Garden City, they were sentenced to hang on April 14, 1965, between midnight and 2:00 A.M. The scaffold was a simple structure made of rough, unfinished lumber located in a jumbled warehouse at Kansas State Penitentiary, in Leavenworth. Inmates called the spot "The Corner." Thirteen steps led to the platform, where a noose dangled over a trapdoor. Fifteen men had been hanged there.

On the night of the fourteenth, the executioner, an anonymous paid volunteer from Missouri, sped through the rain in a black Cadillac. He wore a long, dingy coat and a large felt hat to hide his face. Smith, assuming both Nelle and Truman had denied his request, wrote a hasty note at 11:45 P.M.: "I want you to know that I cannot condemn you for it & understand. Not much time left but want you both to know that I've been sincerely grateful for your friend[ship] through the years and everything else. I'm not very good at these things—I want you both to know that I have become very affectionate toward you. But harness time. Adios Amigos. Best of everything. Your friend always, Perry."[41]

In a hotel nearby, Truman agonized and wept in his room, trying to decide whether he should go or not. Finally, he hurried to the prison in time to say goodbye. A handful of reporters and KBI agents were waiting in the warehouse. Hickock arrived first, trussed in a leather harness that held his arms to his sides. "Nice to see you," he said pleasantly, smiling at faces he recognized. He was pronounced dead at 12:41 A.M. When it was Smith's turn on the gallows, twenty minutes later, Capote became sick to his stomach.

On April 17, Al Dewey submitted the final report on the Clutter murders, ending it with the statement that it was a "joint report of Special Agents Roy Church, C. C. Duntz, Harold Nye and the writer. The executions were witnessed by the above four mentioned agents." An unidentified hand wrote "Closed" on the outside of the folder.[42]

Capote flew home to New York immediately. "Perry and Dick were executed last Tuesday," he wrote to his friend Cecil Beaton. "I was there because they wanted me to be. It was a terrible experience. Something that I will never really get over. One day I will tell you about it—if you can bear it."[43]

To mark the killers' side-by-side graves in row twenty-nine of Mount Muncie Cemetery, Truman paid $70.50 apiece for basic granite headstones.

* * *

With such a macabre event behind her, Lee could look forward to Maurice Crain accompanying her on a visit to her hometown in May. "Nelle Harper and Maurice are leaving Sunday for their trip to Alabama," Annie Laurie Williams wrote to James Mitchell, a British mystery author who wrote under the name James Munro. "Maurice will spend about a week visiting her family and then will fly back to New York. She will stay in Monroeville, Alabama (that is her home as you know) until late August when she comes back to New York to see her plastic surgeon."[44]

Nelle's friends in New York were fascinated by the aura around Monroeville created by the novel.[45] Crain had grown up in small Texas towns, but he wanted to take a gander and compare for himself Nelle's description of Monroeville with fictional Maycomb. A lot had changed, of course. "I don't know what you'd really care to see in Monroeville, except maybe a new courthouse standing beside an old one, or an under- wear factory," Nelle said apologetically to another visitor later that summer.[46] But Crain was not disappointed, especially because Alice and Nelle, both history buffs, arranged for a tour of famous southern battlefields.

Returning from his journey to the Deep South, Crain raved to his wife about the wonderful time he'd had. "Maurice has never expressed to you folks what he felt about the memorable trip," Williams wrote to Alice. "Just being away from the office for awhile helped Maurice and he has been much calmer since he got back. You all were so good to him and he did appreciate it. . . . It is almost seven o'clock and Maurice gets hungry around this time (we used to eat at eight) so I will stop talking and go along to Stouffers with him."[47]

Lately Crain had been getting hungrier earlier. And Williams noticed that even though he scooped up the cake and cookies she put out for teatime, he wasn't gaining any weight. Although no one knew it yet, he was showing early symptoms of cancer from years of heavy smoking.

For the rest of the summer of 1965 in Monroeville, Nelle buckled down again to work. It had been five years since the publication of *To Kill a Mockingbird*. Although novelists often go years between books, she had been trading on her first novel for quite some time. But now she shunned interviews: first, because questions about *To Kill a Mockingbird* had become redundant; second, because she had gone on record a number of times that a second novel was in the offing. So far, it was a promise she hadn't made good on. What she needed was "paper, pen, and privacy," the formula that had produced her first success.

She made one exception to turning down interviews, however. A young Mississippian, Don Keith, approached her about granting one for a small quarterly, the *Delta Review*. She consented to a "visit," not an interview, perhaps because she saw in the earnest young writer a glimpse of herself from her *Rammer Jammer* days.

Keith, who would go on to become a first-rate journalist in New Orleans, provided a remarkably fresh portrait of Nelle, placing her in the context of a writer at work. "When I met her that Sunday afternoon in Monroeville, Alabama, she was the same as I knew she would be. We had spoken twice briefly over the telephone. I had written her two letters; she had written me one. But regardless of the long distance acquaintance, we exchanged hello kisses in that familiar manner characteristic of Southerners. Once inside the modest but comfortable brick house," they settled down to a "long talk over coffee and cigarettes. She consumes both in abundance."

The young visitor was the first to use the term *recluse* in connection with Nelle, but he did so for the sake of denying she was one. "Harper Lee is no recluse," he said. "She is no McCullers or Salinger whose veneer of notoriety cannot be punctured to reveal, after all, another individual. She is real and down-to-earth as is the woman next door who puts up fig preserves in the spring and covers her chrysanthemums in winter.

"During most of our afternoon together, she sat at a card table placed in front of an armchair in the living room. On the table was a typewriter, not new, and an abundance of paper. A stack of finished manuscript lay nearby, work on a new novel." Nelle explained that she hadn't set a deadline for it, and that her publisher, Lippincott, didn't know the entire plot yet. But she hinted that it was set in a southern town again, perhaps Maycomb. Whether Jem, Scout, and Atticus would figure in the story, she wouldn't say.

Also piled near the table were new books, sent by publishers in the hope that she might pen a blurb for their back covers, or even write a review. Alfred A. Knopf had sent her four such requests, for instance, but she never replied.

The conversation turned to another literary project that needed her attention. She was scheduled to leave the next week for New York, where she was to read, before publication, Capote's finished manuscript.

"It must seem a chore," Keith said.

"But one I'm looking forward to," replied Nelle. As always, she was Capote's friend and advocate.[48]

It was a pivotal interview, this final "visit" that Lee consented to. Despite Keith's avowal that "Harper Lee is no recluse," she was in fact becoming one. Granted, she disliked publicity, but unlike most writers she also evinced a continual lack of interest in participating in the literary scene. She didn't accept a post as a writer-in-residence at a college, or speak at a writers' conference, or participate in the Iowa Writers' Workshop, for example, although she knew the director, Paul Engle, well. When friends from Alabama called her and expressed an interest in meeting certain authors during a visit to New York, Lee replied, "I don't know them myself."[49] Once *To Kill a Mockingbird* was launched and sailing on its own, Nelle turned back to being "the woman next door who puts up fig preserves in the spring and covers her chrysanthemums in winter." She was withdrawing into an ordinary life and writing, as she once described Jane Austen, "cameo-like, in that little corner of the world of hers." Perhaps her temperament and interests weren't as suited to the arena of literature as she had once dreamed. Reentering the difficult and demanding fray of public literary life was a sacrifice and, apparently, she was unwilling to make it.

Besides needing to be in New York to read Truman's typewritten manuscript of *In Cold Blood*, it was time for Nelle to let a doctor examine her injured hand and see if surgery would be required. Everyone hoped for a good prognosis. "We were all looking at her hand and were pleased and surprised how beautifully it has healed. We hope when she sees Dr. Stark on the 19th [of September] that he will tell her she doesn't have to have the operation," Williams wrote to Alice.[50]

Lee could hold a pen or pencil again, but her fingers' movement was slightly constricted and her handwriting—normally open and highly legible—looked compressed. Perhaps because of this, she jotted only succinct comments on Capote's pages. Regarding a piece of dialogue, for instance, she noted, "Everybody talks in short sentences. Mannered."[51]

In August, however, *McCall's* magazine published her first piece— "When Children Discover America"—since *Vogue* had carried "Love—In Other Words" in 1961. But the new article, just like the *Vogue* essay, showed none of Nelle's hallmark humor or vividness. In fact, a strong whiff of sanctimony replaced the exuberance that readers would have expected after *To Kill a Mockingbird*. It was as if her high spirits and insouciant wit were being tamped down by too much self-consciousness, perhaps a result of her being in the public eye.

> I do not think the youngest or even the most jaded citizen could go to Washington and through the Capitol or the Smithsonian Institution without having the feeling of yes, we *are* something; yes, we *do* have a history. . . . Younger children may not respond in words, but they will drink everything in with their eyes, and fill their minds with awareness and wonder. It's an experience they will enjoy and remember all their lives; and it will give them greater pride in their own country.[52]

She finished reviewing *In Cold Blood* and then hurried off to Fire Island again to spend time with the Browns, who had returned for another season. She was almost done with a draft of her second novel and hoped to polish it up before showing it to Hohoff.

Capote, meanwhile, was certain he was on the verge of volcanic fame, and he was feeling ecstatic about it. The *New Yorker* would begin serializing *In Cold Blood* at the end of September, in four consecutive issues. Anticipating that this would be his best book yet, he had a huge party in mind, the Black and White Ball, which would set high society on its ear. Even though the date for the ball was more than a year off, he was already dropping tantalizing hints about the exclusive guest list, and promising invitations to those with whom he wanted to curry favor.

So he was stunned when Harold Nye threatened to throw a wrench into everything.

As a perfunctory last piece of business, Truman had mailed Nye a copy of the manuscript. He asked Nye to give it a final read-through for accuracy. But Nye, reading it from beginning to end for the first time, saw that Alvin Dewey, the KBI's "office boy" as he later bitterly characterized him, had been cast as the book's hero. When Truman arrived in Kansas City, right before the first magazine installment was scheduled to run, the disgruntled detective abruptly dug in his heels.

"Truman and I, we got into a heck of a fight," said Nye. "That happened in the Muehlebach Hotel on 12th and Baltimore Avenue when we got together. He brought down, I can't remember—he was an editor of the *New Yorker*, who was also a 'piccolo player'—and my wife and I went over to the hotel and had dinner with them. Well, this came up after our dinner and we went through the manuscript and I had told him I would not approve it, because it wasn't true."

Capote was aghast, and went into a rage reminiscent of one of his boyhood tantrums.

"And we got into a hell of a fight right in the Muehlebach Hotel," said Nye. "He marched me outside and he was screaming. He called me a tyrant and told my wife I was a tyrant. Now, I had been invited to the Black and White Ball and he told me that night, 'Cancel your invitation!' and that I'd never get another one. Never did, of course."[53]

Capote threw aside Nye's objections, and on the strength of his own word and the *New Yorker*'s exhaustive fact-checking, the 135,000-word serial began anyway, on September 25, 1965, beginning with the oft-quoted sentence "The village of Holcomb stands on the high wheat plains of western Kansas, a lonesome area that other Kansans call 'out there.'"

The *New Yorker*'s circulation soared, and sightseers poured down the elm-lined road to the Clutters' old house.[54]

Nelle's physician decided that an operation would be necessary after all; otherwise, scar tissue would permanently impair her hand. "Just a wee note to tell you that Maurice and I will take Nelle Harper to St. Luke's on Sunday," Annie Laurie Williams wrote Alice Lee in September. "Monday Maurice will go up alone to be with Nelle Harper when she comes out from under and opens her eyes. He will then telephone you. And when the doctor says she can be released Maurice will take her back to her apartment and see that she is fed and taken care of until she feels well enough to let him leave. Nelle Harper thinks this is a lot of nonsense, but we don't pay any attention to what she says, as we want to be with her."[55]

The operation was a success.[56] And the timing was perfect, because Lee's high school English teacher Gladys Watson-Burkett was coming to New York at her invitation. The teacher and former student were about to embark on a memorable month-long trip to England on October 8, and Nelle had insisted on paying for the excursion. "It was a thank-you for editing her manuscript," said Sarah Countryman, Gladys's daughter.[57]

"Harper Lee and Gladys got away on schedule yesterday," Williams informed Alice. "Maurice went with them and saw that they got aboard the *Queen Elizabeth* with all their baggage. The day before Nelle Harper brought Gladys in to meet us and we enjoyed our brief visit with her."[58]

A completed second novel had not materialized before Nelle left, and Tay Hohoff was getting tired of the delay. Williams sprang to Nelle's defense: "I told her that I thought it was better the way things turned out about her second book, as she was under pressure and thought she had to write it this summer," she assured Alice.

It doesn't have to be written according [to] her publisher's schedule and I think she should take her time and not try to work on the book until she gets back down to Alabama with her folks. . . . Too many people up here ask too many questions and she seems to feel that she is expected to turn in another manuscript, because everybody says, "Are you working on another novel." I always say "Of course, she is going to write another book but she is not *going to be hurried.*" It is difficult, as you know to follow Mockingbird as this book was such an all-around success that measuring up to that book is almost impossible. *But she is a writer* and her next book will be a success too, and will have some of the flavor of the first one. I am saying all of this to you, because I want you to know that she was depressed when she didn't come back from Fire Island with a finished manuscript. *She doesn't have to be driven by her* publisher to turn in another script, as she is in the driver's seat and can be independent.[59]

Lee returned from England in November. As a parting gift for her favorite teacher, she took Watson-Burkett, Crain, and Williams as her guests to see Beatrice Lillie in Hugh Martin and Timothy Gray's musical *High Spirits*. Watson-Burkett had never seen a Broadway show before, and it was a fitting send-off. Then, a few weeks later, Nelle followed her to Monroeville.

In Cold Blood would be out soon. The magazine serialization had served as a drum roll leading up to publication. For Harper Lee, it would be the end to a long experience. More than five years earlier, she had bucked up Truman in Garden City when he was convinced that they would never get past people's suspicions about them. Then, for two months, she had served as his listening post in town and made friends with the folks he needed to interview. Later, she had accompanied him on return trips: once to attend the trial, and two more times just to go over the territory—sifting, sifting for more information. "Without her deep probing of the people of that little town, I could never have done the job I did with it."[60] And finally, she had tightened up his manuscript while she was supposed to be working on her second novel.

So when, in January 1966, she opened the first edition of *In Cold Blood*, she was shocked to find the book dedicated to her, a patronizing gesture in light of her contribution—"With Love and Gratitude," it said. And, out of the blue, she found she had to share Capote's thanks with his longtime lover, Jack Dunphy.

Lee was not a woman who was quick to anger or demanding of attention. Still, "she was very hurt that she didn't get more credit because she wrote half that book—really upset about that. She told me several times," recalled R. Philip Hanes, who became friends with her later that year.[61] She was "written out of that book at the last minute," maintained Claudia Durst Johnson, a scholar who has published extensively about *To Kill a Mockingbird*. Not even the perfunctory acknowledgment page paid tribute to Nelle's large and important contribution.[62]

Capote's failure to appreciate her was more than an oversight or a letdown. It was a betrayal. Since childhood, Truman had been testing their friendship, perhaps because, deep down, he believed that no one, including Nelle, really liked him—not since his parents had withdrawn their love. He was constantly showing off to get people's attention and approval, all the while gauging their response. But hurting her so gratuitously, perhaps to see what she would do, spoke volumes about whether she could trust him. She would remain his friend, but their relationship had suffered its first permanent crack.

If Capote suspected the amount of damage he had done to their lifelong friendship, he doesn't seem to have taken special steps to repair it. For instance, he could have counteracted the rumors that he had written all or part of *To Kill a Mockingbird*, but he never went to any strenuous lengths to do so.[63] And later, when *In Cold Blood* didn't win a National Book Award or a Pulitzer Prize, he used a little trick of backhanding his friend's success by asking interviewers if they'd ever heard of her book. What he did to Nelle was the beginning of his deliquescing into the sad person he became at the end of his life.

Harper Lee's disappointment over the *In Cold Blood* affair was soon to be compounded by another incident. In 1966, the Hanover County School Board in Richmond, Virginia, ordered all copies of *To Kill a Mockingbird* removed from the county's school library shelves. In the board's opinion, the novel was "immoral literature."[64]

The episode began when a prominent local physician, father of a Hanover County student and a county Board of Education trustee, protested that a novel about rape was "improper for our children to read." On the strength of his criticism, the board voted to ban *To Kill a Mockingbird* from the county schools. The next day, the *Richmond News-Leader* editorialized about the board's "asinine performance" and created a Bumble Beadle Fund, named for the officious guardian of children's morals in *Oliver Twist*. The first fifty students of the local high school who requested a copy of *To Kill a Mockingbird* would receive one gratis, courtesy of the newspaper.

For almost two weeks, the controversy went back and forth on the letters-to-the-editor page, until the *News-Leader* called a halt by allowing Nelle to have the last word. She fired with both barrels.

> Surely it is plain to the simplest intelligence that "To Kill a Mockingbird" spells out in words of seldom more than two syllables a code of honor and conduct, Christian in its ethic, that is the heritage of all Southerners. To hear that the novel is "immoral" has made me count the years between now and 1984, for I have yet to come across a better example of doublethink. I feel, however, that the problem is one of illiteracy, not Marxism. Therefore I enclose a small contribution to the Beadle Bumble Fund that I hope will be used to enroll the Hanover County School Board in any first grade of its choice.[65]

Eventually, *To Kill a Mockingbird* was restored to Hanover County school libraries because of a technicality in board policy. But the Richmond debate over the book's suitability for young readers was the first of many in the ensuing years. As more schools added *To Kill a Mockingbird* to their reading lists, the book also joined the list of the one hundred novels most often targeted for banning.

Despite indications that Lee was close to finishing her second book, the spring of 1966 found her accepting another responsibility. President Lyndon Baines Johnson had appointed her to the National Council on the Arts. It was going to be a long commitment, six years, which would cut into her writing time when she was already far behind in delivering a second manuscript to Hohoff. But it's likely that she accepted the appointment because Gregory Peck had urged her to say yes.

How the council would function was left in the hands of the chairman, theatrical producer Roger Stevens. One morning, during the council's first meeting, Stevens went for a walk with council member and industrialist R. Philip Hanes, Jr. " 'We can't be all going off the council at the same time,' he said, 'so we're going to have two-year terms, four-year-terms, and six-year terms. I'll draw names out of a hat and see what happens. But I'll tell you right now, your number's going to be six! And Gregory Peck—he's a hack actor—he's going to be a number two.'"

"Well," recalled Hanes, "Gregory hadn't been on there a year before he took off for several months and he went to every single repertory theater in America: to Providence, to Cleveland, to San Francisco, to Houston. He went to every single one and saw at least one play, sometimes two. And he came back to the council and produced a huge written report. Stevens was stunned!"[66] As a result of Peck's research, repertory theater companies and the training of young actors occupied an equal place beside larger initiatives on the council's agenda. Then, probably because Peck was now in a position to pull some strings, the number of members on the council increased from twenty-four to twenty-six, to make room for the abstract painter Richard Diebenkorn and for Harper Lee.

"Gregory just worshipped her," said Hanes. "Often he would be seated studying his papers, and when Harper would walk in, he would jump up like a bolt of lightning and pull out her chair."[67]

Although the nation had more pressing needs than putting money behind the arts—particularly with the Vietnam War claiming American lives everyday—"If anything," said council member and sculptor Jimilu Mason, "we felt we had to do more in the arts to counteract the effects of the war."[68] Lee reserved her comments at council meetings for times when she believed she needed to speak up. "She was quiet, unassuming—concise, terse, powerful, and gained the love and respect of all. She only spoke when she had something to say. It was always something important and always heeded. And often her remarks were wry. She would seldom say more than just a sentence, but they would drop down like a small bomb. She had the total respect of Roger Stevens."[69] When she couldn't be found during a social hour before dinner, she could often be spotted with John Steinbeck, standing in a corner discussing favorite books.[70]

Though she wasn't by nature a joiner, Lee would do favors for friends such as Peck, provided there was no fanfare about it. Students at

Monroe County High School became accustomed to seeing the Pulitzer Prize–winning author making an annual visit to Marjorie Nichols's English class to discuss *To Kill a Mockingbird*. They were often so awed by her that they didn't know what to say.

She "was very frazzled," said one, "she was matronly, she was kind of disheveled. She was a person who didn't seem to care about appearances. She wore a beige skirt with the blouse tucked in unevenly. She dressed like a woman who seemed much older, not like a woman who spent time in New York. She had a loud voice and she was rather brusque. She just took over the class. After talking a little bit about the writing of the book, she asked if there were any questions, but of course there weren't any because we were too intimidated. So, with a remark like, 'See you next week at bridge, Marj!' she left."[71]

Interestingly, the novel was not taught throughout the Monroe County school system, despite the story being set in Monroeville. Although it was on the approved reading list, few teachers used it in their classrooms. A resident and former teacher said there was a "certain reluctance to get into the controversial issues of race relations, rape accusations, and so on. Some also felt that perhaps some local folks did not at that time regard the book as great literature. Plus, there may have been more people in the 1960s and '70s who would have thought they recognized their family members as characters in the novel and been offended."[72]

In addition to her annual visits to the local high school, Lee also accepted an invitation from another close friend, Anne Gary Pannell, president of Sweet Briar College, to speak to Professor William Smart's creative writing classes. Smart had only recently joined the faculty as a young instructor, and was nervous about squiring Nelle around the campus for several days. When the train pulled into the station with Lee aboard in late October, Smart studied the passengers as they descended to the platform.

"Are you Harper Lee?" he said cautiously to a stout woman with salt-and-pepper hair.

"I sure am!" she said and handed him her suitcase.[73]

The eighty students who attended her talks received never-to-be-repeated insights into her experience about the craft of writing.

"It's absolutely essential that a writer know himself," Lee began, "for until he knows his abilities and limitations, his talents and problems, he will be unable to produce anything of real value. Secondly, you must be able to look coldly at what you do. The writer must know for whom he writes, why he writes, and if his writing says what he means for it to say. Writing is, in a way, a contest of knowing, of seeing the dream, of getting there, and of achieving what you set out to do. The simplest way to reach this goal is to simply say what you mean as clearly and precisely as you know how."

In answer to a student's question about her typical workday, Nelle described a regime that must have made some of the young listeners quail. She said that when she was writing *To Kill a Mockingbird*, she had stayed at her desk six to twelve hours a day and ended up with, perhaps, one page of finished manuscript. "To be a serious writer requires discipline that is iron fisted. It's sitting down and doing it whether you think you have it in you or not. Everyday. Alone. Without interruption. Contrary to what most people think, there is no glamour to writing. In fact, it's heartbreak most of the time."

And to disabuse the novice writers listening to her of the notion that merely completing a novel would guarantee its publication, she added, "it's just as hard to write a bad novel as it is to write a good one. And if a writer does come up with a manuscript worthy of publication, it is assured that many pages of unpublished material have preceded it."[74]

Given the tone of her remarks, and her description of the demands of authorship, perhaps she was venting her frustration over failing to complete the second novel. Annie Laurie Williams had been alternately encouraging, unctuous, bantering, optimistic, quick to come to her defense, and confident that Harper Lee would deliver. But she didn't.

Lee's retreat and predictions about when the novel would be done became background noise. In 1962, when Williams and Crain were pressing her for a quick follow-up to *To Kill a Mockingbird*, another young woman had come to Williams, eager to do whatever was necessary to become a bestselling author. On the day of the appointment, she kept changing outfits over and over, trying to look like what she thought a high-powered literary agent would expect. She was a former television actress and she knew the importance of dressing the part.

The meeting went well, and afterwards she wrote excitedly in her diary that Williams had agreed to take her as a client. "As an actress," Williams reminded her, "when you're up for a part, if the producer says no—that's it. But with a book, if a publisher says no—you send it to another publisher. . . . It only takes one yes to make a hit."

The young woman was Jacqueline Susann. Her first novel, *Valley of the Dolls* (1966), became one of the most popular in American publishing history, with thirty million copies sold. She followed it up with *The Love Machine* (1969) and *Once Is Not Enough* (1972), becoming the first author to have three consecutive novels ranked first on the *New York Times* bestseller list. Critics dismissed her books as trash; some libraries refused to carry them; but she produced, and by the time she died at fifty-six of lung cancer, she had made herself and Annie Laurie Williams very, very rich.

On November 28, 1966, all of New York society was agog at Truman Capote's Black and White Ball, held at the Plaza Hotel. It was, Truman told the press, a "little masked ball for Kay Graham [president of the *Washington Post* and *Newsweek* magazine] and all my friends."[75] Five hundred and forty of his friends had received invitations, but the red-and-white admission tickets were printed only the week before, to prevent forgeries. Stairways and elevators were blocked, except for one elevator going up to the ballroom. From its doors emerged the glitterati of the times: politicians, scientists, painters, writers, composers, actors, producers, dress designers, social figures, and tycoons. Truman invited ten guests from Kansas, too, including Alvin and Marie Dewey and the widow of Judge Roland Tate. Secret Service agents made a mental note of everyone getting off the elevator, and the guests were announced as they entered the ballroom.

Nelle received an invitation, but she didn't attend. Perhaps her absence was an indication of how much she wanted to distance herself from *In Cold Blood* and everything associated with it, or maybe the crush of glamorous people was more than she could bear.

* * *

By January 1968, Maurice Crain's cancer had progressed to a point that "I have been urged by my doctors to curtail my activities somewhat in the future," he wrote to a writer who had submitted a manuscript for review. "I do not feel it would be fair to you or to my present clients to undertake any new projects at this time."[76]

Nelle was in limbo about what to do. Her novel was still unfinished, and Crain, who was not only her agent but also one of her dearest friends, was ill. He had been her bulwark against pressure from Lippincott to hurry up. He was the first one she saw when she opened her eyes after the surgery on her hand, and now he needed that kind of support. Naturally, however, Annie Laurie Williams wanted to spend more private time with her husband, and the two went for long weekends alone to the Old Stone House as often as they could.

Turning to another old friend to ease her worries, Lee temporarily patched up things with Capote, and the two of them went on a sentimental trip through Alabama.[77]

Despite the pleasure excursion, thoughts of death weren't far from Nelle's mind. A colleague on the National Council of the Arts, René D'Harnoncourt, director of the Museum of Modern Art, was hit while walking and killed by a drunk driver. "The news of René's death has no doubt reached you," she wrote to fellow council member Paul Engle, director of the Iowa Writers' Workshop. "A sad cruel thing. I for one shall miss him sorely. There is nothing of the slightest interest to report from Alabama."[78]

In spite of his illness, Crain continued to go into the office. He enjoyed his work and wouldn't hear of taking it easy. Characteristically, he put up a front of gruffness, even as his cancer treatments took their toll on his energy. An agent sent him a proposal for a book about deserters from the war in Vietnam. Crain, a former War World II bomber crewman and prisoner of war, sent back a reply that crackled with contempt: "It would be hard to find a subject which would interest me less or which I think less deserving of treatment at book length than the confused and bewildered Army deserters who have inflicted themselves upon the Swiss. Has it occurred to you that the younger generation has produced an extraordinarily high proportion of jerks—a much higher proportion than our own? The material is returned herewith."[79]

Six months later, Maurice was too ill to go into the office any longer. Because there were still commitments with authors and publishers that had to be shepherded to completion, Annie Laurie ran both her dramatic rights agency and Maurice's literary agency by herself. While she did that, Nelle took care of Maurice. There were hospital visits to make, errands to run, and appointments to keep with doctors. "Nelle was there for him," said his niece, Joy Hafner-Bailey. "There was no choice—Annie Laurie had to keep the business running."[80] When he became bedridden, Lee stayed with him most of the day until Annie Laurie could return in the evening.

On April 23, 1970, he died at age sixty-eight.

"I don't know whether you know my sad news. My husband died last April of cancer, so I have been 'going it alone' now for the past sad months," Williams wrote to a friend in barely decipherable handwriting that suggests she was still emotionally distraught.[81]

Lee disappeared from view. The death of her older friend had robbed her of her most valuable advocate and upset the balance of her relationship with Williams. The two women stopped seeing each other very often, probably because being together conjured up too many painful memories. Not long after Crain's death, Williams received a request asking if Horton Foote's screenplay of *To Kill a Mockingbird* could be adapted for the professional theater market. After not receiving an answer from Nelle for months, Williams wrote her a testy note, "Will you please tell me what I should say to Lucy Kroll? I hope that sometime soon you will have dinner with me."[82]

It's conceivable that the relationship between Nelle and Crain was something more than deep friendship. Because although Crain was a considerate man, it's hard to limit his role to agent in light of what he did for Nelle. Not only was he the first person she saw when she awoke from surgery; he was the one who cared for her at home while she was recuperating; he made a special trip out to Fire Island for the purpose of paying her a visit; he called her regularly, perhaps as often as once a week; he waved her off on the *Queen Elizabeth* for her celebratory trip to Britain; and, finally, he went to Alabama to meet her extended family. Despite all this, among his papers at Columbia University, there is not a single piece of correspondence from Nelle. It's as if the collection was scoured clean of the relationship. Yet, in the papers of Fred Gipson, another of Crain's clients, there are half a dozen letters from Crain, a few of which have Harper Lee as their main subject. The clues about the relationship are suggestive, but inconclusive. Even Capote was intrigued. In December 1961, he wrote to Alvin and Marie Dewey, "About Nelle. I am rather worried about her. *Just between us*, I have good reason to believe that she is unhappily in love with a man impossible to marry etc."[83]

Annie Laurie began to suffer health problems, and she lost interest in the agency. In September 1971, her sister Pamela Barnes informed Erskine Caldwell's wife, Virginia, "Annie Laurie intended writing you a personal letter but unfortunately she fell and fractured a rib and has been in the hospital. However, she asked me to write you and tell you that we are giving up our office . . . and have been trying to return books and scripts to authors."[84]

Lee's surrogate family, the community that had sustained her through the creation of her first novel and whom she had relied upon for guidance when she was a beginning writer, was growing smaller. She continued to see the Browns regularly whenever she was in New York, but their friendship was unrelated—except for the unforgettable Christmas loan she repaid—to her career as a writer. Maurice Crain had passed away and Annie Laurie Williams was living with relatives, having turned over care of the Old Stone House to her sister Fern. Truman's place in Nelle's life was uncertain because he was drinking and using drugs heavily, a result of strain caused by *In Cold Blood*, he said. Nelle was prepared to stand by him, but he was difficult, even to people who genuinely cared about him.

Getting a finished manuscript to Tay Hohoff no longer mattered, either, because Hohoff had retired from Lippincott in the early 1970s. Besides, the bloom was off the rose as far as bringing out another novel from Nelle Harper Lee was concerned. It had been more than ten years since *To Kill a Mockingbird*.

Hohoff was on her own since the death of her husband, Arthur, several years earlier. On the evening of January 4, 1974, her son-in-law, Dr. Grady Nunn, daughter Torrey, and granddaughter, also named

Tay, went to her apartment in New York to urge her to move in with them in Tuscaloosa, Alabama. "It was hardly an ideal solution," Dr. Nunn remembered. "Tay loved Manhattan, and the Deep South was a far cry from what she was accustomed to. But it would have worked. She had the heartfelt assurances of our affection and welcoming embrace. And she knew from visits with us in Tuscaloosa over the years that we attracted and were attracted to the kind of people with whom she was comfortable. Tay accepted our invitation, and it was settled."

The next morning, the Nunn family came to talk more about the arrangements, but Hohoff had passed away. "There was no response when we knocked on Tay's door. In the next few days we were gratefully kept busy doing all the things that had to be done and calling all the people who had to be notified. It fell to me to call Nelle Lee with the news."

And so she was deprived of the editor whom she trusted and who, many believe, had urged her on in the heavy revisions of the manuscript that became *To Kill a Mockingbird*.[85]

About the same time, a strange thing happened. Peter Griffiths, a film producer visiting Monroeville for the BBC, asked Alice Lee what ever happened to the second novel her sister was supposed to have been working on. According to Alice, just as Nelle was finishing the novel, a burglar broke into her apartment in New York and stole the manuscript.[86]

It's hard to believe that someone would make off with a ream of paper; besides, they were looking in the wrong place, as it turned out.

twelve

The Golden Goose

"Not just no, but *hell* no."
—HARPER LEE

Glimpses of Harper Lee during most of the 1970s and '80s were as infrequent as sightings of rare southern birds in New York's Central Park. In 1967 she moved to a new apartment, still on the Upper East Side, only her third address since arriving in the city almost twenty years earlier. All of the apartments where she had lived were within a fifteen-minute walk of one another, and none was particularly luxurious. She wasn't living like a rich person; that wasn't her style. The new place—a four-story brick building—would have looked quite ordinary to most passersby. "I couldn't pick it out from a hundred others," said a visiting friend.[1] It seemed the perfect camouflage for someone who wanted to go unnoticed. Lining her side of the street were a dozen stunted trees, which served more as identifiers of where residents should put their garbage cans once a week than as adornments for the neighborhood. The usual commercial properties interrupted the eye's sweep of the block where there was a dry cleaner's, a travel agency, and a restaurant that served wild game. The only hint of community was a storefront church.

Inside Lee's apartment, 1E, the décor was unexceptional, too. There were no indications that she was the author of a book that had sold nearly ten million copies by the late 1970s. A visitor trying to describe it years later could recall no particulars.

Slowly, Harper Lee's world was becoming more circumscribed. Although she continued her migratory pattern of returning to Monroeville every October and staying until spring, she stayed close to familiar haunts while in New York. "I honestly, *truly* have not the slightest idea *why* she lives in New York," said Capote in an interview. "I don't think she ever goes *out*."[2] When a friend visiting from Alabama suggested that they meet downtown for dinner, Nelle objected, "My God, I wouldn't go into downtown Manhattan for the world!"[3] Any new venture seemed to make her hesitate. Several times over the years she phoned Louise Sims, an acquaintance from her earliest days in New York, to set up a lunch date. But if Louise said, "I'll have to call you back," Nelle would reply "Okay, I'll get back to you," and hang up without giving a phone number where she could be reached. Horton Foote marveled that for years Nelle lived within blocks of mutual friends of theirs without ever contacting them.[4]

Instead, she preferred friends from long ago. She corresponded regularly with Ralph Hammond, a writer from her days on the *Rammer Jammer* at the University of Alabama. ("I've got a whole drawerful of letters from Nelle," he liked to boast, "she's my best friend in all of Alabama.")[5] And Joy Brown could always be relied on for shopping trips and jaunts to secondhand bookstores. But Nelle's oldest friend, Truman, whose ties spanned both Monroeville and New York, seemed to be undergoing a slow-motion breakdown she was unable to stop. Fears and regrets assailed him. When *People* magazine requested an interview in 1976, he brought Nelle along for comfort. As he was describing his unhappy childhood, she interjected that a kindergarten teacher in Monroeville had smacked his palm with a ruler because he knew how to read.

"It's true!" Capote wailed.

Glancing protectively at him, Nelle explained, "It was traumatic."[6]

Truman's deterioration became newsworthy in July 1978 when he appeared as a guest on *The Stanley Siegel Show* TV program in New York.[7] During the first few minutes of the program, he seemed all right, but gradually his speech became slurred and hesitant. Clearly, there were problems.

"What's going to happen unless you lick this problem of drugs and alcohol?" Siegel asked.

Seconds of dead air followed while Truman tried to rally himself. Finally, he replied in a croaky voice, "The obvious answer is that eventually I'll kill myself."

Thoughts of suicide preoccupied him because of an emotionally disastrous situation he'd gotten himself into. Between 1975 and 1976, *Esquire* magazine ran installments of *Answered Prayers,* the title taken from a remark by St. Teresa of Avila that answered prayers cause more tears than those that remain unanswered. Truman claimed he had been working on the book for years, but at other times said he'd tossed it off as a lark. It was a public shellacking of many of his friends from the glittering social world—Jackie Kennedy, Babe Paley, and Johnny Carson—who had once embraced him.

Revenge was swift. Knowing how much Truman cherished his role as raconteur to the rich and famous, they simply turned their backs on him. He was no longer included in their lives. Perversely, he proved that no one really liked him by making himself persona non grata.

He hung on for eight more years, washing up now and then like driftwood in hospital emergency rooms, until he died in 1984 in the home of Joanna Carson, Johnny Carson's ex-wife. His last words were for his mother.[8]

Lee, along with Al and Marie Dewey, attended Capote's memorial service in Los Angeles, where the first chapter of *In Cold Blood* was read aloud as a tribute. Afterward, they went to the home of one of Truman's friends from happier times, the novelist Donald Windham. When Windham asked Nelle during dinner when the last time she'd spoken to Truman was, she had to say she hadn't heard from him in a very long while.

"In my opinion," said Dolores Hope, her Kansas friend, "the strain in her friendship with Capote came with his continuing debauchery—alcohol and drugs—and with his sordid treatment of longtime friends, associates and celebrities in his book, never completed, *Answered Prayers*."[9]

Truman's death ended a long chapter in Nelle's life. But it also spun her thoughts back twenty-five years to those Kansas days when she'd been the most creative. In 1960, she had been his "assistant researchist," contributing to one of the most sensational and highly regarded books in American literature, while simultaneously her first novel, *To Kill a Mockingbird*, was just months away from publication. That brief period had been the apogee of her writing life thus far.

And so in the mid-1980s, retracing her steps over familiar ground, Nelle embarked on a book project that resembled *In Cold Blood*. It would be a nonfiction novel based on a serial murder case in Alabama she'd read about involving a man accused of killing relatives for their insurance money. And this time, unlike *In Cold Blood*, the book and the credit would belong wholly to her. The working title she chose was *The Reverend*.[10]

The story revolves around W. M. "Willie Jo" Maxwell, a veteran of World War II, born and raised in east Alabama. During the mid-1970s, in addition to working in the wood pulp business, he did some preaching on the side in black churches in Alexander City and became known as the Reverend Maxwell. One night, Tom Radney, Sr., an attorney and former state senator, received a call from Maxwell. "You've got to come out here to my home," Maxwell pleaded, "the police are saying I killed my wife." Mrs. Maxwell had been found tied to a tree about a mile outside of town and murdered.

Radney agreed to take the case. Fortunately for the reverend, the woman next door provided him with an alibi, and he was found not guilty. From a portion of his late wife's insurance policy Maxwell paid Radney's fees. Later, he married the woman next door.

"A year or so passed," said Radney, "and then the new wife showed up dead."

Again, Maxwell asked Radney to defend him. During the trial, the jury was persuaded that there was no evidence linking Maxwell to the murder. He was acquitted and paid Radney from his second wife's insurance policy.

The third time Maxwell was charged with murder was in connection with his brother, who was found dead by the side of a road. The district attorney argued that Maxwell, either by himself or with someone's help, had poured liquor down his brother's throat until he died of alcohol poisoning. But the jury wasn't convinced and returned another verdict of not guilty. Maxwell was his brother's beneficiary and had another lump sum due him. The Alexander City Police Department began referring to Radney's law offices as the "Maxwell Building."

The fourth death involved Maxwell's nephew, discovered dead behind the wheel of his car. Apparently, he had run into a tree. The following day, Radney, retained again as Maxwell's attorney, inspected the crash site. "Not even the largest trees were more than two inches around," he said. "It was obvious that hitting those little trees didn't kill the reverend's nephew. However, the state could not prove the cause of death. I remember having a pathologist on the witness stand. I asked him, 'C'mon, what did he die of?' And the reply was, 'Judge, I hate to tell you, but we don't know what he died of.'" Maxwell left the courtroom a free man and settled with Radney with proceeds from his nephew's insurance policy.

The fifth death touching the reverend was reported on the front page of the *Alexander City Outlook* on June 15, 1977. According to police, Shirley Ellington, Maxwell's teenage niece, had been changing a flat tire when her car fell off the jack and killed her. After reading the news story, Radney decided, "I've had enough." When Maxwell showed up at his offices, his erstwhile attorney turned him down.

"Mr. Radney, you're not being fair to me," Maxwell protested. "I have done nothing wrong. You've got to defend me."

Radney later recalled the next few minutes clearly. "I said, 'Reverend, enough's enough. Maybe you're innocent, you never told me anything differently, and I'll never say a word against you, but I will not defend you anymore.' In the meantime, the area behind my office building was filled with cameras and reporters from Birmingham, Montgomery, and Columbus, Georgia. A newswoman was standing behind his car, and the last thing I heard the reverend say as he got into his big Chrysler was, 'Ma'am, if you don't move, I'm going to run over you.'"

The police waited to arrest Maxwell, hoping he might do or say something during his niece's funeral service that would incriminate him. Instead, a scene both awful and comic took place. Nelle decided it would make the perfect beginning to *The Reverend*.

A week after Shirley Ellington's death, three hundred people gathered for her memorial service in the chapel of the House of Hutcheson funeral home. One of the teenager's uncles, Robert Burns from Chicago, took a seat in the pew behind Maxwell. As the organist was playing and the choir singing in the loft, Burns took out a .45 from his suit jacket and shot Maxwell point blank in the back. For a moment, Maxwell dabbed at his forehead with a handkerchief while blood spilled from his mouth. Then he fell to the floor, dead. Suddenly, all the mourners made for the doors, but finding police blocking the exits, they pushed back inside.

"Two or three ladies, little heavy ones," said Radney, "tried to get out the windows and got stuck. The preacher didn't stop preaching, he just got under the pulpit. The organist got under the organ and kept playing, and the choir in the choir loft kept singing—nothing stopped. The next day, police found more than a dozen guns and twice as many knives scattered under the pews."

That's where Nelle would end her first chapter.[11]

Radney defended Burns, after first checking with the Alabama Bar Association to determine that it wouldn't be a conflict of interest. Since Maxwell was dead, there was none. The jury was out twenty minutes and came back with a verdict of not guilty. The judge sent Burns on his way. As court adjourned, the district attorney mused aloud that he must be the only prosecutor in the United States to have lost a first-degree murder case when there were three hundred witnesses.

The Maxwell killings were tailor-made for someone with Nelle's experience. Moreover, Radney was "really excited about the possibility of a book or movie" when she contacted him about giving the story an *In Cold Blood* treatment. He agreed to share all his files going back to the beginning, when he first met the reverend. For the movie version, she said she wanted him to play the defense counsel. Gregory Peck would probably get the lead, she said.[12]

For about a year she made her writing headquarters the Horseshoe Bend Motel in Alexander City, where she pored over the records of the trials and took notes on the setting, the same way Truman had closeted himself at the Wheatlands Motel outside Garden City. Then she shifted to her sister Louise's house in Eufaula for three months.[13] Louise, though never especially interested in Nelle's writing, was glad for company, since her husband, Herschel, was in poor health. During the next few years, Nelle would call Radney with updates on how the book was progressing, sometimes saying that it was practically done. "The galleys are at the publishers; it should be published in about a week," she would say.

But nothing materialized. According to Jack Dunphy, Capote's former lover, Nelle couldn't find a satisfactory structure for the material. About 1984, Radney finally concluded, "she's fighting a battle between the book and a bottle of Scotch. And the Scotch is winning."[14] It may have been so. Shortly before his death that year, Capote remarked about Lee's drinking. It "was a problem in that she would drink and then tell somebody off—that's what it amounted to. She was really a somebody. People were really quite frightened of her."[15]

Impatient with being put off over and over, Radney went to New York to retrieve his files. After that, he gradually stopped hearing from Nelle. "Don't bring up writing," a friend of hers cautioned William Smart, the Sweet Briar College professor whose creative-writing classes Nelle had addressed years earlier. He, too, was going to meet her in the city. "She's very sensitive about that."[16]

Nelle's conflicted feelings about writing, the past, and the invasiveness of publicity came to a head in 1988 with the publication of Gerald Clarke's bestselling *Capote: A Biography*. Reminiscing to Clarke about growing up next door to the Lees, Capote claimed that Mrs. Lee had twice tried to drown two-year-old Nelle in the bathtub. "'Both times Nelle was saved by one of her older sisters,' said Truman. 'When they talk about Southern grotesque, they're not kidding!'"[17]

Nelle was outraged. There was no more vulnerable or painful side of her life he could have touched on.

She wrote to Caldwell Delaney, an old friend and former director of the Museum of Mobile, "Truman's vicious lie—that my mother was mentally unbalanced and tried twice to kill me (that gentle soul's reward for having loved him)—was the first example of his legacy to his friends. Truman left, in the book, something hateful and untrue about every one of them, which more than anything should tell you what was plain to us for more than the last fifteen years of his life—he was paranoid to a terrifying degree. Drugs and alcohol did not cause his insanity, they were the result of it."[18] Newscaster Paul Harvey repeated the story of Mrs. Lee on his program in 1997, this time, provoking a public broadside from Alice. "It was a fabrication of a fabrication," Alice told the *Mobile Register*, a "pack of lies. My mother was the gentlest of people. According to the broadcast, I was one of the ones who saved Nelle from drowning. It is false. How would you feel if someone told a story that in essence accused your deceased mother of being an attempted murderer?"[19]

Protecting her legacy became important to Nelle as the chances of her publishing again diminished. At one point, her cousin Dickie Williams asked her, " 'When are you going to come out with another book?' And she said, 'Richard, when you're at the top there's only one way to go.' "[20]

Meanwhile, Monroeville had realized its singular advantage as the birthplace of the author who had written one of the most popular and influential novels of the twentieth century. By 1988, the National Council of Teachers of English reported that *To Kill a Mockingbird* was taught in 74 percent of the nation's public schools. Only *Romeo and Juliet*, *Macbeth*, and *Huckleberry Finn* were assigned more often. In addition, as the lightly fictionalized setting for Nelle's novel, Monroeville enjoyed a second distinction that no other town could claim.

In 1990, on the thirtieth anniversary of the publication of *To Kill a Mockingbird*, Monroeville staged its first production of the play based on the novel, which had just that year been licensed for amateur theatricals.[21]

The Monroeville staging of *To Kill a Mockingbird* had charms that no other production could have matched. Audience members sat in chairs and risers placed outside the courthouse, next to sidewalks where Nelle had roller-skated as a child. Huge pecan trees provided a natural canopy above the sets representing porches on the street where the Finches live. The cast, consisting of residents—businesspeople, farmers, students—rehearsed for weeks in the evenings, trying to recapture the Depression in Alabama, though few could personally recall it. Some hoped that Nelle might make an encouraging appearance at their inaugural opening night, but they were destined to be disappointed. "She sort of hates publicity," said Julie Fallowfield, Lee's agent at McIntosh and Otis. "The book stands. Which in a way is wonderful."[22]

The first act unfolded under trees by the side of the courthouse, where mockingbirds can be heard singing cascades of brilliant notes in the branches. When Atticus raised a rifle to shoot an imaginary mad dog in the distance, the children in the audience gleefully covered their ears. *Bang!* echoed off the storefronts on the square. For the scene in which Atticus defies a lynch mob bent on kidnapping his client, the courthouse's side door doubled as the entrance to the jailhouse. Across the street was the actual jail Nelle had in mind.

During intermission, the actor playing the sheriff called the names of twelve white males in the audience for jury duty—the only citizens eligible to serve under the laws of Alabama in the 1930s. Coolers heaped with ice, a welcome anachronism, provided drinks and snacks during the break to combat the weather, which, as early as May, was already muggy.

Once inside the courthouse for the start of the second act, the audience settled into the pewlike benches. Up in the "colored" gallery members of a local black church sat and watched, a poignant reminder of how things once were. In the jury box, a dozen white men prepared to hear the case.

Everyone knew the trial's outcome, although in the stuffy courtroom built in 1903 with one ceiling fan turning tiredly high above, there was a sense that the sins of history could be reversed if only the jury would find Tom Robinson not guilty. But while the jury was sequestered in a hot, dark stairway to "deliberate," the sheriff informed them that no verdict except the "right one" would be tolerated.[23] The foreman then led the jury back into the courtroom and Robinson was again convicted for a crime he hadn't committed.

The play was such a success—both in attendance and for the boost it gave civic pride—that the following year, 1991, the Monroe County Heritage Museum—a consortium of local history museums—hired a director to further capitalize on Monroeville's link with *To Kill a Mockingbird*. In light of such a tribute to the novel and its creator, few could have anticipated that it would be the start of an uneasy relationship between Nelle and the town.

As the annual theatrical performances of *To Kill a Mockingbird* in Monroeville became more popular, and the Monroe County Heritage Museum tended to put more emphasis on Monroeville's link to Harper Lee, the author was not pleased to see that her birthplace was getting on the bandwagon, so to speak. It augured more requests for autographs, more fan mail, and more occasions when strangers would quiz her about the book. At a Christmas party one year in Monroeville, an out-of-towner began chatting her up about *To Kill a Mockingbird*. She turned on her heel and walked away.[24]

By now Nelle was in her seventies and weary of any attention connected with *To Kill a Mockingbird*. She had put that far behind her, along with the film. Rarely could invitations to receive honors induce her to depart from her well-worn paths. Twice, Huntingdon College invited her in the 1990s to attend graduation. She never replied.[25] The University of Alabama succeeded in awarding her an honorary degree in 1993—perhaps the appeal for Nelle was closure after never having graduated—but all she would say to the audience was, "Thank you."

The distance she felt from her only published novel was unmistakable in a foreword to the thirty-fifth anniversary edition in 1993. "Please spare *Mockingbird* an Introduction," she wrote.

> As a reader I loathe Introductions. To novels, I associate Introductions with long-gone authors and works that are being brought back into print after decades of internment. Although *Mockingbird* will be 33 this year, it has never been out of print and I am still alive, although very quiet. Introductions inhibit pleasure, they kill the joy of anticipation, they frustrate curiosity. The only good thing about Introductions is that in some cases they delay the dose to come. *Mockingbird* still says what it has to say; it has managed to survive without preamble.[26]

With dismay, she watched the transformation of Monroeville into the "Literary Capital of Alabama." After volunteers had finished painting twelve-foot-high outdoor murals of scenes from the novel, Nelle pronounced them "graffiti." When a television crew asked to film portions of the play and interview the actors, Nelle responded through her agent, "Not just no, but *hell* no."

"She would give you the shirt off her back," remarked a resident, "but do not try to take it without permission." In fact, it was lack of permission that brought about a showdown between Nelle and the Monroe County Heritage Museum. The trouble arose over a cookbook.

Calpurnia's Cookbook, named for the Finches' cook and housekeeper, was a recipe collection of the kind assembled by churches to raise money. In this case, the idea was that profits from the sale would support the museum. When Nelle got wind that one of her characters' names would soon be appearing beside *To Kill a Mockingbird* pens, coffee mugs, and T-shirts in the courthouse museum gift shop, she threatened to sue. The entire print run of the cookbook, several thousand copies, was pulped.

Yet Nelle's secluded life and decades-long silence continued to exert a fascination for newspaper editors and other media people looking for a good story. Features headlined "What Ever Happened to Harper Lee?" cropped up several times a year. Whether she intended to or not, she created a mystique when she withdrew from the public eye.

It's unusual for an author, an actor, an artist, or a playwright to "loathe" a new introduction to her work; to respond "Hell, no!" to a request to film an amateur play for a few minutes; to write "Go away!" at the bottom of a letter requesting an interview; to call a mural painted by students "graffiti." Harper Lee has never, in sixty years, attended a reunion of the sisters of Chi Omega house at the University of Alabama. "I've written to her many times," said a sorority sister, "and she's never acknowledged receipt of my letter." But a street on campus is named for her.

If they could publish only one book in their lifetime, many authors would choose to write one with as much popularity and influence as *To Kill a Mockingbird*. What could account for Harper Lee's extreme dislike of talking about the novel? She rebuffed attempts by Mary Badham, the child actor who played Scout, to communicate with her. "Mary acts like that book is the Bible," Lee groused.[27]

Could it be that she lacks a sense of ownership?

Tay Hohoff took a long, rambling, discursive, and highly autobiographical manuscript from a young woman who had never published in a national magazine or newspaper, and recrafted it until it went from *Go Set a Watchman*, the "parent of *To Kill a Mockingbird*," as Lee later said, to the novel that sold millions.[28] As the years passed, Lee continued to assure friends, and her agent, that she was working on another one. It was coming along. . . . It was very hard to do. . . . It was almost ready for the publisher. But it never materialized.

Epilogue

The Dike Is Breached

Greed is the coldest of deadly sins, don't you think?

—HARPER LEE, quoted in *The Mockingbird*
Next Door (2014)

In June 2007, Harper Lee didn't arrive for a lunch appointment with friends in New York. They went to her apartment—the one on East Eighty-second Street where she'd lived for over forty years—knocked on the door, and heard faint cries for help coming from inside. They found the eighty-two-year-old author lying on the floor, where she had been for a day, possibly longer, after suffering a stroke.

Her eyesight had been getting worse because she had macular degeneration, and she was losing her hearing. Her glasses were fitted with side panels to widen her frame of vision, and she wore a hearing aid. With the aid of her headgear, she continued taking city buses everywhere, dressed in her favorite outfit for excursions—a running suit, sneakers, and a big purse slung across in front. She frequented used bookstores, favorite diners, and museums, and she was a bleacher bum at Shea Stadium every summer.

But now, in the judgment of friends, it was out of the question for her to keep living alone. While she was in the hospital recovering from the stroke, which weakened her left side, arrangements were made to drive her back to Monroeville to stay. The apartment sold quickly.

The residents of Monroeville had grown accustomed to seeing her in town during the balmy winter months. She had been coming south since the publication of *To Kill a Mockingbird* in 1960, traveling twenty-four hours by Amtrak sleeper car to Birmingham, insisting that friends meet her at the train station to drive her four hours south to Monroeville.

In the one-story brick house she shared with Alice was a small library. There were bookcases in the foyer and in Alice's bedroom. At the end of the hall, the shelves in Nelle's room reached from floor to ceiling. To Harper Lee, a day well spent was a day spent reading.

When she ventured out on errands, the locals had learned how to notice her out of the corner of their eye without imposing. The famous Harper Lee was the woman with short, blunt-cut white hair, combing the aisles at the Dollar General store for bargains. During the week, she might be spotted at the Excel Laundromat waiting for a dryer to become available, or at Whitley Lee Lake sitting beside Alice on a bench, feeding popcorn kernels to the ducks and geese. On Saturdays the sisters frequented Dave's Catfish Cabin for a plate of catfish fillet, sweet tea, and hush puppies from the children's menu. And on Sundays they liked to go to out for coffee after church, or to the country club for brunch. If an old blue Buick was parked outside the post office, then Alice and Nelle were inside getting the mail, which usually brought dozens of letters from readers. They stuffed them into a plastic shopping bag and took it out to the car.

The sisters' weekly rounds weren't hard to figure out, as enterprising journalists sometimes did. The less enterprising only needed to consult the phone book, because Alice Lee's address and home phone were listed. If she declined an interview on her sister's behalf, or if Nelle wrote, "Hell, no," at the bottom of a written request, reporters who arrived on the front step had to gamble that the door would be closed on them, politely but firmly. And woe to any neighbor who pointed out the Lee residence to a stranger; he or she was sure to come in for a "blessing out" with "hell and pepper" from Harper if she found out about it.

"Walking on eggs," an old-timer said—that was part of being her friend. She used to sign books as a favor to shops on the square, but when she heard that customers were selling them online for more than eight thousand dollars each, she stopped.[1]

To forestall any unnecessary unpleasantness, a cadre of retired gentlemen served as Monroeville docents. Their job was to provide a welcome for those interested in Harper Lee, but also to play a kind of shell game with them. Journalists who researched the town ahead of time probably found it puzzling to read the same two or three people quoted over and over, telling the same folksy stories, as if they were going past on a merry-go-round with a friendly wave. If a reporter got a little too warm during his scavenger hunt for Harper Lee, the docents took evasive action. A BBC reporter in town with a camera crew discovered too late that he had been only a few feet away from his quarry during lunch at the country club, but neither of his chaperones let him know. The Britisher shrugged it off as "good fun."

So when Harper Lee returned permanently to Monroeville in late summer 2007, it seemed easy to ensure her privacy—even easier when she moved into an assisted living facility three years later. With royalties of close to a million dollars a year from forty million copies sold of *To Kill a Mockingbird*, plus residuals from the film, she had plenty of options for long-term care; she chose a residence called The Meadows, on Highway Bypass 21, just a few blocks from the town's commercial center. The Meadows resembles an inexpensively built Protestant church, long and narrow like a motel, with a big gabled roof at the center where the entrance is. The staff would insulate her from intrusions (an extra precaution was putting a fictitious name on her hallway door); but there were also encouraging indications in recent years that she had become a little less prickly about being famous.

In 2002, for instance, a journalist for the *Chicago Tribune*, Marja Mills, went to Monroeville to write a feature story about Lee. Others had failed and she was denied an interview, but Nelle agreed to have her photograph taken, and the sisters came to like the young woman; as related in the subsequently published story, Alice even went so far as to confide that Nelle's second novel never got beyond an outline. "I'll put it this way," she said. "When you have hit the pinnacle, how would you feel about writing more? Would you feel like you're competing with yourself?"[2]

It seemed that the ice was broken and the sisters were willing to go on the record with her about their lives. So two years later, Mills, who suffers from lupus, left the pressures of her job at the *Chicago Tribune* and moved to Monroeville. The Lees assisted her with renting the house next to theirs—a gesture of trust never shown to another outsider.

For the next year and a half, Mills participated in the lives of her elderly neighbors. Harper Lee enjoyed meeting for lunch at Radley's Fountain Grille, the name of which she grudgingly tolerated because the octogenarian owner was a friend. Alice set aside time at the law office to visit; and on Sunday afternoons, the threesome went on long drives in country, during which the sisters narrated the history of homes they passed, the families who had lived there, their troubles or successes, and the feuds between people long since dead.

A few juicy tidbits came Mills's way. "Truman was a psychopath, honey," Harper Lee told her. "He thought the rules that apply to everybody else didn't apply to him." About *To Kill a Mockingbird*: "I wish I'd never written the damn thing."

But as might be expected from a pair of ladies who never married, had no children or grandchildren, never traveled widely, and resided in a small town, most of what they said was fairly commonplace.[3] "Oomph. I'm bushed." "I shouldn't have the cheese grits. But I'm going to."

Still, the material gathered was suitable for a memoir, and just to make clear that Mills intended to publish a book, she sent Alice a letter agreement: "This is to confirm, should anyone want such a confirmation, that you and Nelle cooperated with me and, I would add, were invaluable guides in the effort to learn about your remarkable lives, past and present, in the context of your friendships and family, your work, your recollections and personal reflections, your ancestors and the history of the area. By signing below, you confirm this participation and cooperation, and that I moved into the house next door to yours only after I had the blessing of both of you."

Alice signed, and then Mills returned to Chicago to work on *The Mockingbird Next Door* for what turned out to be almost ten years.

Marja Mills's success at breaking the seal on Harper Lee's reclusiveness was followed by more developments of that kind. Two films arising out of renewed interest in Truman Capote appeared in theaters in 2005; Sandra Bullock played Lee in Douglas McGrath's *Infamous*, and Catherine Keener played her in *Capote*, for which Philip Seymour Hoffman won the Oscar for best actor. Bullock was proud of not troubling Lee while she was preparing for the role. "I would never have contacted her. Wouldn't have done it in a million years. I have family that lives very close to Monroeville."[4] Lee commented on *Capote*, but her response wasn't what most would have expected after almost fifty years of silence. There was a mistake in the trial scene in Kansas, she said in a letter printed in the *New Yorker*: the photographer Richard Avedon wasn't present.

It was the beginning of something, though. During May 2006, she appeared in public more times than she had in decades: at the Los Angeles Public Library to accept an award, and at the University of Notre Dame to receive an honorary doctorate, for instance. *O* magazine carried a personal remembrance about how she loved to read as a child. "Now, seventy-five years later in an abundant society where people have laptops, cell phones, iPods, and minds like empty rooms, I still plod along with books. Instant information is not for me. I prefer to search library stacks because when I work to learn something, I remember it."

All of this seemed to augur that Harper Lee might be more approachable as a year-round resident of Monroeville, more of a participant in the spirit of the community trying to live up to its name as "The Literary Capital of Alabama."[5] After all, about thirty thousand visitors come to Monroeville annually to see the courthouse, attend the annual play on the lawn, or buy a few mementoes at the Monroe County Heritage Museum. *Mockingbird* foot traffic keeps the shops on the square and the strip malls humming.

No one would have anticipated that Harper Lee's permanent return

to her hometown would see the playground boss of Monroe County
Elementary School knocking a few heads together.

The Wind Creek Casino and Hotel, a high-rise, Las Vegas–style
entertainment center in Atmore, Alabama, is about an hour south of
Monroeville, and Harper Lee liked to gamble. During the 1980s and
1990s, she vacationed in the resort town of Gulf Shores, on the Gulf
of Mexico, where Jimmy's Casino Shuttle would take her door-to-door
to any of the half-dozen gambling establishments. But Wind Creek is
so much closer, and she didn't have to leave the premises. There's a
spa, a bowling alley, a cinema, a cooking school, and an amphitheater
for live concerts. The fifty-thousand-foot gaming floor has row upon
row of machines all chiming, blinking, speaking, blazing with lights,
and spouting jangling music in the bluish dimness of an eternal casino
night.

Lee's close friend of many years, the Reverend Thomas Lane Butts,
the silver-haired pastor emeritus of the United Methodist Church in
Monroeville, likes to gamble, too. He took her to Wind Creek so they
could drink ("I've seen her drunk as a lord," said a friend) and seek out
"loose slots."[6] As odd as this seems for a clergyman, Reverend Butts
apparently puts a generous construction on Methodism and the responsibilities of one of its ministers. In 1983 he was publicly tried before
thirteen church elders for drunkenness and having an affair with a
married woman. Acquitted on both counts, he was suspended from the
ministry for two years for denying an associate minister due process
before firing him.[7]

Not long after Harper Lee's stroke, he ran into her at Wind Creek
Casino, rolling up and down the aisles in a wheelchair and merrily feeding quarters into the machines. He was glad to see her out and about so
soon after returning to Monroeville. Pushing the wheelchair and putting coins into her right hand, because her left side was paralyzed, was
Tonja B. Carter, whom the reverend knew. She was married to Patrick
Carter, one of three sons of Truman Capote's cousin Jennings Faulk
Carter—evidence once again of how, it is said, "people in small Southern towns are mixed together like blended peanut butter."[8] But the man

accompanying them was someone Butts wasn't familiar with—a short gentleman, bald, and wearing a loud sport shirt with the tail hanging out.

"That's my agent," Lee said. Butts extended his hand. Instead of taking it, however, the man reached up and plucked the reverend's winnings for the night, a $100 voucher, from his sports jacket pocket.

"I'm taking this," he said.

Butts wasn't amused. "You're a real carpetbagger, aren't you?"

"And you're a redneck, aren't you?"

"I certainly am and proud of it," Butts said.

Carter wheeled Harper Lee around and headed her in the direction of Wind Creek's glass-walled steakhouse. Lee's agent gave the voucher back to Butts and strolled after them.[9]

His name was Samuel L. Pinkus, and he was raised in Scranton, Pennsylvania, where his father had been a hospital administrator. After high school, Pinkus went on the bum using his winnings from playing poker to travel around the Middle East. For a few winters he worked as a ski instructor out West. After graduating from Yeshiva University's Benjamin N. Cardozo School of Law, he became an assistant district attorney in Brooklyn and later a copyright attorney providing counsel to the American Society of Composers, Authors and Publishers. While vacationing at a Club Med, he met Leigh Ann Winick, daughter of Eugene Winick, the president of McIntosh & Otis, the literary agency representing Harper Lee.

McIntosh & Otis had inherited Lee from Maurice Crain. When Crain became ill in the mid-1960s, he asked Elizabeth Otis and her partner, Mavis McIntosh, to manage his list of authors, provided each of them approved of the idea. McIntosh & Otis had been in business since the 1920s and were so beloved by John Steinbeck, a discovery of theirs in 1931, that he shared his 1962 Nobel Prize money with them.

Lee's new agency worked the copyright of *To Kill a Mockingbird* through subagents around the world, arranging for licenses and translations, collecting royalties and paying them to her. Their assiduousness in promoting the novel was really the reason it became read worldwide. Their outside legal counsel was Eugene Winick, the attorney of record in several cases involving the literary estates of Thomas Wolfe, Sinclair Lewis, and others. Winick was aggressive about protecting clients from copyright infringement, such as when an advertiser used without permission the name "John Galt," Ayn Rand's protagonist in *Atlas Shrugged*. He went after copyright violators on principle.

In 1984, after McIntosh & Otis had been in business for almost sixty years, Winick became president. He and his wife, Ina, an educational consultant, lived in a rather ordinary suburban home that belied his success. Case in point: four years after taking over the agency, he landed a $10 million contract for Mary Higgins Clark for four novels and a book of short stories.

About that time, his daughter Leigh Ann married Samuel Pinkus, and Winick began to teach his new son-in-law the business. Pinkus was a quick study and showed promise. But as he gained access to some of the agency's best clients, however, something about him changed, as if being the heir apparent entitled him to show off.[10] His style became audacious and flamboyant. One night for the opening of a Broadway play, for instance, he showed up wearing plaid pants, sandals, and a bowling shirt. To a female relative of John Steinbeck's who complained to him about how he was stirring up litigation in connection with Steinbeck's estate, Pinkus replied, "Go fuck yourself."[11]

In 2002, Eugene Winick suffered a traumatic brain injury that affected his memory; Pinkus replaced him at the helm of McIntosh & Otis, pulling down a salary of a million dollars a year, and began cutting his own deals through a side agency called Veritas Media, Inc. that Winick knew nothing about. Pinkus walled off certain clients from review, including review by his sister-in-law, Elizabeth Winick Rubinstein, who handled the agency's foreign, film, and theater rights. Three years later, with Winick threatening a lawsuit, he left the agency in 2005, but was still empowered to act for one of his clients, Harper Lee.

They are provincial women, the Lee sisters, and they have always put themselves in the hands of the comparatively few people they knew and trusted. Most of Harper Lee's friends—in New York, in Monroeville, and those she made while in Kansas helping Capote with *In*

Cold Blood—have passed away. She never taught writing, appeared at a writing conference, accepted a position as writer-in-residence, or served on the board of a foundation except for the stint on the National Council of the Arts in the 1960s, which she undertook as a favor to Gregory Peck. Money from the novel didn't interest her, either—"Well, it doesn't matter because I only make ten percent on it."[12]

She left all of her business affairs to Alice to handle. Beginning with the publication of *To Kill a Mockingbird*, Alice figured her sister's taxes, paying what was owed from their personal joint bank account as if they were paying utility bills. Alice reviewed contracts, too, and the complicated terms regarding returns, reprints, rights, pay schedules, and percentages, before allowing her sister to sign. McIntosh & Otis, during forty years of representing Harper Lee, had never given Alice reason to think they were being treated unfairly. For half that time, their point of contact was agent Julie Fallowfield, until her retirement in 1996. The Lee sisters trusted her and Winick without reservation.[13] They felt the same about Samuel Pinkus after Fallowfield left. Nelle thought he was "the most wonderful agent in the world."[14]

But the way he playfully picked Reverend Butts's pocket at Wind Creek Casino in the summer of 2007 seemed symbolic of the way he rolled now. In early May, while Lee was still in her New York apartment, he had dropped by with some papers to sign. Alice would have preferred to have been consulted, because she knew her sister tended to sign anything anybody put in front of her just to be done with it.[15]

And in fact, Nelle later couldn't recall what had transpired. Pinkus bid her adieu afterward and went outside into a sunny, breezy spring day in New York, knowing he had just succeeded in getting her to sign away all her rights in the copyright of *To Kill a Mockingbird*. The agreement did not recite any consideration for the transfer of her rights, was not notarized, and contained legal language that would try most people's patience—let alone an elderly woman who couldn't see well. Pinkus's intent, claimed Nelle's attorneys in a subsequently filed lawsuit, was not only to secure for himself "irrevocable" interest in the income derived from both the novel and the film but also to assist him in efforts to avoid having to return any money he owed to McIntosh & Otis for commissions.[16]

None the wiser, Harper Lee received the Medal of Freedom from President George W. Bush in a ceremony at the White House that November. Bush praised her "outstanding contribution to America's literary tradition. At a critical moment in our history, her beautiful book, *To Kill a Mockingbird*, helped focus the nation on the turbulent struggle for equality." Still infirm from her stroke, she took the arms of the president, and C-Span founder Brian Lamb, who was seated beside her, to rise from her chair so she could stand for the honor.

But she decided not to keep the medal; she gave it to Sam Pinkus instead, because she told him that he had lost family in the Holocaust. He deserved it, she said, not her.[17]

He visited her often at The Meadows after that, usually unannounced, again needing to conduct business. It was probably during one of those visits that the names "Tonja Carter" and "Samuel Pinkus" replaced Alice Lee as cotrustees of Harper Lee's literary estate and gained decision-making power over her intellectual property. Pinkus also prepared, and had Lee sign, "To whom it may concern" communications that allegedly were designed to protect his, rather than Nelle's, interests. She received royalty checks every six months, but no accompanying information about the number of books printed, shipped, or sold. HarperCollins, her publisher, couldn't get a response from Pinkus about offering *To Kill a Mockingbird* as an e-book. The silence from his corner left Lee "increasingly dissatisfied."[18]

Tonja Carter had been selected to serve as cotrustee with Pinkus because Alice thought her former secretary was wonderful. Clerks and bank tellers in town became accustomed to seeing her run errands for the law office. "Miss Alice just loved her. She's almost like family."[19]

Carter was born in Ohio, coming to Monroeville as a teenager when her father started work at the Alabama River Pulp Company in Perdue Hill, a fifteen-minute drive from Monroeville. Her husband, Patrick, whom she had married in 1990, piloted small airplanes like his father, Jennings, an aerial crop duster in the county for more than forty years. Patrick's private plane service flew out of the single-runway Monroe County Airport three miles south of Monroeville. One of his regular passengers happened to be a close friend of Harper Lee's—George

Landegger, chairman and CEO of Parsons & Whittemore, which owns the pulp mill.

Alice Lee saw a successor in Tonja, someone to carry on the practice. Just as her own father had encouraged her to take "lawyering" in the 1940s, Alice made it possible for her secretary to attend the University of Alabama School of Law, which would have been Harper Lee's alma mater had she graduated. When Tonja graduated in 2006, Barnett & Lee became Barnett, Bugg, Lee & Carter.

That same year, the first version of this biography appeared; the Lee sisters told Reverend Butts they were "very unhappy" about it and told friends not to read it.[20] Setting aside the question of its merits, however, the first life of Harper Lee to be published occasioned quite a few reviews, and invited a fresh reassessment of *To Kill a Mockingbird*.

That millions still loved the book was indisputable. A World Book Day poll in 2006—the poll is held annually in the United Kingdom and Ireland—named it the number one book every adult should read, beating the Bible into second place.

And yet since at least the mid-1990s, assigning the novel in English class had been generating uneasy feelings among some teachers. Integration had made classes more diverse, and some—in particular, black students—argued that Tom Robinson and other black characters—Tom's wife, Helen; Calpurnia; and Reverend Sykes, who admonishes Scout, "Miss Jean Louise, stand up. Your father's passing."—existed for whites in the novel to test their ethics against.[21]

In a lengthy review of this biography for the *New Yorker* titled "Big Bird," the critic and novelist Thomas Mallon argued that the novel that had beguiled millions of readers for decades appeared rather shopworn in postmillennial America. To him, Atticus came off as a "plaster saint"; his conversation with his children "tends toward the stagey and the sententious." Mallon also faulted Lee's twin narrators as a "wildly unstable compound," saying Jean Louise and her nine-year-old self "serve only to jar us out of a past that we've already been seeing, quite clearly, through the eyes of the little girl."

However, the novel's most serious shortcoming in Mallon's view was that it lacked moral complexity regarding racism and injustice. "The one thing that doesn't abide by majority rule is a person's conscience," says Atticus. Mallon speculated that *To Kill a Mocking-bird*'s popularity in classrooms "is less because the novel was likely to stimulate students toward protest than because it acted as a kind of moral Ritalin, an ungainsayable endorser of the obvious."[22]

The fiftieth anniversary of the publication of *To Kill a Mockingbird* in 2010 provided Monroeville with another opportunity to strut as the hometown of the author. Harper Lee's publisher wished to lend a hand, but Samuel Pinkus did not respond to requests for assistance.[23]

Not that it would have mattered, because boosters in Monroe-ville had become accustomed to going it alone. For twenty years, the nonprofit Monroe County Heritage Museum, which manages six local historical sites, had been drawing attention to Lee's association with the town without imposing on her. The museum board was thrilled when she attended a reading by Patricia Neal of Capote's "A Christmas Memory," and sent her flowers afterward. "My dearest friends," she replied, "the roses are spectacular and I love them, sincerely yours, Nelle Harper Lee."[24] But that was the only time Lee put in an appearance.

And it seemed highly unlikely that Lee would be involved in any commemoration of *Mockingbird*'s fiftieth anniversary because, as Alice Lee wrote to Marja Mills, "She doesn't know from one minute to the other what she's told anybody. . . . She's surprised at anything that she hears because she doesn't remember anything that's ever been said about it."[25]

For the celebration there would be games, walking tours, and cake, ice cream, and lemonade served on the courthouse lawn to counter the July heat, followed by a Sunday evening banquet of southern foods: collard greens, cornbread, fried chicken, and Lane Cake. Once again, the Mockingbird Players were cautioned not to deviate from the licensed script—no ad-libbing, in other words. Not only out of deference to the author, but also to avoid a repeat of the episode in 2002 when Lee threatened to sue the museum for trademark infringement in connection with its publication of *Calpurnia's Cookbook*. Although two hundred copies of the cookbook were secretly stored in the museum's attic—perhaps in the fond hope that Lee might relent someday—it was vital to walk on eggshells. Tickets to the play were $50 per person, and sales provided 25 percent of the museum's budget.

In the gift shop, volunteers laid in an extra-heavy supply of souvenirs with tie-ins to *To Kill a Mockingbird*—aprons, T-shirts, fleece vests, infant clothes, hand towels, soaps, wine bags, magnets, glassware, bookmarks, beverage huggers, and more. With thousands of visitors expected for the four-day festival, hope ran high that this would be a banner year.

Against that, background noise about the novel continued. Malcolm Gladwell, writing in the *New Yorker,* described Atticus as an accommodator, not a reformer. A blog post titled "Stuff White People Do: Warmly Embrace a Racist Novel"—and cited in the *Huffington Post*—condemned a National Public Radio piece for implying that whites who reread the novel would come away feeling that "things are oh so much better now." In *Mockingbird*'s defense, the novelist Chimamanda Ngozi Adichie described the story's effect on her when she read it for the first time at age eleven and delighted in its humor; and then how, as an adult, she came to admire it for "its clear-eyed depiction of American tribalism in its three major manifestations: race, class and region."[26]

In any case, the volunteers preparing for the fiftieth-anniversary celebration couldn't afford to think about such things. Twenty percent of Monroeville's residents have incomes below the poverty line. There's no money to repair the original law offices of A. C. Lee on the square, which would cost half a million dollars just to bring up to code.[27] On the site of the ramshackle Boulware house—the original of Boo Radley's place—is an independent gas station; and the rock wall where Nelle and Truman played tightrope between their houses marks the edge of the parking lot of Mel's Dairy Dream drive-up. Unless the town could continue advertising its kinship with *To Kill a Mockingbird* via ticket sales to the annual play, and selling keepsakes from the gift shop, financially the "Literary Capital of Alabama" would have its wobbly legs kicked out from under it. So it was good news for the town when, on Harper Lee's eighty-fifth birthday in April 2011, Penguin Press announced it had purchased Marja Mills's memoir, *The Mockingbird Next Door.* For curious fans, it seemed that at last, after decades, the dike guarding the author's privacy had been breached, because Mills had "written with direct access to Harper and Alice Lee and their friends and family." Readers would be privy to the sisters' memories of growing up in Monroeville, how the novel changed their lives, and so on—a complete departure from the way things had been for so long. Among the optimistic in town, it sounded like a favorable change in Harper Lee weather.

But immediately the next day, Penguin's announcement was challenged. In a terse statement released by Lee's editor at HarperCollins and purportedly written by the author, Lee implied that Mills was taking advantage of her. And because the response was attached to an e-mail from the law offices of Barnett, Bugg, Lee & Carter, it carried a whiff of potential legal consequences.

"Contrary to recent news reports, I have not willingly participated in any book written or to be written by Marja Mills. Neither have I authorized such a book. Any claims otherwise are false."

Alice Lee was taken aback and asked Carter about it. In a letter sent to Mills a month later, Alice related that, without her knowledge, her law partner had written it herself and taken it over to The Meadows for Nelle to sign. She claimed, "Poor Nelle Harper can't see and can't hear and will sign anything put before her by anyone in whom she has confidence," Alice wrote to Mills a month later. "Now she has no memory of the incident. . . . I am humiliated, embarrassed, and upset about the suggestion of lack of integrity at my office." Penguin later released a portion of the letter, with permission, claiming that the Lee sisters had indeed cooperated with Mills. [28]

In October, a meeting took place at Monroeville Bank Trust, which is below the law offices of Barnett, Bugg, Lee & Carter. It lasted an hour; three persons were present. But later, they couldn't agree on what occurred.

There was a visitor from London: the rare books expert Justin Caldwell from Sotheby's, the three-hundred-year-old auction house; Tonja Carter, to whom Alice Lee had recently given power of attorney for her sister; and Samuel Pinkus. Pinkus was there because, although he was no longer her agent—she had finally fired him in January 2009 and replaced him with Andrew Nurnberg Associates in London—he was still coexecutor of her literary estate.[29]

From the bank's vault, a safety deposit box belonging to Lee was carried into a private conference room. Inside were letters, contracts, and personal papers. Caldwell had been invited to make a literary appraisal of what was in there, for insurance purposes, while Carter and Pinkus looked on. But after the two men got down to work, Carter left because she had to run some errands, and so she missed out on an astounding discovery that Caldwell and Pinkus didn't tell her about. That's one version of events.[30]

Another is that Carter and Pinkus presented Caldwell with a gift box from Lord & Taylor, inside of which was an item he needed to see for himself on the premises. This suggests the pair had previously found something valuable of a literary nature and decided it was important enough to call in an expert.[31]

The third version puts all three back in the conference room for an hour, going through Lee's personal papers. In this telling, with Carter fully participating, Caldwell examined two items carefully: a publisher's proof of *To Kill a Mockingbird*, which was not a particularly valuable item, he decided. The other was a lengthy typewritten manuscript. Caldwell read about twenty pages, glancing back and forth between it and a copy of *To Kill a Mockingbird* that Carter had brought into the room. The typed story was set in the fictional town of Maycomb and inhabited by the same people.[32] But the two didn't match: the manuscript lying on the table was the original of *Go Set a Watchman*, which Tay Hohoff had read in 1957.

Alice Lee might have told them that, but she wasn't there. She was one hundred years old and profoundly deaf, and she had broken three ribs in a fall. In December, ill with pneumonia, she entered a nursing home.

The meeting ended and *Go Set a Watchman* was returned to the safety deposit box and locked in the vault again. For the time being, nothing was said publicly.

Tonja B. Carter was the only remaining active partner of Barnett, Bugg, Lee & Carter after Alice Lee left, and beginning in 2012, Harper

Lee became part of litigation that whipped out the doors of her assisted living facility like a Gulf hurricane. First, she sued her agent Samuel Pinkus and others for breach of various fiduciary duties during Pinkus's representation of Lee. The suit alleged that, in order to protect Pinkus's Veritas Media from a judgment his father-in-law sought for commissions owed to McIntosh & Otis, Pinkus had created a series of shell companies that fit inside one another like Russian dolls, each with continually changing bank accounts.

The suit also sought to have all defendants and entities controlled by the defendants assign to Lee whatever rights they owned in the *Mockingbird* copyright and warrant that they had not encumbered the copyright in any way.[33] According to an arbitration award entered against Veritas Media that was referenced in Lee's lawsuit, Pinkus had siphoned off commissions totaling more than half a million dollars that were due to McIntosh & Otis.[34] About his son-in-law's behavior, Eugene Winick said, "It was an absolute betrayal, not only as an employee, but also as a family member."[35]

The following year, Lee filed a federal lawsuit against the Monroe County Heritage Museum, claiming gift shop sales of *Mockingbird*-themed T-shirts, totes, towels, and coffee mugs—many of them also available at the museum's former website www.tokillamockingbird .com—interfered with her efforts to trademark the novel's title, adding that the museum had ignored cease and desist letters for twenty years. The museum's mission was not historical, the suit alleged; its true purpose was to trade on the novel and Lee's renown. "The town's desire to capitalize upon the fame of *To Kill a Mockingbird* is unmistakable: Monroeville's town logo features an image of a mockingbird and the cupola of the Old County Courthouse."[36]

Through its attorney, the museum expressed shock: "Lee's greedy handlers have seen fit to attack the non-profit museum in her hometown that has been honoring her legacy." But as one of the prime movers behind the museum had said some years earlier, "Yes, she has got us by the gonads."[37] The governor of Alabama, Robert J. Bentley, asked George Landegger, the wealthy pulp mill owner and close friend of Harper Lee and the Carters, to broker a settlement. He advised the museum to back down and take its medicine, because it had "pulled

the tiger's tail"; but his efforts were complicated when he was indicted for tax evasion on the basis of having maintained Swiss bank accounts containing millions since the early 2000s.[38] Friends who thought they might suggest reconciling, a "healing," tried to see her at The Meadows, but the staff had been instructed by Carter not to admit visitors whose names were not on a preapproved list. The owner of Radley's Fountain Grille, who had been bringing her potato soup every Thursday, discovered from a letter sent by the law firm that he wouldn't be able to see her any longer, either.

In protest, residents boycotted a new restaurant that had just opened on the town square: the Prop & Gavel—the name referring to the professions of the owners, pilot Patrick Carter and his attorney wife. The restaurant's manager, the Carters' daughter, shut the doors for a year, leaving the salt and pepper shakers still on the tables, and posted a sign saying it was undergoing remodeling, which included turning the empty store beside it into the new offices of Barnett, Bugg, Lee & Carter. During the rehabbing of the old storefront, a large word was discovered under the drywall, painted on the original brick: "Monala," the name proposed by Alice Lee in a contest for the new drugstore on that spot in the 1920s.

Meanwhile, Harper Lee, through her attorney, applied to register her trademarks and offered to sell authorized merchandise to the Monroe County Heritage Museum. The museum refused this proposal. In February 2014, lawyers for both sides filed a joint motion seeking to end the suit under terms that were confidential. As part of the settlement, however, the museum's attorney agreed to publicly apologize on behalf of the museum for any suggestion "that Miss Lee is not in control of her own business affairs."

Six months later, on the evening before the publication of *The Mockingbird Next Door*, the threat of another suit was again in the wind. Through her attorney, Lee stated again that the book was unauthorized. In addition, she denied being friends with Mills and claimed that her sister, who "would have been 100 years old at the time," had been duped into signing something.

"Miss Mills befriended my elderly sister, Alice. It did not take long

to discover Marja's true mission; another book about Harper Lee. I was hurt, angry and saddened, but not surprised. I immediately cut off all contact with Miss Mills, leaving town whenever she headed this way. . . . Neither my attorney nor I have retracted my original statement. Rest assured, as long as I am alive any book purporting to be with my cooperation is a falsehood."[39] The publisher immediately responded by supporting Mills and quoting again from Alice's original letter, clarifying that the April statement "was sent without my knowledge and does not represent my feelings or those of my sister."

Mills said, "I can only speak to the truth, that Nelle Harper Lee and Alice F. Lee were aware I was writing this book and my friendship with both of them continued during and after my time in Monroeville. The stories they shared with me that I recount in the book speak for themselves."

On November 17, 2014, Tonja Carter confirmed that Alice Finch Lee, age 103, had died of natural causes at the Monroe County Hospital. Until her retirement two years earlier, Monroeville's "tax lady" had been the oldest attorney still practicing law in Alabama—possibly in the United States. More than once, she had been asked about her secret to a long life. Her sensible answer was, "I don't do anything to bring on dying."[40]

During her three years of retirement, most of it spent in ill health, Alice tried to catch up on her reading. Even her method of falling asleep for the night was a mental exercise. She began by reciting the names of all the presidents of the United States. If she was still awake when she got to Obama, she started on the vice presidents. After that, if she hadn't drifted off yet, she began on the first ladies and then the governors of Alabama. Her last resort was reciting Alabama's sixty-seven counties and the license plate tag numbers for each one. Almost a century after the event, she could recall, as if it were yesterday, the parade and celebration in Monroeville when she was a child of seven, to welcome home the doughboys who had served in the Great War of 1914–1918. She had been enamored of the free cake.[41]

The morning of the funeral there was a small earthquake centered near Tuscaloosa, a coincidence that a few mourners sorrowfully made light of as a sign of "Miss Alice's passing" at the First United Methodist Church during the service that afternoon. It was a partly cloudy day in the sixties, the kind of temperate winter weather that had always brought Harper Lee home to Alabama. Seated in a wheelchair at the front, she was heard babbling and muttering loudly to herself. She was eighty-eight, the last of the Lee siblings, and had said many times to Reverend Butts, who was in attendance, that she didn't know what she would do without Alice.

During the service, friends and family members went to the front of the church to recall Alice's devotion to the church and the community. She was the first woman to chair the Alabama–West Florida Council on Ministries and the first to chair the Board of Directors of the United Methodist Children's home. She was legal counsel to her own church after joining her father's law firm, and taught adult Sunday school classes for over sixty years. As a "Pink Lady" volunteer in the evenings for the local hospital, she was one of the first to reach five hundred hours of service. In 1992, the Alabama–West Florida Conference of the United Methodist Church established the Alice Lee Award for women who have demonstrated outstanding leadership in the United Methodist Church. The Chamber of Commerce chose her as Monroeville's Woman of the Year and the Kiwanis Club created its Citizen of the Year award just for her.

As Butts listened to the tributes, he couldn't help but think that the recent problems surrounding Harper Lee and her novel "never would have developed if Alice was still handling things. Her sister adored her."[42]

Three months later, in February 2015, HarperCollins announced that a second novel by Harper Lee titled *Go Set a Watchman* had been discovered, in a statement attributed to the author, by "my dear friend and lawyer Tonja Carter," and it was hailed as the most important literary event in a generation.

Nelle Harper Lee followed her sister in death on February 19, 2016, passing away in her sleep at eighty-nine in Monroeville. In keeping with her wish that her funeral not attract attention, the following day private services with a few dozen people attending were held at the First United Methodist Church, where her family had worshipped since she was a child, and she was laid to rest in the church cemetery near her parents and Alice. In every direction is the world that meant the most to her, a world that could be encircled in a leisurely hour's walk with the Lee family headstone as its center.

Lee's attachment to Monroeville was constant and lifelong. Sixty years earlier, living alone in a barely furnished, cold-water flat, she had been overwhelmed with homesickness. "New York streets shine wet with the same gentle farmer's rain that soaks Alabama's winter fields. . . . I missed Christmas away from home, I thought. . . . I missed the sound of hunting boots, the sudden open-door gusts of chilly air that cut through the aroma of pine needles and oyster dressing. I missed my brother's night-before-Christmas mask of rectitude and my father's bumblebee bass humming 'Joy to the World.'"

It wasn't the hardship of being lonely and without money that made her yearn to go home. If that were true, then after becoming famous and wealthy she wouldn't have returned to southern Alabama for months at a time every year. She did so because she had a profound love of place. That's why Lee's readers recognize her characters and the town of Maycomb. It's a place they feel sure they've been to, and where they'd always like to be. It was where they belonged, where people knew them—where they felt loved.

Lee often said that *To Kill a Mockingbird* was a love story, meaning Scout's boundless love for her father. And when Scout has grown into a young woman in *Go Set a Watchman*, it's love again that makes Jean Louise forgive Atticus for being imperfect. Love was the alpha and omega of life, and should be in all relationships, the lens through which we look at others. She believed that she could say it no plainer, and when she was asked why she didn't write more, she didn't see the need to restate the importance of love in different words: "I have said what I wanted to say, and I will not say it again."

Notes

1. The Making of Me

1. Harper Lee, "Christmas to Me," *McCall's*, December 1961, 63.
2. Orville Prescott, "Books of The Times," *The New York Times*, 21 January 1948.
3. Geoffrey Mohan, "Levittown at Fifty: Suburban Pioneers," in "Long Island: Our Story," *Newsday,* 28 September 1997.
4. Robert Daley, "It's Like a Plate of Spaghetti Under New York Streets," *Chicago Tribune*, 7 February 1960, 20.
5. Truman Capote, *Breakfast at Tiffany's* (New York: Random House, 1950), 1.
6. "Rubbish in Manhattan Streets" (letter to the editor), *The New York Times*, 11 May 1949, 28.
7. At Mount Holyoke's 125-year anniversary commemoration, on November 8, 1962, Lee received an honorary doctorate. During the ceremony, her bookstore experience was mentioned. Most sketches of her adult life begin with her working at an airline.
8. Eugene Walter, as told to Katherine Clark, *Milking the Moon* (New York: Three Rivers Press, 2001), 93.
9. Drew Jubera, "To Find a Mockingbird," *Dallas Times Herald*, n.d. (1984).
10. Harry Hansen, "Miracle of Manhattan—1st Novel Sweeps Board," *Chicago Tribune*, 14 May 1961, D6.
11. Kay Anderson, e-mail to author, 15 March 2004. As a student at Monroe County High School, Anderson heard Harper Lee tell the story to her English class of throwing the manuscript out the window, which Alice Lee denied. Several other

former students heard the same story over the years. The "for better or for worse" remark is from Newquist, *Counterpoint*, 405.

2. "ELLEN" SPELLED BACKWARD

1. George Thomas Jones, "Young Harper Lee's Affinity for Fighting," Swiss Education, www.swisseduc.ch, 7 December 1999.
2. Ibid.
3. Freda Roberson Noble, e-mail to author, 18 September 2002.
4. George Thomas Jones, "Queen of the Tomboys," in *Happenings in Old Monroeville*, vol. 1 (Monroeville, AL: Bolton Newspapers, 1999), 125.
5. Truman Capote, "The Thanksgiving Visitor," in *A Christmas Memory, One Christmas, and The Thanksgiving Visitor* (New York: Modern Library, 1996).
6. Kathy McCoy, *Monroeville: The Search for Harper Lee's Maycomb* (Charleston, SC: Arcadia Publishing, 1999), 69.
7. *Harper Lee's Maycomb*, 26.
8. Lee, *To Kill a Mockingbird*, 144.
9. M. Thomas Inge, *Truman Capote: Conversations* (University of Mississippi Press, 1987), 316.
10. Charles Ray Skinner, interview with author, 22 December 2002.
11. Marie Rudisill, with James C. Simmons, *The Southern Haunting of Truman Capote* (Nashville, TN: Cumberland House, 2000), 192.
12. Clark, *Milking the Moon*, 40.
13. Patricia Burstein, "Tiny, Yes, But a Terror? Do Not Be Fooled by Truman Capote in Repose," *People Weekly*, 10 May 1976, 12–17.
14. "Ninth Annual Catalogue of the Alabama Girls' Industrial School, Montevallo, Alabama, 1904–1905" (Montgomery, AL: The Brown Printing Co.), 20. Reprint. London: Forgotten Books, 2013.
15. Harper Lee to Caldwell Delaney, 30 December 1988. Private collection.
16. *National Archives and Records Service*, College Park, MD, Fifteenth Alabama Infantry files. I am also indebted to the Johnston County (North Carolina) Genealogical and History Society, and to the genealogists Kevin L. Privette, Margaret Lee, Larry Kea, and Tiffany Harmon for sharing their research about the Virginia, North Carolina, and Alabama Lees.
17. Edward L. Ayers, *The Promise of the New South: Life After Reconstruction* (Oxford University Press, 2007), 3.
18. Kathy Painter McCoy, *Letters from the Civil War: Monroe County Remembers Her Rebel Sons* (Monroeville, AL: Monroe County Heritage Museum, 1992). Monroeville would have been sacked by the Union army, except for the timely intervention of two leading citizens. A detachment of Brig. Gen. Thomas J. Lucas's troops was sent to Monroeville to make a raid. Their approach naturally created a wild panic in the village, and women and children crowded terror-stricken to the village hotel. Practically all the able-bodied men had been at the front, and few paroled Confederates had reached home. A judge and lady of the town rode out two or three miles to meet the advancing raiders and ask protection for the homes of the village. An officer in command of the advance guard of

the raiders told them to tell the women and children to go to their homes—he would place a guard at every house to see that no harm befell them. Not a home in the village was pillaged. Commissary stores in houses on the north side of town were burned; but private property, except horses and forage, was respected.

19. "Centennial Edition: 1866–1966," *Monroe Journal*, 22 December 1966, 23C.

20. W. J. Cash, *The Mind of the South* (New York: Knopf, 1941), 61 and 220. "The new men were less likely to be the storekeepers and small merchants who had led the towns in the seventies and eighties, more likely to be educated lawyers and manufacturers." Ayers, 65.

21. Marja Mills, *The Mockingbird Next Door: Life With Harper Lee* (Penguin, 2014), 178.

22. Lee, *To Kill a Mockingbird*, 136.

23. Truman Capote, "Christmas Vacation," in *Conjunctions: 31*, ed. Bradford Morrow and Peter Constantine (New York: Bard College, 1998), 139–77. Capote retitled "Mrs. Busybody" and handed it in as a school assignment in the sixth grade at Trinity School in Manhattan in 1935.

24. Lawrence Grobel, *Conversations with Capote* (New York: New American Library, 1985), 54.

25. Rudisill, interview with author, 15 December 2005.

26. Charles Ray Skinner, interview with author, 22 December 2002.

27. Mary Tucker, interview with Monroe County Heritage Museum, Monroeville, AL, 7 July 1998.

28. Thomas Daniel Young, introduction to part III of *A History of Southern Literature*, ed. Louis D. Rubin, Jr., et al. (Baton Rouge, LA: Louisiana State University Press, 1985), 262.

29. Rudisill, interview with author, 15 December 2005. The only black person residing in town was a woman who was rumored to be the illegitimate daughter of Judge I. B. Slaughter. Anna Stabler could not be readily identified as black or white because she wore heavy makeup and a wig. Her animated fiddle playing induced the children to draw near. Truman took a particular liking to her. He begged Jenny Faulk to buy him a guitar. Then, when he had mastered a few chords, he would steal through the backyard bushes to strum and sing with Anna. In concert, they sounded like two cats. Truman later took Anna as the model for Catherine in *The Grass Harp*.

30. Betty Martin, interview with author, 5 November 2005.

31. Rudisill, interview with author, 21 December 2005.

32. Said a relative of the novelist Carson McCullers:

> We knew 'colored people' as servants. In both our houses we had a cook who was really a general housekeeper. About half her time was spent with the baby if there was one. She did whatever was necessary at the time. We had a yard man who came about once a week. Our clothes were picked up by a black woman with a wagon. She took them home, boiled them on an outside fire, starched them, ironed them and returned them. Sheets, etc., went to the commercial laundry. Extra help came in for fall cleaning. It was the way of life.

Roberta Steiner, "My Cousin Carson McCullers," *Carson McCullers Society Newsletter*, no. 3. University of West Florida, Pensacola, FL, 2000.

33. Rudisill, interview with author, 21 December 2005.

34. George Thomas Jones, e-mail to author, 11 January 2003.

35. According to Jones, the town historian who knew all the parties involved:

> Arch Persons "came from a fine, well-respected family in Tuscaloosa. His father was a prominent lawyer and a first cousin, Gordon Persons, was once governor of Alabama. Archie first came to Monroeville in the early 1930s as houseguests of two brothers with whom he had become good friends while they were students at the University of Alabama. It was during a visit that he met Lillie Mae. A whirlwind romance ended in marriage . . . followed by the birth of Truman and subsequently by Archie abandoning them in New Orleans. It was at this time that Lillie Mae brought her baby to Monroeville to keep both of them from starving."

Ibid., 3 July 2003.

36. Marie Rudisill, with James C. Simmons, *The Southern Haunting of Truman Capote* (Nashville, TN: Cumberland House, 2000), 61.

37. Gerald Clarke, *Capote: A Biography* (New York: Simon & Schuster, 1988), 14. I am indebted to Clarke's excellent biography of Capote for much of the information about Truman's parents and the Faulk home.

38. Ibid.

39. Rudisill, with Simmons, *Southern Haunting*, 241–42.

40. Truman Capote, *Other Voices, Other Rooms* (1948; reprint, New York: Vintage/Random House, 1994), 132.

41. "Spare the Laurels" (review of *Other Voices, Other Rooms*), *Time*, 26 January 1948.

42. Gloria Steinem, " 'Go Right Ahead and Ask Me Anything' (And So She Did): An Interview with Truman Capote," *McCall's*, November 1967, 76–77, 148–52, 154.

43. *Harper Lee's Maycomb*, 70.

44. Roy Newquist, *Counterpoint* (Chicago: Rand McNally, 1964), 407.

45. To this Miss Lee would undoubtedly respond, "Hell, no!" It's interesting that in *To Kill a Mockingbird* and also in the film version, Scout, Jem, and Dill never have to do a lick of work. Not a chore, not a paper route—nothing.

46. Harper Lee, letter to *O Magazine*, May 2006. Online.

47. Marianne M. Moates, *A Bridge of Childhood: Truman Capote's Southern Years* (New York: Holt, 1989), 116.

48. Randy Schulkers, letter to author, 25 February 2005.

49. Rudisill, with Simmons, *Southern Haunting*, 193.

50. Wayne Greenhaw, "Capote Country," *Alabama on My Mind* (Montgomery, AL: Sycamore Press, 1987), 103. Later, Capote added details to the caper. "Once I ran away with a friend who lived across the street—a girl much older than myself who in later life achieved a certain fame. Because she murdered a half-dozen people and was electrocuted at Sing Sing. Someone wrote a book about her. They called her the Lonely Hearts Killer. But there, I'm wandering again." M. Thomas Inge, *Truman Capote: Conversations* (University Press of Mississippi, 1987), 23. The interview originally appeared in *The Paris Review*, spring-summer, 1957.

51. A classmate of Lee's recalled growing up in Monroeville this way:

> Living in a town like Monroeville was not a pleasure for me. My relatives and friends from there have always been special, but I couldn't wait to get

away. No library, no recreation, no entertainment at all except the local movie and church activities. Believe me, it was a very sterile place to grow up. My friends whose family could afford to take them on trips or to the cities for shows, entertainment, etc., probably have different memories. A number of my classmates were sent to private schools in Atlanta, Birmingham or Mobile. Those of us whose parents struggled to survive, working six days a week, more than eight hours a day, have different memories.

Freda Noble, e-mail to author, 29 April 2003.

The economy in our town was terrible. I say that from the perspective of looking back. At the time, nobody really considered themselves as being poor because, I suppose, everybody was in the same boat. I know that in 1934 my dad, who was the Ford Dealer, only sold five new cars the entire year. It nearly killed him to have to lay off sales personnel and (again looking back) greatly affected his health. Truly, those were the days that tried men's souls.

George Thomas Jones, e-mail to author, 5 August 2004.

52. Jones, "Meyer Katz Found His Dream in Monroeville," *Happenings*, vol. 1, 135.

53. Lee, *To Kill a Mockingbird*, 101.

54. Ibid., 9.

55. "Old Monroe County Courthouse," Monroe County Heritage Museum, Monroeville, AL, n.d., n.p.

56. Truman's dictionary was a gift from Mr. Lee and he kept it for years.

57. George Plimpton, *Truman Capote: In Which Various Friends, Enemies, Acquaintances and Detractors Recall His Turbulent Career* (New York: Anchor, 1998), 14.

58. Harper Lee's first appearance in print was a poem, "Springtime," which appeared in the *Monroe Journal*, 1 April 1937, 3.

59. Newquist, *Counterpoint*, 407.

60. Truman Capote papers, box 7, folders 11–14, New York Public Library. Lee introduces her notes on the research for *In Cold Blood*, "These Notes Are Dedicated To The Author of The Fire and the Flame. . . ."

61. United States Federal Census, 1930, National Archives and Records Administration, T626, 2,667 rolls, Washington, D.C.; also, George Thomas Jones, letter to author, 16 March 2004.

62. "Judge Mick," as he was known around town, had hair as white as duck down. He had a hawklike profile accentuated by a habit of studying things and people with an intense, thoughtful stare. As probate judge of Monroe County, he spent most of his days at the courthouse reviewing and ruling on wills, contested estates, property transfers, and so on. On his father's side he was French, descended from one of the largest slaveholding families in North Carolina. His mother was the daughter of another prominent family—the McCorveys of Scotland, Alabama. His background was a source of personal pride and he liked to advertise it by the way he dressed. In an era when most businessmen toiled in dark, self-effacing three-piece suits, Judge Fountain was dapper. He sported a white suit in summer, a cambric cotton shirt, and a bow tie that provided a spot of color. In autumn and winter, he selected a white, red, or pink camellia from his lush garden and pinned it to his lapel. His mild manner belied his toughness,

though. He had a crease in his forehead from a bullet during a shootout in 1894 when he killed the outlaw Wyatt Tate. "Fountain wore a big coat on that rainy day; Tate's first shot went under Fountain's arm; second shot grazed his fore-head; had a scar there until he died. They wanted to give him a shot of whiskey, but being a Methodist, he was dead set against it—said he'd rather die than drink whiskey." Claude Nunnelly, interview with author, 7 December 2003.

63. George Thomas Jones, e-mail to author, 5 August 2004.

64. Freda Roberson Noble, e-mail to author, 18 September 2002; also, Jones, e-mail to author, 8 October 2002. "My Mother was a friend of Sonny's family when I was very small. She told me that when Sonny was a teenager, he and a couple of friends were caught breaking into a store. His father punished him by tying him to a bed for some time. As a result, Sonny never went outside during daylight again!" (Noble).

65. Skinner, interview with author, 22 December 2002.

66. The drugstore was the Monala. Alice Lee won $50 in a contest for inventing the name; she combined Monroeville with Alabama.

67. George Thomas Jones was the soda jerk; interview with author, August 2004. Jones said Capote had no business being "so uppity. He used to eat butterbeans like the rest of us."

68. "'Luckiest Person in the World,' Says Pulitzer Winner," *Birmingham News*, 2 May 1961.

69. Joseph Blass, e-mail to author, 10 September 2002. Blass caddied for Lee at the golf course.

70. Rudisill, with Simmons, *Southern Haunting*, 190.

71. Cash, 76.

72. Blass, 10 September 2002.

73. "When our local Kiwanis Club was organized in 1947 both A. C. Lee and I were charter members. I always came to the meetings with at least two quarters in my pocket. One for Mr. Lee and the other for my boss, the Superintendent of Education." George Thomas Jones, e-mail to author, 28 October 2002.

74. Blass, 10 September 2002.

75. The *Monroe Journal* was located in an antebellum building made of bricks hand-formed by enslaved workers and fired in kilns on the spot. It's the oldest extant structure in Monroeville.

76. Ayers, 157. There were more blacks than whites in Monroe County, Alabama. The census of 1890 reports the population as 19,685, of whom 8,327 were white; 398 Indians; and 10,960 black. In the Carolinas before the War Between the States, the law required white men to carry arms to church on Sunday when the likeli-hood of an uprising seemed greatest. "We're outnumbered, you know," Atticus reminds Jean Louise in *Go Set a Watchman*.

77. Southern troops during the rebellion called every officer, regardless of rank, Cap'n, including generals. It was all one to them. Bob Ewell in *To Kill a Mocking-bird* does the same to Atticus when he takes the witness stand. "That's m'name, cap'n'."

78. "Centennial Edition: 1866–1966," *Monroe Journal*, December 22, 1966, 22C.

79. Cash, 73.

80. Harper Lee, *Go Set a Watchman: A Novel.* HarperCollins (2015). Kindle edition.

81. William R. Snell, "Fiery Crosses in the Roaring Twenties: Activities of the Revised Klan in Alabama, 1915–1930," *Alabama Review* (October 1970), 256–76.

82. George Thomas Jones, letter to author, 16 August 2004.

83. Consider the views of the nation's twenty-eighth president, Virginia-born Woodrow Wilson. Using the executive office, he rolled back earlier gains in racial equality by segregating the federal workforce. Wilson's racism extended to his scholarly work too, including *A History of the American People* (1902), in which he wrote glowingly of the cause of the Ku Klux Klan. Wilson wrote to a black leader that segregation *benefitted* blacks because it didn't put them into direct competition with whites. At the time, many Americans, including Mr. Lee, would have argued that this was a liberal view of the way American society worked. "Honey," says Atticus in *Go Set a Watchman*, "you do not seem to understand that the Negroes down here are still in their childhood as a people. You should know it, you've seen it all your life. They've made terrific progress in adapting themselves to white ways, but they're far from it yet."

84. A. C. Lee, "This Is My Father's World," 1952. Bounds Law Library, University of Alabama, Tuscaloosa, AL.

85. Cash, 81.

86. Ibid., 127.

87. Caitlan Sumner, "The New Woman of the New South: Gender and Class in 20th Century Southern Women's Literature," master's thesis, University of Alabama, 2013.

88. Rudisill, interview with author, 15 December 2005.

3. Without "Finishing Touches"

1. Dannye Romaine, "Truman's Aunt: A Bio in Cold Blood," *Chicago Tribune*, 5 June 1983, 1–2.

2. "Centennial Edition: 1866–1966," *Monroe Journal*, 22 December 1966.

3. Ibid.

4. Claude Nunnelly, interview with author, 7 December 2003.

5. George Thomas Jones, "Courthouse Lawn Was Once Kids' Playground," in *Happenings in Old Monroeville*, vol. 2 (Monroeville, AL: Bolton Newspapers, 2003), 163.

6. Susan Philipp, interview with author, 9 March 2004.

7. Miss Watson married late in life, and struggled with alcoholism—a consequence perhaps of being marooned in a "tired old town," as Scout calls Maycomb.

8. Freda Roberson Noble, e-mail to author, 25 April 2003.

9. Ibid.

10. Drew Jubera, "To Find a Mockingbird," *Dallas Times Herald*, n.d. (1984).

11. Noble, e-mail to author, 25 April 2003.

12. *Harper Lee's Maycomb*, 41.

13. Joseph Deitch, "Harper Lee: Novelist of South," *Christian Science Monitor*, 3 October 1961, 6.

14. Rev. Thomas Butts, pastor emeritus of First United Methodist Church in Monroeville, introducing attorney Alice Lee for an award given her by the Alabama Bar Association in 2003. The first "Citizen of the Year" award given by the Kiwanis Club of Monroeville—in 1987, when membership was still closed to women—was to Alice Lee.

15. Jubera, "To Find a Mockingbird."

16. Dr. Wanda D. Bigham, letter to author, 9 April 2004.

17. "Election Results," *Monroe Journal*, 12 August 1926, 3.

18. Vernon Hendrix, "Firm Gives Books to Monroe County," *Montgomery Advertiser*, 23 December 1962, 1D.

19. *Journal of the House of Representatives of Alabama*, 1935, House Bill 191, 418–19.

20. Ibid.

21. Elizabeth Otts, "Lady Lawyers Prepare Homecoming Costumes," *Crimson White*, 26 November 1946, 14.

22. Catherine Helms, e-mail to author, 14 June 2003.

23. Jeanne Foote North, e-mail to author, 17 February 2003.

24. Ibid.

25. Catherine Helms, e-mail to author, 18 June 2003.

26. Catherine Helms, interview with author, 29 March 2003.

27. Mary Tomlinson, e-mail to author, 2 November 2005.

28. Helms, e-mail to author, 20 June 2003.

29. Harper Lee, "Nightmare," *Prelude* (Huntingdon College literary magazine), Spring 1945, 11.

30. Harper Lee, "A Wink at Justice," *Prelude* (Huntingdon College literary magazine), Spring 1945, 14–15.

31. Ann Richards, interview with author, 14 March 2003.

32. Florence Moore Stikes, e-mail to author, 26 April 2003.

4. *Rammer Jammer*

1. Mary Anne Berryman, interview with author, 5 February 2003.

2. Jane Benton Davis, interview with author, 8 March 2004.

3. Berryman, e-mail to author, 3 February 2003.

4. Davis, interview with author, 8 March 2004.

5. Barbara Moore, e-mail to author, 13 December 2003. Carney Dobbs was on the *Crimson White* with Harper Lee. "Nelle wouldn't win any beauty contests but she was fun to talk to. She had a very attractive sister [Louise] and that sort of accentuated Nelle's somewhat plain appearance. She really didn't try to look as good as she could." Dobbs e-mail to author, 5 December 2002.

6. Berryman, interview with author, 5 February 2003.

7. Harper Lee, "Caustic Comment," *Crimson White*, 2 August 1946, 2.

8. Ibid.

9. Harper Lee, "Some Writers of Our Times," *Rammer Jammer*, November 1945.

10. Mazie Bryant, "When Harper Lee Mocked *Esquire* (and Writers in General)," *Esquire*, 7 February 2015.

11. Mildred H. Jacobs, interview with author, 7 December 2003.

12. John T. Hamner, "This Mockingbird Is a Happy Singer," *Montgomery Advertiser*, 7 October 1960.

13. Letter to the editor, "Caustic Comment," *Crimson White*, 2 August 1946, 2. In an issue of the *Rammer Jammer*, under a photograph of Lee near a hog, someone unkindly identified the hog as Nelle Lee and vice versa.

14. Ernest Maygarden, e-mail to author, 3 December 2003.

15. "One wonders whether this rough to violent picture of the Mississippi hinterlands and the dark issue of race persecution will have appeal for the public, accustomed—or let us say inured—to race problem stories closer to their own comprehension." *Kirkus Reviews* online archive, 1946. www.kirkusreviews .com.

16. Quoted in Myrlie (Mrs. Medgar) Evers, with William Peters, *For Us, the Living* (Jackson, MS: University Press of Mississippi, 1996), 27.

17. "We Bequeath Our Anti-Klanism," editorial, *Crimson White*, 16 August 1946, 2.

18. "'Little Nelle' Heads Ram, Maps Lee's Strategy," *Crimson White*, 8 October 1946, 1.

19. "Farrah's Eyes Are on You, Barristers," *Crimson White*, 16 August 1946, 8.

20. Harper Lee, "Revision," *Rammer Jammer*, November–December 1945, 18.

21. Elise Sanguinetti, interview with author, 5 November 2005. "Sanguinetti's published fiction—a short story followed by four novels—all center around one upper-class southern family whose members defied popular images of southerners as ignorant, bigoted, poor, and socially inept," according to the *Encyclopedia of Alabama*. *The Last of the Whitfields* (1962) bears a noticeable resemblance to *To Kill a Mockingbird*, published two years earlier.

22. Harper Lee, "Now Is the Time for All Good Men (A One-Act Play)," *Rammer Jammer*, October 1946, 7, 17–18.

23. "I would have joined any group if it helped get me votes," he later said. Black's life and tenure on the Supreme Court has been the subject of a great deal of scholarship and biography. It's surprising, for example, that Black was with the majority who held in *Brown v. Board of Education* that segregation in public schools is unconstitutional.

24. Wayne Greenhaw, "Learning to Swim," in *The Remembered Gate: Memoirs by Alabama Writers*, ed. Jay Lamar and Jeanie Thompson (Tuscaloosa, AL: University of Alabama Press, 2002), 101.

25. "He was a consummate name-dropper. Hudson would go out of his way to meet all famous people he could, getting pictures along the way, etc." Keith Karze, e-mail to author, 16 December 2003. Karze's mother was a friend of Strode's.

26. Greenhaw, "Learning to Swim," 101.

27. Helen Norris, interview with author, 18 March 2004.

28. Thomas Hal Phillips, interview with author, 14 December 2002.

29. Timothy Hoff, "Influences on Harper Lee: An Introduction to the Symposium," *Alabama Law Review* 45 (Winter 1994): 389.

30. Helen Norris, interview with author, 18 March 2004.

31. John T. Hammer, interview with author, 29 April 2005. Hammer said Lee tried to conceal the odor of liquor by chewing on a bit of raw onion.

32. "Edwin was somewhat of a loner until he started playing football at about age sixteen. Very much like Nelle. It seems that high school football brought him 'out of his shell.' He was always friendly and jovial but still was more of a quiet type until his college days." George Thomas Jones, e-mail to author, 6 December 2002.

33. Winzola McLendon, "Nobody Mocks 'Mockingbird' Author: Sales Are Proof of Pudding," *The Washington Post*, 17 November 1960, B12.

34. Mary Lee Stapp, interview with author, 11 March 2004. "Most of the women who were there knew each other, but most of us don't remember her." Olive Landon, interview with author, 16 March 2004.

35. Jane Williams, interview with author, 12 March 2004.

36. Ibid.

37. Jubera, "To Find a Mockingbird."

38. Williams, interview with author, 12 March 2004.

5. To New York City by Way of Oxford

1. Jimmy Faulkner, "How the Monroe Journal Was Purchased from Gregory Peck . . . Sort Of," Jimmy Faulkner's "Mumblings," 26 June 2003. www.siteone.com/columns/faulkner.

2. "A Final Word of Appreciation," *Monroe Journal*, 26 June 1947, 4.

3. "Miss Nelle Lee Chosen to Attend Oxford," *Monroe Journal*, 29 April 1948, 1.

4. "Ten Liners Arrive or Depart Today," *The New York Times*, 30 June 1947, 37.

5. Roy E. Hranicky, interview with author, 6 December 2004. Hranicky was in 4-H and going to a farm in Holland.

6. Robert W. Morgan, Jr., "Letter from France: Notes on Tourists, Students, Francs, and Politics," *Harvard Crimson*, 28 September 1948.

7. Roy E. Hranicky and Lois Belle White, *The Five H's* (privately printed, 1950), 15.

8. Ibid.

9. "Programme for the 1948 Delegacy for Extra-Mural Studies Summer School: 'European Civilization in the Twentieth Century,'" Oxford University Archives (CE 3/384), Bodleian Library, Oxford, England.

10. Marja Mills, "To Find a Mockingbird," *Chicago Tribune*, 28 December 2002, Midwest edition.

11. Ibid.

12. Olga Lee Ryan, letter to author, 22 April 2003.

13. George Thomas Jones, interview with author, 3 August 2004.

14. Dr. Ed Lee, Edwin's son, practiced dentistry in town for many years.

15. "As if evacuating everyone from a home that had become associated with sorrow, Alice sold the bungalow [the setting for *To Kill a Mockingbird*], purchased a brick ranch a few streets away, and settled her grieving father into the smaller house." Drew Jubera, "To Find a Mockingbird: The Search for Harper Lee," Westward, *Dallas Times Herald* (Magazine), 5 February 1984, 3 and 15.

6. *Go Set a Watchman*

1. *House of Flowers* was adapted from a short story by Capote that later appeared in *Breakfast at Tiffany's* (1958), a novella with three short stories.

2. The Chad Mitchell Trio had radio listeners all over the country singing the chorus to Brown's song:

   > 'Cause you can't chop your poppa up in Massachusetts
   > Not even if it's planned as a surprise
   > No you can't chop your poppa up in Massachusetts
   > You know how neighbors love to criticize.

3. Harper Lee, "Christmas to Me," *McCall's*, December 1961, 63. This is one of the few magazine articles Lee ever published.

4. Ibid.

5. Ibid.

6. Annie Laurie Williams papers, Columbia University, box 210, author card files I–Q. As of 2015, Harper Lee hasn't left her papers to any institution, and the Williams collection remains the best source of information about her early career.

7. Don Lee Keith, "An Afternoon with Harper Lee," *Delta Review* (Spring 1966), 40–41, 75, 81–82.

8. "Annie L. Williams, Authors' Agent, Dies," *The New York Times*, 18 May 1977, 94.

9. Leonard Lyons, "Gossip from Gotham," *The Washington Post*, 14 February 1945, 14.

10. Williams papers, unsorted correspondence, 7 January 1961, unsigned, box 194.

11. Dick Stuart, "Williams Is a Magic Name," *Corpus Christi Caller-Times*, 8 June 1955.

12. "Harper Lee: A Journeyman Writer," *The Ottawa Journal*, 11 April 1963, 6.

13. Williams papers, box 210, author card files I–Q.

14. Anne Edwards, *Road to Tara: The Life of Margaret Mitchell* (New York: Ticknor & Fields, 1983), 196. Maurice Crain was raised in Goodnight and Canyon, Texas.

15. Williams papers, box 210, author card files I–Q.

16. "Nelle Harper Lee," in *Current Biography*, ed. Charles Moritz (New York: H. W. Wilson Co., 1961).

17. Harper Lee, "Christmas to Me."

18. Ibid.

19. "Alumna Wins Pulitzer Prize for Distinguished Fiction," University of Alabama *Alumni News*, May–June 1961, n.p.

20. Harper Lee, letter to Huntingdon College, 26 January 1961. Houghton Library.

21. Ray E. Whatley, "The Laborer," sermon delivered at Methodist Episcopal Church, Monroeville, AL, 2 September 1951. Private collection.

22. Ray E. Whatley, "A Brotherhood of Love," sermon delivered at Methodist Episcopal Church, Monroeville, AL, 2 October 1952. Private collection.

23. A. C. Lee, "This Is My Father's World."

24. Ray E. Whatley, "Some Reflections on Race Relations in the South," paper presented to the Commission on Social Concerns of the First Methodist Church, Evanston, IL, 19 April 1965. Private collection.

25. Ray E. Whatley, "My Brother's Keeper," sermon delivered at Methodist Episcopal Church, Monroeville, AL, 8 February 1953. Private collection.

26. Donald E. Collins, interview with author, 1 April 2004. Collins's memoir, *When the Church Bell Rang Racist*, is an insider's view of the struggle to end segregation in the Alabama–West Florida Conference of the Methodist Church, to which the Monroeville church belonged.

27. Ray E. Whatley, "A Review of Personal Experiences in Racial Issues" (contribution to a project in Richmond, Virginia, about the history of integration), 11 January 1994. Private collection.

28. Williams papers, box 210, author card files I–Q.

29. Ari N. Schulman, "The Man Who Helped Make Harper Lee," *The Atlantic Monthly*, 14 July 2015. www.theatlantic.com.

30. Maryon Pittman Allen, e-mail to author, 30 November 2003.

31. To Uncle Jack Finch, Harper Lee gives the hoary arguments about the Lost Cause and states' rights in *Go Set a Watchman*.

> "Now then, Scout," said her uncle. "Now, at this very minute, a political philosophy foreign to it is being pressed on the South, and the South's not ready for it—we're finding ourselves in the same deep waters. As sure as time, history is repeating itself, and as sure as man is man, history is the last place he'll look for his lessons. I hope to God it'll be a comparatively bloodless Reconstruction this time."

And, "It seems quixotic today, with jet airplanes and overdoses of Nembutal, that a man would go through a war for something so insignificant as his state."

32. The Rev. J. O. Malone, interview with author, 13 April 2003. James Agee, visiting Alabama in the 1930s, wrote:

> The school population of this county is five black to one white, and since not a cent of the money has gone into Negro schools. . . . Negro children, meanwhile, continue to sardine themselves, a hundred and a hundred and twenty strong, into stove-heated one-room pine shacks which might comfortably accommodate a fifth of their number if the walls, roof, and windows were tight.

James Agee, *Let Us Now Praise Famous Men* (Mariner Books, 2001), 220.

33. "The one thing that whites had to be careful about was permitting the blacks to cross the line socially. Not so much from a personal standpoint, but to prevent being ostracized by their own race. With blacks this was not true, because all blacks were well aware that they badly needed white friends who could go to bat for them." George Thomas Jones, e-mail to author, 5 October 2002.

34. Dixiecrats, the States' Rights Democratic Party, seceded from the party in 1948 in opposition to its policy of extending civil rights, so adamant were they that the color lines were necessary.

35. "President Eisenhower may have inadvertently verbalized some of the deepest fears of Southerners when he explained in 1954 that segregationists 'were not bad people. All they are concerned about is to see that their sweet little girls are not required to sit in schools alongside some big overgrown Negroes.'" Patrick Chura, "Prolepsis and Anachronism: Emmett Till and the Historicity of To Kill a Mockingbird," *The Southern Literary Journal*, vol. 32, no. 2 (2000), 1.

36. Joseph Crespino, "Atticus Finch Offers a Lesson in Southern Politics," *The New York Times*, 16 July 2015.

37. Harper Lee, *Go Set a Watchman: A Novel*. HarperCollins (2015). Kindle edition.

38. Apparently, the manuscript was submitted under the title "Atticus," according to a corporate history of Lippincott. Perhaps "Atticus" was Crain's suggestion. But for the sake of clarity, *Go Set a Watchman* will be used throughout.

39. Williams papers, box 210, author card files I–Q.

7. TAY HOHOFF EDITS *GO SET A WATCHMAN*

1. Clarissa W. Atkinson, later an associate dean of the Harvard Divinity School, was an assistant editor for Hohoff:

   > "She and Miss Lucy Tompkins and my new boss, Eunice Blake, were the first women I actually knew (as opposed to actresses and people like that) who kept their maiden names after they were married. [Hohoff was married to Arthur Torrey, a literary agent.] When I got married after three years at Lippincott, Miss Hohoff let me know how much she disapproved of my changing my name. I was polite, of course, but I thought she was nuts."

   Neely Tucker, "How 'To Kill a Mockingbird' Came to Be: More Evidence," *The Washington Post*, 18 February 2015.

2. Jonathan Mahler, "The Invisible Hand Behind Harper Lee's 'To Kill a Mockingbird,'" *The New York Times*, 12 July 2015.

3. Tay Hohoff, *Cats and Other People* (New York: Popular Library, 1973), 20.

4. Tay Hohoff, "We Get a New Author," *Literary Guild Book Club Magazine*, August 1960, 3–4. Typical of Hohoff's enthusiasm was her reaction to Nicholas Delbanco's draft of *Grasse 3/23/66* over lunch. "She said, 'It's coruscating, Nicholas!'" he recalled. "I nodded sagely and had no idea what she meant. After she finished her second martini, I had to run home and look the word up myself."

5. Margarite (Ridge) Perrone was the first reader. She recommended Hohoff reject the novel because, among other things, the references to menstruation were offensive. Fernanda Perrone, interview with author, 16 February 2015.

6. Tucker, *The Washington Post*, 18 February 2015.

7. *The Author and His Audience: 175th Anniversary of J. B. Lippincott Company* (Philadelphia: J. B. Lippincott, 1967), 28.

8. Ibid.

9. Karla Nelson, "Off the Shelf: 'Go Set a Watchman' in the Papers of Lee's Literary Agents," newsletter, Columbia University Libraries, 14 July 2015.

10. Wayne Greenhaw, interview with author, 20 March 2004.

11. The long, long section about Methodism is one of the most egregious examples. Even to knowledgeable Christians, it's incredibly abstruse and unrewarding.

12. Both Lett and Lowery were luckless types, human flotsam on the surface of economic hard times. Naomi Lowery, twenty-five, had drifted into Monroe County with her husband, Ira, after living for several years in a fifteen-dollar-a-month rented house in Memphis, Tennessee. Lett, in his early thirties, had served time in the state prison farm in Tunnel Springs, Alabama, draining swamps and cutting roads through wooded areas. The length of his sentence, less than ten years, suggests that he had been convicted of drunkenness or fighting.

13. It may have been that he and Lowery were lovers, or that she was involved with another man who was black. If a white woman became pregnant under those circumstances, it was not uncommon for her to claim rape, or accuse someone other than her lover. John N. Maxwell, who grew up in nearby Beatrice, Alabama, in the late 1930s remembered his father "remarking about a local case in which a black man was accused of molesting a white woman. He said he had the feeling the man wasn't guilty. But later, when the suspect tried to escape, my father said that proved it, the man was guilty. Any educated person today knows that that man was running for his life." John N. Maxwell, interview with author, 9 July 2003.

14. *State of Alabama v. Walter Lett*, State Minutes of the Circuit Court, Monroe County Courthouse, Monroeville, Monroe County, Alabama (1934), 345.

15. "Lett Negro Saved from Electric Chair," *Monroe Journal*, 12 July 1934, 1.

16. C. E. Johnson, M.D., to Hon. B. M. Miller, governor, 20 July 1934, Death Cases (Executions, Reprieves and Communications) by Gov. B. M. Miller, Alabama State Archives, Montgomery, AL.

17. G. M. Taylor, M.D., to Hon. B. M. Miller, governor, 23 July 1934, Alabama State Archives, Montgomery, AL.

18. Readers, teachers, and scholars tend to assume Lee turned to the Scottsboro Boys trials in 1931–1937 for the novel that became *To Kill a Mockingbird*. The Scottsboro "boys"—black teenagers, with none older than nineteen—were accused of raping two white girls in boxcars on the Southern Railroad freight run from Chattanooga to Memphis, as the train crossed the Alabama border on March 25, 1931. But Lee, writing to biographer Hazel Rowley (*Richard Wright: The Life and Times*, 2001) said that she did not have so sensational a case as the Scottsboro Boys in mind, "but it will more than do as an example (albeit a lurid one) of deep-South attitudes on race vs. justice that prevailed at the time." Hazel Rowley, "Mockingbird Country," *Australian's Review of Books*, 22 April 1999.

19. "Negro law," not taught in any law school or codified in any statute book was a blur that whipped past black defendants. Part show, part legal twaddle, it rested largely, wrote the southern historian Leon Litwack in *Trouble in Mind* (1998), "on custom, racial assumptions, the unquestioned authority of whites, and a heavy dose of paternalism."

20. "Centennial Edition: 1866–1966," *Monroe Journal*, 22 December 1966.

21. George Thomas Jones, e-mail to author, 24 October 2003.

22. *The Author and His Audience*, 28.

23. Truman Capote, letter to Alvin and Marie Dewey, 12 August 1960. In *Too Brief a Treat: The Letters of Truman Capote*, ed. Gerald Clarke (New York: Random House, 2004), 290.

24. "Negro Accidentally Killed Last Friday," *Monroe Journal*, 16 February 1933, 1.

25. "Mad Dog Warning Issued for State," *Monroe Journal*, 28 June 1934, 2.

26. Capote, letter to Alvin Dewey III, 4 July 1964, in Clarke, *Too Brief*, 401.

27. Claude Nunnelly, interview with author, 7 December 2003.

28. Dr. Grady Nunn, letter to author, 1 December 2003.

29. Peschock, T. Madison. "A Well-Hidden Secret: Harper Lee's Contributions to

Truman Capote's *In Cold Blood*." PhD dissertation, Indiana University of Pennsylvania, 2012.

30. "Harper Lee Gets Scroll, Tells of Book," *Birmingham News*, 12 November 1961, n.p.

31. *The Author and His Audience*, 29.

32. Susan Philipp, interview with author, 9 March 2004.

33. Nicholas Delbanco, e-mail to author, 10 November 2004.

34. Marie Faulk Rudisill, interview with author, 21 December 2005.

35. Dr. Nunn, e-mail to author, 1 December 2003.

36. Sarah Countryman, interview with author, 9 March 2004.

37. *Harper Lee's Maycomb*, 44.

38. Fernanda Perrone, interview with author, 16 February 2015. Perrone's mother, Margarite, was the first reader of *Go Set a Watchman*.

39. *The Author and His Audience*, 28. It was Lee's decision to appear as "Harper Lee" on the cover. She never liked it when people pronounced her name "Nellie." Winzola McLendon, "Nobody Mocks 'Mockingbird' Author: Sales Are Proof of Pudding," *The Washington Post*, 17 November 1960, B12.

40. Clarke, *Capote*, 319.

8. "See NL's Notes"

1. George Plimpton, "The Story Behind a Nonfiction Novel," *The New York Times*, 16 January 1966, accessed at www.nytimes.com/books/97/12/28/home/capote-interview.html.

2. Capote papers, New York Public Library, Manuscripts and Archives Division, box 7, folders 11–14, n.d. These folders contain dated but not numbered typewritten notes by Harper Lee.

3. Ibid., 16 December 1959.

4. Alvin A. Dewey as told to Dolores Hope, "The Clutter Case: 25 Years Later KBI Agent Recounts Holcomb Tragedy," *Garden City* (Kansas) *Telegram*, 10 November 1984, compact disc.

5. Ibid.

6. Ibid.

7. Ibid.

8. Ibid.

9. Clarke, *Capote*, 322.

10. Crystal K. Wiebe, "Author Left Mark on State," *Lawrence Journal*, www.ljworld.com, 3 April 2005.

11. Jon Craig, "The Clutter Family Murders, November 14–15, 1959," unpublished paper, Washburn University, 5.

12. Wiebe, "Author Left Mark."

13. Truman Capote papers, Library of Congress, Manuscript Division, box 4, ac. 14, 213, research material/interviews.

14. Harold Nye, interview with author, 30 December 2002.

15. "Scene of the Crime: Twenty-Five Years Later, Holcomb, Kansas Remembers 'In Cold Blood,'" *Chicago Sunday Tribune*, 11 November 1984, 33.

16. Ibid.

17. "In Cold Blood: An American Tragedy," *Newsweek*, 24 January 1966, 59–63.

18. Capote papers, New York Public Library, box 7, folders 11–14, 26 December 1959.

19. Bill Brown, letter to author, 10 February 2003.

20. Capote papers, New York Public Library, box 7, folders 11–14, n.d.

21. Clarke, *Capote*, 323.

22. Cliff Hope, interview with author, 5 April 2005.

23. Harold Nye, interview with author, 30 December 2002.

24. Capote papers, New York Public Library, box 7, folders 11–14, 20 December 1959.

25. Truman Capote, *In Cold Blood* (1965; reprint, New York: Vintage, 1994), 70.

26. Craig, "Clutter Family Murders," note 1. Clutter's remark comes from his files examined by the Finney County Sheriff's Department.

27. Capote papers, New York Public Library, box 7, folders 11–14, 20 December 1959.

28. Cliff Hope, interview with author, 5 April 2005.

29. Capote papers, Library of Congress, box 4, ac. 14, 213, research material/interviews; also, Capote papers, New York Public Library, box 7, folders 11–14, 20 December 1959.

30. Capote papers, New York Public Library, box 7, folders 11–14, 20 December 1959.

31. Ibid.

32. Melissa Lee, "Brother, Friends Object to Portrayal of Bonnie Clutter by Capote," *Lawrence Journal*, www.ljworld.com, 4 April 2005.

33. Capote papers, Library of Congress, box 4, ac. 14, 213, research material/interviews.

34. Capote papers, New York Public Library, box 7, folders 11–14, 20 December 1959.

35. Capote, *In Cold Blood*, 17.

36. Capote papers, New York Public Library, box 7, folders 11–14, 20 December 1959.

37. Ibid.

38. Ibid.

39. Ted Hall, letter to author, 21 October 2002.

40. Capote papers, Library of Congress, box 4, ac. 14, 213, research material/ interviews.

41. C. B. Palmer, "A Farmer Looks at Farming 1954," *The New York Times Magazine*, 1 August 1954, 8, 23, 24.

42. Harold Nye, interview with author, 30 December 2002.

43. Capote papers, New York Public Library, box 7, folders 11–14, n.d.

44. Pat Johnson, letter to author, 23 October 2002.

45. Capote papers, New York Public Library, box 7, folders 11–14, n.d.

46. Ibid.

47. Ibid., 15 January 1960.

48. Ibid., 19 December 1959.

49. Ibid., 20 December 1959.

50. Ibid., 19 December 1959.

51. Ibid., 18 December 1959.

52. Ibid.

53. Nathaniel Pennypacker, "Massacre of the Clutter Family," *Front Page Detective*, April 1960, 76.

54. Capote, *In Cold Blood*, 13. Capote also preferred not to delve into the homeo-erotic overtones in Smith and Hickock's relationship. *In Cold Blood* is "a book by a gay man about a gay man [Perry Smith]," argues Ned Stuckey-French in his excellent reappraisal of the novel, "Queer Blood," appearing in *The Los Angeles Review of Book*s, 4 May 2015.

55. Plimpton, "Nonfiction Novel." Capote has been credited with creating a new genre, the nonfiction novel; Lee used the word he preferred, *reportage*, to describe it, which gained some currency in connection with the New Journalism in the 1960s.

    Plimpton's 1966 article begins: "'In Cold Blood' is remarkable for its objectivity—nowhere, despite his involvement, does the author intrude. In the following interview, done a few weeks ago, Truman Capote presents his own views on the case, its principals, and in particular he discusses the new literary art form which he calls the nonfiction novel. . . ."

    The laurel, however, for the nonfiction novella (it was thirty-one thousand words) goes to John Hersey's *Hiroshima* (1946) which was serialized in the *New Yorker* beginning August 31, 1946. "Hiroshima" traced the experiences of six residents who survived the blast of August 6, 1945, at 8:15 A.M. Forty years after its publication, Hersey said in a letter to the historian Paul Boyer, "The flat style was deliberate, and I still think I was right to adopt it. A high literary manner, or a show of passion, would have brought me into the story as a mediator; I wanted to avoid such mediation, so the reader's experience would be as direct as possible." Paul Boyer, *By the Bomb's Early Light* (New York: Pantheon, 1985), 208.

56. Cliff Hope, interview with author, 5 April 2005.

57. Hope, *Garden City*, 61.

58. Hope, "The Clutter Case."

59. Dolores Hope, letter to author, 8 June 2005.

60. Plimpton, "Nonfiction Novel."

61. Hope, *Garden City*, 23.

62. Alvin A. Dewey as told to Dolores Hope, "Finding the Killers 'Gave Me Peace of Mind,'" *Hutchinson News*, 11 November 1984, 7B.

63. Crystal K. Wiebe, "'To Kill a Mockingbird' Author Helped Truman Capote Break the Ice in Kansas," *Lawrence Journal*, www.ljworld.com, 3 April 2005.

64. Holly Hope, interview with author, 17 February 2005. Harold Nye maintained that Dewey and others in town, charmed by Capote, formed a clique. Said Nye, "In 1989 at the KBI 50th anniversary Marie Dewey made several comments including an apology from the Dewey family of any hard feelings that had resulted from the Clutter investigation. A little late, Sweetie." Harold Nye, e-mail,

16 February 2003. Dolores Hope defended Al Dewey's friendship with Lee and Capote. "I think perhaps his professionalism, education, and experience with the FBI might have contributed to the resentment of some of the local lawmen after he became 'famous.' I always thought he was well liked and respected before the fame came." Hope, e-mail to author, 4 May 2005.

65. Dewey and Hope, "Finding the Killers," 16B.

66. Harold Nye, interview with author, 30 December 2002.

67. Capote papers, New York Public Library, box 7, folders 11–14, 26 December 1959.

68. Ibid.

69. Ibid.

70. Ibid., box 7, folder 8. Folder 8 contains some of Capote's notes.

71. Dewey and Hope, "Finding the Killers," 7B.

72. Capote papers, New York Public Library, box 7, folder 8.

73. Ibid., box 7, folders 11–14, n.d. (probably 31 December 1959).

74. Ibid., box 7, folder 8, n.d. (probably 31 December 1959).

75. Hope, "The Clutter Case."

76. Plimpton, *Capote*, 172.

77. Dan Holt, *Kansas Bureau of Investigation, 1939–1989* (Marceline, MO: Jostens, 1990), 70.

78. Capote papers, New York Public Library, box 7, folder 8, n.d.

79. Capote papers, New York Public Library, box 7, folders 11–14, n.d.

80. Ibid., 2 January 1960.

81. Ibid., box 7, folder 7, n.d.

82. Plimpton, "Nonfiction Novel."

83. Dolores Hope, letter to author, 21 February 2005.

84. Capote, *In Cold Blood*, 20.

85. George Steiner, "A Cold-Blooded Happening," *The* (U.K.) *Guardian*, 2 December 1965.

86. Capote papers, New York Public Library, box 7, folders 11–14, 3 January 1960.

87. Capote papers, Library of Congress, Washington, D.C., box 4, ac. 213, interviews.

88. Harold Nye, interview with author, 30 December 2002.

89. Capote papers, New York Public Library, box 7, folders 11–14, 5 January 1960.

90. Ibid.

91. Ibid.

92. Ibid.

93. Truman Capote, letter to Alvin and Marie Dewey, 12 August 1960. In Clarke, *Too Brief*, 276.

94. Bill Brown, letter to author, 10 February 2003.

95. Capote papers, New York Public Library, box 7, folders 11–14, 6 January 1960.

96. Capote, *In Cold Blood*, 248.

97. Capote papers, New York Public Library, box 7, folder 8, 7 January 1960.

98. Ibid., box 7, folders 11–14, 7 January 1960.

99. Capote, *In Cold Blood*, 31.

100. Clarke, *Capote*, 326.

101. "In Cold Blood," *Newsweek*, 26 January 1966, 59–63.

102. Guy Louis Rocha, "Truman Capote's *In Cold Blood*: The Nevada Connection," *Las Vegas Review Journal*, 18 April 1999.

103. Capote, *In Cold Blood*, 244.

104. Capote papers, New York Public Library, box 7, folders 11–14, 7 January 1960.

105. Ibid., 9 January 1960.

106. Ibid., 11 January 1960.

107. Capote papers, Library of Congress, box 4, ac. 14, 421, 11 January 1960.

108. Capote papers, New York Public Library, box 7, folders 11–14, 11 January 1960.

109. Ibid., 11 January 1960.

110. Ibid.

111. Plimpton, "Nonfiction Novel."

112. Capote papers, New York Public Library, box 7, folders 11–14, 11 January 1960.

113. Ibid.

114. Ibid.

115. Harold Nye, interview with author, 30 December 2002.

116. Capote papers, Harold Nye to Truman Capote, 27 June 1962, New York Public Library, box 7, folder 8.

117. Ibid., box 7, folders 11–14, 15 January 1960.

118. Bill Brown, letter to author, 10 February 2003.

119. Harold Nye, interview with author, 30 December 2002.

120. Plimpton, *Capote*, 171.

121. Newquist, *Counterpoint*, 405.

122. Truman Capote, letter to Cecil Beaton, 21 January 1960, in Clarke, *Too Brief*, 276–77. Capote was not the only one with that idea—Starling Mack Nations (Mack Nations), a Kansas-born newspaper publisher, was trying to beat his time on a book deal.

Starting in March 1961, Nations began interviewing Hickock and Smith in the penitentiary, too. Hickock, seeing that Smith and Capote were collaborating on a book, told Nations he would cooperate exclusively with him. When Nations agreed, he excitedly proposed a grandiose plan. "I believe I informed you before that I would be perfectly willing to agree to an arrangement on a fifty-fifty split basis. I realize that your expenses will be considerable in the event of your traveling to New York City. I agree that the most expedient method of selling the book would be a personal appearance before the publisher, and an oral sales talk is by far superior to one by mail. Time is a very important factor as far as my future benefit is concerned, and I also am aware that this could possibly be a hindrance in our obtaining the maximum sales price for the material." A contract was drawn up in the early summer of 1961; over the next six months, Nations wrote a book-length manuscript, "High Road to Hell," a portion of which appeared in the December issue of *Male* magazine, adding to Capote's anxiety that the story would slip through his hands. Nations had difficulty finding a publisher, however. The manuscript was lost after Nations was killed in an automobile accident on Christmas Eve, 1968. His papers are available at the Kansas State Historical Society.

123. "Harper Lee Gets Scroll, Tells of Book," *Birmingham News*, 12 November 1961, n.p.

124. Don Kendall, "Clutter Sale Has Big Crowd," *Garden City* (Kansas) *Telegram*, 21 March 1960, 1.

125. Elon Torrence, interview with author, 6 May 2005. Torrence is a former Associated Press reporter who attended the trial.

126. Capote papers, New York Public Library, box 7, folders 11–14, 22 March 1960.

127. Ibid.

128. Ibid.

129. Ibid., 19 March 1960.

130. Mack Nations, "America's Worst Crime in Twenty Years," *Male*, December 1961, 30–31, 76–83.

131. Elon Torrence, interview with author, 6 May 2005.

132. Nations, "America's Worst Crime," 76–83.

133. Capote papers, New York Public Library, box 7, folders 11–14, n.d.

134. Mark Besten, "Too Hot for You? Take a Dip in Cold Blood," *Louisville Eccentric Observer*, 1 August 2001, 16.

9. *MOCKINGBIRD* TAKES OFF

1. Truman Capote, letter to David O. Selznick and Jennifer Jones, early June 1960, in Clarke, *Too Brief,* 284.

2. John Beechcroft, "To Kill a Mockingbird," *Literary Guild Book Club Magazine*, August 1960, 1–2.

3. Newquist, *Counterpoint*, 405.

4. "Traffic Ticket Report," *Saturday Review*, 6 August 1960.

5. "Mocking Bird Call," *Newsweek*, 9 January 1961, 83.

6. Michael Stillman, "19th Century Shop Offers Selections from New York Antiques Show," *Americana Exchange*, November 2004.

7. Williams papers, undated news release, early January 1960, box 86.

8. Frances Nettles, "Addenda," *Monroe Journal*, 16 June 1960, n.p.

9. Glendy Culligan, "Listen to That Mockingbird," *The Washington Post*, 3 July 1960, E6. It was also about this time that the legend began, erroneously, that Harper Lee was related to General Robert E. Lee. In an undated letter, Williams wrote to her, "Yesterday we grabbed a copy of *Newsweek* off the stands and raced through the pages until we saw your smiling face then read what we think is a good piece. As a relative of General Lee, we must remember to bow a little lower next time we see you."

10. Williams papers, Williams to Truman Capote, 3 August 1960, box 41.

11. Alden Todd, interview with author, 20 November 2004.

12. R. A. Dave, "*To Kill a Mockingbird*: Harper Lee's Tragic Vision," *Indian Studies in American Fiction* (Calcutta: The MacMillan Company of India Limited, 1974), 311–23.

13. Francine Prose, "I Know Why the Caged Bird Cannot Read: How American High School Students Learn to Loathe Literature," *Harper's Magazine*, September 1999. Reviewers in 1960 didn't touch on the significance of Scout's wanting to

be treated like a boy—like an equal. "Jem told me I was being a girl, that girls always imagined things, that's why other people hated them so, and if I started behaving like one I could just go off and find some to play with."

14. Minor anachronisms in the story, for those interested: the Works Progress Administration did not exist until 1935, but it's mentioned in the novel's fourth chapter, which is set in 1933. Eleanor Roosevelt violated segregation law in 1938 by sitting with black audience members at the Southern Conference on Human Welfare in Birmingham, but the episode angers Mrs. Merriweather during the fall of 1935. "I think that woman, that Mrs. Roosevelt's lost her mind—just plain lost her mind coming down to Birmingham and tryin' to sit with 'em."

15. Chura, "Prolepsis and Anachronism." Parallels worth noting that Chura points out: Emmett Till was killed on August 28, 1955, and his body found on August 31; Tom Robinson's death took place when "August was on the brink of September." Attorney Gerald Chatham, the prosecutor in the Till case, died a year later. Hearing the news that Robinson had been killed, Alexandra reacts angrily to the town's seeming disregard for her brother's health: "I just want to know when this will ever end. . . . It tears him to pieces . . . it tears him to pieces. . . . They're perfectly willing to let him wreck his health doing what they're afraid to do." Emmett Till's mother collapsed when she saw her son's body; Helen Robinson, informed that Tom is dead, "just fell down in the dirt. Just fell down in the dirt, like a giant with a big foot just came along and stepped on her."

16. Gunnar Myrdal, *An American Dilemma: The Negro Problem and Modern Democracy* (New York: Harper & Brothers, 1947).

17. Margaret Hunt Gram, "Matters of State: American Literature in the Civil Rights Era." PhD dissertation, Harvard University, 2013. The point needs to be raised, however, that Radley might not have been arrested, but Tom Robinson was, because Boo is white.

18. Capote, letter to Alvin and Marie Dewey, 10 October 1960, in Clarke, *Too Brief*, 299.

19. "Mocking Bird Call," *Newsweek*, 9 January 1961, 83.

20. Williams papers, W. D. Weinman to Harper Lee, 8 August 1965, box 86. Responses like these to the novel were to be expected. In 1949, Rodgers and Hammerstein wrote a song called 'You've Got to Be Carefully Taught' for their hit show *South Pacific*, in which a soldier sings: 'You've got to be taught to be afraid / Of people whose eyes are oddly made, / And people whose skin is a different shade, / You've got to be carefully taught.' When the show toured the American South, demands were made that the song be cut; Rodgers and Hammerstein flatly refused.

21. Hudson Strode papers, letter to Nelle Harper Lee, 24 January 1961, Hoole Library, University of Alabama, Tuscaloosa, AL, box 1121, folder 158.

22. Wayne Greenhaw, interview with author, 20 March 2004.

23. Capote, letter to Andrew Lyndon, 6 September 1960, in Clarke, *Too Brief*, 291.

24. "Mocking Bird Call," 83.

25. Williams papers, unsigned letter to Harper Lee from secretary in Williams's office, 7 January 1961, box 86.

26. Dannye Romine Powell, "A Visit with Capote's Aunt, Uncle," *Charlotte Observer*, 30 May 2006, n.p.

27. Charles Ray Skinner, interview with author, 22 December 2002.

28. Joel P. Smith, "'Mockingbird' Author Looking for Characters?," *Eufaula (Alabama) Tribune*, 8 September 1960, 4.

29. Williams papers, letter to Harper Lee, and her reply, 5 January 1961, box 86.

30. Nelle Harper Lee to Leo R. Roberts, January 1960, Archives and Information Center, Houghton Library, Huntingdon Collection, Montgomery, AL.

31. Max York, "Throngs Greet Monroe Writer," *Montgomery Advertiser*, 13 September 1960, 3A.

32. Hendrix, "Author's Father Proud of 'Mockingbird' Fame." Nelle's sister Louise was unimpressed by all the hoopla surrounding her sister's novel and didn't think much of Nelle's talent, either. She told her son's teacher that *To Kill a Mockingbird* was just "ridiculous." Emma Foy, interview with author, 5 July 2003.

33. *Journal of the 1964 General Conference of the Methodist Church* (Nashville, TN: Methodist Publishing House, 1964), 1272.

34. Reverend Thomas Lane Butts, remarks at "Maud McLure Kelly Award Luncheon" (award given to Alice Lee, Mobile, AL, 18 July 2003).

35. Ibid.

36. Hendrix, "Author's Father Proud of 'Mockingbird' Fame."

37. Williams papers, Robert P. Richards to Williams, 8 November 1960, box 86.

38. Frances Kiernan, "No Apologies Necessary," *The Atlantic Monthly*, April 2001.

39. Williams to Nelle and Alice Lee, 28 January 1961, Williams papers, box 86.

40. Williams to Alan Pakula, 16 November 1960, Williams papers, box 86.

41. Williams to "Boaty" Boatwright, 25 June 1962, Williams papers, box 86.

42. Williams to George Stevens, with note attached from Harper Lee, 8 August 1960, Williams papers, box 86.

43. Maurice Crain to Alice Lee, 22 March 1961, Williams papers, box 86.

44. Maurice Crain to Fred and Tommie Gipson, 7 April 1961, Fred Gipson papers, Harry Ransom Humanities Research Center, University of Texas at Austin, box 18, folder 4.

45. Murray Schumach, "Prize for Novel Elates Film Pair," *The New York Times*, 19 May 1961, 26.

46. "'Luckiest Person in the World,' Says Pulitzer Winner," *Birmingham News*, 2 May 1961, n.p.

47. "State Pulitzer Prize Winner Too Busy to Write," *Dothan* (Alabama) *Eagle*, 2 May 1961, n.p.

48. Strode papers, box 1211, folder 158.

49. "Luckiest Person," n.p.

50. Capote to Alvin and Marie Dewey, 22 May 1961, in Clarke, *Too Brief*, 317.

51. Nelle Lee to Helen Waterman, 20 November 1961, Caldwell Delaney papers, University of South Alabama Archives, Mobile, AL.

52. Plimpton, *Capote*, 14.

53. "Senate Lauds Pulitzer Winner," *Montgomery Advertiser*, 20 May 1961, 7A.

54. James B. McMillan, review of *To Kill a Mockingbird* by Harper Lee, *Alabama Review,* July 1961, 233.

55. Note to Harper Lee, 12 July 1961, Williams papers, box 86.

56. "Luckiest Person," n.p.

10. "Oh, Mr. Peck!"

1. Reed Polk, letter to author, 10 July 2003.

2. Scott McGee, Kerryn Sherrod, and Jeff Stafford, "To Kill a Mockingbird: The Essentials," Turner Classic Movies, www.turnerclassicmovies.com.

3. Deitch, "Novelist of the South," 6.

4. Charles S. Watson, *Horton Foote: A Literary Biography* (Austin: University of Texas Press, 2003), 114. Miss Lee didn't quite feel "indifference," as she claimed. In a letter to Helen Waterman, a friend in Mobile, dated November 20, 1961, Lee wrote: "Please forgive the long silence from Monroeville. I had to do some things that had to be done as soon as I returned—the most pressing task was doctoring the movie script" (Caldwell Delaney papers, University of South Alabama).

5. Don Noble, *Bookmark: Interview with Horton Foote,* videocassette, Alabama Center for Public Television, Tuscaloosa, AL, 27 August 1998.

6. *To Kill a Mockingbird: Then and Now,* videocassette, Prince William County Public Schools, Manassas, VA, 25 April 1997.

7. M. Jerry Weiss, *Photoplay Guide: "To Kill a Mockingbird,"* NCTE Studies in the Mass Media (Champaign, IL: National Council of Teachers of English, 1963), 18.

8. *To Kill a Mockingbird* (commentary section), Universal City, CA: Universal Home Video, 1998, compact disc.

9. Williams papers, Williams to George Stevens, 23 May 1961, box 86.

10. Jones, "Stand Up, Monroeville, Gregory Peck Is Passin'," *Happenings,* vol. 2, 159–60.

11. Gary Fishgall, *Gregory Peck: A Biography* (New York: Scribner, 2002), 233.

12. Jones, "Stand Up," *Happenings,* vol. 2, 160.

13. Ibid., 160–61.

14. Dolores Hope, e-mail to author, 15 October 2002. "My impression of the Pulitzer time is that people who had come to know Truman here in Kansas just had a gut feeling that Truman would have his nose out of joint about it. He always made sure he was the center of attention at any gathering here that I know of. Nelle knew him so well and she was anything but an attention getter herself. In fact, she shunned it. She would change the subject as quickly as she could when people exclaimed about her book and the prize. She was the exact opposite of Truman, being more interested in others than she was in herself."

15. Thomas McDonald, "Bird in Hand," *The New York Times,* 6 May 1962, 149.

16. Jane Kansas, "To Kill a Mockingbird and Harper Lee: Why the Site?," mockingbird.chebucto.org/why.html.

17. "Brock Peters, 'To Kill a Mockingbird' Actor, Dies at 78," *USA Today,* 23 August 2005.

18. *To Kill a Mockingbird* (commentary section), compact disc.

19. Barbara Vancheri, "Author Lauded 'Mockingbird' as a 'Moving' Film," *Pittsburgh Post-Gazette*, 20 February 2003.

20. Philip Alford, interview with author, 21 May 2004.

21. Murray Schumach, "Film Crew Saves $75,000 on Shacks," *The New York Times*, 19 January 1962, 26.

22. Jane Kansas, "To Kill a Mockingbird and Harper Lee: The Film," mockingbird.chebucto.org/film.html. Lee's remark about the set is from Bob Thomas, "Harper Lee Returns Visit, Sees Movie Sets, Hollywood," *Monroe Journal*, 4 May 1961.

23. Newquist, *Counterpoint*, 406.

24. Gipson papers, Tommie Gipson to Maurice Crain, 19 February 1962, box 18, folder 4.

25. Gipson papers, Maurice Crain to Tommie Gipson, 20 February 1962, box 18, folder 4.

26. Kansas, "To Kill a Mockingbird and Harper Lee: The Film."

27. Philip Alford, interview with author, 21 May 2004.

28. Ibid.

29. Vernon Hendrix, "Firm Gives Books to Monroe County," *Montgomery Advertiser*, 23 December 1962, n.p.

30. E. L. H., Jr., "The Obvious Is All Around Us," *Birmingham News*, 22 April 1962, n.p.

31. Capote, letter to Alvin and Marie Dewey, 5 May 1962, in Clarke, *Too Brief*, 348.

32. Joy Hafner-Bailey, interview with author, 21 December 2005.

33. Williams papers, Harold Hayes, *Esquire* editor, to Nelle Harper Lee (regarding "Dress Rehearsal," submitted by Lee), 27 October 1961, box 86.

34. Fishgall, *Gregory Peck*, 236.

35. Ibid.

36. Watson, *Horton Foote*, 143.

37. Fishgall, *Gregory Peck*, 236.

38. *To Kill a Mockingbird* (commentary section), compact disc.

39. Capote, letter to Alvin and Marie Dewey, 16 August 1962, in Clarke, *Too Brief*, 361.

40. Strode papers, Elise Sanguinetti to Hudson Strode, box 1211, folder 161.

41. Darryl Pebbles, interview with author, 9 February 2005.

42. "Harper Lee" Program from 1962 Founders Day, Mount Holyoke College Archives and Special Collections, South Hadley, MA, Honorary Degrees: Citations, folder 6.

43. "Chicago Press Call," *Overpress*, Chicago Press Club, March 1963.

44. Capote, letter to Donald Cullivan, 11 December 1962, in Clarke, *Too Brief*, 372.

45. Judith Martin, "To Lady Bird Johnson Alabama Is New Kin," *The Washington Post*, 10 December 1962, B4.

46. Ibid.

47. Williams papers, "Author Praises Picture Made from Prize Novel," *The New York Times*, n.d., n.p.

48. *To Kill a Mockingbird* (commentary section), compact disc.

49. Williams papers, Williams to Alice Lee, 16 February 1963, box 86.

50. *To Kill a Mockingbird* (commentary section), compact disc.

51. Dean Shackelford, "The Female Voice in *To Kill a Mockingbird*: Narrative Strategies in Film and the Novel," in *To Kill a Mockingbird: Modern Critical Interpretations*, ed. Harold Bloom (Philadelphia: Chelsea House, 1999), 121.

52. *Newsweek*, film review of *To Kill a Mockingbird*, 18 February 1963, 93.

53. Bosley Crowther, "Screen: 'To Kill a Mockingbird,'" *The New York Times*, 15 February 1963, 10.

54. Colin Nicholson, "Hollywood and Race: *To Kill a Mockingbird*," in *Cinema and Fiction: New Modes of Adapting, 1950–1990*, ed. John Orr and Colin Nicholson (Edinburgh: Edinburgh University Press, 1992), 97.

55. Andrew Sarris, *Village Voice*, 7 March 1963.

56. Weiss, *Photoplay Guide: "To Kill a Mockingbird,"* 18.

57. Capote, letter to Alvin and Marie Dewey, 15 February 1963, in Clarke, *Too Brief*, 382.

58. Williams papers, Williams to Alice Lee, 16 February 1963, box 86.

59. Boyle, "Harper Lee Running Scared," n.p.

60. Williams papers, Williams to Alice Lee, 25 March 1963.

61. Dorothy and Taylor Faircloth, interview with author, 17 March 2003.

62. Joseph Blass, letter to author, 10 September 2002.

63. Dorothy and Taylor Faircloth, interview with author, 17 March 2003. The Monroe Theater, the town's only movie theater, burned down the year after the premier and was never rebuilt.

64. S. Jonathan Bass, *Blessed Are the Peacemakers: Martin Luther King, Jr., Eight White Religious Leaders, and the "Letter from Birmingham Jail"* (Baton Rouge, LA: Louisiana State University Press, 2001), 102–3.

65. Vernon Hendrix, "Harper Lee Cries for Joy at Peck's Winning of Oscar," *Montgomery Advertiser*, 10 April 1963.

66. Moates, *Bridge of Childhood*, 11.

11. Unfinished Business

1. Williams papers, Williams to Alice Lee, 21 June 1963, box 86.

2. Ibid.

3. Strode papers, Therese Strode to Peggy (unidentified), 22 June 1963, box 1209, folder 48.

4. "Chicago Press Call."

5. Virginia Van der Veer Hamilton, *Alabama: A History* (reprint, New York: Norton, 1984).

6. Kay Wells, interview with author, 5 November 2005.

7. Allison, "Woman of the Year," n.p.

8. Donald Collins, interview with author, 1 April 2004.

9. Sam Hodges, "To Love a Mockingbird," *Mobile Register*, 8 September 2002.

10. Wes Lawrence, "Author's Problem: Friends," *Cleveland Plain Dealer*, 17 March 1964, n.p.

11. Williams papers, Williams to Alice Lee, 6 September 1963, box 86.

12. Williams papers, Alice Lee to Williams, 9 September 1963, box 86.

13. Williams papers, Williams to Alice Lee, 21 October 1963, box 86.
14. Ibid.
15. Newquist, *Counterpoint*, 208.
16. Amelia Young, "Her Writing Place Is Secret: 'Mockingbird' Author Working on Second Book," *Minneapolis Star*, 26 May 1963, n.p., Williams papers, box 86.
17. Lawrence, "Author's Problem."
18. James B. Simpson, *Simpson's Contemporary Quotations* (New York: Houghton Mifflin, 1988).
19. Boyle, "Harper Lee Running Scared," n.p.
20. Deitch, "Novelist of the South," 6.
21. Williams papers, Alice Lee to Williams, 14 November 1963, box 86.
22. Capote to Alvin and Marie Dewey, 14 February 1964, in Clarke, *Too Brief*, 393.
23. Young, "Her Writing Place Is Secret."
24. Ibid.
25. Capote to Bennett Cerf, 10 September 1962, in Clarke, *Too Brief*, 363.
26. Capote papers, New York Public Library, Harold Nye to Capote, 27 June 1962, box 7, folder 9.
27. Capote papers, Library of Congress, Washington, D.C., box 7, ac. 14, 213: research material/interviews. Robert J. Kaiser to Clifford R. Hope, Jr., 14 January 1963.
28. Capote to Alvin and Marie Dewey, 23 May 1964, in Clarke, *Too Brief*, 397.
29. Patrick Smith, "An Outspoken Critic," *Lawrence Journal*, www.ljworld.com, 5 April 2005.
30. "Scene of the Crime: Twenty-Five Years Later, Holcomb, Kansas Remembers 'In Cold Blood.'" *Chicago Sunday Tribune*, 11 November 1984, 34.
31. Don Lee Keith, "An Afternoon with Harper Lee," *Delta Review* (Spring 1966), 41.
32. Harold Nye, interview with author, 30 December 2002.
33. Newquist, *Counterpoint*, 412.
34. Williams papers, Williams to Alice Lee, 3 August 1964, box 86.
35. Ibid.
36. Williams papers, Williams to Alice Lee, 1 September 1964, 86.
37. Brigadier General Jack Capps (Ret.), letter to author, 1 July 2006.
38. Gus Lee, *Honor and Duty* (reprint, New York: Ivy Books, 1994), 149–50.
39. Ibid.
40. Joy Hafner-Bailey, interview with author, 15 December 2005.
41. Clarke, *Capote*, 354.
42. Holt, *Kansas Bureau of Investigation*, 71.
43. Capote to Cecil Beaton, 19 April 1965, in Clarke, *Too Brief*, 421.
44. Williams papers, Williams to Alice Lee, 7 May 1965, box 86.
45. *Harper Lee's Maycomb*, 19.
46. Keith, "An Afternoon with Harper Lee," 82.
47. Williams papers, Williams to Alice Lee, 7 June 1965, box 86.
48. Keith, "An Afternoon with Harper Lee."
49. Jubera, "To Find a Mockingbird."

50. Williams papers, Williams to Alice Lee, 5 August 1965, box 86.

51. Capote papers, New York Public Library, box 9, folder 1.

52. Harper Lee, "When Children Discover America," *McCall's*, August 1965, 76–79.

53. Nye, interview with author, 30 December 2002.

54. Wayne Lee, "Emotions Mixed Among Clutter Participants," *Hutchinson News*, 31 October 1965, n.p.

55. Williams papers, Williams to Alice Lee, 15 September 1965, box 86.

56. Williams papers, Williams to Alice Lee, 28 September1965, box 86.

57. Sarah Countryman, interview with author, 9 March 2004.

58. Williams papers, Williams to Alice Lee, 8 October 1965, box 86.

59. Ibid.

60. Wayne Greenhaw, e-mail to author, 1 November 2005.

61. R. Philip Hanes, interview with author, 6 December 2004.

62. Michael Shelden, "The Writer Vanishes," *Daily Telegraph*, 12 April 1997, n.p. When asked about Lee's help with *In Cold Blood*, Capote said, "She kept me company when I was based out there. I suppose she was with me about two months altogether. She went on a number of interviews; she typed her own notes, and I had these and could refer to them." Plimpton, "The Story Behind a Non-Fiction Novel," *The New York Times*, 16 January 1966.

63. David Kipen, e-mail to author, 23 November 2005. Mr. Kipen is the former National Endowment for the Arts Literature director.

64. "Mr. Bumble and the Mockingbird," editorial, *Richmond News-Leader*, 5 January 1966, 12.

65. "Author Harper Lee Comments on Book-Banning," *Richmond News-Leader*, 15 January 1966, 10.

66. R. Philip Hanes, interview with author, 6 December 2004.

67. Ibid.

68. Jimilu Mason, interview with author, 18 February 2005.

69. R. Philip Hanes, interview with author, 6 December 2004.

70. Ibid.

71. Darryl Pebbles, interview with author, 9 February 2005.

72. Sarah Dyess, letter to author, 10 December 2004.

73. William Smart, interview with author, 2 July 2004.

74. Karen Schwabenton, "Harper Lee Discusses the Writer's Attitude and Craft," *Sweet Briar News*, 28 October 1966, 3.

75. Charlotte Curtis, "Capote's Black and White Ball: 'The Most Exquisite of Spectator Sports,'" *The New York Times*, 29 November 1966.

76. Williams papers, Maurice Crain to Ann Brun Ash, 3 January 1968, box 146, folder Ca.

77. Wayne Greenhaw, letter to author, 23 March 2005.

78. Paul Engle papers, Special Collections Department, University of Iowa Libraries, Harper Lee to Paul Engle, 20 August 1968, box 9.

79. Williams papers, Maurice Crain to Ted Lloyd, 24 February 1969, box 149, folder L.

80. Joy Hafner-Bailey, interview with author, 15 December 2005.

81. Williams papers, Williams to May Lou (unidentified), December 1970, box 149, folder L.
82. Williams papers, Williams to Harper Lee, 11 March 1971.
83. Capote to Alvin and Marie Dewey, 3 December 1961, in Clarke, *Too Brief*, 332–33.
84. Williams papers, Pamela Barnes to Mrs. Erskine Caldwell, 13 September 1971, box 146, folder C-Cu.
85. Dr. Grady H. Nunn, letter to author, 4 January 2005.
86. Peter Griffiths, letter to author, 26 April 2005. Mr. Griffiths was a researcher for the BBC in 1982, which visited Monroeville for a documentary about *To Kill a Mockingbird*.

12. THE GOLDEN GOOSE
1. Tom Radney, interview with author, 14 November 2005.
2. Jubera, "To Find a Mockingbird."
3. Tom Radney, interview with author, 14 November 2005.
4. Jubera, "To Find a Mockingbird."
5. Ralph Hammond, interview with author, 20 March 2005.
6. Burstein, "Tiny, Yes."
7. James Wolcott, "Tru Grit," *Vanity Fair*, October 2005, 166.
8. Clark, *Capote*, 547.
9. Dolores Hope, e-mail to author, 13 October 2002.
10. Tom Radney, interview with author, 14 November 2005.
11. Ibid.
12. Drew Jubera, " 'Mockingbird' Still Sings Despite Silence of Author Harper Lee," *Atlanta Journal-Constitution*, 26 August 1990, M1 and M3.
13. Emma S. Foy, interview with author, 5 July 2003.
14. Jubera, "To Find a Mockingbird."
15. Ibid.
16. William Smart, interview with author, 2 July 2004.
17. Clarke, *Capote*, 22.
18. Harper Lee to Caldwell Delaney, 30 December 1988. Robert Hicks, author of *Widow of the South* (New York: Warner Books, 2005), found this letter between the pages of a used copy of Clarke's *Capote*.
19. "Story of Attempted Drowning Called False, Angers Harper Lee," *Tuscaloosa News*, 25 September 1997.
20. *Harper Lee's Maycomb*, 86.
21. As far back as 1965, Christopher Sergel, owner of Dramatic Publishing for schools, had tried to persuade Annie Laurie Williams to allow an adaptation, saying that "Schools all across the country continue to write to us with requests for a dramatization of *To Kill a Mockingbird*—it is much more requested than *any* other book." It wasn't until 1990 that Sergel received permission from Lee. Williams papers, Christopher Sergel to Williams, 5 January 1965, box 149, folder L.
22. "Harper Lee, Read but Not Heard," *The Washington Post*, 17 August 1990.

23. The author participated as a juror during the play in Monroeville in May 2003.
24. Roy Hoffman, "Long Lives the Mockingbird," *The New York Times*, 9 August 1998, BR31.
25. Dr. Wanda Bigham, former president of Huntingdon College, letter to author, 25 May 2004.
26. Harper Lee, foreword to the thirty-fifth-anniversary edition of *To Kill a Mockingbird* (New York: HarperCollins, 1995).
27. Kathy McCoy, former director of the Monroe County Heritage Museum, e-mail to author, 11 August 2004.
28. Alexander Alter, "Harper Lee, author of 'To Kill a Mockingbird,' Is to Publish a Second Novel," *The New York Times*, 3 February 2015.

EPILOGUE: THE DIKE IS BREACHED

1. In April 2005, a first edition of Lee's novel sold for $19,000 at Swann Galleries in Manhattan.
2. Mills, "A Life Apart," *Chicago Tribune*, 13 September 2002.
3. Boris Kachka in *New York* magazine summarized what Mills concluded about Harper Lee: "unconfident in her looks and therefore unconcerned; witty and garrulous within the strict limits she sets for talk; conservative by northern standards; cranky and principled; moody but predictable." "The Decline of Harper Lee," July 2014. www.vulture.com.
4. T. Madison Peschock, "A Well-Hidden Secret: Harper Lee's Contributions to Truman Capote's *In Cold Blood*." PhD dissertation, Indiana University of Pennsylvania, 2012.
5. "The literary capital of Alabama doesn't read" was Lee's retort. Marja Mills, *The Mockingbird Next Door* (New York: Penguin Press, 2014), 217.
6. Mark Seal, "To Steal a Mockingbird," *Vanity Fair*, July 2013, 108.

> "She once said to me when we were up late one night, sharing a bottle of scotch: 'You ever wonder why I never wrote anything else?' And I said, 'Well, along with a million other people, yes.' "I espoused two or three ideas. I said maybe you didn't want to compete with yourself. She said, 'Bull ... Two reasons: one, I wouldn't go through the pressure and publicity I went through with *To Kill a Mockingbird* for any amount of money. Second, I have said what I wanted to say and I will not say it again.' "

Greg Richter, "Friend Finds Why Harper Lee Didn't Write Again," *The Birmingham* (Alabama) *News*, 7 August 2011.

7. "Suspension Upsets Methodist Minister," *Lubbock* (Texas) *Evening Journal*, 25 April 1983.
8. Maryon Pittman Allen, e-mail to author, 30 November 2003.
9. Seal, "To Steal a Mockingbird."
10. Ibid.
11. Ibid. The remark was made to the wife of Thomas Steinbeck, the author's son and heir and the administrator of his estate.
12. Ibid. Her apparent lack of largesse in her hometown is a sore point with some residents, where one in four live below the poverty line. "Are the streets paved with gold?," asked a Monroeville booster bitterly. "Does every kid have a computer?"

George Thomas Jones, e-mail to author, 29 September 2002. However, her sister and Reverend Butts said, "Lee donates large sums to charity, according to Alice, who manages her sister's financial affairs. The attorney declined to give details. Butts says she discreetly disburses some of the charity through their church in Monroeville. 'She has educated so many people who have no idea' that she was their benefactor." Mills, "A Life Apart."

13. *Nelle Harper Lee v. Samuel L. Pinkus et al.*, U.S. District Court, Southern District of New York, 3 May 2013. Case number 1:13-cv-03000. "During its decades of representation, M and O acted appropriately and in Harper Lee's interests, handling the kinds of activities that are the business of a literary agent. . . . M and O conferred with Harper Lee and her lawyer (her sister, Alice Lee) about publishing opportunities before securing them on Harper Lee's behalf." ¶ 19.

14. Mark Seal, "To Steal a Mockingbird."

15. Ibid.

16. *Lee V. Pinkus*, ¶ 13 (Pinkus had "engaged in a scheme to dupe Harper Lee, then 80 years old with declining hearing and eyesight, into assigning her valuable [To Kill a Mockingbird] copyright to VMI for no consideration"; ¶ 63 ("Pinkus engineered such a transfer as part of a scheme to secure to himself an irrevocable interest in the income stream from Harper Lee's copyright and to avoid his legal obligations to M&O under the arbitration decision.")

17. Seal, "To Steal a Mockingbird."

18. *Lee v. Pinkus*, ¶ 31, 39. Lee's interest in an e-book of *To Kill a Mockingbird* seems to indicate that she had changed her mind since declaring in *O* magazine four years earlier "that some things should happen on soft pages, not cold metal."

19. Monroe Country circuit clerk William R. "Bob" McMillan, quoted in Jacob Gershman, "Meet the Lawyer Who Found Harper Lee's New Novel," *The Wall Street Journal*, 4 February 2015.

20. Peschock, "A Well-Hidden Secret," 21. "They told friends not to read it" was told to the author by persons who said they knew Harper Lee.

21. Scott Martelle, "Educators Take a Hard Look at 'To Kill a Mockingbird,'" *Los Angeles Times*, 21 June 2000. Martelle reported, "We make whiteness invisible— 'We're not a race, black people are,' said Ricker-Wilson, a white Philadelphia native who wrote about her experience in the academic *English Journal*, published by the National Council of Teachers of English.

    "Rather than drop *Mockingbird*, though, she recommends pairing it with books on similar topics by black authors. Among those: Mildred D. Taylor's *Roll of Thunder, Hear My Cry*, about a black girl coming of age in the South in the '30s; Ouida Sebestyen's *Words by Heart*, narrated by a young black girl living in a small Southwestern town; and Walter Dean Myers' *The Glory Field*, tracing five generations of a family from Africa through American slavery."

22. Thomas Mallon, "Big Bird," *The New Yorker*, 29 May 2006. Auburn University history professor Wayne Flynt, an oft-quoted spokesperson for Lee and the novel expresses another view: "Popular acclaim for the novel owes much to the message of tolerance that Lee proclaimed during an intolerant age. Atticus's admoni-

tion to his children that they will never understand a person until they consider life from his or her point of view is viewed as trite by some critics, but the novel's message had profound effects for Jews in Prague, homosexuals in Berlin, and gypsies in eastern Europe who had been the victims of Nazi oppression. . . . Hundreds of thousands of American teachers have chosen to teach *To Kill a Mockingbird*, deciding that Harper Lee's values represent the best of humanity: tolerance; kindness; civility; justice; the courage to face down community or family when they are wrong; and the compassion to love them despite their flaws." Wayne Flint, "To Kill a Mockingbird," Encyclopedia of Alabama, online, 16 May 2007.

23. *Lee v. Pinkus*, ¶ 57.
24. Paul Lewis, "Lawsuit Divides Town Which Inspired Classic Novel, 'To Kill a Mockingbird,'" *The* (U.K.) *Guardian*, 1 November 2013.
25. David A. Graham, "Can Alabama Determine What Harper Lee Wants?," *The Atlantic Monthly*, 12 March 2015. www.theatlantic.com.
26. Chimamanda Ngozi Adichie, "Rereading: To Kill a Mockingbird by Harper Lee," *The* (U.K.) *Guardian*, 9 July 2010.
27. Anne Marie Bryan (director, Monroeville Chamber of Commerce), e-mail to author, 10 August 2015.
28. Boris Kachka, "The Decline of Harper Lee," *New York* magazine, 3 February 2015; and Michelle Dean, "How Unauthorized is the New Book About Harper Lee?," 18 July 2014.
29. According to the suit that Lee later brought against Pinkus, HarperCollins wasn't notified that he was no longer her agent, and foreign subagents and subsidiary publishers continued to receive instructions for another year that were drafted to look as if they had come from Harper Lee, directing them not to provide financial information or royalties without her permission to any other company except Pinkus's Veritas Media.
30. Debra Cassens Weiss, "Lawyer's Account of Discovery of Harper Lee's 'Watchman' Book Differs from that of Sued Agent," *American Bar Association Journal*, 14 July 2015. www.abajournal.com.
31. Serge F. Kovaleski and Alexandra Alter, "A New Account of 'Watchman's' Origin and Hints of a Third Book," *The New York Times*, 13 July 2015. Talk of a third and fourth book surfaced briefly. www.nytimes.com.
32. Shekhar Bhatia, "Did Harper Lee's lawyer purposely hold on to the manuscript of Go Set a Watchman for years—until she had control of the author's affairs? New account claims she knew all about book in 2011," *The* (U.K.) *Daily Mail*, 17 July 2015. dailymail.co.uk.
33. *Lee v. Pinkus* lawsuit, Prayer for Relief.
34. Ibid., Appendix A. The arbitrator did not find that Pinkus had "treated VMI's corporate assests as his own, or that he had undercapitalized the corporation, or that he did not respect corporate formalities, or that he, in any other way, abused the privilege of doing business in the corporate form, to implicate the doctrine of piercing the corporate veil." The copyright case was settled in September 2015.
35. Kachka, "The Decline of Harper Lee."

36. *Nelle Harper Lee v. Monroe County Heritage Museum, Inc.* U.S. District Court, Southern District of Alabama, 10 October 2013. Case number 1:13-cv-00490-WS-B.

37. Jones, e-mail to author, 29 September 2002.

38. George Thomas, "CEO and Chairman of International Pulp Mill Company Pleads Guilty in Manhattan Federal Court to Hiding Over $8.4 Million In Secret Swiss Bank Accounts," United States Attorney's Office, Southern District of New York, press release, 20 January 2015.

39. Jocelyn McClurg, "Harper Lee Denies She Cooperated with New Biography," *USA Today*, 15 July 2014. The book is not a biography; it's a memoir.

40. Mary McDonagh Murphy, "Harper Lee's Sister, Alice, Is 100, Still Practices Law, and Remembers Everything," The Daily Beast, 1 April 2012. Murphy is the producer of the documentary *Hey, Boo: Harper Lee and* To Kill a Mockingbird.

41. Elaine Woo, "Lawyer Alice Lee Dies at 103; Sister of 'To Kill a Mockingbird' Author," *Los Angeles Times*, 22 November 2014; and Alice Lee, letter to author, August 2004.

42. Ibid.

Bibliography

AWARDS, HARPER LEE

Pulitzer Prize (1961)

Brotherhood Award of the National Conference of Christians and Jews (1961)

Alabama Library Association Award (1961)

Bestsellers Paperback of the Year Award (1962)

Member, National Council on the Arts (1966)

Best Novel of the Century, Library Journal (1999)

Alabama Humanities Award (2002)

ATTY Award, Spector Gadon & Rosen Foundation (2005)

Los Angeles Public Library Literary Award (2005)

Honorary degree, University of Notre Dame (2006)

American Academy of Arts and Letters (2007)

Presidential Medal of Freedom (2007)

BOOKS

The Author and His Audience: *175th Anniversary J. B. Lippincott Company*. Philadelphia: J. B. Lippincott, 1967.

Ayers, Edward L. *The Promise of the New South: Life After Reconstruction*. New York: Oxford University Press, 1992.

Bass, S. Jonathan. *Blessed Are the Peacemakers: Martin Luther King, Jr., Eight White Religious Leaders, and the "Letter from Birmingham Jail."* Baton Rouge, LA: Louisiana State University Press, 2001.

Bloom, Harold, ed. *To Kill a Mockingbird: Modern Critical Interpretations.* Philadelphia: Chelsea House Books, 1999.

Capote, Truman. *Breakfast at Tiffany's.* New York: Random House, 1950.

―――. "The Thanksgiving Visitor," in *A Christmas Memory, One Christmas, and The Thanksgiving Visitor.* New York: Modern Library, 1996.

―――. *In Cold Blood.* 1965. Reprint, New York: Vintage, 1994.

―――. *Other Voices, Other Rooms.* 1948. Reprint, New York: Vintage, 1994.

Cash, W. J. *The Mind of the South.* New York: Alfred A. Knopf, 1941.

Clarke, Gerald. *Capote: A Biography.* New York: Simon and Schuster, 1988.

―――, ed. *Too Brief a Treat: The Letters of Truman Capote.* New York: Random House, 2004.

Collins, Donald E. *When the Church Bell Rang Racist: The Methodist Church and the Civil Rights Movement in Alabama.* Macon, GA: Mercer University Press, 1998.

Dixon, Wheeler Winston. *Film Talk: Directors at Work.* New Brunswick, NJ: Rutgers University Press, 2007.

Fisher, Jerilyn, and Ellen S. Silber, eds. *Women in Literature: Reading Through the Lens of Gender.* Westport, CT: Greenwood, 2003.

Fishgall, Gary. *Gregory Peck: A Biography.* New York: Scribner, 2002.

Fleming, Walter L. *Civil War and Reconstruction in Alabama.* New York: Peter Smith, 1949.

Flynt, Wayne. *Alabama in the Twentieth Century.* Tuscaloosa, AL: University of Alabama, 2004. Accessed online at Questia, 5 October 2015.

Grant, Barry Keith, ed. *American Cinema of the 1960s: Themes and Variations.* New Brunswick, NJ: Rutgers University Press, 2008.

Griffith, Lucille. *Alabama: A Documentary History to 1900.* Tuscaloosa, AL: University of Alabama Press, 1968.

Grobel, Lawrence. *Conversations with Capote.* New York: New American Library, 1985.

Hamilton, Virginia Van der Veer. *Alabama: A History.* 1977. Reprint, New York: Norton, 1984.

Hohoff, Tay. *A Ministry to Man: The Life of John Lovejoy Elliot.* New York: Harper, 1959.

―――. *Cats and Other People.* New York: Popular Library, 1973.

Hollowell, John. *Fact and Fiction: The New Journalism and the Nonfiction Novel.* Chapel Hill, NC: University of North Carolina Press, 1977.

Holt, Dan. *Kansas Bureau of Investigation, 1939–1989.* Marceline, MO: Jostens, 1990.

Hope, Holly. *Garden City: Dreams in a Kansas Town.* Norman, OK: University of Oklahoma Press, 1988.

Horton, Andrew. *Henry Bumstead and the World of Hollywood Art Direction.* Austin, TX: University of Texas Press, 2003.

Hranicky, Roy E., and Lois Belle White. *The Five H's.* Privately printed, 1950.

Inge, Thomas M. *Truman Capote Conversations.* Jackson, MS: University of Mississippi Press, 1987.

Johnson, Claudia Durst. *To Kill a Mockingbird: Threatening Boundaries*. New York: Twayne, 1994.

———. *Understanding To Kill a Mockingbird: A Student Casebook of Issues, Sources, and Historic Documents*. Westport, CT: Greenwood, 1994.

Jones, George Thomas. *Happenings in Old Monroeville*. Volume 1. Monroeville, AL: Bolton Newspapers, 1999.

———. *Happenings in Old Monroeville*. Volume 2. Monroeville, AL: Bolton Newspapers, 2003.

Lee, Harper. *To Kill a Mockingbird*. 1960. Reprint, New York: Warner Books, 1982.

Litwack, Leon F. *Trouble in Mind: Black Southerners in the Age of Jim Crow*. New York: Alfred A. Knopf, 1998.

Malin, Irving. *Truman Capote's In Cold Blood: A Critical Handbook*. Belmont, CA: Wadsworth, 1968.

McCorvey, Thomas Chalmers. *Alabama Historical Poems*. Birmingham, AL: Birmingham Publishing Company, 1927.

Moates, Marianne M. *A Bridge of Childhood: Truman Capote's Southern Years*. New York: Holt, 1989.

Monroeville: Literary Capital of Alabama. Charleston, SC: Arcadia Publishing, 1998.

Monroeville: The Search for Harper Lee's Maycomb. Charleston, SC: Arcadia Publishing, 1999.

Moore, Albert Burton, ed. *History of Alabama and Her People*. 3 vols. Chicago: American Historical Society, 1927.

Morrow, Bradford, and Peter Constantine, eds. *Conjunctions: 31. Radical Shadows: Previously Untranslated and Unpublished Works by 19th and 20th Century Masters*. New York: Bard College, 1998.

Nance, William L. *The Worlds of Truman Capote*. New York: Stein and Day, 1970.

Newquist, Roy. *Counterpoint*. Chicago: Rand McNally, 1964.

New York City Guide and Almanac, 1957–1958. New York: New York University Press, 1957–58.

O'Neill, Terry, ed. *Readings on* To Kill A Mockingbird. San Diego: Greenhaven Press, 2000.

Owen, Thomas McDory. *History of Alabama and Dictionary of Alabama Biography*. 4 vols. Chicago: S. J. Clarke, 1921.

Plimpton, George. *Truman Capote: In Which Various Friends, Enemies, Acquaintances and Detractors Recall His Turbulent Career*. New York: Anchor, 1997.

Roman, James. *Bigger Than Blockbusters: Movies That Defined America*. Westport, CT: Greenwood, 2009.

Rubin, Louis D., Jr., et al., eds. *A History of Southern Literature*. Baton Rouge, LA: Louisiana State University Press, 1985.

Rudisill, Marie, with James C. Simmons. *Truman Capote: The Story of His Bizarre and Exotic Childhood by an Aunt Who Helped Raise Him*. New York: William Morrow, 1983.

Sellers, James B. *History of the University of Alabama*. Revised and edited by W. Stanley Hoole. Tuscaloosa, AL: University of Alabama Press, 1975.

Shaffer, Thomas L., and Mary M. Shaffer. *American Lawyers and Their Communities: Ethics in the Legal Profession*. Notre Dame, IN: University of Notre Dame Press, 1991.

Sharpless, Rebecca. *Cooking in Other Women's Kitchens: Domestic Workers in the South, 1865–1960*. Ed. Waldo E. Martin and Patricia Sullivan. Chapel Hill, NC: University of North Carolina Press, 2010.

Sielke, Sabine. *Reading Rape: The Rhetoric of Sexual Violence in American Literature and Culture, 1790–1990*. Princeton, NJ: Princeton University Press, 2002.

Strode, Hudson. *Spring Harvest: A Collection of Stories from Alabama*. New York: Alfred A. Knopf, 1944.

Stuckey, W. J. *The Pulitzer Prize Novels: A Critical Backward Look*. Norman, OK: University of Oklahoma Press, 1966.

Thomas, G. Scott. *A New World to Be Won: John Kennedy, Richard Nixon, and the Tumultuous Year of 1960*. Santa Barbara, CA: Praeger, 2011.

Tindall, George Brown. *The Emergence of the New South 1913–1945. A History of the South*. Compiled and edited by Wendell Holmes Stephenson and E. Merton Coulter. Vol. X. Baton Rouge, LA: Louisiana State University Press, 1967.

Walter, Eugene (as told to Katherine Clark). *Milking the Moon*. New York: Three Rivers Press, 2001.

Watson, Charles S. *Horton Foote: A Literary Biography*. Austin, TX: The Jack and Doris Smothers Series in Texas History, Life, and Culture, University of Texas Press, 2003.

Watson, Fred S. *Piney Woods Echoes: A History of Dale and Coffee Counties, Alabama*. Enterprise, AL: Elba Clipper, 1949.

White, E. B. *Here Is New York*. New York: Harper & Brothers, 1949.

Williams, R. B., III. *The Day the Barn Almost Burned and Other Stories of Deep South Plantation Life in the 1940s*. Montgomery, AL: Court Street Press, 2000.

ARTICLES

Adams, J. Donald. Speaking of Books (column). *The New York Times*, 2 June 1963, 27.

Adams, Phoebe. Review of *To Kill a Mockingbird* by Harper Lee. *The Atlantic Monthly*, August 1960, 98–99.

Allison, Ramona. "'Mockingbird' Author Is Alabama's 'Woman of the Year.'" *Birmingham Post Herald*, 3 January 1962.

"Alumna Wins Pulitzer Prize for Distinguished Fiction." University of Alabama *Alumni News*, May–June 1961.

Ames, Lynn. "Dispelling Misconceptions Between the North and the South." *The New York Times*, 5 May 1996, WC2.

"Annie L. Williams, Authors' Agent, Dies." *The New York Times*, 18 May 1977, O4.

"Annie Williams, Agent Who Sold 'Gone With the Wind.'" *The Washington Post*, 20 May 1977, C8.

"Arts Council to Mull Grants, 1967 Budget." *The Washington Post*, 11 February 1966, B3.

"Author Harper Lee Comments on Book-Banning." *Richmond News-Leader*, 15 January 1966, 10.

Beechcroft, John. "To Kill a Mockingbird." *Literary Guild Book Club Magazine*, August 1960, 1–2.

Bennett, Barbara. "On Harper Lee: Essays and Reflections." *The Mississippi Quarterly* 60.2 (2007), 429ff.

Best, Rebecca H. "Panopticism and the Use of 'The Other' in To Kill a Mockingbird." *The Mississippi Quarterly* 62.3–4 (2009), 541ff.

Besten, Mark. "Too Hot for You? Take a Dip in Cold Blood." *Louisville Eccentric Observer*, 1 August 2001, 16.

Blass, A. B. "Mockingbird Tales." *Legacy*, Fall/Winter 1999, 22.

Boyle, Hal. "Harper Lee Running Scared, Getting Fat on Heels of Success." *Birmingham News*, 15 March 1963.

Brady, Dave. "Harper Lee; Top Scientists Are Competition for 'Bear.'" *The Washington Post*, 26 May 1963, C6.

Brian, Denis. "Truman Capote," in *Truman Capote Conversations*, ed. Thomas M. Inge. Jackson, MS: University of Mississippi Press, 1987, 210–35.

Brinkmeyer, Robert H., Jr. "Scout Comes Home Again." *Virginia Quarterly Review*, Fall 2015, 217–21.

"Brock Peters, 'To Kill a Mockingbird' Actor, Dies at 78." *USA Today*, 23 August 2005.

Buder, Leonard. "Opportunities for Study in Europe." *The New York Times*, 11 April 1948, E11.

Burstein, Patricia. "Tiny, Yes, But a Terror? Do Not Be Fooled by Truman Capote in Repose." *People Weekly*, 10 May 1976, 12–17.

Carroll, Maurice. "New York Plays Upbeat Host to Delegates." *The New York Times*, 12 July 1976, 1.

Cep, Casey N. "Harper Lee's Abandoned True Crime Novel." *The New Yorker*, 17 March 2015.

Chalfin, Richard. "The Day Harper Lee Came to See Me." *New York Observer*, 4 December 2000, 5.

"Chicago Press Call." *Rogue*. Chicago Press Club. December 1963.

Childress, Mark. "Looking for Harper Lee." *Southern Living*, May 1997, 148–50.

"Christopher Sergel, Publisher of Plays and Playwright, 75." *The New York Times*, 2 May 1993, B7.

Chura, Patrick. "Prolepsis and Anachronism: Emmet Till and the Historicity of To Kill a Mockingbird." *The Southern Literary Journal* 32.2 (2000).

Clemons, Walter. "The Last Word: The Pulitzer Non-Prize for Fiction." *The New York Times*, 6 June 1971, BR55.

Cobb, Mark Hughes. "Native Stars Fall on Alabama Hall of Fame." *Tuscaloosa News*, 17 March 2001.

Cooper, Rand Richards. "Literary Conceits: 'The Squid and the Whale' & 'Capote.'" *Commonweal*, 2 December 2005, 28ff.

"Countries—One Brings Tractor Order." *The New York Times*, 5 October 1948, 28.

Crespino, Joseph. "Atticus Finch Offers a Lesson in Southern Politics." *The New York Times*, 16 July 2015.

"Crime Scenes Revisited; 'Infamous,' 'King' Die at Box Office." *The Washington Times*, 3 May 2007.

Crimmins, Margaret, and Nancy L. Ross. "Kennedy Center's Opening—It'll Be a Starry Night." *The Washington Post*, 5 September 1971, 135.

Crowther, Bosley. "Screen: 'To Kill a Mockingbird.'" *The New York Times*, 15 February 1963.

Culligan, Glendy. "Listen to That Mockingbird." *The Washington Post*, 3 July 1960, E6.

Curtis, Charlotte. "Capote's Black & White Ball: 'The Most Exquisite of Spectator Sports.'" *The New York Times*, 29 November 1966, 53.

Daley, Robert. "It's Like a Plate of Spaghetti Under New York Streets." *Chicago Tribune*, 7 February 1960, 20.

Dare, Tim. "Lawyers, Ethics, and *To Kill a Mockingbird*." *Philosophy and Literature* 25 (April 2001), 127–41.

Deitch, Joseph. "Harper Lee: Novelist of South." *Christian Science Monitor*, 3 October 1961, 6.

Eder, Maciej, and Jan Rybicki. "Go Set a Watchman While We Kill the Mockingbird in Cold Blood." Computational Stylistics Group blog, n.d.

Erisman, Fred. "The Romantic Regionalism of Harper Lee." *Alabama Review* 26 (1973), 122–36.

"Exchange Students Sail: But Only 105 Leave on *Marine Jumper* Under U.S. Plan." *The New York Times*, 7 June 1947, 29.

Faulkner, Jimmy. "How the Monroe Journal Was Purchased from Gregory Peck . . . Sort Of." Jimmy Faulkner's "Mumblings." 26 June 2003. www.siteone.com/columns/faulkner.

Feeney, F. X. "A Tale of Three Parties." (Review) *Truman Capote: In Which Various Friends, Enemies, Acquaintances and Detractors Recall His Turbulent Career* by George Plimpton. *LA Weekly*, February 1998. www.laweekly.com.

"1st Novel Wins Pulitzer Prize." *The Washington Post*, 12 May 1961, A3.

Gilbert, Jim. "Cold, Cold Mockingbird." *Mobile Register*, 13 May 2001.

———. "Cold, Cold Mockingbird: Postscript." www.weirdplots.com. March 2002.

Going, William T. "Truman Capote: Harper Lee's Fictional Portrait of the Artist As an Alabama Child." *Alabama Review* 42.2 (April 1989), 136–49.

Greenhaw, Wayne. "Capote Country," in *Alabama on My Mind*. Montgomery, AL: Sycamore Press, 1987.

———. "Learning to Swim," in *The Remembered Gate: Memoirs by Alabama Writers*, ed. Jay Lamar and Jeanie Thompson. Tuscaloosa, AL: University of Alabama Press, 2002.

———. "Teacher and Friend," in *Alabama on My Mind*. Montgomery, AL: Sycamore Press, 1987.

Grelen, Jay C. "Freaking Out the Talented Harper Lee." *Sun News* (Myrtle Beach, SC), 31 December 2002, C1.

H., E. L., Jr. "The Obvious Is All Around Us." *Birmingham News*, 22 April 1962.

Hamner, John T. "This Mockingbird Is a Happy Singer." *Montgomery Advertiser,* 7 October 1960.

Hansen, Harry. "Miracle of Manhattan—1st Novel Sweeps Board." *Chicago Tribune,* 14 May 1961, D6.

"Harper Lee Gets Scroll, Tells of Book." *Birmingham News,* 12 November 1961.

"Harper Lee, Read but Not Heard." *The Washington Post,* 17 August 1990.

"Harper Lee Twits School Board in Virginia for Ban on Her Novel." *The New York Times,* 16 January 1966, 82.

"Harper Lee's First Novel Sets the Whole Book World on Fire!" (advertisement). *The New York Times,* 17 July 1960, 228.

Hatoum, Sarah. "Go Set a Watchman by the Numbers: Harper Lee's New Novel Proves Popular, Divisive." *Library Journal,* 1 September 2015, 14, 16, 17.

Hechinger, Fred M. "Censorship Found on the Increase." *The New York Times,* 16 September 1986, C7.

Hendrix, Vernon. "Author's Father Proud of 'Mockingbird' Fame." *Montgomery Advertiser,* 7 August 1960.

———. "Firm Gives Books to Monroe County." *Montgomery Advertiser,* 23 December 1962.

———. "Harper Lee Cries for Joy at Peck's Winning of Oscar." *Montgomery Advertiser,* 10 April 1963.

Hodges, Sam. "To Love a Mockingbird." *Mobile Register,* 8 September 2002.

Hoff, Timothy. "Influences on Harper Lee: An Introduction to the Symposium." *Alabama Law Review* 45 (Winter 1994), 389.

Hoffman, Roy. "Long Lives the Mockingbird." *The New York Times Book Review,* 9 August 1998, 31.

Hohoff, Tay. "We Get a New Author." *Literary Guild Book Club Magazine,* August 1960, 3–4.

"Honors Are Given 13 Women by Mount Holyoke College." *The New York Times,* 11 November 1962, 53.

"John Megna, 42, 'Mockingbird' Star." *The New York Times,* 7 September 1995, B17.

Johnson, Claudia Durst. "The Secret Courts of Men's Hearts: Code and Law in Harper Lee's *To Kill a Mockingbird." Studies in American Fiction* 19 (Autumn 1991), 129–39.

Johnson, Hubert A. *To Kill a Mockingbird,* uncorrected proof, printed Spring 1960, Special Collections, University of Virginia.

Jones, George Thomas. "Courthouse Lawn Was Once Kids' Playground," in *Happenings in Old Monroeville.* Volume 2. Monroeville, AL: Bolton Newspapers, 2003.

———. "Queen of the Tomboys." *Monroe Journal,* 6 May 1999.

———. "Stand Up, Monroeville, Gregory Peck Is Passin'," in *Happenings in Old Monroeville.* Volume 2. Monroeville, AL: Bolton Newspapers, 2003.

———. "Young Harper Lee's Affinity for Fighting." EducETH.ch (The English Page). 7 December 1999. www.educeth.ch/english/readinglist/leeh/remin.html#fight.

Jubera, Drew. "'Mockingbird' Still Sings Despite Silence of Author Harper Lee." *Atlanta Journal-Constitution,* 26 August 1990, M1, M3.

———. "To Find a Mockingbird." *Dallas Times Herald,* n.d. (1984).

Keith, Don Lee. "An Afternoon with Harper Lee." *Delta Review* (Spring 1966), 40–41, 75, 81–82.

Kemp, Kathy. "Mockingbird Won't Sing." *News & Observer* (Raleigh, NC), 12 November 1997, E1.

Krebs, Albin. "Truman Capote Is Dead at 59; Novelist of Style and Clarity." *The New York Times*, 28 August 1984.

Lapsley, James N. "Cultural Alienation: *In Cold Blood.*" *Theology Today,* July 1966, 210–15.

Lawrence, Wes. "Author's Problem: Friends." *Cleveland Plain Dealer*, 17 March 1964.

Lazenby, Permilia S. "First United Methodist Church, Monroeville, Alabama: History" (church booklet). n.p., 1979.

Lee, Gus. *Honor and Duty.* Reprint, New York: Ivy Books, 1994.

Lee, Harper. "Springtime." *Monroe Journal*, 1 April 1937, 3.

———. "Nightmare." *Prelude*, Spring 1945, 11.

———. "A Wink at Justice." *Prelude*, Spring 1945, 14–15.

———. "Some Writers of Our Times." *Rammer Jammer*, November 1945, 14.

———. "What Price Registration?" *Crimson White*, 13 June 1946, 2.

———. "Caustic Comment" (column). *Crimson White*, 28 June 1946, 2 August 1946, 16 August 1946.

———. "Now Is the Time for All Good Men" (one-act play). *Rammer Jammer*, October 1946, 7, 17–18.

———. "Alabama Authors Write of Slaves, Women, GIs." *Crimson White*, 1 October 1946, 2.

———. "Christmas Means to Me." *McCall's*, December 1961, 63.

———. Foreword to the 35th anniversary edition of *To Kill a Mockingbird*. New York: HarperCollins, 1995.

Lee, Melissa. "Brother, Friends Object to Portrayal of Bonnie Clutter by Capote." *Lawrence Journal-World*, 4 April 2005. www.ljworld.com.

Lee, Wayne. "Emotions Mixed Among Clutter Participants." *Hutchinson News*, 31 October 1965.

"Lett Negro Saved from Electric Chair." *Monroe Journal*, 12 July 1934, 1.

Letter to the editor. "Caustic Comment." *Crimson White*, 2 August 1946, 2.

Letter to the editor. "Spreading Poison." *Atlanta Journal*, 7 February 1961.

"Literary-est Part of US Is South." *Crimson White*, 29 March 1947, 5.

"'Little Nelle' Heads Ram, Maps Lee's Strategy." *Crimson White*, 8 October 1946, 1.

Lubet, Steven. "Reconstructing Atticus Finch." *Michigan Law Review* 97.6 (1999), 1339–62.

"'Luckiest Person in the World,' Says Pulitzer Winner." *Birmingham News*, 2 May 1961.

Lyell, Frank H. "One Taxi-Town." *The New York Times*, 10 July 1960, BR5.

Lyons, Leonard. "Gossip from Gotham" (column). *The Washington Post*, 14 February 1945, 14.

"Mad Dog Warning Issued for State." *Monroe Journal*, 28 June 1934, 2.

Maples, Ann. "Novels Look Bright Under the Tree." *The Washington Post*, 27 November 1960, C16.

"Marine Tiger to Make Quick Turnaround and Substitute for Marine Jumper." *The New York Times*, 9 September 1948, 55.

Martin, Judith. "To Lady Bird Johnson Alabama Is New Kin." *The Washington Post*, 10 December 1962, B4.

McCoy, Kathy. "*To Kill a Mockingbird*: The Great American Novel." *Legacy*, Monroe County Heritage Museum, 1994, 22–25.

McDonald, Thomas. "Bird in Hand." *The New York Times*, 6 May 1962, 149.

McGee, Scott, Kerryn Sherrod, and Jeff Stafford. "To Kill a Mockingbird: The Essentials." Turner Classic Movies. www.turnerclassicmovies.com.

McLendon, Winzola. "Nobody Mocks 'Mockingbird' Author: Sales Are Proof of Pudding." *The Washington Post*, 17 November 1960, B12.

McMillan, James B. Review of *To Kill a Mockingbird* by Harper Lee. *Alabama Review*, July 1961, 233.

Mills, Marja. "A Life Apart: Harper Lee, The Complex Woman Behind 'A Delicious Mystery.'" *Chicago Tribune*, 13 September 2002.

"'A Ministry to Man: The Life of John Lovejoy Elliot,' a Biography by Tay Hohoff." *The New York Times*, 7 January 1959, 30.

"Miss Nelle Lee Chosen to Attend Oxford." *Monroe Journal*, 29 April 1948, 1.

Mitgang, Herbert. "Books of the Times" (column). *The New York Times*, 13 July 1960, 33.

"Mocking Bird Call." *Newsweek*, 9 January 1961.

"Mockingbird Film May Begin in Fall." *Birmingham News*, 2 May 1961.

Mohan, Gary. "'Suburban Pioneers' in 'Long Island: Our Story.'" www.newsday.com. 2005.

Monroe Journal (Centennial Edition). 22 December 1966.

Morgan, Robert W., Jr. "Letter from France: Notes on Tourists, Students, Francs, and Politics." *Harvard Crimson*, 28 September 1948.

"Mr. Bumble and the Mockingbird." Editorial. *Richmond News-Leader*, 5 January 1966, 12.

Murray, Jennifer. "More Than One Way to (Mis)Read a Mockingbird." *The Southern Literary Journal* 43.1 (2010), 75ff.

Nations, Mack. "America's Worst Crime in Twenty Years." *Male*, December 1961.

"Negro Accidentally Killed Last Friday." *Monroe Journal*, 16 February 1933, 1.

"Negro Held for Attacking a Woman." *Monroe Journal*, 9 November 1933, 1.

"Nelle Harper Lee," in *Current Biography*, ed. Charles Moritz. New York: H. W. Wilson Co., 1961.

Nichols, Lewis. "In and Out of Books" (column). *The New York Times*, 25 December 1960, BR8.

———. "In and Out of Books" (column). *The New York Times*, 14 May 1961, BR8.

Nicholson, Colin. "Hollywood and Race: *To Kill a Mockingbird*," in *Cinema and Fiction: New Modes of Adapting, 1950–1990,* ed. John Orr and Colin Nicholson. Edinburgh: Edinburgh University Press, 1992.

"Novelist Lee to Join Arts Unit." *The Washington Post*, 28 January 1996, C3.

O'Hagan, Andrew. "Good Fibs." *London Review of Books*, 2 April 1998. www.lrb.co .uk/v20/n07/ohag01_.html.

"One Version of the Harper Lee Story." Harperlee@yahoogroups.com (listserv), 11 October 2005.

Otts, Elizabeth. "Lady Lawyers Prepare Homecoming Costumes." *Crimson White*, 26 November 1946, 14.

Palmer, C. B. "A Farmer Looks at Farming 1954." *The New York Times Sunday Magazine*, 1 August 1954.

Park, Mary Jane. "Truman's Aunt Tiny." *St. Petersburg Times*, 3 October 2000. www.sptimes.com/News/100300/Floridian/Truman_s_Aunt_Tiny.shtml.

Pennypacker, Nathaniel. "Massacre of the Clutter Family." *Front Page Detective*, April 1960.

Plimpton, George. "The Story Behind a Nonfiction Novel." *The New York Times*, 16 January 1966. www.nytimes.com/books/97/12/28/home/capote-interview.

Prescott, Orville. "The Best of the Year: A Critic's Choice." *The New York Times*, 4 December 1960, BR3.

———. "Books of the Times" (column). *The New York Times*, 15 August 1960, 21.

"A Prize Novel Is Removed from School Reading List." *The New York Times*, 4 December 1977, 26.

"Prize Winner Remembered as Deflater of Phoniness." *Montgomery Advertiser*, 4 May 1961.

Rhodes, Matthew W. "Truman Capote." *Legacy*, Monroe County Heritage Museum, 1994, 26–31.

Robertson, Nan. "Johnsons Hail the Creative Life with a Dinner at White House," *The New York Times*, 14 December 1966, 55.

Rocha, Guy Louis. "Truman Capote's *In Cold Blood*: The Nevada Connection." Nevada State Library and Archives, Department of Cultural Affairs. dmla.clan.lib.nv.us/docs/nsla/archives/spec-feat.htm.

Romine, Dannye. "Truman's Aunt: A Bio in Cold Blood." *Chicago Tribune*, 5 June 1983, sec. 5, 1–2.

Rowley, Hazel. "Mockingbird Country." *Australian's Review of Books*, April 1999.

"Scene of the Crime: Twenty-Five Years Later, Holcomb, Kansas Remembers 'In Cold Blood.'" *Chicago Sunday Tribune*, 11 November 1984.

"School Reading Lists Shun Women and Black Authors." *The New York Times*, 21 June 1989, B6.

Schultz, William Todd. "Why Did Truman Capote Write Answered Prayers?" www.Psychobiography.com. Schultz Publications, 12 February 2016.

Schumach, Murray. "Film Crew Saves $75,000 on Shacks." *The New York Times*, 19 January 1962, 26.

———. "Prize for Novel Elates Film Pair." *The New York Times*, 19 May 1961.

Schwabenton, Karen. "Harper Lee Discusses the Writer's Attitude and Craft." *Sweet Briar News*, 28 October 1966, 3.

Segal, Victoria. "Writing Crime: A Grisly Tale of Art and Murder Revels in Its Own Gloominess." *NewStatesman*, 27 February 2006, 48.

"Senate Lauds Pulitzer Winner." *Montgomery Advertiser*, 20 May 1961.

"Severe Snowstorm Hits East, Stalls Traffic, Shuts Schools; Many Firms Close Early." *Wall Street Journal*, 4 March 1960.

Shackelford, Dean. "The Female Voice in *To Kill a Mockingbird*: Narrative Strategies in Film and the Novel," in *To Kill a Mockingbird: Modern Critical Interpretations*, ed. Harold Bloom. Philadelphia: Chelsea House, 1999.

Smith, Joel P. "'Mockingbird Author Looking for Characters?'" *Eufaula* (Alabama) *Tribune*, 8 September 1960.

Smith, Patrick. "An Outspoken Critic." *Lawrence Journal-World*, 5 April 2005, www.ljworld.com.

Spike (columnist). "Scaring Harper Lee, No Time to Die, The Leaf Player Revisited." *Online Journalism Review*, 8 January 2003. Annenberg School for Communication, University of Southern California.

"State Pulitzer Prize Winner Too Busy to Write." *Dothan* (Alabama) *Eagle*, 2 May 1961.

Steinem, Gloria. "'Go Right Ahead and Ask Me Anything.' (And So She Did): An Interview with Truman Capote." *McCall's*, November 1967, 76–77, 148–52, 154.

Steiner, George. "A Cold-Blooded Happening." *The* (U.K.) *Guardian*, 2 December 1965.

"Story of Attempted Drowning Called False, Angers Harper Lee." *Tuscaloosa News*, 25 September 1997.

"Strange Gods (Like TV) Buried in Church Rite." *The Washington Post*, 13 July 1962, A3.

Stuart, Dick. Williams is a Magic Name." *Corpus Christi Caller-Times*, 8 June 1955, 15.

"Tay Hohoff, Author, Lippincott Officer." *The New York Times*, 12 January 1974, 36.

"Ten Liners Arrive or Depart Today: Seven Vessels, Bringing 4,596 Passengers, Due from Europe and the Near East." *The New York Times*, 30 June 1947, 37.

"The Redemption of Atticus Finch." *Southern Cultures* 6.4 (2000), 1–4.

"They All Had a Ball at Capote's Party." *The Washington Post*, 30 November 1966, D2.

"$300,000 Is Paid for 'Moon Is Down': Record Price Given by Fox for Screen Rights to the Drama by John Steinbeck." *The New York Times*, 29 April 1942, 27.

"Traffic Ticket Report." *Saturday Review*, 6 August 1960.

Vancheri Barbara. "Author Lauded 'Mockingbird' As a 'Moving' Film." *Pittsburgh Post-Gazette*, 20 February 2003.

"Wealthy Farmer, 3 of Family Slain." *The New York Times*, 16 November 1959, 7.

"We Bequeath Our Anti-Klanism," Editorial. *Crimson White*, 16 August 1946, 2.

Weiler, A. H. "New Midtown Showcase—Other Film Matters." *The New York Times*, 29 January 1961, X7.

Weiss, M. Jerry. *Photoplay Guide: "To Kill a Mockingbird."* NCTE Studies in the Mass Media. Champaign, IL: National Council of Teachers of English, March 1963.

Wells, Hannah. "Reimagining to Kill a Mockingbird: Family, Community, and the Possibility of Equal Justice under the Law." *Law & Society Review* 48.2 (2014), 488ff.

White, Jean M. "The Council on the Arts: Beginning a Second Decade." *The Washington Post*, 4 September 1974, B1.

Whitley, Carla Jean. "Small-Town Q&A: Amanda McMillan." *Crimson White*, 9 October 2003.

Wiebe, Crystal K. "Author Left Mark on State." *Lawrence Journal-World*, 3 April 2005. www.ljworld.com.

———. "'To Kill a Mockingbird' Author Helped Truman Capote Break the Ice in Kansas." *Lawrence Journal-World*, 3 April 2005. www.ljworld.com.

Wolcott, James. "Tru Grit." *Vanity Fair*, October 2005.

Woodard, Calvin. "Listening to the Mockingbird." *Alabama Law Review* 45 (Winter 1994), 563–85.

Yoder, J. Wes. "Debating the Details: Some Residents of Monroeville Prefer to Ponder the Fine Points of Famous Novel." *Expressions* (online magazine), Auburn University Journalism Department, 2001.

York, Max. "Throngs Greet Monroe Writer." *Montgomery Advertiser*, 13 September 1960.

Young, Amelia. "Her Writing Place Is Secret: 'Mockingbird' Author Working on Second Book." *Minneapolis Star*, 26 May 1963.

Young, Thomas Daniel. Introduction to Part III in *A History of Southern Literature*, ed. Louis D. Rubin, Jr., et al. Baton Rouge, LA: Louisiana State University Press, 1985.

Zoerink, Richard. "Truman Capote Talks About His Crowd." *Playgirl*, September 1975, 50–51, 54, 80–81, 128.

THESES AND PhD DISSERTATIONS

Adkins, Christina Katherine. "Slavery and the Civil War in Cultural Memory." Harvard University, 2014.

Gram, Margaret Hunt. "Matters of State: American Literature in the Civil Rights Era." Harvard University, 2013.

Peschock, T. Madison. "A Well-Hidden Secret: Harper Lee's Contributions to Truman Capote's *In Cold Blood*." Indiana University of Pennsylvania, 2012.

Power, Cathy Kelly. "Thirteen Ways of Looking at a Mockingbird: A Collection of Critical Essays." Georgia State University, 1996.

Richards, Gary Neal. "Another Southern Renaissance: Sexual Otherness in Mid-Twentieth Century Fiction." Vanderbilt University, 1996.

Sumner, Caitlan. "The New Woman of the New South: Gender and Class in 20th Century Southern Women's Literature." Master's thesis, University of Alabama, 2013.

Webb, Theresa Ellen. "The Aesthetics of Justice in Contemporary American Film." Unpublished dissertation, University of California–Los Angeles, 2002.

MEDIA

Dewey, Alvin A., as told to Dolores Hope. "The Clutter Case: 25 Years Later KBI Agent Recounts Holcomb Tragedy." Compact disc. *Garden City* (Kansas) *Telegram*, 10 November 1984.

Noble, Don. "Bookmark: Interview with Horton Foote." Videocassette. Alabama Center for Public Television, Tuscaloosa, AL, 27 August 1998.

"To Kill a Mockingbird" (commentary section). Compact disc. Universal City, CA: Universal Home Video, 1998.

"'To Kill a Mockingbird': Then and Now." Videocassette. Prince William County Public Schools, Manassas, VA, 25 April 1997.

Acknowledgments

A number of institutions made their archives available: the Alderman Library at the University of Virginia; Mount Holyoke College Archives and Special Collections; the New York Public Library, Manuscripts and Archives Division; the Hoole Library and Bounds Law Library at the University of Alabama; the Huntingdon College Archives and Information Center; the Columbia University Rare Book and Manuscript Library; the National Archives and Records Service, College Park, Maryland; the University of Montevallo Carmichael Library; the Rare Book, Manuscript, and Special Collections Library at Duke University; the University of South Alabama Archives; the Library of Congress Manuscript Reading Room; the Harry Ransom Humanities Research Center at the University of Texas at Austin; the Oxford University Archives, Bodleian Library; the Special Collections and Archives, Ralph Brown Draughon Library, Auburn University; the Alabama Department of History and Archives; the University of Iowa Special Collections; the University of North Carolina at Chapel Hill,

Special Collections, Randall Library; the Wisconsin Historical Society; the Fales Library and Special Collections at New York University; the Evergreen Public Library, Lucy C. Warren Heritage Section, Evergreen, Alabama; the Finney County Public Library, Garden City, Kansas; and the Johnston County Genealogical and Historical Society, Smithfield, South Carolina.

In particular, I thank these people for their assistance: Phillip Alford, former senator Maryon Pittman Allen (D-Alabama), Emily H. Anthony, Mary Nell Atherton, Mary Badham, Joy Hafner-Bailey, Mary Anne Berryman, the Hon. Otha Lee Biggs, A. B. Blass, Jr., Joseph Blass, Bill Brown, Joy Brown, Martha Brown, Gerald Clarke, Donald Collins, Sarah Countryman, Caroline Crawford, Jane Benton Davis, Nicholas Delbanco, Carney Dobbs, Sarah Dyess, Dorothy and Taylor Faircloth, Emma S. Foy, Tom Gardner, John Greaves, Wayne Greenhaw, Jay Grelen, Peter Griffiths, Ralph Hammond, John T. Hamner, R. Philip Hanes, Catherine Helms, James Hood, Cliff Hope, Delores Hope, Holly Hope, Roy E. Hranicky, Mildred H. Jacobs, George Thomas Jones, Olive Landon, Vincent Lauria, Katie Law, Gus Lee, Jimilu Mason, John N. Maxwell, Ernest Maygarden, Sara Anne McCall, Kathy McCoy, Betty McGiffert, Daniel J. Meador, Barbara Moore, Mike Nations, Helen Norris, Jeanne Foote North, Dr. Grady H. Nunn, Claude Nunnelly, Harold Nye, Emma Medlock Panske, Darryl Pebbles, Sue Philipp, Thomas Hal Phillips, Mary Ann Pickard, L. Reed Polk, Thomas Radney, Sr., Emily Wheelock Reed, Ann Richards, Freda Roberson, Douglas Roberts, Tina Rood, Marie Faulk Rudisill, Elise Sanguinetti, Marion Goode Shirkey, Louise Sims, Charles Ray Skinner, William Smart, Mary Lee Stapp, Florence Moore Stikes, Harriet Swift, Polly Terry, Alden Todd, Mary Tomlinson, Elon Torrence, Mary Tucker, Kay Wells, Ray E. Whatley, Jane Williams, Carter Wilson, and Robert Woolridge.

Jeff Kleinman at Folio Literary Management and Serena Jones, senior editor at Henry Holt, were instrumental in seeing this revision through to the end.

Index

About the Author

CHARLES J. SHIELDS's biography of Harper Lee, the first ever published, became a *New York Times* bestseller, a Literary Guild Selection, and a Book-of-the-Month Club Alternate. His young adult biography of Harper Lee, *I Am Scout* (Owl 2008; reprinted 2015), was chosen as an ALA Best Book for Young Adults, a Bank Street Best Children's Book of the Year, and a Junior Literary Guild Selection. In 2011, Shields published *And So It Goes: Kurt Vonnegut, A Life* (Holt), a *New York Times* and *Washington Post* notable nonfiction book of the year.

He and his wife, Guadalupe, reside in Charlottesville, Virginia.